IFIP Advances in Information and Communication Technology 310

IFIP – The International Federation for Information Processing

IFIP was founded in 1960 under the auspices of UNESCO, following the First World Computer Congress held in Paris the previous year. An umbrella organization for societies working in information processing, IFIP's aim is two-fold: to support information processing within its member countries and to encourage technology transfer to developing nations. As its mission statement clearly states,

> *IFIP's mission is to be the leading, truly international, apolitical organization which encourages and assists in the development, exploitation and application of information technology for the benefit of all people.*

IFIP is a non-profitmaking organization, run almost solely by 2500 volunteers. It operates through a number of technical committees, which organize events and publications. IFIP's events range from an international congress to local seminars, but the most important are:

- The IFIP World Computer Congress, held every second year;
- Open conferences;
- Working conferences.

The flagship event is the IFIP World Computer Congress, at which both invited and contributed papers are presented. Contributed papers are rigorously refereed and the rejection rate is high.

As with the Congress, participation in the open conferences is open to all and papers may be invited or submitted. Again, submitted papers are stringently refereed.

The working conferences are structured differently. They are usually run by a working group and attendance is small and by invitation only. Their purpose is to create an atmosphere conducive to innovation and development. Refereeing is less rigorous and papers are subjected to extensive group discussion.

Publications arising from IFIP events vary. The papers presented at the IFIP World Computer Congress and at open conferences are published as conference proceedings, while the results of the working conferences are often published as collections of selected and edited papers.

Any national society whose primary activity is in information may apply to become a full member of IFIP, although full membership is restricted to one society per country. Full members are entitled to vote at the annual General Assembly, National societies preferring a less committed involvement may apply for associate or corresponding membership. Associate members enjoy the same benefits as full members, but without voting rights. Corresponding members are not represented in IFIP bodies. Affiliated membership is open to non-national societies, and individual and honorary membership schemes are also offered.

Achim Rettberg   Mauro C. Zanella
Michael Amann   Michael Keckeisen
Franz J. Rammig (Eds.)

Analysis, Architectures and Modelling of Embedded Systems

Third IFIP TC 10 International
Embedded Systems Symposium, IESS 2009
Langenargen, Germany, September 14-16, 2009
Proceedings

 Springer

Volume Editors

Achim Rettberg
Carl v. Ossietzky University Oldenburg, OFFIS
Escherweg 2, 26121 Oldenburg, Germany
E-mail: achim.rettberg@iess.org

Mauro C. Zanella
Michael Amann
Michael Keckeisen
ZF Friedrichshafen AG
88038 Friedrichshafen, Germany
E-mail: {mauro.zanella, m.amann, michael.keckeisen}@zf.com

Franz J. Rammig
University of Paderborn
Fürstenallee 11, 33094 Paderborn, Germany
E-mail: franz@upb.de

CR Subject Classification (1998): C.3, C.2, D.4.7, C.2.4, J.2

ISSN   1868-4238
ISBN-10   3-642-04283-X Springer Berlin Heidelberg New York
ISBN-13   978-3-642-04283-6 Springer Berlin Heidelberg New York

springer.com

© IFIP International Federation for Information Processing 2009
Softcover reprint of the hardcover 1st edition 2009

Typesetting: Camera-ready by author, data conversion by Scientific Publishing Services, Chennai, India
Printed on acid-free paper   SPIN: 12755752   06/3180   5 4 3 2 1 0

Preface

This book presents the technical program of the International Embedded Systems Symposium (IESS) 2009. Timely topics, techniques and trends in embedded system design are covered by the chapters in this volume, including modelling, simulation, verification, test, scheduling, platforms and processors. Particular emphasis is paid to automotive systems and wireless sensor networks. Sets of actual case studies in the area of embedded system design are also included.

Over recent years, *embedded systems* have gained an enormous amount of processing power and functionality and now enter numerous application areas, due to the fact that many of the formerly external components can now be integrated into a single System-on-Chip. This tendency has resulted in a dramatic reduction in the size and cost of embedded systems. As a unique technology, the design of embedded systems is an essential element of many innovations.

Embedded systems meet their performance goals, including real-time constraints, through a combination of special-purpose hardware and software components tailored to the system requirements. Both the development of new features and the reuse of existing intellectual property components are essential to keeping up with ever more demanding customer requirements. Furthermore, design complexities are steadily growing with an increasing number of components that have to cooperate properly. Embedded system designers have to cope with multiple goals and constraints simultaneously, including timing, power, reliability, dependability, maintenance, packaging and, last but not least, price.

The significance of these constraints varies depending on the application area a system is targeted for. Typical embedded applications include consumer electronic, automotive, medical, and communication devices.

The International Embedded Systems Symposium (IESS) is a unique forum to present novel ideas, exchange timely research results, and discuss the state of the art and future trends in the field of embedded systems. Contributors and participants from both industry and academia take active part in this symposium which fosters research relations and collaboration between academic researchers and industry representatives worldwide. The IESS conference is organized by the Computer Systems Technology committee (TC10) of the International Federation for Information Processing (IFIP).

IESS is a true inter-disciplinary conference on the design of embedded systems. Computer science and electrical engineering are the predominant academic disciplines concerned with the topics covered in IESS, but many applications also involve civil, mechanical, aerospace, and automotive engineering, as well as various medical disciplines.

In 2005, IESS was held for the first time in Manaus, Brazil. In this initial installment, IESS 2005 was very successful with 30 accepted papers ranging from specification to embedded systems application. IESS 2007 was the second edition of the symposium held in Irvine (CA), USA, with 35 accepted papers and 2 tutorials ranging from analysis, design methodologies to case studies from automotive and medical applications.

IESS 2009 was held in Langenargen, Germany, at Schloß Montfort a historic castle. The castle is located by the Bodensee. The articles presented in this book are the result of a rigorous double-blind review process implemented by the Technical Program Committee. Out of 46 valid submissions, 28 papers were accepted for publication, yielding an overall acceptance rate of 60.8%.

The strong technical program led to a very successful IESS 2009 conference.

First and foremost, we thank our sponsors ZF Friedrichshafen AG, the Carl von Ossietzky University Oldenburg, and the Paderborn University for their generous financial support of this conference. Without these contributions, IESS 2009 would not have been possible in its current form.

We would also like to thank IFIP as the organizational body for the promotion and support of the IESS conference.

Last but not least, we thank the authors for their interesting research contributions and the members of the Technical Program Committee for their valuable time and effort in reviewing the articles.

September 2009

Achim Rettberg
Mauro C. Zanella
Michael Amann
Michael Keckeisen
Franz J. Rammig

Organization

IFIP TC10 Working Conference: International Embedded Systems Symposium (IESS), September 14–16, 2009, Schloß Montfort, Langenargen, Germany

General Chairs

Achim Rettberg
Mauro C. Zanella

General Co-chair

Franz J. Rammig

Technical Program Chair

Michael Amann

Local Arrangements Chair

Michael Keckeisen

Technical Program Committee

Samar Abdi	University of California at Irvine, USA
Christian Allmann	Audi Electronics Venture, Germany
Michael Amann	ZF Friedrichshafen, Germany
Richard Anthony	The University of Greenwich, UK
Jürgen Becker	University of Karlsruhe, Germany
Christophe Bobda	University of Potsdam, Germany
Florian Dittmann	TWT, Germany
Rainer Doemer	University of California at Irvine, USA
Cecilia Ekelin	Volvo Technology Corporation, Sweden
Rolf Ernst	Technical University Braunschweig, Germany
Masahiro Fujita	University of Tokyo, Japan
Andreas Gerstlauer	University of Texas Austin, USA
Marcelo Götz	UFRGS, Brazil
Joerg Henkel	University of Karlsruhe, Germany
Uwe Honekamp	Vector Informatik, Germany
Marcel Jackowski	USP, Brazil

Michael Keckeisen	ZF Friedrichshafen, Germany
Kane Kim	University of California at Irvine, USA
Bernd Kleinjohann	C-LAB, Germany
Hermann Kopetz	Technical University Vienna, Austria
Horst Krimmel	ZF Friedrichshafen, Germany
Jean-Claude Laprie	LAAS, France
Thomas Lehmann	HAW Hamburg, Germany
Armin Lichtblau	Mentor Graphics, Germany
Patrick Lysaght	Xilinx Research Labs, USA
Roger May	Altera, UK
Wolfgang Nebel	Carl von Ossietzky University Oldenburg, Germany
Mike Olivarez	Freescale Semiconductor, USA
Frank Oppenheimer	OFFIS, Germany
Carlos Pereira	UFRGS, Brazil
Franz Rammig	University of Paderborn, Germany
Achim Rettberg	Carl von Ossietzky University Oldenburg, Germany
Carsten Rust	Sagem Orga, Germany
Stefan Schimpf	ETAS, Germany
Juergen Schirmer	Robert Bosch GmbH, Stuttgart, Germany
Gunar Schirner	University of California at Irvine, USA
Aviral Shrivastava	Arizona State University, USA
Joachim Stroop	dSPACE, Germany
Hiroyuki Tomiyama	Nagoya University, Japan
Ansgar Traechtler	University of Paderborn, Germany
Flavio R. Wagner	UFRGS, Brazil
Wayne Wolf	Georgia Institute of Technology, USA
Mauro Zanella	ZF Friedrichshafen, Germany
Jianwen Zhu	University of Toronto, Canada

Organizing Committee

Achim Rettberg, Mauro C. Zanella, Michael Amann, Michael Keckeisen

Co-organizing Institution

IFIP TC 10, WG 10.2 and WG 10.5

Sponsors

ZF Lemförder GmbH
Carl von Ossietzky University Oldenburg
University Paderborn

Table of Contents

Modelling

Transaction Level Modelling

Scheduling and Real-Time Systems

Simulation, Verification and Test

Platforms and Processors

Automotive Systems

Case Studies

Wireless Sensor Networks

Tutorials

State Machine Based Method for Consolidating Vehicle Data

Florian Dittmann[1], Konstantina Geramani[1], Victor Fäßler[1], and Sergio Damiani[2]

[1] TWT GmbH Science & Innovation, Bernhäuser Str. 40 -42,
73765 Neuhausen, Germany
{florian.dittmann,konstantina.geramani,
victor.faessler}@twt-gmbh.de
[2] Centro Ricerche Fiat S.C.p.A., Strada Torino, 50
10043 Orbassano (TO), Italy
sergio.damiani@crf.it

Abstract. The increasing number of information and assistance systems built into modern vehicles raises the demand for appropriate preparation of their output. On one side, crucial information has to be emphasized and prioritized, as well as relevant changes in the driving situation and surrounding environment have to be recognized and transmitted. On the other side, marginal alterations should be suitably filtered, while duplications of messages should be avoided completely. These issues hold in particular when assistance systems overlap each other in terms of their situation coverage. In this work it is described how such a consolidation of information can be meaningfully supported. The method is integrated in a system that collects messages from various data acquisition units and prepares them to be forwarded. Thus, subsequent actions can be taken on a consolidated and tailored set of messages. Situation assessment modules that rely on immediate estimation of situations are primary recipients of the messages. To meet their major demand—rapid decision taking—the method generates events by applying the concept of state machines. The state machines form the anchor to merge and fuse input, track changes, and generate output messages on higher levels. Besides this feature of consolidating vehicle data, the state machines also facilitate the transformation of continuous data to event messages for the rapid decision taking. Eventually, comprehensive driver support is facilitated, also enabling unprecedented features to improve road safety by decreasing the cognitive workload of drivers.

Keywords: automotive domain, time-triggered, event-triggered, information fusion, state machines, data aggregation, architectures and models.

1 Introduction

The number of advanced driver assistance systems (ADAS) and in-vehicle information systems (IVIS) is constantly increasing in modern vehicles. Despite ADAS and IVIS systems are implemented to the benefit of the driver, a not proper integration within ADAS/IVIS easily can impose a hard-to-manage workload. At the same time,

A. Rettberg et al. (Eds.): IESS 2009, IFIP AICT 310, pp. 1–11, 2009.

interoperation between those systems should be fostered to exploit their capabilities for improving road safety. Meaningful combination of their output could even lead to more useful information with potential added benefit to the safety. For example radar and vision for the lane detection can cooperate to better describe the scenario ahead.

The method was designed and developed in the course of the European Commission funded I-WAY project [9], where it forms the pre-processing system for a situation assessment module. The situation assessment module takes over the responsibility to finally rate incoming information by rapid decision taking, performing tailored user warning. Besides reducing the complexity, the pre-processing module was also decided to be implemented for becoming a clear-defined boarder between time-triggered or continuous information and event messages on higher levels.

To achieve the overall demands of meaningfully combining and consolidating vehicle data, well-thought-out organization of the information issued by IVIS and ADAS is required. Only then, their output can undergo a rapid assessment and combination to become beneficial for the driver. In particular, a situation assessment system that takes vehicle status as input and intends to warn drivers in a sensible way will operate best if the information is available in a well-organized style. Hence, appropriate information fusion and subsequent filtering should take place to allow for presentation of messages in a consolidated manner.

The increasing number of ADAS and IVIS systems to be integrated has to be taken into account: this can be met by fostering a well-defined and modular architecture to manage the complexity. To organize the data meaningfully and facilitate rapid decision making, it is proposed a suitable transformation of information to higher levels as inevitable key factor, reflected in the overall architecture. The objective of the fusing thereby is to combine input information of different sources over time and only forward significant messages.

In this work, a method based on state-machine approach to meet the above requirement of transforming information fusion to a higher level is presented. The method derives from a dedicated unit for processing and consolidating the vehicle relevant data. The unit takes over the responsibility to merge and fuse, filter and suppress, generate and trigger output tailored to the requirements of subsequent systems, which decide when and in which way to display the information. The state machine combines time- and event-triggered input and allows the issuing of messages in an event-based style. In some cases the exploitation of state machines facilitates the method to transform information fusion to a higher level.

The unit was implemented to be portable, generic and suitable for multiple purposes. The rest of the paper is organized as follows. In the next two sections, we review related work and give an overview of the architectural integration. The application of the state machines is discussed in section 4 on the method details. Section 5 shows an exemplary implementation before section 6 concludes the work.

2   Related Work

Information fusion in the automotive domain can be found in several works, for example [2], [3]. These works often focus on advanced driver assistance systems. A tracking based information fusion technique is presented in [15]. It tracks data of sensors having complementary or/and redundant field of views. The technique of multi-level fusion for vehicular environment recognition is discussed in [14]. Here fuzzy operators are used and confidence levels are introduced. In [16] the architecture of the SASPENCE project is presented, which introduced separate fusion modules for individual features in a vehicle. A layered data-fusion process is discussed in [17]. Object as well as situation refinement is targeted. In [18], a step based interaction and communication assistant is presented, which defines a technique how to process information for HMI in vehicles.

In general, information fusion fundamentally discusses the combination of data extracted from multi sensors systems. Basically, two or more sensors S_i shall be utilized appropriately to achieve a performance L that outperforms the simple addition of their single performances L_i [1]. A comprehensive overview on techniques and methods of information fusion is given in [10]. Information fusion for multimedia data analysis is discussed in [11]. While the application area is different, the methods and concepts of the reference are very valuable for this work. More recently, there has been a push to extend systems to multiple sensing modalities. Multi-sensor fusion using complementary sensing modalities greatly increases the robustness of sensing systems [4].

Fundamental consideration on time vs. event triggered processing is extensively covered in [7]. Targeting the domain of safety-critical applications, [5] discusses requirements concerning the transformation from the time to the event domain. Reference [12] gives an overview on the same issue for the automotive domain from the control theory point of view, while [6] discusses whether to use time- or event triggered communication as a non-functional feature that requires early consideration in the development process.

To conclude, substantial work on information fusion also in the automotive domain has been done. The approach presented in this paper builds on the results and complements them by exploiting a state machine based method that allows for generating tailored event-triggered messages for processing and decision making on higher levels.

3 Architectural Integration

The objective of the method is the preparation and provision of high-level output for subsequent systems, particularly fusing input information of different sources over time and only forwarding significant messages. By evaluating these high level messages rapid decision making can take place. Actions necessary to be performed can be issued, e.g., generating warning messages to the driver. The method therefore performs advanced information fusion by applying a transformation from time-triggered to event-triggered, a transformation from the space-time domain to the event domain. This can be abstractly described as follows:

$$XYZ \text{ and } dX/dt, dY/dt, \text{ and } dZ/dt, c \rightarrow \text{ event}, \tag{1}$$

where XYZ denotes the physical location of data (e.g. critical objects referring to the vehicles environment), dX/dt denotes the temporal changes of these coordinates, and c other conditions. The latter covers global changes like entering a tunnel, which can be derived from digital maps based on GPS localization. State machines thereby become the primary technique to facilitate the transformation form the (continuous) input data into event messages (see Section 4).

On top of this basic behavior, other features are added to the overall performance: first of all, a tracking of raw monitoring information over time helps to increase the level of confidence and to detect wrong messages concerning the surrounding environment of a car. This tracking mechanism introduces a memory in the system; as consequence a more reliable decision becomes possible and multiple sources basically can increase the data's reliability and the confidence level. Concepts of temporal redundancy are exploited therefore.

The method implements early sensor fusion: environmental information gained by multiple acquisition modules are analyzed and combined to generate high-level data, with potential higher reliability. To avoid data degradation, the implementation reflects a negotiation to a canonical reference base to combine data from different monitoring sources.

For maintenance and complexity reasons, the method is enveloped in five logical steps, which each take over a significant part of the overall processing. The steps then are executed cyclic, triggered by newly arriving input data. Figure 1 depicts the logical steps and indicates their order of execution. The two core steps *information fusion* and *event generation* are preceded by a *basic plausibility analysis*, which ensures valid data in terms of range, resolution, etc. In the two surrounding steps, data from acquisition units is received and decoded, as well as encoded and send to listening systems.

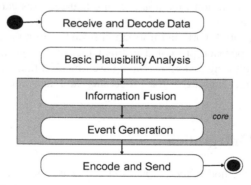

Fig. 1. Logical steps of the processing architecture

Well-defined communication techniques are used for interaction with the input and output systems. The overall communication architecture was designed to allow for seamless integration of additional input devices, enabling future extensions. Newly arriving messages trigger the cyclic behaviour, irrespective of their origin or source. The architecture thus allows producing synergy between different products / systems from different vendors. Eventually, it provides at least a means how to synchronize input data.

Besides the physical communication requirements, also the timing characteristics of the communication are of special concern: the system shall operate in vehicles on roads requiring real-time behaviour. A solid strategy was developed and integrated to target the real-time requirements. It is based on time stamps that are crucial to prevent

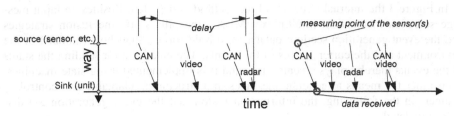

Fig. 2. Messages over the time axis

wrong behavior. Figure 2 depicts the situation along a time axis showing the message travelling times. In the example, different messages travelling times can impose a false ordering of messages when they arrive at the unit. Time stamps then ensure a correct sorting.

4 Method Details

The method has to handle sources of input in an adequate manner, fuse the information when appropriate, generate events and send messages. The general concept of information fusion thereby is based on: physical redundancy (the same kind of information is given by multiple sensors); temporal/knowledge based redundancy (the same sensor is monitored over time and conclusions are drawn by referring to an expected behaviour of the sources). Moreover, the exploitation of the concept of temporal redundancy (information is tracked over time and historical knowledge is taken into account to generate events) is realized giving to the system the capability to take memory / history.

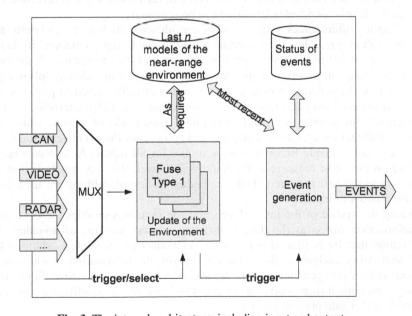

Fig. 3. The internal architecture: including input and output

In Figure 3 the internal structure of the method is depicted. Besides an input message selection mechanism (multiplexer MUX), the pillars are: the fusion strategies and the event generation section; databases to hold former snapshots (models) of the environment and the current status of the events. The data base for holding the status of the events thereby plays a central role and it is implemented using state machines. It becomes the means to generate messages in a structured, adaptable and controlled manner. In the following, the information fusion and the event generation are discussed in detail.

4.1 Information Fusion

The information fusion step evaluates input data and combines them into a virtual representation of the environment, which is also used to track the environment. It is implemented as internal database holding the last n models. The virtual representation has a double functionality: it does not only hold the results of the information fusion, it also becomes an input for the information fusion itself: new states are calculated by referring to previous situations, adding memory to the system.

The update of the environment is done by referring to multiple sources, exploiting the redundancy of them, also using temporal redundancy of the same source. The fusion thereby also includes an advanced plausibility analysis taking place on a higher level. The analysis performs checks on the physical logic of the data. For example, input data that denotes a high velocity is only accepted, if the RPM (rates per minute) of the engine also has shown some high values in the close past.

Eventually, the system performs an information fusion based on newly arriving data and old data, originating from multiple sensors (complementary redundancy) or the same sensors (temporal redundancy) over time. The structure allows information storing also in the case that it is of no relevance at the time when it is received. Obviously at this level redundant information can be removed.

Information often comes with a level of confidence, which is used to perform the merging with previous levels, generating a more reliable representation. By keeping not only the current but also some previous "images of the environment", the system can merge objects that vanish in one "image" and reappear in a closely following one at a later time. In general, incoming information is already related to previous information in terms of temporal redundancy. Monitoring signal characteristics over time also can help to identify untypical behaviour. Thus, peaks of values, which could describe malfunctioning, can be sorted out and ignored for the event generation.

There is not a unique fusion technique usable for all inputs. As consequence, depending on the input message at the multiplexer level, the appropriate fusion algorithm is selected and triggered. Thus, individual fusing algorithms are used for the variable sources of input.

During the update of the internal structure the system resembles the data core of the information fusion as the data of different sensors merging all together. False information thereby is filtered before event messages are generated, adding a high-level plausibility analysis to the method. However, the information is not abstracted (as done in the event generation step), but packed as densely as possible. For example, messages on critical road conditions ahead, which are issued by different sources, are merged together into one single data.

4.2 Event Message Generation

The event message generation step implements, with the fusion technique that here is not described, the core of the method. It refers to the virtual representation of the environment, evaluates the current values and issues events, transforming the low (raw) input data to a higher level of abstraction. Thereby, also the amount of information for a listening system is reduced. For example, an HMI can make rapid decision and issue appropriate messages, thereby also becoming compliant to principles of the EU project AIDE, which is currently undergoing an ISO standardization process. Nevertheless, the immediate transmission of alarm from a monitoring system (e.g. radar) is foreseen also. On the other hand a level of criticalness is forwarded for rapid decisions to subsequent units. The level allows for rating the events in a more consolidated manner. Besides these functional requirements, the event generation method focuses on reaching real-time requirements, by guaranteeing predictable decisions within a given time-frame.

The method relies on state machines. Each state defines an event and when entering the state an event message is sent. The decision to change a state is based on decision trees. Figure 4 displays the concept. The process of classification thus relies on these trees, where a priori knowledge is used to decide on the tree structure. The deterministic depth / length of the decision trees thereby allows guaranteeing the real-time behaviour.

The system reacts on changes in the environment and triggers new assessments. The process is state based, i.e., the differences between current and previous environmental conditions are detected and suitable events are prepared. Figure 5 displays an example for lane change events. Please note that the reduced number of states describing the location of vehicles allows for rapid decision making on issuing warning messages to drivers. Summarizing the concept behind the state machine of Figure 5, the vision system produce only information on the vehicle position in the lane, the proposed system takes care to evaluate the lane change.

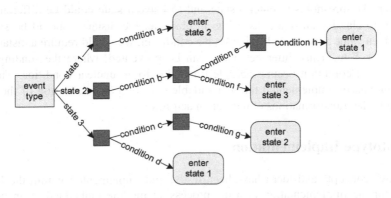

Fig. 4. The concept of decision trees for the state changes

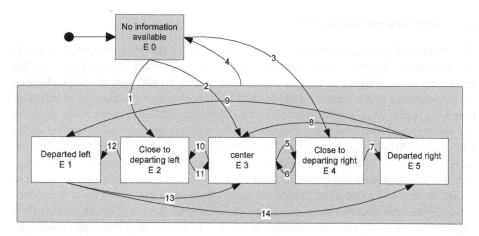

Fig. 5. Exemplary Event Generation

The decision trees to be followed are hidden behind the transitions of the state machine and identified by numbers in the figure. A table is used to hold the details on the decision trees. The source of information for the event message generation—exploited by the decision trees—is twofold: on one hand, the virtual representation of the environment—as presented above—serves as major source of input; on the other hand also the previous state of the events is required, avoiding the sending of the same event twice.

In the end, periodic updated data is transformed into events in this stage, marking the final boarder-line between the time-triggered and the event-triggered domain. As monitoring systems often operate on a cyclic behaviour, and therefore transmit information periodically, the method thus generates event-triggered messages

The occurrence of an event changes the conditions of the system. For example, the same events should not be sent twice (directly following each other), rather a minimum interval should be respected. The state machine ensures this functionality. Moreover, the thresholds to enter a state and to leave a state could be different. For example, to classify an object as being an obstacle, the distance should be smaller than a given value x m; while leaving such a condition, we would require a distance of at least $x + Y$ m. Thus, jitter behaviour can be prevented, where the sending of a specific event condition occurs multiple times due to an unclear condition. This requirement can be implemented through suitable selection and definition of the rules attached to the transformations of the state machines.

5 Prototype Implementation

The above concepts and ideas have been tested and implemented within the I-Way project for the implementation of a pre-processing module embedded to an overall architecture of a decision support system [8, 13].

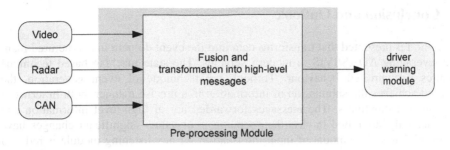

Fig. 6. Pre-processing module: prototype implementation

The decision for implementing a pre-processing module has been made upon the need to bundle data gathered from the near and medium range of a vehicle, including the vehicle itself and providing them on a higher level to the decision support system.

The scope of the pre-processing module is to facilitate the decision making process and enable fast reactions to issue alerts on time by reducing the overall data traffic of the final system. The advantage in that case is that higher reliability is achieved while the probability of error detection in the final system is reduced and the confidence in sensor observations is increased. Moreover, the combining and pre-processing of the above gathered information within a separate module gives the overall system both modularity and reduced complexity, permitting by this way easier integration and faster testing. Further possibilities as detecting the plausibility of the collected data have also been explored in order to secure the correctness of the final decisions at the end system and to avoid overlap of the collected data.

The processed data are derived from physically separated sources (Radar, video and vehicle network CAN), sending their outputs to the pre-processing system for decoding, fusing and transformation (ref. to Figure 6). The decision to enhance video information with radar and CAN data is justified upon the fact that video detection algorithms strongly depend on weather and lighting conditions thus need to be complemented with other sensing modalities.

The communication is based on TCP/IP messages sent via Sockets. The distribution of the modules to multiple and different hosts thus becomes possible, only requiring Ethernet access for the communication. For receiving messages, the unit runs one single server at a single port. Each input device has to start a client and connect to the server of the unit. The server thereby was designed to accept multiple connections of different clients at the same time. For the output messages, the unit itself starts a client and requests a connection to a server. Again, this connection is kept alive and messages (events) are transmitted directly.

Event generation state machines have been implemented for event messages classified into object detection, narrow road, and lane change as well as weather conditions. The method has been selected as it permits much more reliable and robust situational awareness.

6 Conclusion and Outlook

A method is presented that transforms data into the event domain in a structured manner leveraging ADAS/IVIS in modern vehicles. The state machine based technique ensures a controlled behaviour. Through the technique of event generation, the method achieves the submission of information in a precise manner, both in terms of content and timeliness. The messages forwarded are of high-level information and they are only submitted in case their sending is of value—significant changes have occurred. Thus, the amount of input information for any listening module is reduced to a well manageable amount. Moreover, real-time requirements are respected during the design and implementation. The modular structure of the method allows for easy extensions and maintainability.

As an enhancement to the current system, the thresholds for the decision trees could be made adaptable during run-time. The listening system then can ask for more fine or coarse grain information, depending on current conductions. Thereby, an in-field adaptation and customization can be achieved. Moreover, the straight forward technique of decision trees could be replaced by more complex decision making techniques like support vector machines or Bayesian networks. However, real-time capabilities as given for the deterministic decision trees have to be ensured also for support vector machines or Bayesian networks.

To conclude, the method resembles a technique to achieving safety for all in a cost efficient and effective manner. It proposes a technique for consolidating vehicle data to be forwarded as high level events. The events can be used for rapid decision making by modules that issue tailored messages to the benefit of drivers and the safety on roads in general.

Acknowledgements. The work was partially funded by the European Commission, Information Society Technologies (IST) as part of the project I-WAY: IST-2004-027195.

References

1. Luo, R.C., Kay, M.G.: Multisensor integration and fusion in intelligent systems. IEEE Trans. On Systems, Man, And Cybernetics 19(5), 901–931 (1989)
2. Kopf, M., Simon, J.: A concept for a learn-adaptive advanced driver assistance system. In: Conference on Cognitive Science Approaches, Neubiberg (September 2001)
3. Yoshida, T., Kuroda, H., Nishigaito, T.: Adaptive driver-assistance systems. Hitachi Review 53(4) (November 2004)
4. Ploetner, J., Trivedi, M.: A Multimodal Approach for Dynamic Event Capture of Vehicles and Pedestrians. In: VSSN 1996 Proceedings of the 4th CM international workshop on Video surveillance and sensor networks (October 2006)
5. Obermaisser, R.: Event-Triggered and Time-Triggered Control Paradigms. Springer Series: Real-Time Systems Series, vol. 22 (2005)
6. Scheler, F., Schröder-Preikschat, W.: Time-Triggered vs. Event-Triggered: A matter of configuration? In: MMB Workshop Proceedings GI/ITG Workshop on Non-Functional Properties of Embedded Systems Nuremberg, pp. 107–112. VDE Verlag (2006)

7. Kopetz, H.: Event-triggered versus time-triggered real-time systems. In: Karshmer, A.I., Nehmer, J. (eds.) Dagstuhl Seminar 1991. LNCS, vol. 563, pp. 87–101. Springer, Heidelberg (1991)
8. Rigas, G., Katsis, C.D., Bougia, P., Fotiadis, D.I.: IWAY: Towards Highway Vehicle-2-Vehicle Communications and driver support. In: The IEEE Conf. on Systems, Man, and Cybernetics (2008)
9. Rusconi, G., Brugnoli, M.C., Dosso, P., Kretzschmar, K., Bougia, P., Fotiadis, D.I., Salgado, L., Jaureguizar, F., De Feo, M.: I-WAY, intelligent co-operative system for road safety. In: IEEE Intelligent Vehicles Symposium, June 13-15, pp. 1056–1061 (2007)
10. Nakamura, E., Loureiro, A., Frery, A.: Information Fusion for Wireless Sensor Networks: Methods, Models, and Classifications. ACM Computing Surveys 39(3), Article No. 9 (2007)
11. Wu, Y., Chang, E., Chang, K., Smith, J.: Optimal multimodal fusion for multimedia data analysis. In: 12th ACM International Conference on Multimedia, pp. 572–579 (2004)
12. Albert, A.: Comparison of Event-Triggered and Time-Triggered Concepts with Regard to Distributed Control Systems, Embedded World, Nuremberg, Germany, pp. 235–252 (2004)
13. Dittmann, F., Geramani, K., Rigas, G., Katsis, C., Fotiadis, D.: Towards Advanced Information Fusion for Driver Assistant Systems of Modern Vehicles. In: Proceedings of the 68th IEEE Vehicular Technology Conference (VTC), Calgary, Alberta, Canada, September 21-24 (2008)
14. Lindner, P., Scheunert, U., Richter, E.: Multi Level Fusion for Environment Recognition. ProFusion2 e-Journal 2, 24–30 (2008)
15. Floudas, N., Tsogas, M., Amditis, A., Polychronopoulos, A.: Track Level Fusion for Object Recognition in Road Environments. ProFusion2 e-Journal 2, 16–23 (2008)
16. Tango, F., Saroli, A., Cramer, H., Floudas, N., Da Lio, M., Biral, F.: The SASPENCE Project: data-fusion and other data-processing modules. ProFusion2 e-Journal 2, 31–35 (2008)
17. Ahlers, F., Schendzielortz, T., Tango, F., Lytrivis, P., Zott, C., Fürstenberg, K.: Data Fusion Structure for the SAFESPOT Platforms. ProFusion2 e-Journal 2, 48–58 (2008)
18. http://www.aide-eu.org/

Automatic HW/SW Interface Modeling for Scratch-Pad and Memory Mapped HW Components in Native Source-Code Co-simulation[*]

Héctor Posadas and Eugenio Villar

University of Cantabria
ETSIIT, Av. Los Castros s/n,39005 Santander, Spain
{posadash,villar}@teisa.unican.es

Abstract. Native execution of instrumented code is commonly used for early, high-level SW simulations. SW code developed for a target platform is executed in a host computer for fast functional verification and performance estimations. However, as the native platform is different than the target platform, directly writing the peripheral registers or handling scratch pad memories makes the native execution to crash. Previous works require manual recoding to solve this problem. This paper presents a library that automatically solves the problem of simulating directly, fixed memory accesses. HW accesses are detected at run-time in the native execution and redirected to a target platform model. Thus, native HW/SW co-simulation is performed without any recoding effort. Both peripherals only requiring data transfers and peripherals also requiring communication event delivery are automatically managed.

Keywords: High-level modeling, native co-simulation, HW/SW interface, memory access, scratch-pad modeling.

1 Introduction

The constant increase of embedded system complexity is making early, high-level system co-simulations more and more important. Efficient design flows for HW/SW systems requires virtual platforms where the SW code can be developed meanwhile the HW platform is being optimized. Virtual platforms allow designers to verify the SW code functionality. Furthermore, performance information can be obtained to explore the best system architecture, resource mapping or platform configuration.

To obtain early and fast virtual platform models, native execution of the SW code are used. In this simulation technology the SW code is annotated with time information and executed in the host computer together with a TLM model of the target platform. Native execution is much faster than other SW modeling techniques, so it is really useful at the first design steps. Design space exploration, resource allocation and platform requirement dimensioning can be efficiently performed. The target

[*] This work was supported by the Spanish MICyT and EC through MULTICUBE FP7-216693 and the TEC2008-04107 projects.

A. Rettberg et al. (Eds.): IESS 2009, IFIP AICT 310, pp. 12–23, 2009.

platform model provides the functionality associated to the HW peripherals to allow correct system execution. The platform model also contains timing information of the HW components. Thus, not only the functional behavior, but also the performance effects can be considered in the system co-simulation.

One of the main problems in native co-simulation is the modeling of HW/SW communication. When directly executing the SW code in the host computer, HW transfers are delivered to the host peripherals, not the target platform model. Thus, the native execution crashes. Previous works require manual recoding the SW to solve the problem. When the HW accesses are performed through system calls, it is feasible. However, when HW is accessed directly reading and writing bus addresses the solution is not valid. In target platforms without MMU, HW accesses are performed through pointer accesses.

HW accesses through pointers are used for HW peripherals, shared memory regions and scratch-pads. When the scratch-pad is controlled by the user, not by the compiler, pointers are set in the code to refer to the scratch pad memory area. These pointers are scattered along the code. In that case, manual recoding is really inefficient, time consuming and error prone. This recoding is even unfeasible if pointer addresses are not fixed but resolved at runtime. Thus, at compilation time it is unknown if the pointer accesses a peripheral or not.

The solution is also valid for Software in the Loop (SiL) simulations. The usual approach for enclosing the interaction between the system and the physical environment is the Hardware in the Loop (HiL) test. Unfortunately, most of the hardware components needed for the test process are available quite late.

To solve that, SiL test has been proposed. Instead of the usage of physical interfaces, software interfaces provided by the operating system are used to connect the SW and the environment model. However, when accessing peripherals through pointers, it is required a method to detect and handle these accesses as if they was performed as system calls. Summarizing, the problem is mainly the same than for virtual platforms.

The only generic way to easily solve this problem is modifying the way the native execution is performed, not the code itself. It is required a method to automatically redirect the HW accesses to the platform model instead to the host peripherals. To redirect the accesses it is required to handle both data value transfers and communication events or only data (Fig 1). This depends on the type of HW component:

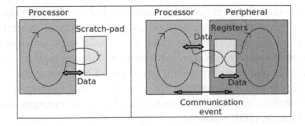

Fig. 1. Types of Processor-HW communication

- When accessing HW components like an scratch-pad or a shared memory, only data value management is required. Scratch-pad memories do not perform any functional operation when the processor accesses the data. Thus, in a native co-simulation it is not required deliver a communication event.
- When accessing a HW peripheral, a read or write access usually implies a peripheral action. For example, when some data is delivered to a co-processor, the co-processor must start computing. Thus, these communications does not only requires transferring the values between processor and peripherals; the event must be delivered to the peripheral. Only that way the peripheral model starts performing the adequate actions.

Applying this behavior to native co-simulations is a really difficult task. HW accesses modeled with direct pointer operations do not provoke any event. In the host computer, this is just a read or write operation in a variable.

This paper proposes an automatic technique to dynamically detect data transfers and deliver communication events in native co-simulations. HW accesses from the SW code are detected and redirected at run-time to access a virtual platform model. The technique has been applied to SystemC simulations. As a result, some SW codes developed for target platforms have been simulated in a native co-simulation, without any recoding effort. Data values and communication events are handled independently. This separation allows minimizing the simulation overhead, as not all HW peripherals require both solutions.

Once presented the state of the art, data value management is presented in section 3. Detection and delivering of communication events is described in section 4. The application of these techniques in a native co-simulation environment is presented in section 5.

2 Related Work

Integrating models of the HW processors in the system simulation allows obtaining very accurate performance estimations. Commercial tools have solved this challenge [1][2] using ISS that can be connected with a SystemC platform. However, integration of processor models produces a large overload when modeling SW-centric systems. The speed is deeply decreased when running binary code over an ISS with respect to executing directly the source code in the simulation. As a consequence, several approaches have been proposed to improve the results provided by commercial tools. In [3] a SystemC infrastructure developed to model architectures with multiple ARM cores is presented. This approach provides a wide set of tools that allow designers to efficiently design SW applications (OS ports, compilers, etc.). However, it cannot be used to evaluate platforms not based on ARM processors.

In [4] a generic design environment for multiprocessor system modeling is proposed. The environment enables transparent integration of instruction-set simulators and prototyping boards. GDB's remote debugging features are used to include ISSs in the co-simulation environment.

Another improvement proposed is the modification of the OS running over the ISS. As the OS is in fact the interface between SW applications and the rest of the system, it can be used to save simulation time. In [5], a technique based on virtual synchronization is presented to faster execute several SW tasks in the ISS. Only application tasks run over the ISS. The OS is modeled in the co-simulation backplane. However, although these simulations have improved the simulation speed with respect to commercial tools, the use of an ISS still implies a large overload. Thus, to obtain really fast simulations, the best option is to integrate SW source code directly in the system simulation. ISS accuracy cannot be obtained, but it can be given up in exchange of speed up when dimensioning the system at the first steps of development.

Several estimation and annotation techniques have been developed to model SW at in native co-simulation [6-10]. Even commercial tools have been developed to automatically estimate and annotate the SW code [11]. However, SW cannot be adequately modeled only using these techniques. SW requires an OS to execute. When several SW tasks run in the same processor, they cannot run at the same time. They have to be scheduled adequately. Furthermore, SW/SW communication commonly uses mechanisms not included in SystemC. Thus, OS models are required in the simulation environment to model SW execution.

Several works on OS modeling for SW native simulations from abstract OS [12-14] to real OS [15-16] have been proposed. These works also dedicate a large effort in accurately integrating time annotation and OS modeling with HW/SW communication, especially for HW interrupt management. In fact, communication in native simulations has been specifically considered in some works [16-18]. However all this works use function calls to perform communications. Accesses through pointers are not solved in any of them. In case the code contains this kind of accesses manual recoding is unavoidable.

To overcome this limitation, in this paper, an automatic way to perform communication between native simulation and virtual platform models is presented. The technique eliminates the need of SW recoding.

3 Memory Remapping of HW Data Values

In native co-simulations the operating system prevents the application code to access specific HW addresses. When the SW code tries to access a fixed HW address, the memory management unit (MMU) detects a failure as there is no a physical address associated to the required virtual address. As a consequence, the memory management system provokes a segmentation fault. The way to solve the problem is to force the operating system to create a page of virtual memory at the desired memory address. Thus, when the SW under simulation wants to read or write the HW values, values are correctly stored in the host memory.

To force the native operating system to create this memory page, the standard POSIX "mmap" function can be used. The "mmap( )" function shall establish a mapping between a process' address space and a file, shared memory object, or typed memory object. The format of the call is as follows:

"pa=mmap(addr, len, prot, flags, fildes, off);"

The mmap( ) function shall establish a mapping between the address space of the process at an address "pa" for "len" bytes to the memory object represented by the file descriptor "fildes" at offset "off". The value of pa is an implementation-defined

Table 1. Possible "flag" and "prot" values for mmap function

Symbolic Constant	Description	Symbolic Constant	Description
MAP_SHARED	Changes are shared.	PROT_READ	Data can be read.
MAP_PRIVATE	Changes are private.	PROT_WRITE	Data can be written.
MAP_FIXED	Interpret addr exactly.	PROT_EXEC	Data can be executed.
		PROT_NONE	Data cannot be accessed.

function of the parameter "addr" and the values of flags. A successful mmap( ) call shall return "pa" as its result. To indicate how the system obtains "pa" from "addr", the parameter "flags" is used (Table 1). Parameter flags provide information about the handling of the mapped data. The value of "flags" is the bitwise-inclusive OR of these options.

To ensure that the memory page created will provide support to the HW addresses required by the SW code under simulation, the option MAP_FIXED must be selected. The parameter "prot" determines whether read, write, execute, or some combination of accesses are permitted to the data being mapped. The "prot" shall be either PROT_NONE or the bitwise-inclusive OR of one or more of the other flags in the following table. For modeling HW memory addresses, PROT_READ and PROT_WRITE flags must be activated.

To apply this solution to a co-simulation infrastructure, it is required to call this function when the platform model is being created. When a peripheral is instantiated, the associated memory address in the target platform is decided. Then the "mmap" function must be called, for the specified address and the indicated memory length. The required code can be shown in figure 2. In that code, a file is created to store the information of the associated memory. It is important to note that the maximum size of the mapped memory is equivalent to the size of the associated file. As a consequence, if an empty file is used, no values can be read or written. The solution applied is to assign a size of "len" to the file before calling "mmap". To do so, the standard POSIX function "ftruncate" is used.

If the initial address does not correspond with the beginning of a memory page, special management is required. Memory pages always start in an aligned position. Thus the memory activated will start at the corresponding aligned address and will cover "len" bytes. To adjust the addresses, there are two possibilities. First the "offset" parameter can be used to indicate where exactly the mapped memory area must start. The second solution is to increase "len" with the offset of "addr". In the proposed code (fig 2) the second solution has been used. Furthermore, for debugging purposes is interesting to note that the values stored in the scratch-pad model can be shown by reading the associated file.

The solution is really effective when modeling scratch-pad memories in native co-simulations. It automatically allows executing SW code using fixed HW addresses

```
void initialize_periph (void *addr, int len){
  fd = open("tmp.txt",O_CREAT|O_RDWR,0x01b6);
  ftruncate(fd,get_page_size());

  len += addr - page_aligned(addr);
  mmap(addr,len,PROT_READ|PROT_WRITE,MAP_FIXED|MAP_SHARED,fd,0);
}
```

Fig. 2. Code for mapping the HW model memory

with a negligible simulation overhead. As no cache misses or any other event is provoked internally by scratch-pad memories, only the ability of reading and writing values at these addresses is required. More specific details of internal scratch-pad operation are not handled at high level.

4 Capturing Communication Events

HW peripherals as co-processors require receiving information about the communication events. Peripherals are not designed to make polling of any variable. They react to read or write accesses from the system processors. High-level models of the HW peripherals used in native co-simulations emulate their operation mechanisms in the same way. When applying the technique presented in the previous section, the storage is done but the peripheral does not receive any event informing that a read/write operation has been performed in their registers.

The only way to produce the event is to not apply the solution of the previous section at the beginning of the simulation and let the simulation crash. When the simulation is going to crash due to the segmentation fault, the error can be captured, solved and then the simulation can continue. The result of that process is that the HW access is detected and the event can be sent to the peripheral model. When the SW tries to access an invalid memory address, the native operating system raises a SIGSEGV signal. This signal can be captured with an appropriate signal handler. This prevents the program to terminate. However, the HW access cannot be performed at the signal handler. Neither the access type (read/write) nor the value are known at the handler.

To obtain the data, the memory remapping technique transfer presented in the previous section is used. At the signal handler the memory mapping is activated and the code returns to repeat the pointer access. To perform a correct access, in reading accesses, the read transfer to the virtual platform is done first, updating the adequate memory address. Thus, when retrying the pointer read, the value obtained is correct. For writing accesses, the pointer access is performed first, and after that the value written is sent to the virtual platform.

Performing an "mmap" allows retrying the instruction, but once an access has been performed, the memory page is active and further accesses are not detected. To solve that, the memory page must be unmapped. However, when the code returns to the failed instruction and it continues normally, that is, without unmaping the page. A possible solution is to create a parallel thread that wait a certain time and then unmaps the page. However, this is a really unsafe solution. There is no guarantee that there

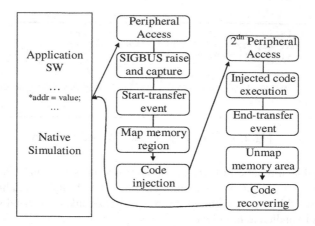

Fig. 3. Process for complete handling of HW accesses directly using pointers

will be no more accesses before the unmap step, and even there is no guarantee that the unmap is done once the application SW code continue the native simulation.

To unmap the memory page properly, the SW code itself must do it. Just after the memory access is performed, the page must be unmapped. To do that, the original SW code must be modified. The solution applied is to dynamically inject code after the load/store assembler instruction that provoked the error. This injected code disables the memory page, re-establish original SW code and continues the execution. As a consequence, the HW access is performed, the peripheral model is informed and the simulation status returns to the correct point to detect new accesses. Although the memory page is unmapped the data stored are not lost. The values are saved in the file associated to the memory page. The entire process is summarized in figure 3.

Detecting if a pointer access is a reading or a writing one is also complex. A possible solution is to disassemble the binary code of the instruction provoking the error, but this solution is non portable. Furthermore, in x86 processors both reading and writing accesses are performed with "mov" instructions, so it is not easy to distinguish both.

The portable solution is to force the system to raise different signals for read and write accesses. When executing an I/O pointer access, a SIGSEGV signal is obtained if the memory address has not been mapped. If the address has been mapped but the associated file has 0 size, a SIGBUS signal is raised. Thus at initialization the address is only activated for reading accesses with an empty file. Thus, a SIGSEGV raises at writing accesses (there is no writing permission) and a SIGBUS raises at reading accesses (there is no area in the associated file).

4.1 Capturing Signals

When the peripheral address is accessed, the memory manager of the native operating system raises a SIGBUS or a SIGSEGV signal. These signals can be captured using an interrupt handler that can be loaded using the standard POSIX "signal" function.

```
void signal_handler(int sig, siginfo_t* info, void* data){

    bus_address = (int)info->si_addr;
    if(!is_HW_addr(bus_address)) raise(SIGINT);

    unmmap(bus_address);
    file = get_no_empty_file(bus_address);
    mmap(bus_address, LEN, PROT_READ|PROT_WRITE, MAP_FIXED, file, 0);

    if(is_read = (sig == SIGSEGV))
        * bus_address=bus_read(bus_address);
    Inject_code(data);
}
```

Fig. 4. Signal handler for SIGBUS and SIGSEGV signals

The handler (fig 4) obtains the address provoking the error and checks that it is a valid I/O access. Using the data address the required memory region can be mapped to allow a retry. The active memory mapping with read-only access and an empty file is replaced by a read/write access with a valid file. Once the memory is mapped, the code injection must be performed.

4.2 Code Injection

To guarantee the memory region is unmapped properly, a new code must be injected after the peripheral access. To inject the code (fig 5), the memory region where the code will be placed is declared a read/write region, using the "mprotect" function call. Then the original code is saved in a buffer and the new code is injected.

```
void Inject_code(ucontext_t *ucp){
    struct sigcontext *sc;
    sc = (&(ucp->uc_mcontext))->gregs;
    as_addr = sc->eip + instruct_size(sc->eip);

    mprotect( page, getpagesize(), PROT_READ|PROT_WRITE|PROT_EXEC );

    memcpy(backup, as_addr, injectSize);
    memcpy(as_addr, &injectStart,  injectSize);
}
```

Fig. 5. Code in charge of performing the code injection

To make the solution portable for C-based simulation environments, the code to be injected is also written in C, avoiding specific assembler code. Two "asm volatile" marks are added to the C code to know where it starts and ends. The code injected has to be small (fig 6). The injected code is composed just by two function calls: one to get the current context and one to perform the writing access and the system recovering.

```
int (*getContext)(ucontext_t *ucp)=&getcontext;
void (*recoverFunction)() = &recoverFunction;

asm volatile( "injectionStart:" );

(*callGetContext)( &uc_auxiliar_ucp );
(*callreturningFunction)( );

asm volatile( "injectionEnd:" );
```

Fig. 6. Code to be injected

4.3 System Recovering

The recovering function (fig 7) starts performing a writing access in the HW platform model if required. Then the function unmaps the memory region using the "unmmap" function, and maps the address in read-only mode with an empty file. The original code is recovered using a "memcpy" function call, and the processor status is restored, continuing with the normal execution. The restoring of the processor status is preformed using the "setcontext" function from the "asm/sigcontext.h" library. When restoring the instruction pointer, the execution jumps to the initial code, after the pointer access.

```
void recoverFunction(){

    if(!is_read) bus_write(bus_address,*bus_address);

    unmmap(bus_address);
    file = get_empty_file(bus_address);
    mmap(bus_address, LEN, PROT_READ, MAP_FIXED, file, 0);

    memcpy(as_addr, backup, injectSize);
    setcontext(&uc_auxiliar_ucp);
}
```

Fig. 7. Function that recovers the initial status to continue the simulation

5   Application into a Native Co-simulation Tool

The solutions presented above have been applied to a state-of-the-art native co-simulation infrastructure to check their validity. SCoPE tool has been selected for this purpose. The selected infrastructure provides facilities to generate HW platform models (fig 8). Performance estimations of the SW code and the entire system can be obtained. The infrastructure also provides a complete RTOS model. This RTOS model allows directly executing SW code developed for a target platform. Recoding of the system calls is not required to perform the SW native simulation.

When applying the solutions proposed in this paper with the SCoPE features, the target SW code can be automatically simulated. The access to both SW (RTOS) and HW resources (peripherals) is dynamically handled by the simulation engine. To

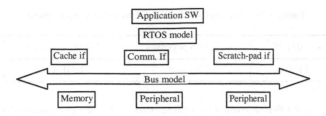

Fig. 8. Platform model built using SCoPE tool

extend SCoPE with the proposed solutions for HW communication modeling, it is required to load the bus error signal handler and to create a module that generates the required bus accesses when the communication events are delivered. To do so, the functions "bus_model->transport" can be used to send the transfers through the bus of the platform model. No other modifications have been required. This means that the proposed solutions can be also easily applied to any other native co-simulation infrastructure.

To show the usefulness of the proposed solutions, an example of a GSM system has been proposed. The GSM system is composed of the coder and the decoder. Each part contains several tasks that can be executed concurrently (fig 9). Input and output values are sent and received using specific I/O HW components. The code has been prepared for an ARM based platform running uclinux. Using SCoPE and the proposed extensions, the target code was automatically integrated in the native co-simulation without any additional effort. However, this automation increases simulation time. To obtain the simulation overhead three different simulations have been performed:

- A coder without I/O HW accesses (all SW)
- A coder with I/O HW accessed by function calls
- A coder with I/O HW accessed through pointers

The result obtained is that the pointer access technique proposed in this paper duplicates the simulation time cost of I/O accesses w.r.t HW communication techniques based on function calls (Table 2).

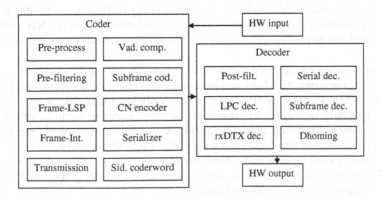

Fig. 9. Coder – decoder task graph

Table 2. Simulation time for the GSM coder (285 frames)

All SW	Function accesses	Pointer accesses
11.3 sec	12.1 sec	13.0 sec

Table 3. GSM Performance information: time, power and processor utilization

Estimated time (sec)	MonoP	SMP	HMP	Net
Proc 1	60.2 s	32.2	55.08s	55.15s
Proc 2	-	28s	5.2s	5.5s
Total	63.6s	34.7s	59.8s	60s
Estimated Energy (mJ)	MonoP	SMP	HMP	Net
Proc 1	149	80	142	136
Proc 2	-	69	77.4	13
Total	153.4	218.1	219.4	218.2
Processor utilization	MonoP	SMP	HMP	Net
Proc 1	95%	92%	92%	93,00%
Proc 2	-	82%	9%	8%

The code has been used to explore different platform architectures in order to select the best one. Mono-processor architecture, multiprocessor symmetric and heterogeneous architectures, and network-based architectures has been explored. The obtained results are shown in the following table (Table 3).

Although the estimation technique is not part of this work, it is interesting to note that source-level estimation techniques have demonstrated to obtain errors lower than the 20% in timing and processor power consumption. This is considered a sufficient accuracy for system dimensioning and analysis at first steps of development.

6   Conclusions

Automatic integration of SW code developed to target platforms can be integrated in native co-simulations. To do so, direct I/O communications from the SW code must be intercepted and redirected to virtual platform models instead of the native host peripherals.

I/O communications has been divided in two groups for native modeling: communications only requiring data load and store and communications required generating events. Modeling accesses to HW components only requiring data storage management can be easily performed by using the memory mapping facilities of the native operating system. Modeling access requiring event generation needs handling the memory faults and injecting additional code in the original execution.

Both techniques can be done using standard functions. The use of functions contained in the POSIX standard has been demonstrated. This characteristic makes the solution portable to a wide range of host computers, as Linux or Unix. The solution requires only setting a signal handler so they can be easily applied to any simulation engine.

References

1. Coware Platform Architect, http://www.coware.com
2. ARM Realview Development Suite, http://www.arm.com
3. Benini, L., Bogliolo, A., Menichelli, F.: MPARM: Exploring the Multi-Processor SoC Design Space with SystemC. Journal of VLSI Signal Processing (2005)
4. Benini, L., Bertozzi, D., Bruni, D., Drago, N., Fummi, F., Ponzino, M.: SystemC cosimulation and emulation of multiprocessor SoC design. IEEE Computer (April 2003)
5. Yi, Y., Kim, D., Ha, S.: Fast and time-accurate cosimulation with OS scheduler modeling. Design Automation of Embedded Systems (8) (2003)
6. Kirchsteiger, C., Schweitzer, H., Weiss, R., Pistauer, M.: A Software Performance Simulation Methodology for Rapid System Architecture Exploration. In: ICECS (2008)
7. Schnerr, J., Bringmann, O., Viehl, A., Rosenstiel, W.: High-Performance Timing Simulation of Embedded Software. In: Proc. of DAC (2008)
8. Brandolese, C., Fornaciari, W., Salice, F., Sciuto, D.: Source-level execution time estimation of C programs. In: Proc. of CoDes (2001)
9. Kempf, T., Karur, K., Wallentowitz, S., Meyr, H.: A SW Performance Estimation Framework for Early SL Design using Fine-Grained Instrumentation. In: Prof. of DATE (2006)
10. Hwang, Y., Abdi, S., Gajski, D.: Cycle approximate Retargetable Performance Estimation at the Transaction Level. In: Proc. of DATE (2008)
11. InterDesign Technologies, FastVeri, http://www.interdesigntech.co.jp/english/
12. Gerstlauer, A., Yu, H., Gajski, D.D.: RTOS Modeling for System Level Design. In: Proc. of DATE. IEEE, Los Alamitos (2003)
13. He, Z., Mok, A., Peng, C.: Timed RTOS modeling for embedded System Design. In: Proc. of RTAS. IEEE, Los Alamitos (2005)
14. Yoo, S., Nicolescu, G., Gauthier, L.G., Jerraya, A.A.: Automatic generation of fast timed simulation models for operating systems in SoC design. In: Proc. of DATE (2002)
15. Hassan, M.A., Yoshinori, S., Takeuchi, K.Y., Imai, M.: RTK-Spec TRON: A Simulation Model of an ITRON Based RTOS Kernel in SystemC. In: Proc of DATE (2005)
16. Castillo, J., Fernández, V., Posadas, H., Quijano, D., Villar, E.: SystemC Platform Modeling for Behavioral Simulation and Performance Estimation of Embedded Systems. In: Behavioral Modeling for Embedded Systems and Technologies: Applications for Design and Implementation. IGI international (ed.)
17. Wieferink, A., Leupers, R., Ascheid, G., Meyer, H., Michiels, T., Nohl, A., Kogel, T.: Retargetable generation of TLM bus interfaces for MPSoC platforms. In: CODES+ISSS 2005 (2005)
18. Gerin, P., Guérin, X., Pétrot, F.: Efficient Implementation of Native Software Simulation for MPSoC. In: Proc. of DATE (2008)

Modelling of Device Driver Software by Reflection of the Device Hardware Structure

Thomas Lehmann

HAW Hamburg, Berliner Tor 7, 20099 Hamburg, Germany
thomas.lehmann@haw-hamburg.de

Abstract. Embedded systems are highly optimised to operate in the physical world they are embedded to. Hence, dedicated peripheral devices are designed which need support by a device driver to raise the level of abstraction for the application programmer. Even with methods of hardware/software co-design, devices and drivers are still designed by two designer groups. This paper depicts a systematic approach to design the coarse grained structure of the device driver by reflection and mapping of the internal structure of the device hardware. Even though common operating systems are programmed in a functional programming language, means of object-oriented programming languages and design pattern are applied.

1 Introduction

Device drivers are adaptors between an application and peripheral devices integrated in an operating system (OS). They have to provide dedicated services towards the application (see Fig. 1) and hides away which services are performed in hardware and which in software, either by the driver or by helper functions of the operating system (see Fig. 2).

Embedded systems are highly optimised systems. Special hardware is designed to adapt to the physical world the device is embedded to. Hardware near programming is a complex task, because of various reasons. Hardware is parallel, software is sequential. Software design paradigms (such as layering[1]) are different from hardware designs paradigms (such as a hierarchy of components[2]). Low-level access to the device is operating systems and target dependent. The developer of a device driver struggles with various problems, next to the problem to find a straight-forward model for the inside of the device driver.

A key question for the software side is, how to structure or to model the device driver to rapidly create a driver prototype? Following the idea of agile software

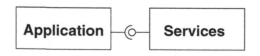

Fig. 1. Expected perspective of the application

A. Rettberg et al. (Eds.): IESS 2009, IFIP AICT 310, pp. 24–31, 2009.

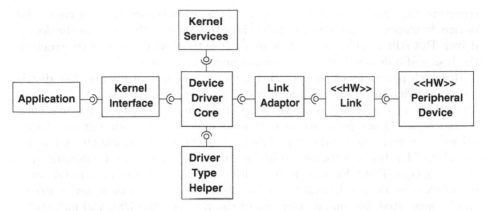

Fig. 2. Relation of application, device, driver, and OS-services

development, this prototype doesn't need to have high performance. It has to demonstrate the combined features at an early stage of development.

A nowadays approach is to build the device driver as part of a hardware/software co-design. Here a model of the whole service functionality is the starting point and device and driver are generated. But still devices are designed by a hardware group and a software group needs to integrate the hardware by providing the device driver for integration. For instance, there are many devices available as IP-Core[3], but there is no corresponding device driver available. Especially, if the controlled system is a medical device, you will never find a standard device driver.

In this paper, an approach for modelling the device driver software based on an analysis of peripheral device structures is described. Hardware structures are identified and the corresponding software models are described. The paper starts with a discussion of other approaches. The approach shown in this paper starts with a description of the main idea and than shows how to reflect and map hardware interfaces and components to corresponding software interfaces and components. The modelling ends with an outline of other useful software structures in this field. The paper ends with a summary and an outlook.

2   Other Approaches

Even though device drivers are 'normal' software, less guidance can be found to model software in the field of device drivers.

Books on this topic deal on the one hand side with a very general view on device drivers. They cover operating systems in general (such as [1]) and hence can give only a rough idea how common device drivers, such as file system drivers, are designed. The second category of books deals with drivers in the environment of dedicated operating systems like Linux[4] or Microsoft Windows[5]. These books focus on the interface (function calls) towards the application, the services the operating system provides for device drivers, and how to coarse grained structure the driver to fit into the operating system kernel. In both cases, the device developer can get a rough idea on how to structure the inside of the device driver. But still no guideline on how to analyse the device and how to structure the inside of a device driver based on the analysis is given.

Research papers focus on operating systems and special features like distribution, configuration or real-time scheduling. Some with separation into User Mode Driver and Kernel Mode Drivers[6] and the refactoring[7] towards such a separation. Other publications deal with a design flow support for device driver[8] or with the synthesis of interface between components[9], following the idea of hardware/software co-design. One group has derived a domain specific language (DSL) for a dedicated class of device drivers by analysis of a set of existing device drivers[10]. So for that class of devices a device driver can be generated, but on an extension of the features, the DSL will lack statements to support that new feature, because it has been constructed by reverse engineering.

In summary, most literature on device drivers is on how it is and only few hidden hints or guidelines are given on how to model device driver software for a dedicated device.

3   Approach of Structural Reflection

Nowadays operating systems, such as Linux, Microsoft Windows, or VxWorks, follow a layering paradigm as internal structure and use a non-object-oriented programming language like C. Other non-common operating systems already make use of the object-oriented paradigm, such as BeOS[11], DReAMs[12] or JNode[13].

Along with the object-oriented paradigm come ideas like Model Driven Design [14], Design Pattern[15], Aspect Oriented Programming[16], and Domain Specific Languages[10] based on the object-oriented concepts. The object-oriented paradigm is a powerful paradigm which is established in application programming and only on the rising in the field of operating systems, due to some drawbacks. Nevertheless, a modelling or structuring approach for device driver software should follow the object-oriented paradigm. An object-oriented model with appropriate restrictions can translated to a non-object-oriented paradigm for the use in common operating systems.

Object-oriented software is a structure of interacting components or objects with a strong separation of concerns. On the hardware side, digital devices are a graph of interacting digital components which are hierarchically organised. Usually, no layering approach is used to structure hardware whereas it is a common architectural pattern in software.

The approach to structure the internal software of the device driver is to map structures and interface identified in hardware to corresponding structures and interfaces in software, which follow the object-oriented paradigm. The graph of interacting hardware components has to be identified and mapped to a graph of interacting objects on the software side. Interfaces between hardware components have to be mapped to appropriate interfaces in software.

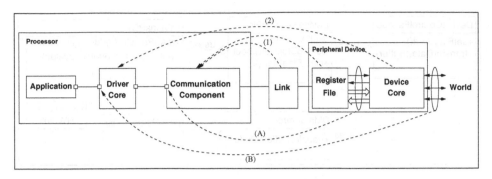

Fig. 3. Reflection of interfaces (A and B) and components (1 and 2)

So on a coarse grained level,

- register file and link maps to communication component (see Fig. 3,1),
- interface between register file and device core maps to interface between driver core and communication component (see Fig. 3,A),
- device core to driver core (see Fig. 3,2), and
- interface to the outside world maps to API of driver, extended by whole service functionality (see Fig. 3,B).

The next subsection will describe this mapping in more detail.

3.1   Register File and Communication Component

The register file is the interface between the device core and the communication link to the processor. A corresponding part on the software side, the communication component, has to hide away this interface and provide the driver core a transparent access to the device core. The objective of the communication component is to cover the communication topology between processor and device even if other devices are involved in the communication, such as serial links like serial peripheral interface (SPI).

The communication component needs to cover the transport via the communication link of various technology (e.g. bus or serial link) and topology (e.g. bus line or star with hubs). If the register file is accessible in a memory space manner, direct communication channels can be provided here. If other devices are involved on the path to the register file, the querries for the register file need to be encoded/decoded for the whole path. Thus the communication component works as an adaptor to device drivers which is responsible to handle the communication via the communication link to the device register file. Along with the access means, management components needs to be integrated. In case the communication link has the ability for hot-plugging, the communication link needs to be monitored and in the case of an interruption the deriver core needs to be informed on the event.

The communication component is either realised by a single object or a set of objects, whereas one object is a facade class[15] with an appropriate interface.

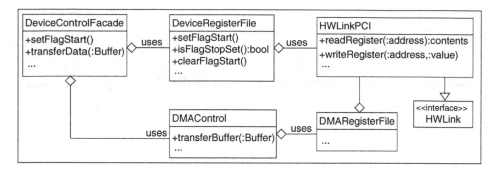

Fig. 4. Example for the class hierarchy for a device driver

Depending on information exchange characteristics between the register file and the device core, additional elements need to be added, as depict in the next section.

3.2   Interface of the Communication Component

The communication component has to provide an interface towards the driver core and adapt to the interface of the communication link.

On the hardware side, via the register file signals to the device core can be set, states of signals can be read, or data is transferred. This interface is reflected to the interface between the communication component and the driver core (see Fig. 3). The provided functionality via this interface is to manipulate the signals and to query the signal states.

In comparison to simple signals, the interfaces for the transfer of data sets must support the kind of data flow demanded by the hardware. The communication pardims used in the hardware must be handled here. Buffers with random access, such as shared memory, have a different data flow than FIFO-buffers. In both cases, a synchronisation means must be provided. For instance, the FIFO buffer can only be read, if data is available. For shared memory, access control means must be provided to avoid collisions. Hence, the communication component needs a control component for each buffer type to provid seamless data transfer. The flow control is handled by dedicated classes, which are part of the communication component facade class (as depict in Fig. 4).

From the perspective of object-orientation, the communication component is an adaptor that hides away the communication via the registers and the communication path between processor and register file. The adaptor can be seen as a delegator as well, because it forwards service requests to the device core. Furthermore, the level of abstraction can be lifted from programming on bit-mask level to query methods, such as *isFlagStopSet()*. The driver core now uses this interface to communicate with the device core transparently.

3.3   Device Driver Core

The device driver has to provide dedicated services with the support of the hardware device. The driver core, that corresponds to the device core, communicates via a transparent communication component with the device core. On the other side, it provides an application programmer interface and uses services of the operating system (see Fig. 3). The driver core has multiple objectives: It has to add missing functionality, it has to cover multiple functionality, it has to restrict functionality, and it has to adapt functionality, like filtering.

Here only a few hints can be derived from the hardware structure, because functionality is not realised by structure only, more by the interaction of the implemented functionality inside the components. Nevertheless, the software part needs to communicate with a dedicated component of the hardware via other components to provide a total functionality. So as reflection, on the software side a chain of software components needs to be created, which cover the (inverse) communication of their associated hardware component, to have a transparent communication to the destination.

Another typical pattern are parallel buffers which in combination with a consuming component. For instance, the message buffers of a CAN-controller. A buffer is selected for consuming depending on a dedicated algorithm. As inverses of the selection component in hardware, a dispatcher to select the message buffer needs to be provided on the software side.

3.4   Device Driver API

The driver core needs to be designed to provide in combination with the device core a dedicated service. If the service does not communicate with the physical world outside the device, the interface needs to provide the access means which are required by components implemented in the driver core.

If communication to the outside world is involved, these services can be put into two classes which have different effect on the interface design:

- End-points of the device shall be controlled by the driver, so access near to the physical level shall be provided. An API towards the application can be directly derived, because driver and device have to provide a transparent access in cooperation. As a simple example, the logical level of a hardware pin of a parallel interface shall be controlled. The API is simply to set the level. The driver must transparently configure the hardware to gain this access to the pin level.
- The other class of API is an abstraction of the device end-point to a higher level. As an example, a Full-CAN controller provides message boxes as interface an has an internal selection policy for the messages. In contradiction to the first class, here not the level on the send lines shall be controlled, but a service which allows messages to send. The driver core has to provide an API for sending messages. Still it is partially reflection of the hardware, because the structures look similar, functionality is different and at a higher level of abstraction.

For some devices, a mixture of abstraction levels is provided by the application interface, depending on the knowledge towards the outside world.

4 Additional Design Patterns

In the following sections, additional patterns are depict or discussed in more detail. Design Patterns[15] are an easy to understand descriptions for solutions in software. In the area of device driver design, some of these patterns can be either applied or used to describe parts of the design, not only for the driver but for parts outside the device driver system as well.

IRQ-Handling. The publisher subscriber pattern[15] in combination with the chain of responsibility pattern[15] fits well to the handling of interrupt requests (IRQ). Interrupt requests are often collected from their hardware source by a chain of OR-elements to a single destination inside the processor (see for instance PowerPC-architecutre[17,18]). The processor branches to the main interrupt handler, which identifies the source and calls the interrupt service routine. The inverse pattern for the collection structure is a dispatcher pattern, for which code can be automatically generated[18]. Destination needs to be registered and assigned to a certain event they are interested in (Publish-Subscriber-Pattern). In some cases, the origin cannot be determined by the publisher itself, so subcomponents (subscriber) need to gather more specific information them self. All subscriber are informed in a chain of responsibility and they check the assigned interrupt source.

Device and Driver Management. Devices and driver management is usually part of the operating system. Device types are identified, corressponding drivers are load, configured and used. This management can be modelled with the multiton and the factory pattern[15]. The factory creates the driver object structure, configures the driver objects including linking to the corresponding device. Depending on the number of devices of the same class, only that number of corrsponding driver objects are created. The management features of the factory can include means of device identification and creation of the correct version of driver for the identified sub-class or sub-version of the device. Driver versions are implemented by inheritance of a base version and means of polymorphism are applied.

5 Conclusion and Future Work

This paper has discussed how to derive a first software model for a device driver for a new hardware device. The software structure and the interfaces has been derived from the interfaces in hardware and the coarse grained structure of the interacting components by reflection. Design Patterns have been applied to ease the software design. The resulting driver will not have high performance, but can be use for first integration in the sense of rapid prototyping.

As future work, a more fine grained reflection of the hardware functionality shall be explored. This requires an appropriate description of the hardware as well as the required total functionality.

References

1. Tanenbaum, A.S.: Moderne Betriebssysteme, 3rd edn. Prentice Hall, Englewood Cliffs (2009)
2. Reichardt, J., Schwarz, B.: VHDL-Synthese, 4th edn. Oldenbourg-Verlag, Munchen (2009)
3. Open cores. Internet (2009), http://www.opencores.org
4. Jonathan Corbet, A.R., Kroah-Hartman, G.: Linux Device Drivers, 3rd edn. O'Reilly, Sebastopol (2005)
5. Oney, W.: Programming the Microsoft Windows Driver Model, 2nd edn. Microsoft Press Books, Redmond (2002)
6. Purohit, A., Wright, C.P., Spadavecchia, J., Zadok, E.: Cosy: Develop in user-land, run in kernel-mode. In: HotOS, pp. 109–114 (2003)
7. Ganapathy, V., Balakrishnan, A., Swift, M.M., Jha, S.: Microdrivers: A new architecture for device drivers. In: HotOS 2007: Proceedings of the 11th Workshop on Hot Topics in Operating Systems, San Diego, California, USA, USENIX Association, May 2007, pp. 85–90 (2007)
8. Lehmann, T.: Towards Device Driver Synthesis. PhD thesis, University of Paderborn (2003)
9. Ihmor, S.: Modeling and automated synthesis of reconfigurable interfaces. Doktorarbeit, University of Paderborn (2006)
10. Thibault, S., Marlet, R., Consel, C.: A Domain-Specific Language for Video Device Drivers: from Design to Implementation. Technical report, Institut National de Recherche en Informatique et en Automatique (1997)
11. Team, T.B.D.: BeOS Advanced Topics-The Official Documentation for the BeOS. O'Reilly, Sebastopol (1998)
12. Ditze, C.: Towards Operating System Synthesis. PhD thesis, University of Paderborn (2000)
13. Jnode - Java new operating system design effort. Internet (2009), http://www.jnode.de
14. Object management group - omg. Internet (2009), http://www.omg.org
15. Gamma, E.: Entwurfsmuster. Addison-Wesley, Reading (1996)
16. Kiczales, G., Lamping, J., Mendhekar, A., Maeda, C., Lopes, C.V., Loingtier, J.M., Irwin, J.: Aspect-Oriented Programming. In: Aksit, M., Matsuoka, S. (eds.) ECOOP 1997. LNCS, vol. 1241, pp. 220–242. Springer, Heidelberg (1997)
17. Shanley, T.: PowerPC System Architecture. MindShare Inc., Addison-Wesley Publishing Company, Reading (1995)
18. Lehmann, T., Zanella, M.: Modeling and software synthesis of interrupt systems. In: GI/ITG/GMM Workshop: Methoden und Beschreibungssprachen zur Modellierung und Verifikation von Schaltungen und Systemen, Tübingen, GI/ITG/GMM (February 2002)

An Infrastructure for UML-Based Code Generation Tools

Marco A. Wehrmeister[1], Edison P. Freitas[3], and Carlos E. Pereira[2]

[1] Instituto de Informática, [2] Dep. de Engenharia Elétrica
Universidade Federal do Rio Grande do Sul, Porto Alegre, Brazil
mawehrmeister@inf.ufrgs.br, cpereira@ece.ufrgs.br
[3] School of Information Science, Computer and Electrical Engineering,
Halmstad University, Halmstad, Sweden
edison.pignaton@hh.se

Abstract. The use of Model-Driven Engineering (MDE) techniques in the domain of distributed embedded real-time systems are gain importance in order to cope with the increasing design complexity of such systems. This paper discusses an infrastructure created to build GenERTiCA, a flexible tool that supports a MDE approach, which uses aspect-oriented concepts to handle non-functional requirements from embedded and real-time systems domain. GenERTiCA generates source code from UML models, and also performs weaving of aspects, which have been specified within the UML model. Additionally, this paper discusses the *Distributed Embedded Real-Time Compact Specification* (DERCS), a PIM created to support UML-based code generation tools. Some heuristics to transform UML models into DERCS, which have been implemented in GenERTiCA, are also discussed.

Keywords: UML, Aspect-Oriented Design (AOD), code generation, aspects weaving, distributed embedded real-time systems.

1 Introduction

The design of embedded systems is not a trivial task. The domain of embedded real-time systems presents many specific requirements (e.g. deadlines for tasks accomplishment, energy consumption, reduced footprint, etc.) that do not specify system's functionalities but are tightly related to them. Such requirements are called non-functional requirements. Traditional approaches, such as object-orientation or the structured analysis, do not have specific abstractions to deal with these requirements, whose treatment is usually found intermixed with the handling of functional requirements. This situation leads to problems such as tangled and scattered handling, which hinder the reuse of previously developed artifacts (e.g. models or code). To solve the above-mentioned problems, some proposals can be found in the literature, such as subject-oriented programming [2] and Aspect-Oriented (AO) programming [3], which provide special constructions to specify and encapsulate non-functional requirements handling into single elements.

A. Rettberg et al. (Eds.): IESS 2009, IFIP AICT 310, pp. 32–43, 2009.

However, solving these problems only at implementation level is not sufficient to deal with the mentioned complexity. Abstraction level increase is an old but widely accepted idea to help with such quest. Thus, embedded systems community is looking for new techniques/approaches, such as Model-Driven Engineering (MDE) [1], aiming at the management of complexity in the design of distributed embedded real-time systems. An important issue to allow the use of MDE in embedded systems design is tool support [1]. Automatic transformation from a Platform Independent Model (PIM) to a Platform Specific Model (PSM) is a key issue to make models the main artifact during the whole development cycle instead of source code. Additionally, it avoids errors coming from manual transformations, and also helps to keep specification and implementation synchronized. Code generation from high-level models can be seen as a transformation of PIM into PSM, but instead of using meta-model to meta-model transformations (i.e. transforming meta-model elements from a PIM into PSM meta-model elements), it applies the translation of meta-model elements into text representing source code in a target language.

The aim of this paper is to extend the discussion presented in [18] by providing details on key elements of a tool called *Generation of Embedded Real-Time Code based on Aspects* (GenERTiCA). GenERTiCA has been developed to support the *Aspect-oriented Model Driven Engineering for Real-Time systems* (AMoDE-RT) approach [4], which uses concepts from the AO paradigm to deal with non-functional requirements since early design phases. Besides code generation, GenERTiCA also performs aspects weaving into both the generated code and the input model to provide non-functional requirements handling as specified in aspects' adaptations. Therefore, in addition to the discussion on code generation and aspects weaving processes, this text also presents the *Distributed Embedded Real-Time Compact Specification* (DERCS), a PIM created to represent system's structure, behavior, and non-functional requirements handling (in terms of AO elements). Moreover, heuristics to transform UML into DERCS models are also discussed.

This text is organized as follows: section 2 provides details on DERCS; section 3 presents the transformation from UML to DERCS models; section 4 discusses GenERTiCA's code generation and aspects weaving processes; section 5 discusses some related works. Concluding remarks and future work are discussed in section 6.

2 Meta-model for Code Generation and Aspects Weaving

AMoDE-RT approach [4] uses UML as specification language for systems' PIM, representing its structure, behavior, and non-functional requirements handling in a platform independent fashion using aspects provided by the *Distributed Embedded Real-time Aspects Framework* (DERAF) [7]. Furthermore, designers use MARTE profile [8] to specify real-time features. UML has been chosen due to its acceptance as a standard, wide use in software community, and increasing interest by embedded systems community. Additionally, there are several academic and commercial CASE tools (supporting UML modeling) available to be used. However, for code generation purposes, UML has a weakness: its meta-model is huge and ambiguous, i.e. the same feature can be specified in distinct perspectives using distinct diagrams, which most often overlap each other making it a source of inconsistencies. Such inconsistencies could be partially verified using model consistency checking/testing techniques. However, despite its importance, this paper does not discuss model checking.

To address the mentioned specification problem, GenERTiCA transforms UML models into a new PIM called *Distributed Embedded Real-time Compact Specification* (DERCS). DERCS' meta-model is simpler than the UML one, but it provides the same information as UML models, i.e. system's structure, behavior and non-functional requirements handling, which is specified independently from functional requirements handling by using AO constructions. In addition, it is worth to mention that DERCS has been proposed to assist code generation tools design.

In DERCS, system structure is specified in the same way as in UML, i.e. objects are the fundamental entity. They represent system's elements, whose interaction and performed actions provide the expected functionality. Objects can be active or passive. The former kind represents objects that have their own execution flow (i.e. their own thread), such that they execute actions concurrently with other active objects. Usually, the active objects are compared to concurrent processes, and hence also have characteristics such as execution pattern (e.g. periodic, aperiodic, or sporadic), priority, deadlines, and others. On the other hand, passive objects execute actions sequentially as response to messages sent by other objects (passive or active). Additionally, objects can be deployed in different nodes, representing computing resources (i.e. a unit with processor, memory, network infrastructure, etc.) or a hardware unit upon which object execute their behavior. These concepts are similar to those available in UML and MARTE meta-models.

The behavior semantics of DERCS is to execute a sequence of actions in response to: (i) messages exchanged among objects, (ii) application events or (iii) state-related events. Objects, which can be deployed in the same (i.e. local objects) or different nodes (i.e. remote objects), interact by exchanging messages. After receiving a message, an object executes the behavior associated with this message. In DERCS, this behavior semantics is always the same, independently if the message has been sent from a remote or local object. The description on "how" to implement this communication is defined in the mapping rules according to the target platform. GenERTiCA selects (based on DERCS information) the appropriate script for each sending message action. For events, the behavior semantics is similar, i.e. the behavior associated with an event is triggered after the recognition of this event's occurrence.

Furthermore, DERCS can represent not only send message action, but also other actions, such as assignments, evaluation of expression, state transitions, creation and destruction of objects. These actions represent an adaptation of UML 2.x meta-model's behavioral elements (e.g. actions).

The most important difference between DERCS and UML 2.x meta-model is the representation of aspects and their adaptations. Fig. 1 shows a fragment of DERCS meta-model that is related to AO concepts. Aspects provide structural and behavioral adaptations, which modify system's elements that have been selected through joint points. Inside the UML model, joint points are specified as *Join Point Designation Diagrams* (JPDD) [9]. JPDDs are "compiled" during the UML-to-DERCS transformation to create instances of the *JoinPoint*, which contain a list of elements selected by the JPDD. The following elements can be selected: (i) classes, (ii) attributes, (iii) methods, (iv) behaviors, (v) actions, (vi) objects, and (vii) nodes. All of these elements are descendents of the *BaseElement* meta-model class.

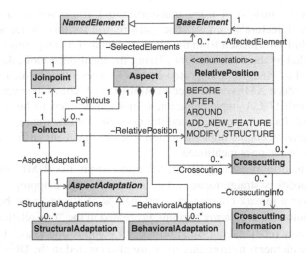

Fig. 1. DERCS elements related to non-functional requirements

Aspects' adaptations are linked with join points through *Pointcut* instances, which are obtained from *Aspects Crosscutting Overview Diagram* (ACOD) [4][10]. Adaptations are applied in the selected element at a *RelativePostion*, which can be before or after a certain point in the execution flow, or enclosing a behavior or action, or even modifying the structure or adding new features to an element. In this sense, DERAF aspects provide pre-defined adaptation semantics that shall be used to specify the non-functional requirements handling. *StructuralAdaptations* and *BehavioralAdaptations* are created according to aspects' adaptations that have been specified in ACOD.

Finally, it is important to highlight that DERCS tries to simplify the meta-model of UML 2.x by grouping structural and behavioral information, instead of having this information spread over different meta-model elements of different diagrams. More specifically, the modeled dynamic behavior (i.e. action sequences) described in different diagrams (i.e. activity, interaction and state diagrams) are grouped together into an instance of *Behavior* meta-model element. Moreover, AO-related meta-model elements separate the handling of function from non-functional requirements already in modeling level. Hence, this separation can be carried until the aspects weaving phase. This is an important contribution for the improvement of model elements reusability, as presented in [10]. Additionally, this separation is also helpful to mapping rules description since it allows designers to concentrate efforts in one concern at each time.

3   UML-to-DERCS Transformation

Once the distributed embedded real-time system is modeled using UML, MARTE and DERAF, it is possible to transform the UML model into a DERCS model. GenER-TiCA performs this transformation automatically using pre-defined heuristics.

GenERTiCA has been implemented as a plug-in to the Magic Draw CASE tool [15], which provides an API to access the UML 2.x meta-model. Hence, the transformation from UML to DERCS (as well as DERCS meta-model itself) was written as "normal Java code" instead of using transformations frameworks, such as Acceleo [13] and OpenArchitectureWare [14]. The main reason for this choice was the possibility to access full information from the UML model and its diagrams using an MOF [17] API (provided by the modeling tool). Using the mentioned tools, the UML model must be exported as XMI to be imported as other representation, such as EMF [16], which could introduce XMI version incompatibility problems. However it is worth to mention that GenERTiCA implementation is not constrained to be a plug-in for a specific case tool. Its source code is modular enough to allow the replacement of the current transformation engine implementation to other one using different transformation frameworks as the ones mentioned.

The transformation of structural specification from the UML meta-model to DERCS meta-model is straightforward, i.e. is a one-to-one mapping, as depicted in Table 1. However a remark concerning relationships of classes must be written. For one to many relationships, an array attribute is created in the "one relationship-end" to represent the "many relationship-end". Further, for composition associations, methods to add or remove elements to/from this array are also created in the DERCS model.

Considering the behavior specified in the UML model, GenERTiCA analyzes sequence diagrams to find actions that are executed within the context of methods. It also identifies branches in the execution flow as well as loops. This is achieved using a call stack-based mechanism similar to one implemented in computer programs. Reserved words are used to indicate actions that are different from message sending, allowing the specification of assignments or expression evaluations actions within sequence diagrams. During the evaluation of sequence diagrams, objects are also "discovered". On the other hand, their deployment is performed according to information obtained from deployment diagram.

Table 1. Mappings between structural elements of UML and DERCS meta-model

UML meta-model	DERCS meta-model
Class	Class
Property	Attribute
Type ou PrimitiveType	DataType sub-class
VisibilityKind	Visibility
Operation	Method
decorated with <<getter>>	Method, Behavior, ReturnAction
decorated with <<setter>>	Method, Parameter, Behavior, AssignmentAction
Parameter	Parameter
ParameterDirectionKind	ParameterKind
Association	Attribute, Method, Behavior, ReturnAction, AssignmentAction, Parameter
if any association end defines AggregationKind as composite	Além dos acima, CreateObjectAction, DestroyObjectAction
Lifeline ou InstanceSpecification	
related to class decorated with <<SchedulableResource>>	ActiveObject
classes without stereotype or decorated with <<MutualExclusionResource>> or <<Resource>>	PassiveObject

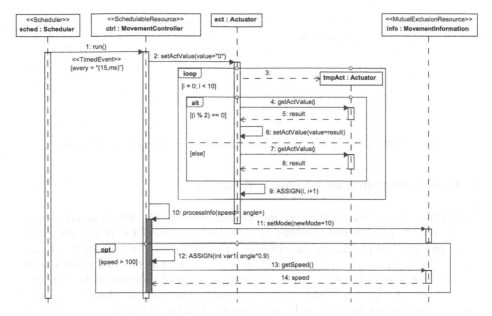

Fig. 2. Specification of system behavior using a sequence diagram

Fig. 2 depicts a sequence diagram that illustrates an example of system behavior modeling. From this diagram, transformation heuristics can infer the behavior of three methods: (i) *MovementController.run()*; (ii) *Actuator.setActValue()*; (iii) *Movement Information.processInfo()*. For (i), the behavior has two send message actions (related to messages 2 and 10). The behavior of (ii) is more complex having a object creation action (message 3), a branch, three send message actions (messages 4-8) and an assignment action (message 9). Considering (iii), its behavior has two send message actions (messages 11 and 13), an assignment action (message 12) and a branch.

An important part of UML-to-DERCS transformation heuristics is the creation of AO related elements in DERCS model. Aspects are specified in ACOD, which is a special kind of class diagram. Each class annotated with <<Aspect>> stereotype is transformed into an aspect. Structural and behavioral adaptations, and also pointcuts are represented as instances of the *Operation* meta-class in the UML meta-model. They are transformed into instances of, respectively, *StructuralAdaptation*, *BehavioralAdaptation* and *Pointcut* meta-classes of DERCS.

However the most critical part of the transformation is the evaluation of JPDDs to create *JoinPoint* instances, and also to select elements according the search criteria specified by JPDD. In spite of the expressiveness provided by JPPD to select join points, in current version of the UML-to-DERCS transformation heuristics, JPDD specification is constrained to simple selections. Hence, DERCS elements that can be selected are: (i) *Class*; (ii) *Attribute*; (iii) *Method*; (iv) *Node*; (v) *SendMessageAction*; (vi) *ReturnAction*; (vii) *CreateObjectAction*; (viii) *DestroyObjectAction*; (ix) *Behavior*. Fig. 3 depicts a JPDD that selects the active objects' behaviors that are associated to methods that are executed cyclically. Therefore, when this JPPD is evaluated, all instances of DERCS' *Behavior* meta-model element, which match with the specified selection criteria, are gathered into the join point created to represent this JPDD.

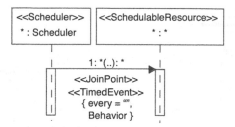

Fig. 3. JPDD: selection of active objects' behavior that is triggered periodically

4   Code Generation and Aspects Weaving

GenERTiCA is a tool created to support the AMoDE-RT [4], which separates concerns related to requirements handling by using aspects from DERAF [7] along with UML and MARTE profile [8]. At modeling phase the (informal) semantics of each aspect adaptation are platform independent, i.e. it is defined how the system is affected by adaptations but there are no definitions on how to implement such adaptations in a given platform. These adaptations implementations are done as mapping rules scripts that use services and constructions available in the target platform. A discussion on aspects implementation has been provided in [18] and [20].

GenERTiCA's code generation approach is based on mapping rules scripts that are described in XML files. Mapping rules for different platforms can be specified in a single XML file. GenERTiCA chooses the appropriate mapping rules according to objects deployment information available in DERCS model. Fig. 4 depicts organization of mapping rules in the XML file.

There are two kinds of mapping rules: *Application* and *Platform Configuration*. The former represents the mapping rules to generate the application source code, i.e. code that implements system's expected behavior according to application requirements; code describing how objects are connected and how they interact, as well as how the application handles system's non-functional requirements. On the other hand, the *Platform Configuration* branch contains scripts that are responsible to customize services provided by the platform, onto which the application runs. Such customization can be seen as an "on/off switch" for platform services. Depending on how the platform can be customized, GenERTiCA can create configuration files, and/or to tailor APIs' source code, using information from DERCS model, e.g. list of aspects specified in the ACOD.

The XML format was chosen due to its organization, as a tree structure, that facilitates the reuse of previously developed scripts, as well as the organization of the produced scripts. Leafs contain scripts, which are in fact the ones responsible to perform the translation from DERCS elements to source code, and also to weave aspects adaptations into the generated code or input model (i.e. DERCS model). By using XML, the designer can create repositories to store implementations of DERAF aspects, as well as mapping rules that have been previously created and validated. It is an easy task to describe a script to map, for example, actions that represent message exchanged between remote objects using a given API, and reuse it in a futher project that uses the same API and/or target platform.

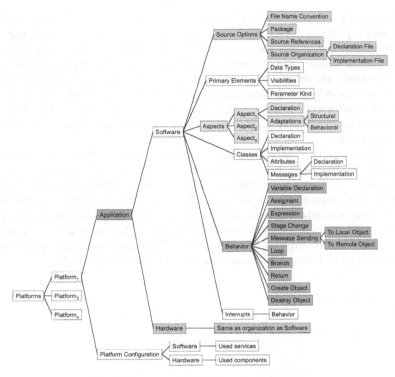

Fig. 4. Strcuture of mapping rules XML files

Simplicity was one of the aims for the description on how to map DERCS elements into source code. GenERTiCA adopts an approach that uses small scripts that are responsible to generate fragments of source code (for each single element of DERCS), which are combined into source code files. On other words, scripts in XML tree's leafs need only to access information from few elements (or just a single one), keeping the focus and aim of the mapping rule, instead of creating complex scripts that can generate the whole source code. The scripting language used in GenERTiCA is the *Velocity Template Language* (VTL) [11], an open source and wide used scripting language. VTL was chose because it allows writing any kind of text, into which one can specify simple commands to customize the text produced after script execution. Thus, VTL accomplishes GenERTiCA requirement for generating code for different languages. For examples of VTL scripts, interested readers are referred to [18] and [20].

To perform the code generation/aspects weaving, GenERTiCA implements the algorithm depicted as an activity diagram in Fig. 5. GenERTiCA traverses the list of DERCS' elements (e.g. classes, attributes, methods, behaviors, etc.), looking for a script that matches with the selected element, according to the tree hierarchy of the XML file. Once the script is found, it is executed, generating a fragment of text representing the source code for the selected element. In addition, GenERTiCA verifies if any aspect affects the selected element, i.e. it checks if this element is contained in the selection list of any join point. If this is the case, all pointcuts, which are related to that join point, are evaluated to find which adaptations must be applied in the selected element.

Adaptations' scripts are executed and modify the generated code fragment, i.e. the aspect weaving is performed. This algorithm repeats until all elements are evaluated.

It is important to highlight that, due to VTL, leaf nodes contain scripts that allow the generation of source code fragments for different languages such as C/C++, Java, VHDL, SystemC, and others. These generated code fragments are merged to create source code files, which are compiled or synthesized by external tools. The script language has full access to information about system objects using DERCS meta-model (see section 2). Therefore, it is possible to construct specialized and also complex mapping rules.

VTL allows scripts to access methods available by any object registered in the scripting engine. Therefore, aspect adaptation scripts can perform modifications in the DERCS model (i.e. aspects model weaving) by means of accessing methods available in DERCS API. Aspects model weaving allows an early evaluation of the impact caused by aspects adaptations in the model. Thus, tools such as design space exploration tools could evaluate different implementations of the same aspect in order to chose one that best fits with system requirements. For details on design space exploration at modeling level using UML, interested readers should refer [12].

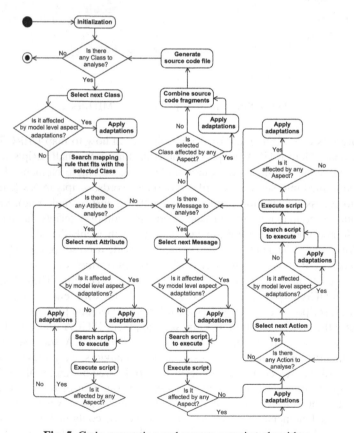

Fig. 5. Code-generation and aspects weaving algorithm

5 Related Work

Code generation is not a new topic. The idea of using computers to generate code from some higher abstract specification comes since the beginning of the use of computers. Several works aiming at distinct domains have been done in this subject. In general, it can be stated that techniques vary from the sort of input specification, passing through the way to perform code generation, until the amount of generated code and the target language. In order to keep the focus on the generation of code for distributed embedded real-time systems, this section discusses a small fraction of recent related works.

CoSMIC [5] provides generative tools that work with a set of Domain Specific Modeling Languages (DSML) in order to provide a component-based implementation for a distributed embedded real-time system. DSML are interesting options for distributed embedded real-time systems design, however user-made languages introduce some problems due to the lack of standardization for concepts and language constructions. In our approach we use a standard and well-accepted modeling language like UML that overcomes such problems. Besides, the CoSMIC's AO-related tools work with aspect like AO languages does, i.e. aspects, joinpoints, pointcuts are specified as text instead of using a graphical notation as our approach does. However, besides not using graphic representations for AO concepts, these tools can also modify the input model.

SysWeaver [6] is a toolset for analyzing non-functional requirements, automating design choices (design space exploration), and also to generate code for distributed embedded real-time systems, which are specified using Mathlab/Simulink. Basically, the difference from that work is that our work deals with distributed embedded real-time systems specification in terms of OO and AO concepts, instead of specifying functional and para-functional properties. In addition, our code generation approach seems to be more flexible to generate code for different target languages due to ability of VTL's scripting engine, which recognizes commands within any normal text, and also due to the approach of using small script dedicated to a specific element of the input model.

6 Conclusions and Future Work

The proposed work addresses the problem of automatic code generation for distributed embedded real-time systems. The presented infrastructure deals with functional and non-functional requirements using concepts of AO paradigm in order to improve the separation of concerns on their handling.

GenERTiCA is a code generation tool capable to deal with aspects during the code generation process. The adopted approach uses small scripts to produce code fragments that are merged to create source code files. Besides code generation, GenERTiCA can also perform aspects weaving at model and implementation levels. Hence, it is possible to perform aspects weaving in the input model, as well as in the generated source code. GenERTiCA's approach supports the use of AO concepts together with non-AO languages, e.g. C/C++, SystemsC, VHDL, since AO concepts are specified in the model, and aspects are implemented as mapping rules that uses constructions available in the target laguage.

GenERTiCA takes a UML model as input, transforming it into a DERCS model, which has a simplified meta-model (compared with the UML one) to provide information on system structure, behavior, and non-functional requirements handling (as DERAF aspects). Additionally, a set of mapping rules organized in a XML file is also used as input to GenERTiCA. With this approach, scripts previously developed can be easily reused in further projects [20], reducing the design time. Once a set of mapping rules is created and validated to a given platform, it can be easily reused into other projects that use the same target platform. As presented in [20], GenERTiCA has been successfully used in some case studies to generate RTSJ code from UML models, as well as C++ code for the ORCOS [21].

As future work, other case studies are being developed, as well as mapping rules for other target platforms (e.g. EPOS [19], RTAI, and VHDL) are being created. The implementation of transformation heuristics needs to be improved to support other JPDD selections. Other possible future work is to modify GenERTiCA implementation to use one of the open source transformation engines mentioned in this text. Additionally, the presented methodology is intended to guide the development of adaptable and flexible middleware aiming at its use in wireless sensor networks. The use of aspect-oriented concepts will allow the aggregation of different features to the middleware as they are required, and this way, promoting the desired flexibility and adaptability.

References

1. Selic, B.: The Pragmatics of Model-Driven Development. IEEE Software 20(5), 19–25 (2003)
2. Ossler, H., Tarr, P.: Using Subject-Oriented Programming to Overcome Common Problems in Object-Oriented Software Development/Evolution. In: 21st International Conference of Software Engineering, pp. 687–688. IEEE Computer Society Press, Los Alamitos (1999)
3. Kiczales, G., et al.: Aspect-Oriented Programming. In: Aksit, M., Matsuoka, S. (eds.) ECOOP 1997. LNCS, vol. 1241, pp. 220–242. Springer, Heidelberg (1997)
4. Wehrmeister, M.A., et al.: An Aspect-Oriented Approach for Dealing with Non-Functional Requirements in a Model-Driven Development of Distributed Embedded Real-Time Systems. In: 10th IEEE International Symposium on Object and Component-Oriented Real-Time Distributed Computing, pp. 428–432. IEEE Computer Society, Los Alamitos (2007)
5. Gokhale, A., et al.: Model Driven Middleware: A New Paradigm for Deploying and Provisioning Distributed Real-time and Embedded Applications. Journal of Science of Computer Programming: Model-Driven Architecture (2004)
6. Niz, D., et al.: Model-based Development of Embedded Systems: The SysWeaver Approach. In: 12th IEEE Real-time and Embedded Technology and Applications Symposium, pp. 231–242. IEEE Computer Society, Los Alamitos (2006)
7. Freitas, E.P., et al.: DERAF: A High-Level Aspects Framework for Distributed Embedded Real-Time Systems Design. In: Moreira, A., Grundy, J. (eds.) Early Aspects Workshop 2007 and EACSL 2007. LNCS, vol. 4765, pp. 55–74. Springer, Heidelberg (2007)

8. OMG. UML Profile for Modeling and Analysis of Real-time and Embedded Systems (MARTE) (2005), http://www.omg.org/cgi-bin/doc?ptc/2007-08-04
9. Stein, D., et al.: Expressing Different Conceptual Models of Join Point Selections in Aspect-Oriented Design. In: 5th International Conference on Aspect-Oriented Software Development, pp. 15–26. ACM Press, New York (2006)
10. Wehrmeister, M.A., et al.: A Case Study to Evaluate Pros/Cons of Aspect- and Object-Oriented Paradigms to Model Distributed Embedded Real-Time Systems. In: 5th International Workshop on Model-based Methodologies for Pervasive and Embedded Software, pp. 44–54. IEEE Computer Society, Los Alamitos (2008)
11. The Apache Velocity Project, http://velocity.apache.org/engine/releases/velocity-1.5/
12. Oliveira, M.F.S., et al.: Early Embedded Software Design Space Exploration Using UML-Based Estimation. In: 7th IEEE International Workshop on Rapid System Prototyping, pp. 24–32. IEEE Computer Society, Los Alamitos (2006)
13. Acceleo, http://www.acceleo.org
14. openArchitectureWare, http://www.openarchitectureware.org/
15. Magic Draw tool, http://www.magicdraw.com/
16. Eclipse Modeling Framework, http://www.eclipse.org/modeling/emf/
17. OMG, Meta Object Facility (MOF), http://www.omg.org/mof/
18. Wehrmeister, M.A., et al.: GenERTiCA: A Tool for Code Generation and Aspects Weaving. In: 11th IEEE International Symposium on Object and Component-Oriented Real-Time Distributed Computing, pp. 234–238. IEEE Computer Society, Los Alamitos (2008)
19. Fröhlich, A.A., Wanner, L.F.: Operating System Support for Wireless Sensor Networks. Journal of Computer Science 4(4), 272–281 (2008)
20. Wehrmeister, M.A.: An Aspect-Oriented Model Driven Engineering Approach for Distributed Embedded Real-Time Systems, Ph.D. Thesis, Federal University of Rio Grande do Sul, Brazil (2009)
21. Organic Reconfigurable Operating System, https://orcos.cs.uni-paderborn.de/orcos/

A Configurable TLM of Wireless Sensor Networks for Fast Exploration of System Communication Performance

Ines Viskic and Rainer Dömer

Center for Embedded Computer Systems
University of California, Irvine
iviskic@uci.edu, doemer@uci.edu

Abstract. Transaction Level Modeling (TLM) is seen as an efficient Embedded System modeling technique to reduce the simulation time in large and complex designs. This is achieved by abstracting away pin- and cycle- accurate details from communication transactions, which reduces the number of events that need to be simulated.

In this paper, we apply TLM principles to communication modeling in Wireless Sensor Networks (WSN). Modeling and simulating wireless communication is critical in exploration and optimization of WSNs as it enables evaluation of system design choices early in the design process.

Unlike on-chip bus modeling, wireless communication modeling is broadcast-based and unreliable, which requires distributed medium access arbitration and timeout/retransmission capabilities. We present two TLMs of TDMA and CSMA/CA protocols. Our models are scalable to large networks and flexible in parameters and protocol configuration. Our experiments demonstrate insights to how adjusting protocol parameters in various network configurations affects the overall WSN performance.

1 Introduction

Advances in hardware and wireless network technologies have enabled widespread and cost effective deployment of WSNs. WSNs are scalable and robust ad-hoc networks of embedded sensing and transmitting devices that represent a new paradigm in system communication. Their applications include surveillance, natural phenomena detection (e.g. wind, flood, fire), GPS and traffic monitoring, all of which have differing requirements and operating conditions. With growing application complexity and expanding design space, WSNs are becoming more difficult to design and optimize. With modeling and simulating the WSN, the designer is able to observe the effects of taken design choices early and can optimize the configuration prior to system implementation.

Network communication is paramount to the functioning of a WSN. The selection of an appropriate communication protocol greatly effects the performance of the entire system. Therefore, modeling and simulating WSN communication is very useful in predicting the overall system behavior.

A. Rettberg et al. (Eds.): IESS 2009, IFIP AICT 310, pp. 44–56, 2009.

This paper reports on the modeling of two popular broadcast protocols for wireless communication: *Carrier Sense Multiple Access with Collision Avoidance* (CSMA/CA) and *Time Division Multiple Access* (TDMA). CSMA/CA is part of the 802.11 standard for wireless communication based on medium sensing and collision avoidance. TDMA is a protocol that divides the time-share of the medium among the users and allocates time slots to each one. Both protocols have properties that benefit certain types of traffic profiles, but are a limiting factor in other deployment conditions. We present a TLM [7], [11] configurable for both protocols and compare their performance on a set of performance indicators.

The rest of the paper is structured as follows: related work is addressed in Section 2. Section 3 and Section 4 describe the components of a wireless sensor network and the broadcast communication protocols, respectively. Our modeling of WSN and its broadcast channels is outlined in Section 5. Finally, we present the experimental setup and analysis of the performed simulations in Section 6 and end the report with concluding remarks in Section 7.

2   Related Work

The widespread application of wireless communication systems (e.g., PDAs, cellphones, WSN, etc.) has generated significant research for their efficient modeling. With respect to the modeling objective, several approaches can be found.

The authors of [6] use SystemC [9], [8] modules to simulate and analyze the performance of the Bluetooth standard at behavioral level. The goal of their simulations is to identify noise levels and creation of a piconet in presence of noise in the channel. Similarly, we use SystemC to model communication primitives of wireless broadcast protocols at transaction level (TL), but with the objective of protocol performance estimation and network configuration.

The methodologies presented in [3] and [10] model WSN to validate the configuration before synthesis. As such, in [3] only TDMA is supported and [10] focuses on automatic code generation for sensor nodes. In [14] and [12], modeling provides insight into power dissipation and computational bottlenecks, respectively. This paper addresses the issue of design exploration and qualitative analysis of WSN communication. The objective is to identify the trade-off of various protocols and their configurations.

NS-2 is a network simulator engine traditionally used to model TCP/IP networks but has recently included features for wireless communication modeling. [2] uses NS-2 together with SystemC to model and simulate a large set of heterogeneous networked embedded systems (both wireless and wired). With respect to wireless network modeling, different network configuration parameters of NS-2 can be set (node distance and speed, power dissipation per transmisson). However, only a general statistical parameters (such as packet loss rate) are available for modelling communication. Also, the application is abstracted with statistical data of message transmission rate over a period of time. In contrast, our model includes the actual functionality of each node as an executable specification in SystemC and therefore will help in identifying the optimal configuration parameters of the actual application at hand.

3   WSN Architecture Components

A WSN consists of a set of sensor devices (nodes) communicating with the base station via a wireless communication protocol. Sensor devices sense the environmental phenomena and transmit the measured data to the base station, while the base station gathers and processes the obtained data. An example WSN is shown in Figure 1. All components contain embedded processors and radio-frequency (RF) transceivers for local data processing and broadcasting, respectively. The capacities of memory units in each component determine the amount of sensing history. Additionally, the sensor devices contain sensing HW and local power supplies (battery).

With regards to the mobility of sensor nodes, we classify WSN as static or dynamic [13]. Static WSN consists of stationary components and is initialized for operation with a set-up infrastructure communication phase where the nodes exchange their status information (node location, available memory size, battery matter, etc). In the operational phase, the sensors regularly transfer the sensed (and locally processed) data to the base station. On the other hand, a dynamic WSN

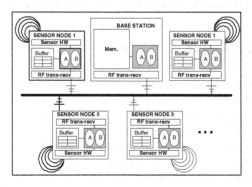

Fig. 1. Example of a Wireless Sensor Network

is characterized with mobile sensor nodes and/or base station, with multiple set-up communication phases for updating the nodes on network's status. This paper addresses static WSN, where the models contain a single infrastructure phase followed by an operational phase. Further, our current TLMs are limited to one-hop WSN, with a single base station and multiple sensor instances. A multi-hop topology, on the other hand, contains multiple base stations with broadcasting capabilities. However, our TLM can be extended to support multi-hop WSN by supplying the current base station implementation with (a) a broadcasting method and (b) support for multiple instantiations.

4   WSN Communication Protocol

Regardless of the specific functionality of a WSN, its performance greatly depends on the efficiency of the underlying communication mechanism. Therefore, one of the most important aspects in configuring a WSN is selection of an appropriate communication protocol.

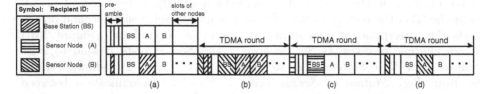

Fig. 2. TDMA protocol. (a) Sensor node A to Base Station transmission, (b) Sensor nodes A and B transmitting to Base Station and Base Station transmitting to Sensor node B, (c) Base Station transmitting to Sensor node A, (d) Sensor node A transmitting to Sensor node B.

In selecting WSN communication, we must take into account the unique features and application requirements of sensor networks, such as limited memory and computational capacities, and proneness to node failure. Therefore, traditional end-to-end communication that requires single and double handshake mechanisms are generally not suitable for WSN. Furthermore, due to strict requirements for power conservation and failure recovery, the WSN should not implement protocols with demand-based QoS, large message overheads, and/or long link setup delays. Finally, WNS should tolerate unreliable and faulty transmissions, which makes broadcast communication with best-effort transport and timeout capabilities desirable.

At TL, the broadcast protocols are described within the Data Link Layer that covers the MAC (Media Access Control) and the Physical Layer, as specified in the ISO OSI reference model. With regards to the mode of medium access, we model representatives of protocols with both random access and fixed allocation channel access.

4.1 Time Division Multiple Access (TDMA)

TDMA is a communication protocol that allows multiple transmitters to access a single radio-frequency (RF) channel by dividing channel access into time slots and allocating each to a specific transmitter (fixed allocation medium access). This time separation ensures that multiple users will not experience interference from other simultaneous transmissions and substantially improves the efficiency and quality of wireless communication.

Figure 2 illustrates the TDMA protocol. The figure shows the RF channel timeline divided among N transmitters: we highlight only Sensor Nodes A, B, and a Base Station, for clarity. Each TDMA transmission (in figure: TDMA round) is separated into a single *preamble* slot (with N sub-slots) and N data slots. Each transmitter announces its intent to transmit by broadcasting the recipient's ID during its *preamble* sub-slot. All transmitters scan the *preamble* to identify whether they are someone's recipient. If so, the recipient expects to receive the data during the sender's data slot. On the other hand, if the transmitter does not read its ID in the *preamble*, it will sleep for the duration of N data slots to conserve energy.

For example, in the first TDMA round (Figure 2(a)), *Sensor node A* broadcasts the ID of the recipient (*Base Station*) in its *preamble* sub-slot, and broadcasts the corresponding data during its data slot. Round two (Figure 2(b)) shows multiple receives, as *Sensor node A* and *Sensor node B* send to *Base Station* while *Base Station* sends to *Sensor node B*. Figure 2(c) shows a transfer from *Base Station* to *Sensor node A*. Finally, communication between two sensors is shown in Figure 2(d), where *Sensor node A* is sending to *Sensor node B*.

The main weakness of the TDMA protocol is in the amount of wasted bandwidth in a low traffic environment, since the time slot is allocated to a transmitter whether or not the transmission is scheduled. For example, only Figure 2 (b) shows the full utilization of the TDMA round. In contrast, Figure 2 (a), (c) and (d) show $N - 1$ data slots left unused since only a single node transmits in each round.

4.2   Carrier Sense Multiple Access (CSMA/CA)

Carrier Sense Multiple Access (CSMA) protocol has a random medium access strategy that is best suited for applications with light traffic load and short delay data exchange, as it allows transmissions as soon as the sender senses a free medium. However, interference occurs if more than one transmitter sense the medium free and decide to transmit at once.

In order to circumvent interference of multiple simultaneous broadcasts, protocol 802.11. uses a *Collision Avoidance* mechanism together with a *Positive Acknowledge* scheme, i.e. CSMA/CA.

Collision Avoidance senses that the medium is free for a specified time (i.e. Distributed Inter Frame Space) before trying to transmit the data. In addition, a Positive Ack scheme is used to assure the transmitted packets are indeed received. If the sender does not receive an acknowledgement of the packet by the receiver, it will retransmit the packet. In case the receiver experienced node failure, the sender will recover by aborting further transmissions after a specified number of retransmission attempts.

Exponential Random Backoff Algorithm is a mechanism to resolve contention for the shared medium access between transmitters. The same algorithm runs on each transmitter independently of each other, generating a random period (M_i) from the *Backoff interval(i)*. M_i is the time transmitter i will wait before sensing the medium again. The waiting time needs to be at least long enough to allow the transmitter to determine whether the medium has already been accessed by another transmitter.

After each unsuccessful attempt to transmit, the transmitter i increases its *Backoff interval(i)* exponentially until it reaches the *Linear interval(i)* (a user defined parameter). After that, the increase continues linearly. As previously stated, each transmitter has only *n_tries* attempts before aborting further transmissions.

5   Transaction Level Modeling of WSN

We model WSN in SystemC [9], which provides module constructs *sc_module* with computational processes (*SC_THREAD*) sensitive to input changes and event oc-curences (*sc_event*). Using SystemC constructs, we implement sensor nodes as ob-jects of class *SensorNode* while the base station is an object in class *BaseStation*. Every component contains one or more concurrent processes that encapsulates a sequential C/C++ code with calls to wireless communication methods.

Our communication methods are modeled based on ISO OSI layering, as shown in Figure 3: at the application level, the processes invoke generic functions *send_msg()* and *recv_msg()* of channel *C_WSN_broadcast* to transfer messages of variable size. In contrast, the MAC layer provides services for fragmenting the message into fixed size packets and forwarding it to either the CSMA/CA (random access) or the TDMA (fixed access) broadcast protocol layers. Further-more, the MAC layer implements the unreliability of WSN communication as follows: based on the probability of a successful broadcast, the sender's MAC

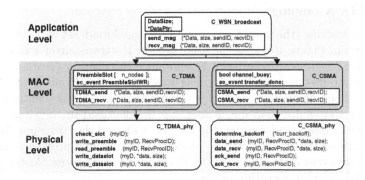

Fig. 3. Overview of our Broadcast Channel Model

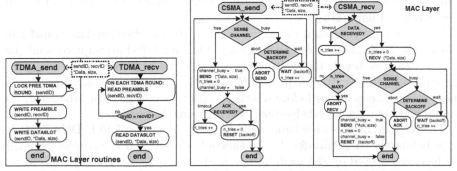

(a) TDMA functionality at the MAC Level.

(b) CSMA/CA func. at the MAC Level.

Fig. 4. TL modeling for broadcast protocols

layer randomly determines whether it will forward the packet to lower layers for broadcasting. As a consequence, the broadcasts of the packets discarded by the MAC layer are considered to have failed. The success/fail rate of the broadcast is a user defined parameter (in percentages).

In case of CSMA/CA broadcast, the processes use channel *C_CSMA*, invoking communication routines with built-in timeout and retransmission mechanisms. We use *sc_event transfer_done* to denote the start and end of transaction, and a *channel_busy* variable to detect packet collision. The physical layer primitives of the CSMA (encapsulated in channel *C_CSMA_phy*) model the exponential backoff algorithm and the data byte and acknowledge transfers.

TDMA broadcast, on the other hand, divides the radio frequency into time slots alotted to different transmitters which announce their intent to transmit during their *preamble* sub-slots. Therefore, the model of the TDMA channel at the MAC layer (channel *C_TDMA*) has an array *PreambleSlot*, which the transmitters read on every TDMA round and a *sc_event* that occurs on each write to the *PreambleSlot*. The physical layer of the same protocol (channel *C_TDMA_phy*) contains transfer announcement and data transfer routines.

5.1   TDMA Modeling

This section describes the flow of executing a package broadcast with TDMA protocol (as seen in Figure 4(a)). At the sending side, the transmitter waits until its first available *PreambleSlot* sub-slot to announce the transfer (*write_preamble*), then writes into its data slot. The receiver reads the entire *PreambleSlot* array. The index of the array element that contains receiver's ID is identified as its sender. Note that more than one sender can be identified in the same TDMA round. If one or more senders exist, the receiver will read the corresponding data slot(s), otherwise the receiver will go to sleep. The sleeping process is modeled with a *wait* for event *PreambleSlotWR*. On the next *write_preamble*, the process returns to the normal operating mode.

5.2   CSMA/CA Modeling

The send and receive routines for package transfer with the CSMA/CA protocol are shown in Figure 4(b)).

Here, the sender senses if the medium is busy before starting data transfer by testing the boolean variable *channel_busy*. On each failed attempt to send (i.e. *channel_busy* is *true*), the waiting time before the next medium sensing will increase according to the *Exp backoff* algorithm. The sender attempts transmission for *n_tries* times before aborting. After successful data broadcast, the sender expects an acknowledge (*ack*) packet from the receiver.

The receiver, on the other hand, will sense the channel for BROADCAST_DUR time before aborting transfer due to timeout. However, if the correct recipient ID has been sensed on the medium before timeout, the receiver will accept the broadcasted data and initiate sending of an (*ack*) packet.

Note that the unsuccessful acknowledge is considered a failed attempt of transmission: the receiver has limited number of attempts to transmit an *ack* (up to *n_tries* times) before aborting, and the sender will abort waiting for an *ack* after experiencing timeout at most *n_tries* times.

6   Experimental Setup and Analysis

We have modeled the described protocols according to their specification and implemented following a temperature sensoring application [1]. The application senses and logs the temperature value and, if the sensed temperature is beyond the threshold limits (specified by the user), an alarm signal toggles a LED. The platform consists of a base station and N_NODES sensors. The application flow is as follows:

1. Upon starting, the base station enters configuration mode, where the infrastructure is determined and the lower and upper bounds for the normal temperature values are set.
2. Once the threshold values are set, the base station enters operational mode. Each sensor node transmits an average of 16 sensed temperature values (*Avg Value* message) to the base station.
3. Regardless of the sampling period, if the temperature crosses the threshold values, the sensor node transmits a *Critical Value* message.
4. In addition, the base station can query the current average temperature aperiodically and get a reply in the form of a *Avg Value* message.

Figure 1 outlines the WSN implementing the described application. Each network component contains two processes: processes marked with *A* on Figure 1 denote transfer of *'Avg Value'* messages and processes marked *B* encapsulate *'Critical Value'* transmissions. The following experiments simulate the wireless communication of this WSN with both CSMA/CA and TDMA protocols.

6.1   Comparison of Broadcast Protocols

Unlike CSMA/CA protocol, TDMA does not require message acknowledgements, since the fixed schedule among the nodes prevents medium access collisions. However, by pre-allocating the medium access, a significant time of a node can

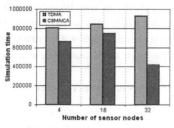

N_SENSOR_NODES	4, 16 and 32
N_PROCESS_PER_NODE	2
N_MSGS	1000
MIN_WAIT	VARIED
MAX_WAIT	VARIED [100 to 1000]
Exp_back-off	32 ns
Linear_back-off	128 ns
N_TRIES	8
SLOT_SENSE	1 ns
SLOT_PREAMBLE	10 ns
SLOT_DATE	100 ns
TDMA_ROUND	32 data slots
TDMA_DELAY	preamble slot

(a) Simulated exe. time   (b) WSN configuration param.

Fig. 5. Experiment 1: Comparison of TDMA and CSMA/CA for the same load

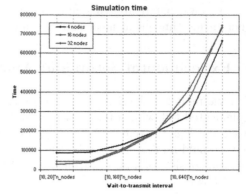

N SENSOR NODES	4, 16 and 32
N_PROCESS_PER_NODE	1
N_MSGS	1000
MIN_WAIT	10
MAX_WAIT	VARIED [100 to 1000]
Exp back-off	32 ns
Linear back-off	128 ns
N_TRIES	8

(a) WSN config. parameters   (b) Scalability of CSMA/CA TLM

Fig. 6. Experiment 2: Dependence of simulated execution time of WSN (with CSMA/CA and decreasing contention) to the WSN size

be wasted on idle waiting for its slot to broadcast. Therefore, **Experiment 1** (Figure 5) compares the CSMA/CA and TDMA communication protocols with regards to (simulated) execution time for 1000 successful broadcast messages.

In Figure 5(a), the x-axis denotes the number of nodes in WSN (4, 16 and 32) and y-axis shows the simulated execution time of the application transmitting 1000 messages from each node. Figure 5(b) presents the full list of configuration parameters for the experiment. As shown in Figure 5(a), even though TDMA protocol needs no retransmissions, broadcasting 1000 messages with TDMA takes more than double the time of CSMA/CA broadcast for the WSN with 32 sensor nodes.

Since CSMA/CA is clearly better suited for the selected WSN model in our experiment set, we will focus on CSMA/CA for the remainder of this paper.

6.2 Scalability of CSMA/CA TLM

Experiment 2 (Figure 6) aims to gauge the scalability of our CSMA/CA communication models by measuring the execution time of sensor networks of different sizes: WSN with 4, 16 and 32 sensor nodes. Each simulation measures sensor nodes broadcasting a total of 1000 messages to the base station using CSMA/CA communication protocol. Further, for each of 3 sensor network configurations (shown in Figure 6(a)), we perform 6 simulations with varied waiting time between two consecutive message broadcasts in each node (in Figure 6(b): wait-time interval), based on:

```
wait-time(node_i) = rand_of [10, a* N_SENSOR_NODES], where:
    N_SENSOR_NODES = 4, 16, 32
                 a = 20, 40, 160, 320, 640 and 1280
```

The function above de-facto configures the level of contention for the WSN communication medium. The longer the wait-time for each transmitter is, the less contention the WSN will experience. For example, the network consisting of

4 nodes simulates broadcast of 1000 messages with 250 messages sent from each node. Each node is programmed to wait between broadcasting two consecutive messages for a random number of [10, 80], [10, 640], [10, 1280], [10, 2560] and [10, 5120] time units (ns).

Figure 6 (a and b) demonstrates that our communication model performs equally well for small and large WSN. The graph shows the increase of (simulated) execution time as contention decreases. As expected, the simulated time of system execution is proportional to the waiting time between two consecutive broadcasts in each node. However, it is virtually independent of the number of nodes in the WSN. We conclude that our communication model scales well for large WSN models.

6.3   Analysis of TLM CSMA/CA

In order to validate the correctness of our modeling approach, **Experiment 3** simulates CSMA/CA protocol on a WSN with configuration listed in Figure 6(a), but with its size fixed to 32 nodes.

The simulated results, shown in Figure 7, confirm the expected behavior of the CSMA/CA protocol: with heavy traffic load and high contention, the majority of broadcast messages will experience collisions. This is evident by the number of retransmissions significantly exceeding the number of successful broadcasts where the wait-to-transmit intervals are ≤ 5120 ns for each node (measure points 1 and 2 in Figure 7).

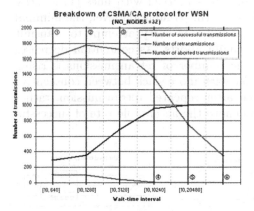

Fig. 7. Experiment 3: Performance of CSMA/CA under decreasing contention

As the contention level decreases, less messages get aborted. However, the WSN still experiences large numbers of retransmissions of messages before each successful transmission. This is demonstrated with the retransmission curve peak at measure point 3 (wait-to-transmit interval = 5120 ns). For networks with sporadic message transfers (wait-to-transmit ≥ approx. 20000), CSMA/CA efficiently transmits ≥ 98% of the total scheduled messages (measure points 4, 5 and 6). Moreover, after point 5 the number of retransmissions is less than the number of successful transfers, falling to less than a third of the successful transfer rate at point 6.

6.4   Configuring an Efficient WSN Supporting CSMA/CA Protocol

The fourth set of experiments (Figure 8 and Figure 9) varies the size of the WSN, the wait-to-transmit interval for each node, and the number of retransmission

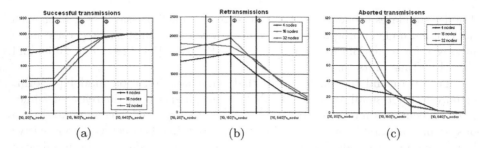

Fig. 8. Experiment 4a: The dependence of transmissions to contention and WSN size. (a) Successful transmisisons, (b) Retransmissions and (c) Aborted transmissions.

attempts (n_tries). Experimenting with values of these parameters, the users can determine a WSN configuration that complies with their specified performance metrics, such as rate of successful, retransmitted or aborted transfers.

Experiment 4a. Varyies the size and wait-to-transfer interval. As the size of WSN increases, the messages need to be transmitted less frequently to decrease contention and avoid collisions. By varying the level of the wait-to-transmit interval, it is possible to identify the threshold size of WSN in which message transfers are of desired/specified efficiency. More specifically, lines (1), (2) and (3) denote characteristic thresholds for our third experiment setup.

In Figure 8(a), (b) and (c), contention levels marked with lines (1) identify the maximal number of aborted transfers. At this contention level, the minimal number of messages is transferred successfully, as every attempt to transmit experiences collision, timeout, and eventually aborts. As contention decreases (from line (1) to (2) in Figure 8(b)), the number of retransmissions is rising until it peaks at line (2). This means that with more slack between consecutive broadcasts, more messages are delivered after repeated retransmission, rather than aborted entirely. Finally, lines (3) denote the acceptable rate of successful

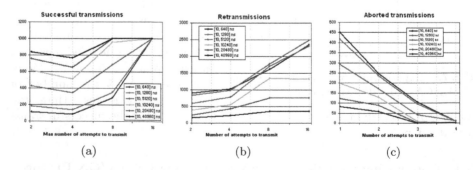

Fig. 9. Experiment 4b: The dependence of transmissions to retransmission attempts and WSN size. (a) Successful transmisisons, (b) Retransmissions and (c) Aborted transmissions.

N_SENSOR_NODES	4, 16 and 32
N_PROCESS_PER_NODE	2
N_MSGS	1000
MIN_WAIT	10
MAX_WAIT	VARIED [100 to 1000]
Exp back-off	32 ns
Linear back-off	128 ns
N_TRIES	2, 4, 8 and 16

Fig. 10. Configuration parameters for experimental setup 4 (a) and (b)

transfers and corresponding numbers for retransmissions and aborted messages. This rate will vary with individual WSN designs, according to their performance specifications. For example, a WSN with 80% successful message transfers and $\leq 10\%$ aborted transfers is accomplished with the wait-to-transmit interval is no less than $160 * n\_sensor\_nodes$.

Experiment 4b: In addition, by experimenting with the maximal number of retransmission attempts before aborting transmissions (n_tries), we can determine the size and/or wait-time interval for most efficient message transfers. The rates of successful transmissions, retransmissions and aborted transmissions, when varying values for n_tries, are shown in Figure 9 (a), (b), (c), respectively. This experiment demonstrates that the value of n_tries for our WSN configuration is at most 8 (for high contention traffic) and at least 4 (for low levels of contention). This is evident from Figure 9 (a), where the change of n_tries from 4 to 8 yields the sharpest rise in the number of successful transfers. During low contention and for $n\_tries \geq 8$, this parameter has little to no effect on the overall WSN performance, as transfers experience a negligible number of retransmissions.

7 Conclusion

We have demonstrated that SystemC TLM can support WSN models. In particular, we describe the TLM of two popular broadcast communication protocols: TDMA and CSMA/CA. A detailed analysis of the CSMA/CA protocol confirms the expected performance of CSMA/CA under varied contention levels and, therefore, validates our modeling approach.

In addition, we demonstrate that applying TLM principles to WSNs is an efficient way to configure WSN systems. By varying the parameters of WSN TLMs, we can quickly explore and identify the WSN configuration that will yield optimal results with regards to the given environment and specified performance metrics.

References

1. Temperature sensor application using st lm135 (2007),
   http://www.st.com/stonline/products/literature/an/11890.htm
2. Alessio, E., Fummi, F., Quaglia, D., Turolla, M.: Modeling and simulation alternatives for the design of networked embedded systems. In: DATE, Nice (2007)

3. Bonivento, A., Carloni, L., Sangiovanni-Vincentelli, A.: Platform based design of wireless sensor networks for industrial applications. In: DATE, Munich (March 2006)
4. Cionca, V., Newe, T., Dadârlat, V.: TDMA protocol requirements for wireless sensor networks. In: Proceedings of the 2nd International Conference on Sensor Technologies and Applications, pp. 30–35 (2008)
5. Clouard, A., Jain, K., Ghenassia, F., Maillet-Contoz, L., Strassen, J.P.: Using Transactional Level Models in a SoC Design Flow. Kluwer Academic Publishers, Dordrecht (2003)
6. Conti, M., Moretti, D.: System level analysis of the bluetooth standard. In: DATE, March 2005, pp. 118–123 (2005)
7. Gajski, D.D., Abdi, S., Viskic, I.: Model based synthesis of embedded software. In: Brinkschulte, U., Givargis, T., Russo, S. (eds.) SEUS 2008. LNCS, vol. 5287, pp. 21–33. Springer, Heidelberg (2008)
8. Ghenassia, F.: TL Modeling with Systemc: TLM Concepts and Applications for Embedded Systems. Springer, New York (2006)
9. Grötker, T., Liao, S., Martin, G., Swan, S.: System Design with SystemC (2002)
10. Mozumdar, M.M.R., Gregoretti, F., Lavagno, L., Vanzago, L., Olivieri, S.: A framework for modeling, simulation and automatic code generation of sensor network application. In: SECON, San Francisco (2008)
11. Schirner, G., Doemer, R.: Quantitative analysis of the speed/accuracy trade-off in transaction level modeling. In: ACM Transactions on Embedded Computing Systems, TECS (2008)
12. Singh, M., Prasanna, V.K.: A hierarchical model for distributed collaborative computation in wireless sensor networks. In: IPDPS (2003)
13. Tilak, S., Abu-Ghazaleh, N.B., Heinzelman, W.: A taxonomy of wireless microsensor network models. In: ACM SIGMOBILE Mobile Computing and Communications Review archive, pp. 28–36 (2002)
14. Zamora, N.H., Kao, J.-C., Marculescu, R.: Distributed power-management techniques for wireless network video systems. In: DATE, Nice (2007)

ConcurrenC: A New Approach towards Effective Abstraction of C-Based SLDLs

Weiwei Chen and Rainer Dömer

Center for Embedded Computer Systems
University of California, Irvine
weiwei.chen@uci.edu, doemer@uci.edu

Abstract. Embedded system design in general can only be successful if it is based on a suitable Model of Computation (MoC) that can be well represented in an executable System-level Description Language (SLDL) and is supported by a matching set of design tools. While C-based SLDLs, such as SystemC and SpecC, are popular in system-level modeling and validation, current tool flows impose serious restrictions on the synthesizable subset of the supported SLDL. A properly aligned and clean system-level MoC is often neglected or even ignored.

In this paper, we motivate the need for a well-defined MoC in embedded system design. We discuss the close relationship between SLDLs and the abstract models they can represent, in contrast to the smaller set of models the tools can support. Based on these findings, we then outline a new approach, called *ConcurrenC*, that defines a true system level of abstraction, aptly fits system modeling requirements, and can be expressed precisely in both SystemC and SpecC. Using the case study of a H.264 video decoder, we demonstrate how the ConcurrenC approach meets the needs and characteristics of a industry size embedded application.

1 Introduction

With applications ranging from portable media players to real-time automotive applications, the complexity of embedded systems is growing rapidly with the increasing number of integrated components that have to cooperate properly and concurrently. Embedded systems also have tight constraints on size, power, and price.

According to the 2007 edition of the International Technology Roadmap for Semiconductors (ITRS) [7], system-level design is a promising solution to improve the design productivity by moving up to a higher level of abstraction. A new modeling approach is needed to enable system design, including simulation, estimation, synthesis, verification, implementation, and design space exploration.

In this paper, we aim to establish a properly aligned relation between three essential ingredients for successful system design, namely (1) a suitable Model of Computation (MoC) for reasoning, (2) an executable System-level Description Language (SLDL) for simulation, and (3) a matching set of design tools for implementation.

After a brief overview about existing MoCs in related work, we discuss the need for a new approach on C-based system design in Section 3. We then outline our approach, called *ConcurrenC*, in Section 4. To demonstrate ConcurrenC, we study in Section 5 a

A. Rettberg et al. (Eds.): IESS 2009, IFIP AICT 310, pp. 57–65, 2009.

H.264 video decoding application and show how the inherent features and characteristics of this application can be naturally reflected in the proposed ConcurrenC MoC.

The contribution of this paper is the identification of needs and requirements of a new MoC that enables effective abstraction of designs specified in C-based SLDLs.

2   Related Work

There has been considerable effort on many MoCs and SLDLs, as well as existing system design flows.

A **Model of Computation (MoC)** is a formal definition of the set of allowable operations used in computation and their respective costs. This defines the behavior of a system at a certain abstraction level to reflect the essential system features. Many different MoCs have been proposed for different domains. Overviews can be found in [4] and [10].

Kahn Process Network (KPN) is a deterministic MoC where processes are connected by unbounded FIFO channels to form a network [9]. **Dataflow Process Network (DFPN)** [11] is a special case of KPN in which the communication buffers are bounded. **Synchronous dataflow (SDF)** is an extended MoC from DFPN that allows static scheduling. While these MoCs are popular for modeling signal processing applications, they are not well-suited for controller applications.

Dataflow Graph (DFG) and its derivatives are MoCs for describing computational intensive systems [1]. Combined with **Finite State Machine (FSM)**, which is popular for describing control systems, FSM and DFG form **Finite-State Machine with Datapath (FSMD)** in order to describe systems requiring both control and computation [5]. **Program-state machine (PSM)** [4] is a FSM extension that supports both hierarchy and concurrency and allows states to contain regular program code.

Transaction-level modeling (TLM) [6] is a well-accepted approach to model digital systems where the details of communication are abstracted. Unfortunately, TLM does not specify a well-defined MoC but relies on the system design flow and the used SLDL to define the details of supported syntax and semantics.

Modern C-based SLDLs, like SystemC [6] and SpecC [5], are available for modeling and describing an embedded system at different levels of abstraction. Both include support for describing several MoCs, including PSM, FSMD, TLM, and general discrete event (DE) simulation. However, neither language defines a formal model behind the plain syntax and execution semantics.

3   Problem Definition

For system-level design, the importance of abstract modeling cannot be overrated. Proper abstraction and specification of the system model is a key to accurate and efficient estimation and the final successful implementation.

Register-Transfer Level (RTL) design is a good example to show the importance of a well-defined model of computation. Designers describe hardware components in hardware description languages (HDL), i.e. VHDL and Verilog. Both languages have strong abilities to support different types of hardware structures and functionalities. By

Table 1. System-level design in comparison with the well-established RTL design

Abstraction Level	Schematics	Language	MoC	Tool
RTL	⊔⊔ ⟍+/-⟋ ⊤	VHDL, Verilog	FSM, FSMD	Synopsys Design Compiler Cadence RTL Compiler ...
ESL	▯ ▯ ▯ ▯ ▯	SpecC, SystemC	PSM, TLM (?) *ConcurrenC !*	SoC Environment [2] Synopsys System Studio ...

using the HDL, designers use FSMs to model controllers or other parts of their design. Thus, FSM plays a crucial role as a formal model behind the languages. In other words, the FSM model in the mind of the designer is described syntactically in the VHDL or Verilog language.

Note that commercial computer aided design (CAD) tools cannot synthesize all the VHDL / Verilog statements. Instead, special design guidelines are provided to restrict the use of specific syntax elements, or to prevent generation of improper logics, e.g. latches.

The importance of the model in system design is the same as in RTL. Table 1 compares the situation at the system level against the mature design methodology at the RTL. RTL design is supported by the strong MoCs of FSM and FSMD, and well-accepted *coding guidelines* exist for VHDL and Verilog, so that established commercial tool chains can implement the described hardware. It is important to notice that here the MoC was defined first, and the coding style in the respective HDL followed the needs of the MoC.

At the Electronic System Level (ESL), on the other hand, we have the popular C-based SLDLs SystemC and SpecC which are more or less supported by early academic and commercial tools [2,3]. As at RTL, the languages are restricted to a (small) subset of supported features, but these *modeling guidelines* are not very clear. Moreover, the MoC behind these SLDLs is unclear. SpecC is defined in context of the PSM MoC [5], but so is SpecCharts [4] whose syntax is entirely different. For SystemC, one could claim TLM as its MoC [6], but a wide variety of interpretations of TLM exists.

We can conclude that in contrast to the popularity of the C-based SLDLs for ESL modeling and validation, and the presence of existing design flows implemented by early tools, the use of a well-defined and clear system-level MoC is neglected. Instead, serious restrictions are imposed on the usable (i.e. synthesizable and verifiable) subset of the supported SLDL. Without a clear MoC behind these syntactical guidelines, computer-aided system design is difficult. Clearly, a well-defined and formal MoC is needed to attack and solve the ESL design challenge.

4   ConcurrenC MoC

We now discuss the close relationship and tight dependencies between SLDLs (i.e. syntax), their expressive abilities (i.e. semantics), and the abstract models they can represent. We will point out that, in contrast to the large set of models the SLDL can describe, the available tools support only a subset of these models. To avoid this discrepancy that clearly hinders the effectiveness of any ESL methodology, we propose a novel MoC, called ConcurrenC, that aptly fits the system modeling requirements and the capabilities of the supporting tool chain and languages.

Generally speaking, ConcurrenC should be a system-level FSM extension with support for concurrency and hierarchy. As such, it falls into the PSM MoC category. The ConcurrenC model needs clear separation of concerns on computation and communication. In the realm of structure abstraction, a ConcurrenC model consists of blocks, channels and interfaces, and fully supports structural and behavioral hierarchy. Blocks can be flexibly composed in space and time to execute sequentially, in parallel/pipelined fashion, or by use of state transitions. Blocks themselves are internally based on C, the most popular programming language for embedded applications. In the realm of communication abstraction, we intentionally use a set of predefined channels that follow a typed message passing paradigm rather than using user-defined freely programmable channels.

Relationship to C-Based SLDLs

More specifically, ConcurrenC is tailored to the SpecC and SystemC SLDLs. ConcurrenC abstracts the embedded system features and provides clear guidelines for the designer to efficiently use the SLDLs to build a system. In other words, the ConcurrenC model is captured and described by using the SLDLs.

Fig. 1 shows the relationship between the C-based SLDLs, SystemC and SpecC, and the MoC, ConcurrenC. ConcurrenC is a true subset of the models that can be described by SpecC and SystemC. This implies that ConcurrenC contains only the model features which can be described by both languages. For example, exception handling, i.e. interrupt and abortion, is supported in SpecC by using the *try-trap* syntax, but SystemC does not have the capability to handle such exceptions. On the other hand, SystemC supports the feature for waiting a certain time *and* for some events at the same time, which SpecC does not support. As shown in Fig. 1, features that are only supported by one SLDL will not be included in the ConcurrenC model.

Moreover, ConcurrenC excludes some features that both SpecC and SystemC support (the shadow overlap area in Fig. 1). We exclude these to make the ConcurrenC model more concise for modeling. For example, ConcurrenC will restrict its communication channels to a predefined library rather than allowing the user to define arbitrary

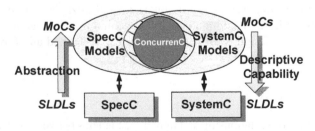

Fig. 1. Relationship between C-based SLDLs SystemC and SpecC, and MoC ConcurrenC

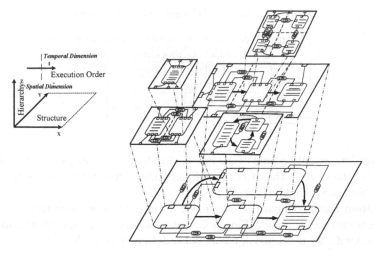

Fig. 2. Visualization of a ConcurrenC Model in three spatial and one temporal dimensions

channels by themselves. This allows tools to recognize the channels and implement them in optimal fashion.

ConcurrenC Features

A ConcurrenC Model can be visualized in four dimensions as shown in Fig. 2. There are three dimensions in space, and one in time. The spatial dimensions consist of two dimensions for structural composition of blocks and channels and their connectivity through ports and signals (X, Y coordinates), and one for hierarchical composition (Z-axis). The temporal dimension specifies the execution order of blocks in time, which can be sequential or FSM-like (thick arrows), parallel (dashed lines), or pipelined (dashed lines with arrows) in Fig. 2.

The detailed features of the proposed ConcurrenC MoC are listed below:

- **Communication & Computation Separation** Separating communication from computation allows "plug-n-play" features of the embedded system [5]. In ConcurrenC, the communication contained in channels is separated from the computation part contained in blocks so that the purpose of each statement in the model can be clearly identified whether it is for communication or computation. This also helps for architecture refinement and hardware/software partitioning.
- **Hierarchy** Hierarchy eliminates the potential explosion of the model size and significantly simplifies comprehensible modeling of complex systems.
- **Concurrency** The need for concurrency is obvious. A common embedded system will have multiple hardware units work in parallel and cooperate through specified communication mechanisms. ConcurrenC also supports pipelining in order to provide a simple and explicit description of the pipelined data flow in the system.
- **Abstract Communications (Channels)** A predefined set of communication channels is available in ConcurrenC. We believe that the restriction to predefined channels not only avoids coding errors by the designer, but also simplifies the later refinement steps, since the channels can be easily recognized by the tools.

Table 2. Parameterized Communication Channels

Channel Type	Receiver	Sender	Buffer Size
Q_0	Blocking	Blocking	0
Q_n	Blocking	Blocking	n
Q_∞	Blocking	–	∞
Signal	Blocking	–	1
Shared Variable	–	–	1

- **Timing** The execution time of the model should be evaluable to observe the efficiency of the system. Thus, ConcurrenC supports wait-for-time statements in similar fashion as SystemC and SpecC.
- **Execution** The model must be executable in order to show its correctness and obtain performance estimation. Since a ConcurrenC model can be converted to SpecC and SystemC, the execution of the model is definitely possible.

Communication Channel Library

For ConcurrenC, we envision two type of channels, channels for synchronization and data transfer. For data transfer, ConcurrenC limits the channel to transfer data in FIFO fashion (as in KPN and SDF). In many cases, these channels make the model deterministic and allow static scheduling. For KPN-like channels, the buffer size is infinite (Q_∞) which makes the model deadlock free but not practical. For SDF-like channels, the buffer size is fixed (Q_n). Double-handshake mechanism, which behaves in a rendezvous fashion, is also available as a FIFO with buffer size of zero (Q_0). Signals are needed to design a 1-N (broadcasting) channel. Furthermore, shared variables are allowed as a simple way of communication that is convenient especially in software. Moreover, FIFO channels can be used to implement semaphore which is the key to build synchronization channels. In summary, ConcurrenC supports the predefined channel library as shown in Table 2.

5   Experiment

In order to demonstrate the feasibility and benefits of the ConcurrenC approach, we use the Advanced Video Coding (AVC) standard H.264 decoding algorithm [8] as driver application to evaluate the modeling features. Our H.264 decoder model is of industrial size, consisting of about 30 thousand lines of code. The input of the decoder is an H.264 stream file, while the output is a YUV file.

ConcurrenC features can be easily used to model the H.264 decoder, see Fig. 3.

- **Hierarchy**: At the top level of the ConcurrenC model, there are three behavioral blocks: **stimulus, decoder, and monitor**. The **stimulus** reads the input yuv file, while the **monitor** receives and displays the decoded stream including signal-to-noise ratio (SNR), system time, and writes the reconstructed frames into the output file. **Decoder** contains multiple blocks for concurrent slice decoding. A stream processing block prepares the settings, n decode units decode slices in parallel, and

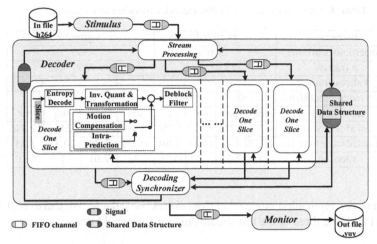

Fig. 3. Proposed H.264 Decoder Block Diagram

the decoding synchronizer combines the decoded slices for output by the monitor. The number of the slice decoders is scalable depending on the number of slices contained in one frame of the input stream file. Inside the slice decode blocks, functional sub-blocks are modeled for the detailed decoding tasks. Hierarchical modeling allows convenient and clear system description.

– **Concurrency**: [12] confirms that multiple slices in one frame are possible to be decoded concurrently. Consequently, our H.264 decoder model consists of multiple blocks for concurrent slice decoding in one picture frame[1].
– **Communication**: FIFO channels and shared variables are used for communication in our H.264 decoder model. FIFO queues are used for data exchange between different blocks. For example, the decoder synchronizer sends the decoded frame via a FIFO channel to the monitor for output. Shared variables, i.e. reference frames, are used to simplify the coordination for decoding multiple slices in parallel.
– **Timing**: The decoding time can be observed by using wait-for-time statements in the modeled blocks. We have obtained the estimated execution time for different hardware architectures by using simulation and profiling tools of the SLDLs.
– **Execution**: We have successfully converted and executed our model in SpecC using the SoC Environment [2].

Table 3 shows the simulation results of our H.264 decoder modeling in ConcurrenC. The model is simulated on a PC machine with Intel(R) Pentium(R) 4 CPU at 3.00GHz. Two stream files, one with 73 frames, and the other with 299 frames are tested. For each test file, we created two types of streams, 4 slices and 8 slices per frame. We run the model by decoding the input streams in two ways: slice by slice (seq model), and slices in one frame concurrently (par model). The estimated execution time is measured by annotated timing information according to the estimation results generated by SCE with a ARM7TDMI 400 MHz processor mapping. Our simulation results show that the

---

[1] We should emphasize that this potential parallelism was not apparent in the original C code. It required serious modeling effort to parallelize the slice decoders for our model.

Table 3. Simulation Results, H.264 Decoder modeled in ConcurrenC

filename	boat.264				coastguard.264			
# macroblocks/frame	396				396			
# frames	73 (2.43 secs)				299 (9.97 secs)			
# slices/frame	4		8		4		8	
max # macroblocks/slice	150		60		150		60	
model type	seq	par	seq	par	seq	par	seq	par
host sim time (s)	4.223	4.258	4.557	4.550	12.191	12.197	12.860	12.846
estimated exec time (s)	11.13	4.43	11.49	**1.80**	18.78	**7.20**	20.31	**3.33**
speedup	1	2.51	1	6.38	1	2.61	1	6.10

parallelism of the application modeled in ConcurrenC is scalable. We can expect that it is possible to decode three of the test streams in real-time (bold times).

6 Conclusion

In this paper, we have discussed the relationship between C-based system description languages and the abstract design models they describe. We argue that a new model of computation is needed behind the syntax of the languages and have outlined a new model of computation, ConcurrenC. ConcurrenC is a concurrent, hierarchical system model of computation with abstraction of both communication and computation, that fits the requirements of both SpecC and SystemC SLDLs. A real-world driver application, H.264 decoder is used to demonstrate how the proposed ConcurrenC approach matches the system modeling requirements.

While we leave the detailed formal modeling for future work, the contribution of this paper is a practical approach at abstract system modeling that fills the gap between the theoretical MoCs KPN and SDF, and the practical SLDLs SpecC and SystemC.

References

1. DeMarco, T.: Structured analysis and system specification, pp. 409–424 (1979)
2. Doemer, R., Gerstlauer, A., Peng, J., Shin, D., Cai, L., Yu, H., Abdi, S., Gajski, D.D.: System-on-chip Environment: A SpecC-based Framework for Heterogeneous MPSoC Design. EURASIP J. Embedded Syst. 2008(3), 1–13 (2008)
3. Embedded System Environment, http://www.cecs.uci.edu/~ese/
4. Gajski, D.D., Vahid, F., Narayan, S., Gong, J.: Specification and Design of Embedded Systems. Prentice Hall, Englewood Cliffs (1994)
5. Gajski, D.D., Zhu, J., Doemer, R., Gerstlauer, A., Zhao, S.: SpecC: Specification Language and Design Methodology. Kluwer Academic Publishers, Dordrecht (2000)
6. Groetker, T., Liao, S., Martin, G., Swan, S.: System Design with SystemC. Kluwer Academic Publishers, Dordrecht (2002)
7. International Semiconductor Industry Association. International Technology Roadmap for Semiconductors, ITRS (2007), http://www.itrs.net

8. Joint Video Team of ITU-T and ISO/IEC JTC 1. Draft ITU-T Recommendation and Final Draft International Standard of Joint Video Specification (ITU-T Rec. H.264 | ISO/IEC 14496-10 AVC). Document JVT-G050r1 (2003)
9. Kahn, G.: The Semantics of a Simple Language for Parallel Programming. Information Processing, 471–475 (1974)
10. Lee, E.A., Sangiovanni-Vincentelli, A.: A Framework for Comparing Models of Computation. IEEE Transactions on Computer-Aided Design of Intergrated Circuits and Systems (TCAD) 17(12) (December 1998)
11. Parks, T.M.: Bounded Scheduling of Process Networks. PhD thesis, Electrical Engineering and Computer Science, University of California, Berkeley (December 1995)
12. Wiegand, T., Sullivan, G.J., Bjontegaard, G., Luthra, A.: Overview of the H.264/AVC video coding standard. IEEE Transactions on Circuits and Systems for Video Technology 13(7), 560–576 (2003)

Automatic Generation of Cycle-Approximate TLMs with Timed RTOS Model Support

Yonghyun Hwang[1], Gunar Schirner[2], and Samar Abdi[3]

[1] University of California, Irvine, USA
yonghyuh@cecs.uci.edu
[2] Northeastern University, Boston, USA
schirner@ece.neu.edu
[3] Concordia University, Montreal, Canada
samar@ece.concordia.ca

Abstract. This paper presents a technique for automatically generating cycle-approximate transaction level models (TLMs) for multi-process applications mapped to embedded platforms. It incorporates three key features: (a) basic block level timing annotation, (b) RTOS model integration, and (c) RTOS overhead delay modeling. The inputs to TLM generation are application C processes and their mapping to processors in the platform. A processor data model, including pipelined datapath, memory hierarchy and branch delay model is used to estimate basic block execution delays. The delays are annotated to the C code, which is then integrated with a generated SystemC RTOS model. Our abstract RTOS provides dynamic scheduling and inter-process communication (IPC) with processor- and RTOS-specific pre-characterized timing. Our experiments using a MP3 decoder and a JPEG encoder show that timed TLMs, with integrated RTOS models, can be automatically generated in less than a minute. Our generated TLMs simulated three times faster than real-time and showed less than 10% timing error compared to board measurements.

Keywords: Transaction Level Modeling, Timed RTOS Modeling.

1 Introduction

The importance of embedded software (SW) in heterogeneous multi-processor systems is increasing with increasing complexity of the systems. Choosing an efficient platform and a suitable SW mapping is essential to meet performance and power constrains. Estimating software performance early in the design flow, e.g. during design space exploration, is essential for achieving an efficient implementation. Traditional ISS-based approaches are performance limited, especially in a multi-processor context. Abstract simulation of SW execution is one key solution for rapid design space exploration and early prototyping.

Important influence factors for SW performance, are the hardware platform (e.g. processor type, memory hierarchy) and, equally important, SW architecture and configuration: task/data granularity, selection of scheduling policy, priority

A. Rettberg et al. (Eds.): IESS 2009, IFIP AICT 310, pp. 66–76, 2009.

distribution and the selection of an appropriate RTOS. Automatic generation of timed TLMs that reflect the effects of the above design choices is needed to enable informed decision in a simulation-based approach.

In order to accurately estimate performance of a SW task three delay contributors have to be modeled: (a) D_{exec}, for execution of straight line code; (b) D_{sched}, for communication and dynamic scheduling (e.g. scheduling of a higher priority task); and (c) D_{sys}, the delay due to the system overhead as a result of dynamic scheduling. Existing dynamic approaches only address (a) D_{exec} and (b) D_{sched}. D_{exec} can be modeled through on-line code profiling, e.g. [16] or off-line profiling and timing annotation of the modeled code, e.g. [13,12]. Modeling of D_{sched} can be addressed by using abstract RTOS models emulating dynamic scheduling, e.g. [16,8,10]. However, current solutions do not model system overhead, i.e. the overhead of executing an RTOS on the target processor remains unaccounted.

Modeling system overhead is essential in guiding the SW developer in parallelizing a given application. Choosing a too fine granularity of Inter-Process Communication (IPC) may unnecessarily increase the number of context switches, thus increase D_{sys} and therefore decrease system performance [4]. With current modeling techniques the negative effects of such a design choice are only discovered when executing on the final system, leading to an expensively long design cycle. To increase efficiency of the design process, system overhead modeling, D_{sys}, is required. In this paper, we present our approach for automatically generating cycle-approximate TLMs that include timed abstract RTOS models, hence reflecting all three delays D_{exec}, D_{sched} and D_{sys}.

This paper is organized as follows. Section 2 presents related work. Section 3 outlines the TLM generation framework, and describes our estimation and annotation approach covering D_{exec}. Section 4 outlines our abstract RTOS model yielding D_{sched}. Section 5 introduces our analysis and modeling of system overhead D_{sys}. Our experimental results, Section 6, show scalability and accuracy based on several design examples. Finally, we conclude the paper and touch on future work.

2   Related Work

Significant research effort has been spent for early performance estimation of multi-processor systems, which can be broadly categorized as static, semi-static and dynamic. Static approaches, such as [17], on one side use purely analytical methods to compute application delays. Dynamic approaches on the other side, use platform models to generate a timed executable model of the design, which later produces the estimation data at run time. ISS and virtual platforms are popular examples of dynamic approaches. Our solution is based on a dynamic approach.

SW performance estimation techniques [13,12,2,3] utilize the execution path of the SW. The common approach is to multiply the cost of operation with the total number of operations executed. Unlike above techniques, [14,5] can take into account the datapath structure. However, they use bus functional models and generate ISS which provides accurate results at the expense of speed. Simplescalar [1] is a well known retargetable ISS that can provide cycle accurate estimation result but is several orders slower than TLM.

Abstract RTOS models have been developed on top of System Level Design Languages (SLDLs) (e.g. SystemC [9], SpecC [7]) to expose the effect of dynamic scheduling. Examples include [8,20], modeling typical RTOS primitives on top of an SLDL, and [16], implementing an POSIX API on top of SystemC. The latter offers an interesting combination of online estimation and RTOS-modeling, which enables an optimized modeling of periodic interrupts. However, the solutions do not include modeling of RTOS overheads, which we address in this paper. An RTOS centric cosimulator using a host compiled RTOS is described in [10], which, however, does not include target execution time simulation.

3   TLM Estimation Framework

Our support for RTOS overhead modeling and integration into TLM is built upon the TLM based design infrastructure proposed by Gajski et al. [6]. In this methodology, the user specifies the system definition consisting of application code and a graphically notated platform specification. The application is expressed as parallel executing C/C++ processes, which communicate through a set of standard communication channels. The framework generates TLMs based on the design decisions to verify system performance and functionality early in the design cycle. The TLMs then serve as an input to cycle accurate synthesis, which produces Pin/Cycle Accurate Models (PCAM) for detailed validation and analysis. After finalizing the design, the PCAMs are used for low level synthesis generating board level prototype design.

Figure 1 shows the architecture and implementation of our timing estimation tool with RTOS support integrated into th framework. The input specification contains untimed C code for each process and and its mapping to PEs in the platform. According to the mapping decisions, the user code is analyzed based on a HW processing unit model (PUM), which characterizes datapath, memory

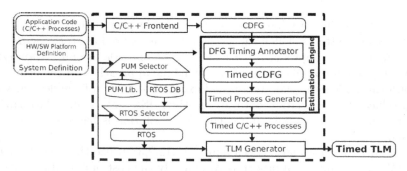

Fig. 1. Estimation Tool Architecture

hierarchy and instruction scheduling of the PE. We have implemented a C/C++ front-end using the LLVM compiler infrastructure [15] which parses the application code into CDFGs. For each basic block of the CDFG, the corresponding DFG is input to an estimation engine. The estimation engine computes the DFG delay by scheduling application instructions based on the PE's PUM. Using the LLVM source transformation API, the estimated delay is then annotated into the CDFG data structure. Subsequently, timed C code is generated for the process using the LLVM code generation API.

During TLM generation, the SW platform definition is used for configuring the abstract RTOS model with overhead delays and scheduling policy. Finally, the annotated C code and the configured RTOS model are compiled and linked with a SystemC programming model of the platform to generate the executable timed TLM. In this paper, we will focus on the timed abstract RTOS aspect. Timed C code generation for single process mapping without dynamic scheduling is described in [11].

4   Abstract RTOS Model

Multiple processes may be mapped to the same processing element, later scheduled by an RTOS on actual HW. For early exploration of dynamic scheduling effects, an abstract RTOS is integrated into the TLM. Each mapped process becomes a virtual process on the abstract RTOS. The RTOS model, as well as the virtual processes are configurable in their scheduling parameters, supporting a validation of the SW configuration (e.g. scheduling policy selection, priority distribution).

As shown in Figure 2, our abstract RTOS executes as an SC_THREAD inside the SC_MODULE of the PE. Each PE runs an own abstract RTOS. The RTOS provides services to start, stop and control virtual processes inside its context. It furthermore communicates with the outside of the processor through the bus interface (provided by an an abstract bus model) and interrupts.

Our RTOS model uses pthreads, native to the host operating system, to provide multiple flows of execution. Each virtual process (i.e. a time annotated process) is executed in an own pthread. The execution of each pthread is controlled by the RTOS model through condition variables to emulate the selected scheduling policy. At any given point in time only one pthread (one virtual

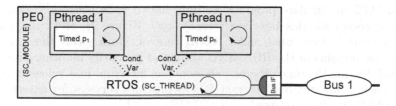

Fig. 2. Threads in Abstract RTOS

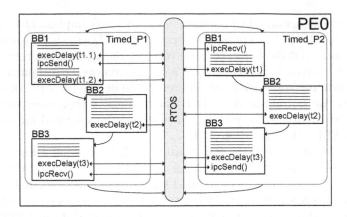

Fig. 3. Abstract RTOS interaction

process) for each PE is released through the condition variable, overwriting the host's scheduling policy.

The abstract RTOS, similarly to an actual RTOS, maintains a Task Control Block (TCB) for each virtual process. Each virtual process is scheduled according to a task state machine, with states such as RUNNING, READY, PENDING, SUSPENDED; and the abstract RTOS maintains the appropriate queues.

Each primitive in the TLM, which could potentially trigger a context switch, is executed under control of the RTOS These primitives include task control and inter-process transactions. Figure 3 shows two virtual processes executing on top of the RTOS model. Interactions with the model are indicated by arrows. The RTOS model provides an fixed API and the TLM generator produces appropriate wrappers for the generated timed process code (Section 3) to utilize this API. To give an example, when a virtual process executes an inter-process transaction (e.g. Figure 3, call *ipcRecv()* in process *Timed_P2*), this transaction is executed under RTOS control. Assuming it contains acquiring a non-available semaphore, the virtual process state is set to PENDING, the next process is selected from the ready queue according to the scheduling policy, set to RUNNING, and released through its condition variable. Finally, the old virtual process suspends by waiting its own condition variable. Note that the actual context switch is performed by pthreads of the host OS, the abstract RTOS only controls their release.

In addition to classical RTOS primitives, our abstract RTOS model provides an API to simulate progress of time due to code execution. Our time annotated code calls this interface (*execDelay()*, Figure 3), and subsequently a *sc_core::wait()* is executed under RTOS control. During this time, the virtual process remains in the RUNNING state and primarily no other process is scheduled. During the time progress, an incoming interrupt may release a higher priority task. Similarly, our abstract RTOS provides services for external bus access, which are the performed under RTOS control.

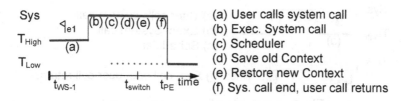

(a) User calls system call
(b) Exec. System call
(c) Scheduler
(d) Save old Context
(e) Restore new Context
(f) Sys. call end, user call returns

Fig. 4. sem_wait() with context switch

5   Modeling of RTOS Overheads

An abstract RTOS exposes the effects of dynamic scheduling. In addition, a system overhead delay model is needed to provide feedback about the overhead in a multi-tasking application, capturing for example the delay due to IPC, context switching and interrupt preemption. Modeling such overheads is essential to guide the developer in partitioning the code (e.g. for deciding granularity of data and communication handling). To illustrate, splitting an application into too many tasks may lead to a system overhead that dominates the application performance (too many context switches and inter-process transactions). The execution time of user code may not be a sufficient indicator for a potential performance bottleneck, which drives the need for modeling RTOS overheads.

Modeling RTOS overhead is challenging as it depends on RTOS, CPU, and CPU configuration (e.g. caching). The analysis is further complicated by a limited source code availability especially for a commercial RTOS , as well as API and structural/organizational differences between implementations. These factors inhibit a static source code analysis or make it prohibitly expensive.

We have developed a time stamping approach to analyze RTOS overheads on RTOS API level without source code analysis. We characterize a RTOS on the actual processor in supported configuration(s). The determined overhead characteristics are stored in our database. As they are independent of processor external HW and independent of the user application, they can be applied in to many designs. Our TLM generator reads the DB to instantiate an abstract RTOS inside a PE model with specific delay parameters.

We developed a special test application that captures time stamps and invokes RTOS primitives in a controlled environment in which we know a priori the scheduling outcome. We use a processor external timer to measure time. The time stamp code and its data are exclusively placed in a non-cached fast local memory (BRAM) to minimize impact on caching and execution time. We disable timer interrupts while analyzing timing unrelated RTOS primitives to eliminate the impact of unexpected interrupts.

Figure 5 and Figure 4 show an example of our analysis based on acquiring a semaphore without and with a context switch. As system calls basically follow the same sequence the example is representative.

In Figure 4, task T_{High} calls *sem_wait()* to acquire non-available sema-phore (a), which results in a context switch to T_{Low}. We record time stamp t_{WS-1}

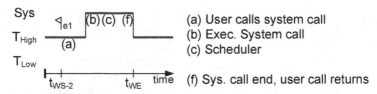

Fig. 5. sem_wait() without context switch

in user mode before the call. Next, the processor mode is switched to system mode, and the system call (the actual semaphore code) is executed (b). Then, the scheduler (c) determines the next task to execute, the current task's context is saved (d), the new task's context is restored (e). Finally, a system call returns (f) in the new task's context. In our application, T_{low} had earlier relinquished the CPU by posting a semaphore to T_{high}. Therefore, the returned system call is a sem_post(), and we record time stamp t_{PE}. Please note, that the code for returning a system call is independent of the call type (e.g. the code is identical for sem_post() and sem_wait() starting at the scheduler call (c)). We can therefore use t_{PE} for analyzing the duration of a sem_wait().

Figure 5 illustrates the case of an available semaphore where no context switch occurs. We record t_{WS-2} before the call. The sequence during the system call is shorter. The scheduler (c) determined no context switch and the system call returns (f) to the same task where we record t_{WE}. Based on these time stamps, we determine the duration for sem_wait(), and for a context switch. We separate these two, in order to simplify abstract modeling and database. Then, only a single delay characterizes each RTOS primitive. Our analysis with these time stamps, after eliminating the overhead of time stamping itself, is as follows:

$$Dur(sem\_wait) = t_{WE} - t_{WS-2}$$
$$Dur(switch) = t_{PE} - t_{WS-1} - Dur(sem\_wait)$$

The duration estimation of sem_wait is the difference between start and end time stamp. We compute the context switch duration based on the duration of the sem_wait with a context switch ($t_{PE} - t_{WS-1}$) and subtract the time for sem_wait() without context switch. We chose sem_wait(), since we expect portion (b), execution of the system call itself, to be minimally dependent on the scheduling outcome as sem_wait() only manipulates the own task state. Conversely, sem_post() shows a variance beyond the estimated context switch duration as it manipulates other task's states.

We analyze other communication and synchronization primitives in a similar manner. For each primitive we measure the time without and with a context switch. After normalizing for the already determined context switch duration, we calculate the average between the two cases to determine the primitive's duration.

In addition to the basic RTOS primitives, we also characterized standard functions that are dependent on the data length. In particular, we have characterized memcpy() as it is frequently used and its code is often heavily optimized. We capture the delay results in a table, and use a linear extension to estimate values beyond the table boundaries.

We store the analyzed RTOS characteristics in our database, with a separate delay for each used RTOS primitives, and the basic context switch.

During TLM generation, the code for instantiating an RTOS is created. The selected RTOS' characteristics are retrieved from the database and the abstract RTOS is configured to reflect the selected RTOS. Upon execution of an abstract RTOS primitive, the characterized delay – without context switch – (e.g. Dur($sem\_wait()$)) is executed. Our abstract task dispatcher, switching between pthreads, is annotated with $Dur(switch)$. We use this basically state less delay model to simplify abstract RTOS implementation maintaining a high simulation performance. While our analysis and modeling approach abstracts away many influences on RTOS overhead (e.g. number of total, waiting, and manipulated tasks, scheduler implementation) and therefore is not cycle-accurate, it already yields valuable feedback for estimating system performance.

6   Experimental Results

To evaluate the benefits of our approach, we have applied it to three designs based on an MP3 decoder, a JPEG encoder and a combined design running both applications. Figure 6 shows the application flow. The MP3 decoder executes in 3 tasks, and JPEG encoder with 5 tasks. The designs originate from an hardware oriented design showing a fine grained task split. All tasks are mapped in the target plaform to the same processor, a Microblaze [19] with 100Mhz, and scheduled by Xilinx's RTOS, Xilkernel [18].

We generate the timed TLMs with timed RTOS using our generation approach. SW binaries were generated for execution on the Xilinx Virtual Platform (XVP) and for execution on the actual processor. Matching hardware designs were synthesized using Xilinx ISE and EDK and downloaded to an Xilinx FF896 board to provide a cycle-accurate reference platform.

Table 1 shows the average accuracy of our abstract models for each of our designs in comparison to cycle-accurate execution on the Xilinx FF896 board. We analyze several abstraction levels providing insight about each delay's contribution. We analyze:

Timed TLM captures D_{exec} at basic block level (Section 3). Tasks may execute concurrently.

TLM w/ RTOS adds an abstract RTOS (Section 4) resolving dynamic scheduling, capturing D_{exec} and D_{sched}.

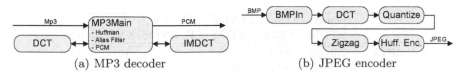

(a) MP3 decoder   (b) JPEG encoder

Fig. 6. Example applications

Table 1. Accuracy of abstract models [%]

	Timed TLM	TLM w/ RTOS	TLM w/ Timed RTOS	XVP
JPEG	-75%	-35.56%	-9.98%	50%
MP3	-41%	-25.95%	5.29%	7%
MP3+JPEG	-83%	-33.25%	-6.20%	37%

TLM w/ Timed RTOS additionally models system overheads (Section 5), reflecting D_{exec}, D_{sched}, and D_{sys}.

In addition to our models, we also compare to the XVP.

Our results show that only modeling D_{exec} is not sufficient for parallel applications. The timed TLM shows 66% average error, up to 83% depending on application parallelizm. Adding dynamic scheduling by an abstract RTOS dramatically improves accuracy. However, with the fine grained IPC, the designs exhibit a significant system overhead and thus the TLM with RTOS underestimates by 32% on average. This result can be compared to other state of the art solutions, which all do not model any RTOS overhead. Adding RTOS overhead modeling reduces the error to less than 10%, yielding already sufficiently accurate timing information. The remaining error is due to our abstract analysis and modeling of RTOS overheads, which we chose in favoring automate ability and simulation speed. Lastly, we compare against the commercial XVP. It significantly overestimates our designs with 31% on average, which can be traced back to inaccurate modeling of memory accesses [11]. Comparing all solutions, our TLM with Timed RTOS yields the most accurate timing estimation. With decreasing system overhead, an even smaller error can be expected. For a single task version of the MP3 decoder our generated TLM exhibited only 0.9% error.

Table 2 summarizes the simulation time in seconds of real-time (or wall clock time). In addition the above discussed models, we also included a purely functional TLM without any timing annotation and execution on real HW.

As expected, native execution on the simulation host yields high performance. Increasing model complexity increases simulation time. The functional TLM executed the fastest (within milliseconds), as it requires the fewest context switches. Executing time annotations *(sc_core::wait())* in the timed TLM, increases simulation time to tens of milliseconds. Our TLM with RTOS model, which models the virtual threads, executes in fractions of a second. No significant increase is

Table 2. Simulation time (real-time) [sec]

	Func. TLM	Timed TLM	TLM w/ RTOS	TLM w/ T. RTOS	XVP	Board
JPEG	0.003	0.02	0.25	0.27	168	0.83
MP3	0.002	0.01	0.08	0.08	60	0.34
MP3+JPEG	0.004	0.04	0.32	0.33	213	1.17

Table 3. Complexity of Models

Feature	JPEG	MP3	MP3+JPEG
# IPC / switch	720 / 1440	392 / 783	1112 / 2225
appl. cycles	53.2E+6	25.0E+6	78.2E+6
system cycles	21.1E+6	10.6E+6	31.7E+6

measurable for reflecting RTOS overheads. Our TLM with timed RTOS executes about 3 times faster than real-time comparing to execution on the Microblaze. In addition, our solution is three orders of magnitude faster than the commercial XVP. These results clearly demonstrate the advantages of our solution, simulating faster than real-time while exhibiting less error than the XVP.

Generation time is an addtional usability aspect. Our TLM generation time is dominated by the SW performance estimation (Section 3), as it executes the LLVM compiler. The additional effort for instanciating the timed RTOS is negligible. The measured total generation time ranges from 1.2 seconds (JPEG) to 33.3 seconds (MP3+JPEG).

In addition to advantages in accuracy and performance, our solution also provides vital statistics. Table 3 shows a small excerpt, listing IPC calls, context switches, as well as number of cycles for executing the application and system (indicating the RTOS overhead). Especially the latter two reveal important information for developing multi-tasking designs. It is alarming for the shown design examples: a significant portion (about 30%) of the total execution time is spend in system overhead. This should urge improving the SW implementation by coarsening granularity – a feedback previously only available when executing on the board.

7   Conclusions

In this paper, we have presented a tool for automatically generating cycle-approximate TLMs. Our approach offers a complete solution for SW simulation including three essential aspects: (a) cycle-approximate retargetable performance estimation for SW execution, (b) dynamic scheduling through an abstract RTOS, and (c) modeling of RTOS overheads. Especially the latter is important as it offers a competitive advantage in guiding developers while designing multi-tasking applications. It exposes performance bottlenecks earlier in the design, thus enabling designing more efficient systems in fewer design cycles.

Results with MP3 decoder and JPEG encoder designs showed that our TLM generation is scalable to complex platforms and simulation results are within 10% of actual board measurements even for applications with high system overhead, while simulating faster than real-time. Our results demonstrate generation of TLMs for fast, early, and accurate estimation.

In future we plan extend our RTOS overhead analysis to finer grained detail using non-intrusive time stamping methods and to extend state dependent overhead modeling.

Acknowledgment

We would like to thank the Center for Embedded Computer Systems at University of California, Irvine for supporting this research.

References

1. Austin, T., Larson, E., Ernst, D.: Simplescalar: an infrastructure for computer system modeling. Computer 35(2), 59–67 (2002)
2. Bammi, J.R., Kruijtzer, W., Lavagno, L.: Software Performance Estimatioin Strategies in a System-Level Design Tool. In: CODES, San Diego, USA (2000)
3. Cai, L., Gerstlauer, A., Gajski, D.: Retargetable Profiling for Rapid, Early System-Level Design Space Exploration. In: DATE, San Diego, USA (June 2004)
4. Cho, Y., Zergainoh, N.-E., Choi, K., Jerraya, A.A.: Low Runtime-Overhead Software Synthesis for Communicating Concurrent Processes. In: RSP, Porto Alegre, Brazil (2007)
5. Chung, M.-K., Na, S., Kyung, C.-M.: System-Level Performance Analysis of Embedded System using Behavioral C/C++ model. In: VLSI-TSA-DAT, Hsinchu, Taiwan (2005)
6. ESE: Embedded Systems Environment, http://www.cecs.uci.edu/~ese
7. Gajski, D.D., Zhu, J., Dömer, R., Gerstlauer, A., Zhao, S.: SpecC: Specification Language and Design Methodology. Kluwer Academic Publishers, Dordrecht (2000)
8. Gerstlauer, A., Yu, H., Gajski, D.D.: Rtos modeling for system level design. In: Proceedings of the Design, Automation and Test in Europe (DATE) Conference, Munich, Germany (March 2003)
9. Grötker, T., Liao, S., Martin, G., Swan, S.: System Design with SystemC. Kluwer Academic Publishers, Dordrecht (2002)
10. Honda, S., et al.: RTOS-Centric Hardware/Software Cosimulator for Embedded System Design. Stockholm (2004)
11. Hwang, Y., Abdi, S., Gajski, D.: Cycle-approximate Retargetable Performance Estimation at the Transaction Level. In: DATE, Munich, Germany (March 2008)
12. Kempf, T., Karuri, K., Wallentowitz, S., Ascheid, G., Leupers, R., Meyr, H.: A SW Performance Estimation Framework for Early System-Level-Design using Fine-grained Instrumentation. In: DATE, Munich, Germany (March 2006)
13. Lajolo, M., Lazarescu, M., Sangiovanni-Vincentelli, A.: A Compilation-based Software Estimation Scheme for Hardware/Software Co-simulation. In: CODES, Rome (1999)
14. Lee, J.-Y., Park, I.-C.: Time Compiled-code Simulation of Embedded Software for Performance Analysis of SOC design. In: DAC, New Orleans, USA (June 2002)
15. LLVM (Low Level Virtual Machine) Compiler Infrastructure Project, http://www.llvm.org
16. Posadas, H., et al.: RTOS modeling in SystemC for real-time embedded SW simulation: A POSIX model 10(4), 209–227 (December 2005)
17. Russell, J.T., Jacome, M.F.: Architecture-level Performance Evaluation of Component-based Embedded Systems. In: DAC, Anaheim, USA (June 2003)
18. Xilinx. OS and Libraries Document Collection (2006)
19. Xilinx. MicroBlaze Processor Reference Manual (2007)
20. Zabel, H., Müller, W., Gerstlauer, A.: Accurate RTOS modeling and analysis with SystemC. In: Ecker, W., Müller, W., Dömer, R. (eds.) Hardware Dependent Software: Principles and Practice (2009)

Transaction Level Modeling of Best-Effort Channels for Networked Embedded Devices

Amal Banerjee and Andreas Gerstlauer

Department of Electrical and Computer Engineering, University of Texas at Austin,
Austin, Texas 78712, USA
{abanerj,gerstl}@ece.utexas.edu

Abstract. We use Transaction Level Modeling techniques to specify and validate best-effort channels for networked embedded devices, to integrate the
generated specification model in system-level design flow, for prototyping, exploration and validation of design alternatives. A best-effort channel does not
provide any guarantees on final data delivery or delivery rate. With more embedded devices existing in networked environments, often sharing a common
communication channel, devices compete with each other for all common network resources, e.g., in a wireless sensor network where low power devices
share a low bandwidth best-effort channel. To examine such systems, we specify Half-Duplex Ethernet using the SpecC language and Transaction Level
Modeling techniques. All models are validated in a multi-station test setup using Ethernet-based network algorithms.

Keywords: Best-effort Channel, Networked Embedded Systems, Transaction
Level Model (TLM), System Level Design Language (SLDL).

1 Introduction

Most of today's embedded systems exist in some form of a networked environment.
Inspired by Ethernet as the most cost-effective local area network technology in general computing, embedded system designers have adapted it for industrial automation.
In order to understand the behavior of these networked embedded devices, for better
control and reliable inter-device communication, more design support and robust
models are essential. For any communication channel in any network, an arbitration
scheme is required to decide which device can use the channel at any given time.
Such schemes could either be centralized (e.g., ARM AMBA bus) or distributed (e.g.,
Ethernet or wireless networks), the latter often in combination with *best-effort* channels. A best-effort communications protocol (e.g., Half-Duplex Ethernet) provides no
guarantees on final data delivery or rate of data delivery. Though replaced by Full-
Duplex Ethernet and variants like Time Triggered Ethernet in wired networks, best-
effort and contention mechanisms resulting in uncertainty and unreliability underlying
the Ethernet protocol are also at the heart of wireless embedded networks [19], e.g.,
mobile device interfaces, wireless local area networks (WLANs) and wireless sensor
networks. As such, modeling concepts developed for Ethernet are applicable to a wide
variety of networked embedded systems.

A. Rettberg et al. (Eds.): IESS 2009, IFIP AICT 310, pp. 77–88, 2009.
© IFIP International Federation for Information Processing 2009

In the ISO/OSI network model, the Ethernet [11] sub-layer of the Data Link layer manipulates frames coming in/going out (from/to Physical layer). In the beginning, Ethernet was half-duplex in nature. A *half-duplex* channel allows two way communication, but only in one direction at a time, i.e., the transmitter must stop before the receiver can reply. A Half-Duplex Ethernet channel has active transmitters and passive receivers. It relies on a contention resolution algorithm, Truncated Binary Exponential Back-Off, that allows a failed transmitter to decide how long to wait before the next transmission attempt. While communication channels have been modeled using networks simulators such as ns-2 [22], these do not allow the modeling of complete systems (hardware and software). In contrast, systems are modeled with a System Level Design Language (SLDL), combined with Transaction-Level Modeling (TLM) techniques. To the best of our knowledge, there are currently no network-oriented TLM channel models.

Transaction-Level Modeling (TLM) [6] allows modeling of digital systems with inter-module communication details abstracted and separated from those of the implementation of computation modules. Communication mechanisms such as busses or FIFOs, are modeled as channels, and modules access them via interfaces. Channel models encapsulate low-level details of the information exchange. Transaction requests occur when modules call interface functions of the channel models. The emphasis is on what data is being transferred, rather than how it is being transmitted. Thus, the system designer can experiment, with different bus architectures (supporting a common abstract interface) without re-coding models that interact with any of the buses. Our choice of the SpecC SLDL [21] supports TLM, along with the crucial concept of time with delta cycles, essential for effective hardware/system and network modeling, unlike traditional network simulators such as ns-2 [22], OPNet [23] or OMNet++ [24].

1.1 Related Work

The Ethernet protocol [11] was developed in a very straightforward way. One of the earliest attempts to specify Half-Duplex Ethernet by Weinberg and Zuck [1] uses Henzinger's real-time models and transition diagrams. Bochmann and Sunshine [2] provide an overview of formal methods used in communication protocol design while Schmaltz and Borrione [3] present an ACL2 logic based scheme for the specification of System-on-Chip (SoC) communication architectures. Georges et al. [4] use concepts of network calculus to formulate a mathematical model of industrial Ethernet, while Shalunov et al. [5] study the properties of half and full duplex Ethernet to devise techniques to detect mismatch between the two modes in a given communication channel and its effects on TCP throughput.

With the emergence of TLM techniques, a number of researchers have applied it to specify existing systems. Cai et al. [6] explain the benefits of the use of TLM techniques. Moussa et al. [7] describe VISTA, a new methodology and tool to analyze SoCs. Klingauf et al. [8] present a generic interconnect fabric for TLM. Wieferink et al. [9] use built-in TLM features of SystemC to propose a methodology for exploring SoC multiprocessor systems. Schirner et al. [10] have proposed some novel techniques to address some of the drawbacks of TLM related to efficient communication modeling. In addition, a number of researchers have applied TLM techniques to analyzing the AMBA bus, mostly with SystemC [14-17]. Bombieri et al. [18] combine SystemC's TLM features with the ns-2 network simulator to analyze voice-over-IP (VOIP) systems using the AMBA bus.

1.2 Goals

Available literature indicates that the focus so far has been on mostly on higher level concepts/theoretical issues and TLM techniques as applied to the analysis of systems using widely used system busses. In contrast, our focus is entirely on best-effort communication channels, which by definition use distributed bus arbitration. Unlike [18], we do not use any network simulator and create our own specification model for a best effort communication channel. Our main goals, based on TLM and SLDL principles, are to combine the two. Specifically:

- Specification and validation of real-world networked embedded systems based on best-effort communication channels, e.g., Ethernet, WLANs and wireless sensor networks.
- Integration of the resulting specification model into the overall system level design process, i.e., a flexible and robust model of networked embedded devices for prototyping of design alternatives, validation of networking effects and rapid, early network-level design space exploration [20].

Networked embedded systems, and wireless networks in particular, often use best-effort communication channels. TLM, with its ability to separate low-level communication details from actual transferred data provides the best means to understand the overall behavior of such a system. In accordance with TLM principles, we design our own abstract Half-Duplex Ethernet channel, including techniques for handling conflicts amongst devices attempting to use the channel simultaneously. The final specification model can be applied as input to system-level design and synthesis tools.

The remainder of this paper is organized as follows. In the next section we introduce our specification/validation model for Half-Duplex Ethernet created with SpecC, with details of how various SpecC language features were used, along with the TLM principles on which the specification model is based. In Section 3 we test the accuracy and validity of our specification model by describing an experiment and its results to analyze the behavior of a widely-used network quality of service (QoS) protocol that operates on Ethernet frames. Finally, we conclude with a brief summary of work performed and future possibilities.

2 Specification and Validation of Half-Duplex Ethernet

The Half-Duplex Ethernet [11] sub-layer of the ISO/OSI Data Link layer is a best-effort protocol, with active senders and passive receivers. Only one of two communicating devices can be sending data at any time. All transmitters share a common channel with maximum specified bandwidth, and transmitters compete with others to gain control of the channel. A transmitter which gains control of the channel has exclusive rights to send data to a receiver of its choice, and can retain control of the channel for as long as it wants. Failed transmitters must wait and use the Truncated Binary Exponential Back-Off algorithm to decide on the duration. Each failed attempt

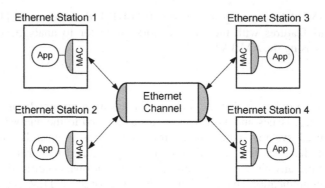

Fig. 1. Basic Ethernet test bench. Four Ethernet stations share a common half duplex Ethernet channel. A media access layer (MAC) in each station implements contention resolution and network access. 'App' is an application exchanging data over the network.

to gain control of the channel is a 'collision'. Each failed transmitter waits for a duration derived from the slot time and the number of failed attempts to retransmit. After i collisions, a random number of slot times between 0 and $2^i - 1$ is chosen. For the first collision, each transmitter might wait 0 or 1 slot times, and after the second collision, each failed transmitter might wait 0, 1, 2, or 3 slot times. The term 'truncated' indicates that the retransmission timeout has a strict upper bound, e.g., for a ceiling of $i=10$, the maximum delay is 1023 slot times. A slot time is the round-trip time interval for one ASCII character and is set at 51.2 μs. As transmission delays can cause transmitting stations to collide, a busy network might have hundreds of senders caught in a single collision set. Because of this, after 16 attempts at transmission of one particular frame, the process is aborted.

Our test bench is shown in Fig. 1. Each station can be configured as sender or receiver, and the test setup consists of two senders talking to two receivers. Fig. 2 shows our implementation of the core Ethernet channel. The challenges in modeling the Half-Duplex Ethernet channel are:

- The channel must correctly detect and handle collisions.
- An Ethernet station that has failed to send a frame in the current attempt has to be able to choose the correct wait duration, depending on the total number of failed attempts so far to send this frame (provided that the total number of failed transmission attempts so far do not exceed a pre-defined limit).

The Truncated Binary Exponential Back-Off algorithm is implemented in each station. Ethernet frames are 128 bytes long, with 64 byte header and 64 byte payload.

2.1 Half-Duplex Ethernet Channel

As per SpecC design principles, the Ethernet channel implements the Ethernet-Interface interface. Ethernet receivers are passive devices, and each waits for a *dataready* event to read data from the channel. Most of the activity on the channel is when a transmitter tries to send a frame.

```
const unsigned int INTER_FRAME_INTERVAL = 10;
const unsigned int SLOT_TIME = 52;
const unsigned int FRAME_PAYLOAD_INTERVAL  = 3328;

interface EthernetInterface
{
    bool send_frame(unsigned char *, unsigned int);
    void recv_frame(unsigned char *);
};

channel EthernetChannel implements EthernetInterface
{
    unsigned int busy;
    unsigned char localbuffer[128];
    unsigned int i;
    bool collision;
    event dataready;

    bool send_frame(unsigned char *frame,
                                  unsigned int stationID)
    {
        while(busy == 2)
            waitfor(SLOT_TIME*64 + INTER_FRAME_INTERVAL);
        if(busy == 1) {
            collision = true;
            return false;
        }
        busy = 1;
        for(i = 0; i < 64; i++) {
            waitfor(SLOT_TIME);
            if(collision) {
                collision = false;
                busy     = 0;
                return false;
            }
        }
        busy = 2;
        waitfor(FRAME_PAYLOAD_INTERVAL);
        memcpy(localbuffer, frame, 128);
        busy = 0;
        collision = false;
        notify(dataready);
        return true;
    }

    void recv_frame(unsigned char *recvframe)
    {
        wait(dataready);
        memcpy(recvframe, localbuffer, 128);
    }
};
```

Fig. 2. SpecC behavior implementing the basic Half-Duplex Ethernet channel

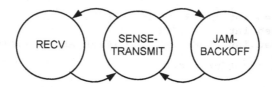

Fig. 3. Ethernet station media access layer state machine

We only consider collisions occurring during sending of the Ethernet header. Once an Ethernet station has successfully transmitted the frame header, it gains control of the channel and does not have to check for frame collisions while sending the payload.

In SpecC, only behaviors are associated with threads, channels are passive. If a behavior calls a channel method it is a regular function call. Any code in the channel (including waitfor statements) is executed in the context of the calling behavior/thread.

Now, let an Ethernet station A want to send a frame. It invokes the *send_frame* function of the Ethernet channel:

1. A checks if the channel's *busy* variable has value 2, which indicates that another Ethernet station is sending its payload. A waits in a loop until *busy* is not equal to 2. During each iteration of the loop, it waits for a time period equal to that required to send a 64 byte payload, plus the mandatory inter frame gap.
2. If instead A finds that the *busy* variable has value 1, then a collision has just occurred. If not, A sets the *busy* variable to 1, and starts to send the 64 byte Ethernet header of the current frame, checking for a collision after sending each header byte.
3. When A has successfully sent the Ethernet header, it sets the *busy* variable to 2, indicating it has acquired complete control over the channel, and starts sending that Ethernet frame payload. On completion, the frame payload contents are copied into a local channel buffer. A resets the status variable *busy* to 0, and sets an event (*dataready*) variable to indicate to all receivers that a frame is available. It is now ready to send/receive any frame to/from any station.

2.2 Media Access Layer

Each Ethernet station is a finite-state machine, with three possible states, JAM_BACKOFF, RECV and SENSE_TRANSMIT, as shown in Fig. 3:

1. Each Ethernet station starts in the SENSE_TRANSMIT state. It invokes the *send_frame* function of the Ethernet channel, which returns a Boolean true if the frame was sent successfully.
2. If the return value is false, the station transitions to the JAM_BACKOFF state. The maximum number of times any station might attempt to re-send a frame is 16. In the JAM_BACKOFF state, the station first waits for a mandatory jam period. It then decides, using the Truncated Binary Exponential Back-Off algorithm and the number of failed attempts so far how long to wait before the next transmission attempt. At the end of the wait period, the Ethernet station

transitions to the SENSE_TRANSMIT state and attempts to send that frame again. If the Ethernet station finds in the JAM_BACKOFF state that the maximum number of transmit attempts for the current frame has exceeded the pre-defined maximum limit, it drops the frame and transitions back to the SENSE_TRANSMIT state in order to send or receive the next frame.

3. The Ethernet station transitions between the SENSE_TRANSMIT and RECV states to send the next frame or to receive frames available on the channel, respectively.

Our specification models for both Half-Duplex Ethernet channels and stations adhere strictly to TLM design concepts and make extensive use of SpecC's detailed time construct, which allows time to be simulated in two nested loops, an outer time loop and inner one for events in each simulation step, called the delta cycle. In addition, the Ethernet channel behavior exploits SpecC's event mechanism to notify receivers when data is available for them.

In accordance with TLM principles, each Ethernet station invokes the *send_frame* function of the Ethernet channel when attempting to send a frame. The channel internally tackles the frame collision and only informs the transmitter if one has occurred (by returning a false value). The transmitter in turn can then decide how long to wait before attempting to retransmit again. The Ethernet channel's underlying data transfer mechanism is transparent to the transmitter.

3 Experiments

We devised a set of experiments with increasing levels of complexity to determine if our specification model for Half-Duplex Ethernet meets design goals. We define the average delay for an Ethernet station (transmitter or receiver) as:

- The average delay for a transmitter is the time interval (averaged over 1000 successful frame transmissions) between the station starting to send a frame (in SENSE_TRANSMIT state) and returning to same state to send the next frame.
- The average delay for a receiver is the time interval (averaged over 1000 successful frame receptions) between the station receiving a frame and it returning to the same state (RECV) to receive the next frame.

As required for the Truncated Binary Exponential Back-Off algorithm, the wait periods after a collision in each Ethernet station are strictly bound between lower and upper limits.

3.1 Channel Model

To simulate realistic network conditions, our specification model includes bursty traffic generators [13]. Bursty traffic is an infinite sequence of frames with sub-sequences of closely spaced (in time) frames interspersed with sub-sequences of widely spaced (in time) frames, i.e., a plot of frames over time shows peaks and plateaus. Bursty traffic has a long tailed (power law) probability distribution and is typically modeled using a Poisson Pareto Burst Processes with heuristics to enable a close fit to observed data. To circumvent the issue of having to choose correct heuristics, a simple power law distribution is used in our setup.

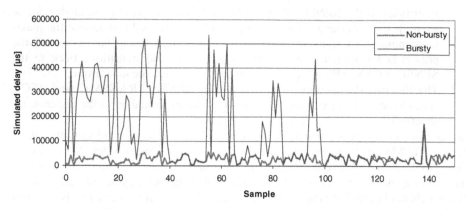

Fig. 4. Bursty and non-bursty average transmitter delays

The effect of adding the power law distributed delays is to increase the average delay in all cases when this delay interval is non-zero, see Fig. 4. This is because the number of collisions increases with the incoming frame rate (bursty traffic). In contrast, when the power law distributed delay interval is zero, the average delay has approximately the same value as if this additional delay is not present at all.

3.2 QoS Application

The next phase of our experiments involves creating specification models for a widely used network quality-of-service (QoS) algorithm that works at the Ethernet layer. QoS algorithms share some common characteristics:

1. Always applied to the interfaces of a router, e.g., WAN and LAN interfaces.
2. QoS features work on the producer-consumer model and rely on non-deterministic queues.

Some common QoS operations on network traffic are:

1. Shaping – delay frames/packets to meet a certain rate
2. Scheduling – rearrange frames/packets for output
3. Classifying – separating traffic into queues
4. Policing – measuring and limiting traffic on queues

With these in mind, the simulated QoS architecture is shown in Fig. 5. One sender and one receiver on each side of a router exchange frames with a receiver and sender on the other, respectively. The Token Source/Token Channel pair for each *EthernetHandler* behavior implements the chosen QoS algorithm, as will be explained shortly.

The router interconnects the two networks consisting of Ethernet channels 1 and 2, where behaviors *EthernetHandler1* and *EthernetHandler2* transfer frames between channels 1 and 2 via router interfaces 1 and 2. QoS algorithms/features are imposed on the router via the Token Source/Token Channel combination for each *EthernetHandler*. Internally, each *EthernetHandler* behavior is an Ethernet station with two ports, one dedicated to transferring frames originating in network 1 to network 2 and vice versa.

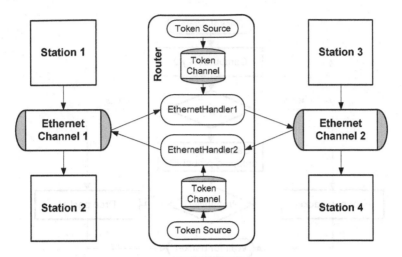

Fig. 5. Simulated Quality of Service architecture

The Token Channel is a non-deterministic custom queue that, in addition to blocking reads and writes, allows the user to check if it is empty – a feature unavailable for any built-in SpecC queue. We define the average delay for a router interface as:

- The time interval (averaged over 1000 successful attempts) between the router interface receiving a frame successfully, sending it out over the other Ethernet channel, and returning to the state where it can receive the next frame.

This is completely independent of the average delay for the basic Half-Duplex Ethernet.

3.2.1 Random Early Detection

Random Early Detection (RED) [12] is used for congestion control and manages queue size intelligently (Fig. 6). Unlike regular queues that drop packets from the tail when they are full, RED does it in a controlled and gradual way.

Once the queue size attains a certain average length, enqueued packets have a finite probability of being marked. A marking probability exceeding a predefined threshold means that the marked packet will be dropped. The marking probability increases linearly with the queue size up to a *maximum dropping probability*. The average queue size used for determining the marking probability is calculated using an Exponential Weighted Moving Average, insensitive to bursts.

When the average queue size is below a preset minimum bound, no packet is marked. When the average queue size exceeds the minimum queue length, the marking probability increases linearly until the average queue size attains the preset maximum queue length. As probability is normally not set to 100%, the queue size might rise above the maximum preset size. Hence, a limit parameter is provided to set a hard maximum for the size of the queue.

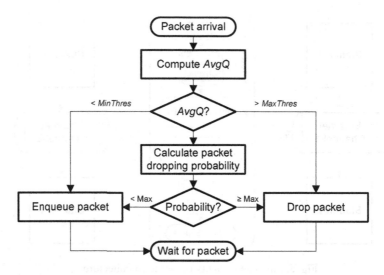

Fig. 6. Random Early Detection (RED) congestion control (*AvgQ*: average queue length, *Max-Thres*: maximum queue length threshold, *MinThres*: minimum queue length threshold)

3.2.2 Experimental Validation

For the purposes of this experiment, the two Token Source behaviors supply marking probabilities to the two *EthernetHandler* behaviors via the token channels. Both token channels are non-deterministic and non-blocking. Each *EthernetHandler* behavior can thus check if a token (marking probability) is available before trying to extract one. Our implementation of the Token Source/Token Channel pair uses the same functions and parameters as in [12] to generate the marking probabilities. This allows us to compare the results generated by our model (specifically queue length and average queue length) with the original ones in [12].

RED uses a number of predefined and computed parameters. The predefined parameters are *maximum dropping or marking probability*, *minimum* and *maximum queue lengths* and *queue weight*. The parameters computed per iteration are *count*, *average queue length*, *queue length* and *dropping or marking probability*. Count is the number of frames since the last marked frame. For our simulation, we used the same values for the predefined parameters as in [12]. In addition, the algorithm uses a linear function of time to determine the time interval since the queue was empty. In our case, we use simple difference in measured times to achieve this effect.

As the average queue length varies between the minimum and maximum thresholds, the packet marking probability varies between 0 and the maximum probability. The final marking probability increases linearly as the count since the last marked packet grows. For each frame that is to be sent out over the Ethernet layer, the average queue length is computed as in [12]. Fig. 7 represents results for queue size and average queue size sampled every 1000 successfully transmitted frames for the first 1000 samples at one of the two router interfaces we implemented using SpecC. All together, simulation of more than 3 million frames successfully transmitted over both router interfaces required 15 minutes of simulation time on a 2.8 GHz Linux workstation.

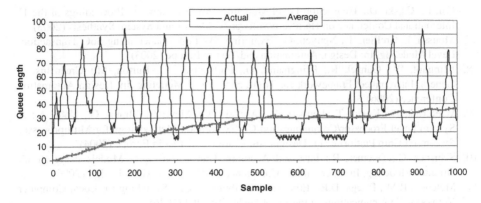

Fig. 7. Queue length and average queue length

4 Summary and Conclusions

Embedded devices are being increasingly deployed in networked environments, often communicating via best-effort channels, e.g., in wireless sensor networks. Using TLM techniques, we have specified and validated a networked embedded system in which devices communicate via a shared best-effort channel, specifically the Half-Duplex Ethernet sub-layer of the ISO/OSI Data Link layer. Our specification model can be easily integrated into the system level design process, using any appropriate toolset for exploration, prototyping and evaluation of design alternatives. To test if our specification model replicates reality, we have validated it using a multi-station bursty traffic scenario and a widely used network QoS protocol that operates at the Ethernet layer. In the future, we plan to deploy our Ethernet channel for modeling of various realistic, large-scale networked systems. In addition, future directions include analysis, customization and optimization of QoS algorithms for applications in typical resource constrained networked embedded system.

References

1. Weinberg, H.B., Zuck, L.D.: Timed Ethernet: Real-Time Formal Specification of Ethernet. In: Cleaveland, W.R. (ed.) CONCUR 1992. LNCS, vol. 630, pp. 370–385. Springer, Heidelberg (1992)
2. Bochmann, G., Sunshine, C.: Formal Methods in Communication Protocol Design. IEEE Transactions on Communications 28(4), 624–631 (1980)
3. Schmaltz, J., Borrione, D.: A Functional Approach to the Formal Specification of Networks on Chip. In: Hu, A.J., Martin, A.K. (eds.) FMCAD 2004. LNCS, vol. 3312, pp. 52–66. Springer, Heidelberg (2004)
4. Georges, J.-P., Rondeau, E., Divoux, T.: Evaluation of Switched Ethernet in an Industrial Context using Network Calculus. In: 4th IEEE International Workshop on Factory Communication Systems, Vasteras, Sweden (August 2002)
5. Shalunov, S., Carlson, R.: Detecting Duplex Mismatch on Ethernet. In: Dovrolis, C. (ed.) PAM 2005. LNCS, vol. 3431, pp. 135–148. Springer, Heidelberg (2005)

6. Cai, L., Gajski, D.: Transaction Level Modeling: An Overview. In: Proceedings of the 1st International Conference on Hardware/Software Codesign and System Synthesis (2003)
7. Moussa, I., Grellier, T., Nguyen, G.: Exploring SW Performance using SoC Transaction-Level Modeling. In: Design, Automation and Test in Europe (2003)
8. Klingauf, W., Günzel, R., Bringmann, O., Partfuntseu, P., Burton, M.: GreenBus: A Generic Interconnect Framework for Transaction Level Modeling. In: Design Automation Conference (2006)
9. Wieferink, A., Kogel, T., Leupers, R., Ascheid, G., Meyr, H., Braun, G., Nohl, A.: A System Level Processor/Communication Co-Exploration Methodology for Multiprocessor System-on-Chip Platforms. In: Design, Automation and Test in Europe (2004)
10. Schirner, G., Doemer, R.: Fast and Accurate Transaction Level Models using Result Oriented Modeling. In: International Conference on Computer Aided Design (2006)
11. Metcalfe, R.M., Boggs, D.R.: Ethernet: Distributed Packet Switching for Local Computer Networks. Communications of the ACM 19(7), 395–404 (1976)
12. Floyd, S. and Jacobson, V.: Random Early Detection Gateways for Congestion Avoidance. IEEE/ACM Transaction on Networking, 1993.
13. Karasaridis, A., Hatzinakos, D.: Network Heavy Traffic Modeling using Alpha-Stable Self-Similar Processes. IEEE Transactions on Communications 49(7), 1203–1214 (2001)
14. Caldari, M., Conti, M., Coppola, M., Curaba, S., Pieralisi, L., Turchetti, C.: Transaction Level Models for AMBA Bus Architecture Using SystemC. In: Design, Automation and Test in Europe: Designers' Forum (2003)
15. Schirner, G., Doemer, R.: Quantitative Analysis of Transaction Level Models for the AMBA Bus. In: Design, Automation and Test in Europe (2006)
16. Pasricha, S., Dutt, N., Ben-Romdhane, M.: Extending the Transaction Level Modeling Approach for Fast Communicating Architecture Exploration. In: Design Automation Conference (2004)
17. Xu, S., And Pollit-Smith, H.: A TLM Platform for System-on-Chip Simulation and Verification. In: VLSI Design, Automation and Test (April 2005)
18. Bombieri, N., Fummi, F., Quaglia, D.: TLM/Network Design Space Exploration for Networked Embedded Systems. In: International Conference on Hardware/Software Codesign and System Synthesis (2006)
19. Andrews, M., Kumaran, K., Ramanan, K., Stolyar, A., Whiting, P., Vijaykumar, R.: Providing Quality of Service Over Shared Wireless Link. IEEE Communications (February 2001)
20. Bonivento, A., Carloni, L., Sangiovanni-Vincentelli, A.: Platform-Based Design for Wireless Sensor Networks. Mobile Networks and Applications 11(4) (August 2006)
21. Gajski, D., Zhu, J., Doemer, R., Gerstlauer, A., Zhao, S.: SpecC: Specification Language and Methdology. Kluwer, Dordrecht (2000)
22. The Network Simulator ns-2, http://www.isi.edu/nsnam/ns
23. OPNET Technologies, Inc.: OPNET Modeler, http://www.opnet.com
24. OMNet++, http://www.omnetpp.org

Modeling Cache Effects at the Transaction Level

Ardavan Pedram*, David Craven, and Andreas Gerstlauer

Department of Electrical and Computer Engineering
University of Texas at Austin,
Austin, Texas, USA
ardavan@mail.utexas.edu, {dcraven,gerstl}@ece.utexas.edu

Abstract. Embedded system design complexities are growing exponentially. Demand has increased for modeling techniques that can provide both accurate measurements of delay and fast simulation speed for use in design space exploration. Previous efforts have enabled designers to estimate performance with Transaction Level Modeling (TLM) of software processors but this technique typically does not account for the effect of memory latencies. Modeling latency effects of a cache can greatly increase accuracy of the simulation and assist designers in choosing appropriate algorithms. In this article, we show the implementation of a cache model and its integration into a processor TLM. We demonstrate a method for extracting information about memory accesses from the final binary and abstracting them into cache model accesses. Our methodology is tested on a common embedded processor application with two algorithms exhibiting different cache behaviors. Our experiments show that the cache model can achieve results comparable to a cycle-accurate ISS, but with very little overhead compared to native, host-compiled code execution.

Keywords: Cache; Transaction Level modeling; System-level design.

1 Introduction

Modern System-on-Chip (SoC) designs are becoming more complex as the capacity of chips is increasing dramatically. Deriving an accurate model for several candidate designs has always been a problem in the limited time given to the vendors to finalize their product.

Traditional Instruction Set Simulators (ISS) provide cycle-accurate precision of the functional and timing behavior, but their simulation speed is prohibitively slow. Thus, these simulators are often unacceptable for exploring the design space in the limited time available.

---

* This research was partially sponsored by NSF grant CCF-0702714. Any opinions, findings and conclusions or recommendations expressed in this material are those of the author(s) and do not necessarily reflect the views of the National Science Foundation (NSF).

A. Rettberg et al. (Eds.): IESS 2009, IFIP AICT 310, pp. 89–101, 2009.

Increasing the level of abstraction in system modeling can increase the simulation speed by two or even three orders of magnitude. Transaction Level Modeling (TLM) [9] is the most commonly used and accepted approach, for abstracting the system behavior both in communication and computation [15]. With this approach the simulation speed is dramatically increased, enabling a larger design space to be covered.

Modern processors contain at least one extra level of memory hierarchy e.g. cache between the CPU and the memory to take advantage of data locality and hide the memory latency. Loading and storing data from the cache incurs much less delay than direct communication with memory. However, due to their dynamic nature, accurate estimates of cache hit/miss rates and associated cache access delays are impossible to obtain statically. Yet, cache effects can have a significant influence on overall software execution performance [11].

Existing high-level, abstract processor TLMs for native, host-compiled execution of computation [15] currently do not take the behavior of a cache into account for execution-delay estimation. As it stands, the simulator back-annotates functions with a simple time-estimate based on the number of cycles the processor takes to complete a given instruction. Each memory access is assumed to take an approximate fraction of the execution delay between CPU and memory.

In order to accurately model a processor, the simulator must also model the behavior of a cache. Two different algorithms of the same application may have different cache access behaviors, which will cause one of them to outperform the other. In the current environment, not only could this not be determined from the TLM estimated delays, the model actually predicts the opposite relative performance for such algorithms because of their higher complexity.

In this paper, we describe our approach to integrating the cache model with a transaction-level model of the processor. We will present the overhead in simulation time and the increase in simulation precision compared to a normal processor TLM simulation.

1.1   Problem Definition

We use a standard system-level design language (SLDL) [5] to obtain TLM simulation results for an ARM processor. Furthermore, we utilize the SWARM ISS [4] to obtain cycle accurate information on execution. Our work is based on an existing processor and operating system model for accurate yet native, host-compiled software execution [15]. However, to the best of our knowledge, none of the existing high-level processor modeling approaches provide a behavioral model of a cache for simulation-time estimation.

A cache simulator is provided and its implementation is discussed as a SLDL channel. Needed addresses are obtained from the final target binary and symbol table. The generated addresses are used in back annotated cache calls. The cache model dynamically updates its status as the simulation is run and returns appropriate delay for each access.

We demonstrate our approach using matrix multiplication as a test application. Matrix multiplication is the foundation of many embedded applications like Discrete Cosine Transform (DCT), and is convenient because it may be implemented with different algorithms with known different cache access behavior [10,8]. We have implemented two matrix multiplication algorithms: a naïve matrix multiplication which exhibits poor cache utilization, and a cache aware matrix multiplication that utilizes the cache to hide memory latencies. We show how the results for the TLM and TLM+cache model differ, and we use SWARM as our reference point for accuracy.

1.2 Outline

The rest of the paper is organized as follows: In Section 2 we discuss the related work. Section 3 describes the design steps taken to refine the application down to its target binary and to use that information for back-annotating cache calls into the TLM code. In Section 4, we give a brief explanation of our cache model and its interfaces. Section 5 introduces our application and presents our results. Finally, Section 6 discusses future work, and we will conclude our paper with a summary in Section 7.

2 Related Work

Traditionally, embedded software is validated using virtual prototyping environments that rely on instruction set simulation of processors [2]. ISS, can provide up to cycle-accurate results, but at the expense of slow simulation speeds, especially in multi-processor contexts. We use the Software ARM (SWARM) simulator [4] as such a cycle-accurate ISS reference to compare our approach against.

To provide fast virtual platform models, there are approaches for native, host-compiled software execution running in a model of the OS and the software environment. Our work extends previous approaches on such high-level, abstract processing modeling [15] based on the SpecC [5] SLDL. Our approach and results are, however, applicable to other processor models [3,14] built on top of other C-based, event-driven SLDLs such as SystemC [6].

There have been similar attempts for high-level modeling of processors with caches for accurate simulation-time measurements. InterDesign Technologies uses a high speed CPU model for hardware/software co-simulation. Their product, FastVeri [1], converts software code into a virtual CPU model in SystemC. To keep cycle accuracy, FastVeri also back-annotates software code with delays from their instruction and data cache emulation. Their process for cache model integration is similar to ours in that the C source code is decomposed into basic blocks. Their approach, however, is proprietary and not easily extensible towards standard system-level design flows.

There are two possible methods for modeling a cache: mathematically or behaviorally. A mathematical cache model involves the derivation and use of cache miss equations for specific code patterns, and their evaluation to produce static delays [13]. While this is fast to simulate, it is necessarily limited to specific algorithms that match code patterns for which such an equation has been derived [7,12]. Being based on static off-line analysis, mathematical models inherently introduce errors into the model, and cannot be extended to handle dynamic effects such as context switching.

3   Methodology

As previously mentioned, current processor models provide no method of modeling memory access latencies. A back-annotation provides execution delays by inserting function calls into user tasks to update the simulation time with static delays . Delays can be obtained through estimation or ISS-based measurements. No runtime analysis or memory latency modeling occurs. We base our work on a processor model that has user tasks wrapped in a hierarchy of behaviors. This hierarchy includes a CPU as an execution unit for user code, a simplified model of an OS consisting of a task scheduler and drivers, a HAL for the OS and finally the hardware core [15]. In order to enable modeling of memory access latency within the TLM simulation, it is necessary to augment this processor model to include a model for a cache.

3.1   Cache Model Integration

As a hardware component, the cache fits most appropriately in the core level of the processor TLM, as shown in Fig. 1. We note that the OS model is very simple, and because it consists of only a task scheduler it makes no memory accesses that reflect real-world behavior. As a result, we cannot model memory activity by the OS itself. User tasks, by contrast, may make many accesses to memory for computation purposes, and we can observe that algorithms selected in the specification exactly reflect those in the resulting code generated for execution on the target platform.

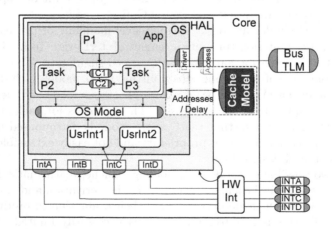

Fig. 1. Processor TLM organization with cache model

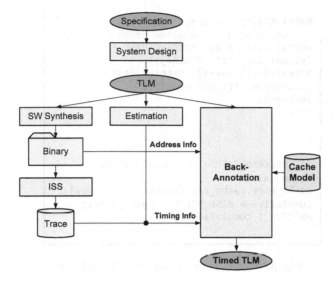

Fig. 2. Design flow

Due to the likelihood of memory accesses that are data-dependent, such as array indexing, it is necessary to model memory behavior at run time when that data is available and the address being accesses can be computed. To accomplish this, we follow the general back-annotation approach and introduce function calls to update the cache model as necessary.

3.2 Base Address Acquisition

Currently, we support access to static global variables/arrays data in our solution. Addresses for our cache model are computed at execution time of the TLM by code that is back-annotated into user behaviors. To compute these addresses, two pieces of information are needed. First, we need the static base address from which the memory offset is calculated, which is available prior to execution. The dynamic offset from this base address is required (in the case of accessing arrays), and this is available only at runtime. Calls to the cache model secondly pass the memory address being accessed and the cache model will return a modeled latency based on whether the data was available in the cache or not.

Obtaining the base addresses requires intimate knowledge of the memory layout of generated code. As shown in Fig. 2, the needed information about memory layout can be obtained from the target binary. This binary is generated starting from the user specification by proceeding through the system-level refinement process down to a TLM of the system. A software synthesis process generates target C code that will run on the final system. This code is then cross-compiled for the target processor to obtain the final target binary. At this point the symbol table with base addresses for global variables has been created. The binary is suitable for simulation on an instruction set simulator to verify results or to obtain accurate information about the execution delay of the various blocks of code.

```
MatrixC[i][j] += sum;
/*__BACKANNOTATED: enqueue cache access*/
accesslist[index]= MatrixC_Base +
(sizeof(int)*(i*MAT_WID+j));
accesslist[index+1]= MatrixC_Base +
(sizeof(int)*(i*MAT_WID+j));
index+=2;
/**/

...

/*__BACKANNOTATED: accumulate BB delays */
cache_delay =
cache_port.cache_call(accesslist, index);
cumulative = BASE_DELAY + cache_delay;
waitfor ( cumulative );
/**/
```

Fig. 3. Back annotated code for a basic block

3.3   Back Annotation

The second step for creating our cache-augmented TLM is to insert the cache model into the basic TLM, and back-annotate it with the proper cache model calls. As seen in Fig. 2, the back annotation process pulls address information from the synthesized binary, basic block timing information either from an estimation tool or from a cycle accurate simulation, and injects API calls to the cache model.

A cache channel is instantiated in the core behavior of the TLM. Back annotation also inserts memory address computations into user code wherever a global variable appears in a statement. Cache calls are inserted to update the model and obtain the memory latency as shown in Fig. 3. Currently, this process is done manually, but we plan to automate this process in the future. The code snippet shows an example of a back-annotated memory address computation and cache model update for a basic block of code.

4   Cache Model Implementation

This section details the process of implementing and integrating the cache model into the processor model. The purpose of integrating the cache model into the TLM is to dynamically update and simulate the behavior of a cache in terms of hit and miss delay. Because memory accesses may be data-dependent, and because the OS model may context-switch between tasks, our cache is maintained dynamically at runtime.

4.1   Cache Model

We use a behavioral modeling approach, which involves the use of data structures that emulate the state of a cache at any point in time. These structures are updated at runtime as memory is accessed. This method allows the user to observe the state of the cache at all times and can model any memory access pattern. Its drawback is a performance penalty due to additional overhead for each memory access to maintain the cache state. We chose to dynamically model a behavioral cache for greater flexibility. Our cache model consists of less than 200 lines of SpecC code and can easily support various cache organizations.

There are two options in the SpecC language for implementing a cache model: as a behavior or as a channel. A behavior consists of a main method, and is associated with an active thread while a channel is a passive component [5]. Since the cache state only needs to be updated when it is being called by a behavior, we chose to build the cache as a SpecC channel. This channel implements an interface that defines *cache_init()* and *cache_call()* functions available for cache communication.

The *cache_init()* function is used to create and initialize the cache model. It is called before the OS is instantiated. It allows the user to configure the cache model based on the number of sets, associativity, and cache line size. The *cache_call()* function provides behaviors a means of updating the cache state and of obtaining cache access delays. To reduce function call overhead, its interface accepts an array of cache accesses containing an ordered sequence of memory accesses with which the cache will be updated and for which a total delay is returned.

4.2   Address Tags Matrix Implementation

Since our cache model only needs to take into account occurrences of cache hits or misses to calculate the delay, we model only functional behavior of the cache, e.g. whether a particular address does or doesn't exist within the cache. For our purposes, we are not concerned with the data that would be stored. As such, our model is simply a matrix of address tags where the rows represent the number of sets and the columns represent the associativity. Fig. 4 shows an example of a typical two-way set associative cache on the left, and our implementation of

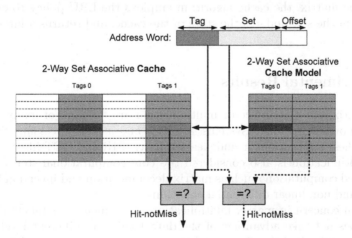

Fig. 4. An example of a typical 2-way set associative cache(left) and our tags matrix representation of the same configuration(right)

it using the tags matrix on the right. As shown in the figure, the tags, set, and offset are determined by the address bits. As described, the cache model on the right does not hold any data.

In a typical cache, there are three types of misses which differ by cause: compulsory, conflict, and capacity [4]. A compulsory miss occurs on a first access, a conflict miss happens when the cache is not associative enough, and a capacity miss means the cache size itself is not large enough. When a miss occurs, a replacement policy is needed to appropriately evict an old tag from the cache and replace it with the new tag. Our model implements the most commonly used algorithm, the Least Recently Used (LRU) replacement policy. In this method, the tag that was the least recently used within a set is evicted from the cache and replaced with the new, most recently used tag. To implement this functionality, we append a current time stamp to each element as it is placed in the address tags matrix. In this way, when a tag needs to be removed from the cache, the element with the smallest time stamp is the least recently used. We define the time stamp variable as an unsigned long long integer, which takes values up to 2^{64}, to ensure that it does not roll over to zero as it increments. This means that the cache must be accessed more than 2^{64} times for a single application before the LRU replacement policy is corrupted.

4.3   Cache Access Implementation

A delay time in cycles is calculated for each address that is passed to the cache model through the address vector. To ensure correct functionality, and therefore correct delay times of the cache, we must constantly maintain the state of the cache model. The $cache\_call()$ function generates an address tag, a set number, and an offset from the address of each cache access. It then searches the specified set in the tags matrix for a matching address tag. If the tag is found it updates the LRU cache status and returns an appropriate hit delay. If the tag is not found in the matrix, the cache algorithm employs the LRU policy to evict one of the tags in the set, updates the state of the cache, and returns a larger cache miss delay.

5   Experimental Results

Matrix-matrix and matrix-vector multiplication are the core of many applications based on solving linear systems, filtering, and media processing. Some examples of these applications include least squares, FIR and DCT filters. Matrix-matrix multiplication is also considered the core computational step for many matrix based computations such as matrix decomposition and inversion for solving linear and non-linear differential equations.

The main concern in matrix multiplication is the memory latency. If the algorithm does not take advantage of the data locality in different levels of the memory hierarchy, it will suffer a performance penalty waiting for data.

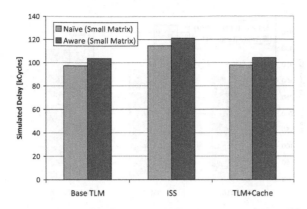

Fig. 5. Small matrix (16 × 16) Simulated delays

We chose to simulate two algorithms, a typical naïve matrix multiplication algorithm and a cache-aware, blocked algorithm. For each algorithm, we simulated both small size matrices that would fit entirely in the cache and large size matrices that could not. Results were obtained from the SWARM instruction set simulator, the TLM simulation, and our back-annotated TLM with cache model. We will discuss results for the small and large data set separately, comparing speed and precision for the three simulation approaches.

5.1 Accuracy

For our experiments, we obtain a base cycle delay from the ISS that does not take into account cache delays and back-annotate this into a basic timed TLM. We compare this against our extended TLM+Cache that reports simulation delay as the sum of this base delay and the delay computed by our cache model. Table 1 summarizes the results gathered for all simulated cases.

To match undocumented target system and simulator characteristics, we need to characterize and calibrate the miss penalty assumed in the reference ISS model. The ISS produces the precise number of cache misses, the number of real cycles, which includes cache miss penalties, and the number of logical cycles, which does not include cache miss delays. We estimate miss penalty by subtracting logical cycles from real cycles and dividing by the number of misses, using large problem sizes with many cache misses to minimize error. From this we obtained a miss penalty of 10 cycles.

Table 1. Accuracy Results

Simulation	Simulated Delay (Cycles)			
	Naive Larger	Aware Large	Naive Small	Aware Small
Base TLM	285,999,032	330,511,500	97,276	103,641
ISS	472,986,462	334,785,093	114,500	121,129
TLM+Cache	469,066,892	395,387,630	97,766	104,131

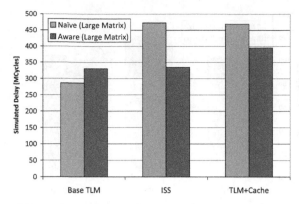

Fig. 6. Large matrix (256×256) simulated delays

For the small data set, we expect the two algorithms to perform similarly. The cache-aware algorithm should hold no advantage for data accesses and may run slightly slower due to increased code complexity over the naïve implementation. As shown in Fig. 5, the difference in performance between the two algorithms remains the same for the the ISS considering cache delays, base TLM cycles, and our cache modeling TLM because both algorithms have approximately the same memory behavior due to the small matrix size.

The large matrix size problem should greatly favor an algorithm that takes advantage of the memory hierarchy. We expect that the cache aware algorithm will amortize the cost of extra instructions by hiding the memory latency penalty. The naïve algorithm exhibits a high cache miss rate and should be heavily penalized in any simulation that takes this into account.

The results in Fig. 6 show that the ISS strongly favors the cache aware algorithm with almost a 30% increase in speed. The cache aware algorithm suffers in the base TLM because of its higher number of instructions. We expected our cache-modeling TLM to eliminate this gap to match the expected relative performance of the two algorithms as seen in the ISS. The cache-modeling TLM correctly reflects the advantage of the cache aware algorithm seen in the ISS.

5.2   Simulation Time

For design space exploration, it is necessary to obtain a variety of simulation results for many different possible implementations. This makes the time to execute the simulator important, as it can be a limiting factor.

As seen in Fig. 7, we incur some overhead over the TLM, but even for large matrix sizes we are no worse than an order of magnitude slower. This penalty is worthwhile considering that the TLM model is very fast, requiring fractions of a second to complete. The ISS, however, is four orders of magnitude slower than the TLM model, and requires more than two hours for a large matrix size. It was frequently the case that we completed back-annotation by hand for our

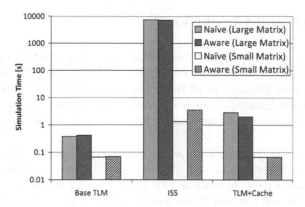

Fig. 7. Model simulation times

TLM with cache and obtained results before the ISS could finish execution. By contrast, our TLM+Cache simulator completes this simulation in just over two seconds.

6 Future Work

Future efforts to integrate cache effects into TLM will need to focus on a few important areas of improvement. These next steps include automation, expansion to track more variables, and additional more realistic testing to determine conditions most favorable to this method.

First, for back-annotation techniques to be useful as a modeling tool, they require implementation as an automated tool. Because we have available detailed information from the target binary during our process, future work may also choose to utilize this information to replace the current estimation tools with one that makes use of the additional detail.

Second, while our results show that tracking only global memory accesses is effective, ideally all variable accesses should be tracked. Hence the ability to trace accesses to stack variables would be desirable and could be achieved by integrating with the OS model to track the stack pointer of each task.

Third, additional testing is necessary to ensure that this technique applies well to a variety of algorithms on a variety of target platforms. We plan to apply the approach to a variety of industrial-strength MPSoC application, e.g. to evaluate performance of different DCT implementations in standard image or video processing algorithms. Larger models with multiple threads could allow us to determine the effects of cache pollution on performance, but to do so may require enhancement of the OS model to allow finer granularity preemptive multitasking than is currently possible. More control over the configuration of the ISS cache model would permit testing the technique against a variety of cache types and sizes. Expanding the set of test cases may also help demonstrate cases in which this technique is most helpful.

7   Summary and Conclusions

In this paper, we showed the implementation and integration of a configurable cache model into the system TLM in order to achieve higher precision for simulation. Our process requires us to refine the specification all the way down to the target processor binary. We gather critical information from the binary code and back-annotate it as input parameters for cache calls in the application code of the TLM.

We selected matrix multiplication as test application because of its well-known behavior under different variations. We chose a cache-aware, blocked matrix multiplication and a naïve algorithm, two algorithms with vastly different cache access behavior, to see how our cache model reflects these behaviors in the simulated cycle counts.

Our experimental result show that the TLM including the cache model does not have a significant simulation time overhead compared to a normal TLM. On the other hand, it is three orders of magnitude faster for large matrix sizes than executing on the ISS.

The TLM with cache accurately shows that extra complexity of cache-aware algorithms is amortized by the reduction in memory access penalty. Our method of back-annotation and cache modeling allows us to model delays with 100% fidelity compared to the ISS while maintaining execution speeds similar to TLM, facilitating rapid, early design space exploration.

References

1. Araki, D., Ito, N., Shinsha, T., Mori, Y.: High speed hardware/software co-verification with cpu model generator from software code. Technical report, InterDesign Technologies Inc (2006)
2. Benini, L., Bertozzi, D., Bogliolo, A., Menichelli, F., Olivieri, M.: MPARM: Exploring the multi-processor SoC design space with SystemC. VLSI Signal Processing 41(2), 169–182 (2005)
3. Bouchhima, A., Bacivarov, I., Yousseff, W., Bonaciu, M., Jerraya, A.A.: Using abstract CPU subsystem simulation model for high level HW/SW architecture exploration. In: ASP-DAC, Shanghai, China (January 2005)
4. Dale, M.: SWARM Instruction Set Simulator,
   http://www.cl.cam.ac.uk/~mwd24/phd/swarm.html
5. Gerstlauer, A., Dömer, R., Peng, J., Gajski, D.D.: System Design: A Practical Guide with SpecC. Kluwer, Dordrecht (2001)
6. Ghenassia, F.: Transaction-Level Modeling with Systemc: Tlm Concepts and Applications for Embedded Systems. Springer, Heidelberg (2006)
7. Ghosh, S., Martonosi, M., Malik, S.: Cache miss equations: an analytical representation of cache misses. In: ICS, Vienna, Austria (1997)
8. Goto, K., van de Geijn, R.A.: Anatomy of high-performance matrix multiplication. ACM Trans. Math. Softw. 34(3), 1–25 (2008)
9. Grotker, T., Li, S., Martin, G., Swan, S.: System Design with SystemC. Kluwer, Dordrecht (2002)

10. Gustavson, F.G., Henriksson, A., Jonsson, I., Kågström, B., Ling, P.: Superscalar GEMM-based level 3 BLAS - the on-going evolution of a portable and high-performance library. In: Kågström, B., Elmroth, E., Waśniewski, J., Dongarra, J. (eds.) PARA 1998. LNCS, vol. 1541. Springer, Heidelberg (1998)
11. Hennessy, J., Patterson, D.: Computer Architecture - A Quantitative Approach. Morgan Kaufmann, San Francisco (2003)
12. Hur, I., Lin, C.: Modeling the cache effects of interprocessor communication. In: PDCS, Cambridge, MA (November 1999)
13. Hwang, Y., Abdi, S., Gajski, D.: Cycle approximate retargettable performance estimation at the transaction level. In: DATE, Munich, Germany (March 2008)
14. Posadas, H., Adamez, J.A., Villar, E., Blasco, F., Escuder, F.: RTOS modeling in SystemC for real-time embedded SW simulation: A POSIX model. Design Automation for Embedded Systems 10(4) (December 2005)
15. Schirner, G., Gerstlauer, A., Dömer, R.: Abstract, multifaceted modeling of embedded processors for system level design. In: ASP-DAC, Yokohama, Japan (January 2007)

Event Stream Calculus for Schedulability Analysis

Karsten Albers[1] and Frank Slomka[2]

[1] INCHRON GmbH, August-Bebel-Strasse 88, 14482 Potsdam, Germany
`karsten.albers@inchron.com`
[2] Department of Embedded Systems/Real-Time Systems, Ulm University, 89069 Ulm,
Germany
`frank.slomka@uni-ulm.de`

Abstract. In the paper we will show the integration of the real-time calculus with
event driven real-time analysis like the periodic or the sporadic task model. For
the event-driven real-time analysis, flexible approximative analysis approaches
where proposed to allow an efficient real-time analysis. We will provide an easy
but powerful approximative description model for the real-time calculus. In contrary to the existing description model the degree of approximation is chooseable
allowing a more accurate description.

1 Motivation

The module-based design processes makes it possible to handle the complexity in software and hardware design. Systems are built using a set of closed modules. These modules can be designed and developed separately. Modules have only designated interfaces
and connections to other modules of their set. The purpose of modularization is to split
the challenging job of designing the whole system into multiple smaller jobs. Another
purpose is to allow the reuse of modules in different designs or use IP components of
third-party vendors.

Each module-based design concept needs a well defined interface-concept for con-
necting the different modules. For developing real-time systems a concept for analysing
the system which can handle the real-time aspects of the different modules separately
and allows to propagate the results through the system is required. One aspect of this
concept is the timing description of events which are produced by one module to trigger
the next following module. Another aspect is the remaining computation capacity for
the next module left over by the previous module.

Consider for example a network packet processor as shown in figure 1. The single
packages are processed by chains of tasks τ which can be located on different processing elements P. The processing elements P can be processors, dedicated hardware or
the communication network. The events Θ triggering the different tasks are equal to
the packages flowing through the network. Each processing unit P uses a fixed-priority
scheduling and the tasks τ on each unit are sorted by their priority level. Each task τ
has, as available capacity, the capacity S' left over by the tasks τ with a higher priority
located on the same processing unit.

The purpose of this paper is to provide an efficient and flexible approach for the real-
time analysis of such a modularized system. Necessary therefore is a powerful and sufficient event model for describing the different time interfaces for the different aspects.

A. Rettberg et al. (Eds.): IESS 2009, IFIP AICT 310, pp. 102–114, 2009.

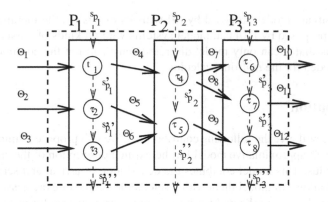

Fig. 1. Network processor example

2 Related Work

The most advanced approach for the real-time analysis of such a modular network is the real-time calculus by [1] and [2]. It is based on the network calculus approach, especially on the concept of arrival and service curves defined by [3] and [4].

The event pattern Θ is modeled by an arrival curve $R_f(t)$ which denotes the number of events arriving within a time interval of length I. $R_f^u(t)$ denotes the upper bound and $R_f^l(t)$ the lower bound for this curve. These functions are sub-additive and deliver for every t the maximum respective the minimum amount of events which can occure in any interval of length t. The service curves $\beta_r^u(t)$ and $\beta_r^l(t)$ model the upper and lower bound of the computational requirements which can be handled by the ressource during a time interval of length t. The real-time caclulus provides equations to calculate the outgoing arrival and service curves out of the incoming curves of a task.

To make it possible to evaluate the modification equations independently from each other, a good finite description for the curves is needed. The complexity of the relationship equations depends directly on the complexity of this description. In [5] and [1] an approximation for the arrival and service curves was proposed in which each curve is described by three straight line segments. One segment describes the initial offset or arrival time, one an initial bursts and one the long time rate. As outlined in [6] this approach is too simplified to be suitable for complex systems. It only has a fixed degree of exactness. No suitable descriptions for the function are known so far.

In this paper we will propose a model for the curves having a selectable approximation error. A trade-off between this degree of accuracy and the necessary effort for the analysis becomes possible.

SymTA/S [7],[8] is another approach for the modularized real-time analysis. The idea was to provide a set of interfaces which can connect different event models. Therefore the different modules can uses different event models for analysis. Unfortunately, the event models for which interfaces are provided are quite simple. In [7] an event model covering all this models was described. The problem of these models is that multiple bursts or bursts with different minimum separation times cannot be handled.

The event stream model proposed by [9] with its extension, the hierarchical event stream model proposed by [10] can model systems with all kinds of bursts efficiently. The problem is that it can only model discrete events and not the continious service function as needed for the real-time calculus.

3 Contribution

In the paper we will give the following contributions. We will propose a simple but flexible and powerful approximative model for the explicit description of the curves of the real-time calculus. This model combines the description of arrival and service curves efficiently and allows to model them with a selectable degree of exactness. Its approximation follows the same scheme like the existing approximation for event models as proposed in [11]. Therefore it is possible to transfer previously existing event models, like the periodic or the sporadic task model, the event stream model, the sporadically task model, the model of SymTA/S or the hierarchical event stream model in this new model. This allows the integration of the approximative analysis for the event models and the real-time calculus to a new powerful overall analysis for distributed systems.

We will outline this transfer methods for the various event models and the resulting real-time analysis for the new model for EDF and static priority scheduling. For the real-time calculus the new model provides a flexible and efficient approximative description of the curves. We will give the first methodology to implement all operations needed by the real-time calculus. This is more accurate than the methodology used in the original literature.

4 Model

In the following we will give a new approximative model for the curves of the real-time calculus allowing a less pessimistic modeling of the curves. It guarantees the approximation error. In [11] such an approximation was proposed for the periodic task model with EDF scheduling. It is now extended to distributed systems and is integrated in the model itself.

We model each curve of the real-time calculus by a test list $Te = \{te\}$ consisting of a set of test-list elements $te = (I, c, G)$ each modeling one segment of the curve. I is an interval determining the start point of the segment, c are costs additionally occuring at the start of the segment and G determines the gradient within the segment and is the increment between the gradient within the segment and the gradient within the previous segment. The total gradient is the sum of all gradients of previous test list elements with an interval $I' < I$.

For example, four events with a distance of 10 to each other and with an execution time of 2 can be modeled by the test list: $Te = \{(0, 2, 0), (10, 2, 0), (20, 2, 0), (30, 2, 0)\}$. The proposed model is not limited to model time discrete events, it can also model the capacity and allows to describe systems with varying capacity over the time. The gradient is useful to model the capacities or the remaining capacities of processing units (PUs). The standard case in which a PU can handle one time unit execution time in one time unit can be modeled by $te = (0, 0, 1)$. More sophisticated service functions like a case in which only half of the processor capacity is available during the first 100 time units can also be described by a few elements $Te = \{(0,0,\frac{1}{2}),(100,0,\frac{1}{2})\}$. Note that the gradients are always only the differences between the resulting gradient and the previous gradient. Therefore in the example the function has a gradient of $\frac{1}{2}$ for the first 100 time units and after them a resuling gradient of 1 for the remaining time.

4.1   Approximation

General event models generate an infinite set of events and would therefore require an infinite number of test-list elements. In the periodic task model for example each task $\tau = (T, cw, d)$ represents an infinite number of jobs sharing the same worst-case execution time cw and relative deadline d and having a periodic release pattern with period T. An approximation is necessary to bound this number of elements and to allow a fast analysis. The idea for the approximation is to consider the first n jobs of a task exactly and to approximate the following jobs by the specific utilization of the task. This approximation can be represented by the test-list model. The selection of the parameter n allows a trade-off between the exactness and the analysis effort. For example a task $\tau = (10,2,6)$ is represented by a test list $Te = \{(0,2,0),(10,2,0),(20,2,0),(30,2,\frac{2}{10})\}$ with 4 as degree of exactness.

Definition 1. *([11]) Let Γ be any taskset bound on any resource ρ. Let ρ_l be the resource with the minimum capacity on which Γ is feasible. An approximation with approximation error ε is a test algorithm which*

1. returns "non-feasible" in those cases in which Γ on ρ is non-feasible
2. returns "feasible" in all those feasible cases in which $\mathcal{C}(\rho) \geq \frac{1}{1-\varepsilon}\mathcal{C}(\rho_l)$
3. can return either "feasible" or "non-feasible" in all cases with $\mathcal{C}(\rho_l) \leq \mathcal{C}(\rho) \leq \frac{1}{1-\varepsilon}\mathcal{C}(\rho_l)$

This idea can be used in a similar way for all other task and event models. Formally, a periodic task τ with $\tau = (T, cw, d)$ and a degree of exactness of n can be transferred into a test list Te with the elements

$$Te = \{(0, cw_\tau, 0), (T_\tau, cw_\tau, 0), (2T_\tau, cw_\tau, 0), ..., (nT_\tau, cw_\tau, \frac{cw_\tau}{T_\tau})\}$$

with deadline d_τ. We can transfer this test list further in a test representing the demand bound function $\Psi(I, \tau)$ for τ by shifting it by the deadline ($Te' = \{(d_\tau, cw_\tau, 0), (T_\tau + d_\tau, cw_\tau, 0), ..., (nT_\tau + d_\tau, cw_\tau, \frac{cw_\tau}{T_\tau})\}$).

The service functions might also require an approximation. But in contrary to above it is necessary to underestimate the original functions. A service function of a processor which is not available every 100 time units for 2 time units due to operation system processes can be modeled with an degree of exactness of 4 by $Te = \{(2,0,1), (100,0,-1), (102,0,1), (200,0,-1), (202,0,1), (300,0,-1), (302,0,\frac{98}{100})\}$.

4.2   Event Bound Function

The amount of events occuring in some intervals I, therefore the value of the real-time calculus curves can be calculated with the following event bound function.

Definition 2. *An event bound function* $\Upsilon(I)$ *gives the amout of events which can occure at most in any interval of length I.*

The calculation can be done as follows:

$$\Upsilon(I, Te) = \sum_{\substack{\forall te_i \in Te \\ I_{te_i} \leq I}} [(I - I_{te_i}) \times G_{te_i} + c_{te_i}]$$

5   Real-Time Analysis

In the following we will show how simple an efficient schedulability analysis can be realized with the introduced model.

5.1   EDF

Schedulability analysis for EDF can be done using the processor demand criteria which was introduced by [12], [13].

Definition 3. *([12]) The demand bound function* $\Psi(I, \Gamma)$ *gives the cummulated execution requirement of those jobs having release time and deadline within I.*

Lemma 1. A task set scheduled with EDF keeps all deadlines if for every intervals $I > 0$ the demand bound function $\Psi(I, \Gamma)$ does not exceed the available capacity $\mathscr{C}(I, \rho)$ for I:$\Psi(I, \Gamma) \leq \mathscr{C}(I, \rho)$

This can be rewritten as:$\mathscr{C}(I, \rho) - \Psi(I, \Gamma) \geq 0$ *Proof:* See [12] and [11]   ∎

Both, the demand bound and the service function can be described by test lists as we have already seen. $\mathscr{C}(I, \Gamma) - \Psi(I, \Gamma)$ can be simplified to one test list. The overall demand bound function of the taskset is the sum of the demand bound functions of the single tasks: $\Psi(I, \Gamma) = \sum_{\forall \tau \in \Gamma} \sum_{\forall te \in Te_\tau} \Psi(I, Te).$

Algorithm 1. Feasibility Analysis

```
Algorithm Superposition
Given: testList Te (sorted with rising I)
r = 0;  G = 0;  I_old = 0;
FOR ALL  (te ∈ Te)
    r := r + (a_te − I_old)G
    IF  (r < 0) THEN ⇒not feasible
    r := r + cw_te
    IF  (r < 0) THEN ⇒not feasible
    I_old := I_te;  G := G + G_te
END WHILE
IF  (G < 0) THEN ⇒not feasible
ELSE  ⇒feasible
```

The demand bound function of a single task can be derived out of the event bound function of this task by shifting this function by the value of the deadline:

$$\Psi(I,\Gamma) = \Upsilon(I-d,\Gamma)$$

So the resulting analysis for EDF reads:

$$\forall I \geq 0 \quad \Upsilon(I,Te') = \mathscr{C}(I,\rho) - \sum_{\forall \tau \in \Gamma} \sum_{\forall te \in Te_\tau} \Upsilon(I - d_\tau, Te) \geq 0$$

For the demand bound function a test list can be calculated out of the test lists of the event bound functions using the shift and add functions as we will define in section 6.

In algorithm 1 we give the short implementation to prove the condition $\Upsilon(I,Te) \geq 0$ for all $I \geq 0$ and therefore to do the real-time analysis.

The best way to do this is to calculate and check the intervals of the test-list elements step-wise in rising order starting by $I = 0$. We have to test each element twice, once after the costs resulting of the previous gradient are added and once after the costs of the element are added. Otherwise, the situation can occure that the costs value can compensate a negative value of the functions which would therefore be undetectable.

5.2   Analysis for Static Priorities

The real-time analysis of systems with static priority scheduling requires another function, the request bound function $\Phi(I,\Gamma)$.

Definition 4. *([12]) The request bound functions $\Phi(I)$ contains the amount of execution time requested by those events having occured within I.*

Events occuring exactly at the end of I are excluded:
$$\Phi(I,Te) = \lim_{I' \nearrow I} \Upsilon(I',Te) = \sum_{\substack{\forall te_i \in Te \\ I_{te_i} < I}} [(I - I_{te_i}) \times G_{te_i} + c_{te_i}]$$

For the analysis it is necessary to consider each task seperatly.

Lemma 2. (similar to [3]) The worst-case response time of a task is given by:

$$r_\tau = min(I|\forall I' > 0 : \mathscr{C}(I',\tau) - \Phi(I',\tau) \geq 0)$$

Schedulability for a job of a task τ is given if $r_\tau \leq d_\tau$.   *Proof:* See [12].   ∎

The schedulability analysis can also simply be done by checking for each $I \geq 0$ and each $\tau \in \Gamma$: $\Psi(I,\tau) \leq \mathscr{C}(I,\tau)$

$\mathscr{C}(I,\tau)$ denotes the capacity available for task τ within I. For the task with the highest priority this is the capacity of the resource $\mathscr{C}(I,\rho)$. For all other tasks it is the remaining part of the capacity after all tasks with a higher priority have been processed. The calculation of this remaining capacity can be done for each task seperately. The problem is that an amount of capacity reached for some intervals I is also available for each larger interval I' even if between I and I' a large amount of computation request occures, so that $\Phi(I',\tau) - \Phi(I,\tau) > \mathscr{C}(I',\tau) - \mathscr{C}(I,\tau)$. No part of this requested computation time can be processed within I as this would require to process it before it is requested.

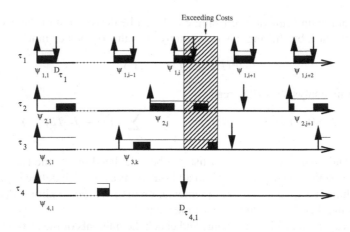

Fig. 2. Exceeding costs

For the calculation of this remaining capacity the exceeding costs function is useful:

Definition 5. *([14]) Exceeding costs $\Upsilon(I,\Gamma)$ denotes those part of the costs requested within the interval I by the taskset Γ which cannot be processed within I with either scheduling due to the late request times.*

See figure 2 for some examples for exceeding costs. For example for the job $\psi_{1,i}$ arriving at time 18 and requesting 4 time units computation time at least 2 time units cannot be processed within $I = 20$ even if the job fully gets the remaining processor time. The exceeding costs get an even higher value taking other jobs into account. Job $\psi_{2,j}$ alone would not contribute to the exceeding costs, but together with job $\psi_{1,i}$ the contribution gets even higher than the contribution of job $\psi_{1,i}$ alone. The reason is that the jobs steal the capacity from each other. Only the sum of the exceeding computation time is relevant not from which task it is requested. The value and the calculation of the exceeding costs is independent of the concrete scheduling.

The exceeding cost function can be used for a simple schedulability analysis for systems with static priorities [14].

Lemma 3. A task set Γ is feasible if for each task $\tau \in \Gamma$ and each $I > 0$:

$$\Psi(I,\tau) + \Phi(I,hp(\tau)) - \Upsilon(I,hp(\tau)) \leq \mathscr{C}(I,\rho)$$

or if τ_{i-1} is the task with next higher priority than τ_i:

$$\Psi(I,\tau_i) + \Phi(I,\tau_{i-1}) - \Upsilon(I,\tau_{i-1}) \leq \mathscr{C}(I,\tau_{i-1})$$

The calculation of the remaining capacity can be therefore done by

$$\mathscr{C}(I,\tau_i) = \mathscr{C}(I,\tau_{i-1}) - \Phi(I,\tau_{i-1}) + \Upsilon(I,\tau_{i-1})$$

Proof: See [14]. ∎

This allows a step-wise calculation of the remaining capacity and also an integration of the analysis for EDF and for fixed priority scheduling to one hierarchical schedulability analysis.

Figure 3 visualizes its calculation. The exceeding costs function starts equally to the difference of the request bound function and the available capacity function ($\Phi(I, \tau) - \mathscr{C}(I, \tau)$). It remains equal to this function until it drops below zero for the first time, e.g. more capacity is available than required by requested jobs. Then the exceeding costs function remains zero until the difference function starts rising again, e.g. new request arrives. Then the exceeding costs function will also rise and run further in parallel to the difference function but with a higher value.

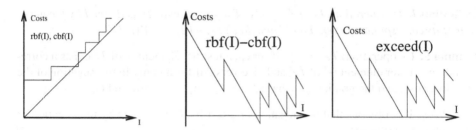

Fig. 3. Calculation of the exceeding costs functions

5.3   Practical Issues

Blocking time, scheduling overhead and the priority inheritance protocol can easily be integrated in the above equations. A blocking time b can be integrated by either adding b to the equations or by integrating the test-list element $te = (0, b, 0)$.

6   Operations and Basic Functions

In the following we will introduce some operations on test-lists and their implementation.

6.1   Adding/Subtracting $(+, -)$

The add-operation for two test lists can be simply realized by a union of the sets of test list elements of the two test lists:

Definition 6. (+ operation) Let Te_A, Te_B, Te_C be test lists. If Te_C is the sum of Te_A and Te_B ($Te_C = Te_A + Te_B$) then for each interval I the equation $\Upsilon(I, Te_C) = \Upsilon(I, Te_A) + \Upsilon(I, Te_B)$ is true.

Lemma 4. (+ operation) The sum $Te_C = Te_A + Te_B$ can be calculated by the union of the event stream elements of Te_A, Te_B: $Te_{new} = Te_A \cup Te_B$

Proof:

$$\Upsilon(I, Te_C) = \Upsilon(I, Te_A) + \Upsilon(I, Te_B)$$
$$= \sum_{\substack{\forall te_i \in Te_A \cup Te_B \\ I_{te_i} \leq I}} [(I - I_{te_i}) \times G_{te_i} + c_{te_i}]$$
$$= \Upsilon(I, Te_A \cup Te_B)$$

■

The resulting test list can be simplified by eliminating test list elements with equal intervals.

Definition 7. *(− operation) Let $Te' = -Te$. The negation of Te is defined by the negation of its corresponding event bound function $\Upsilon(I, -Te) = -\Upsilon(I, Te)$.*

Lemma 5. *(− operation) $Te' = -Te$ if for each test list element te of Te exists a corresponding counter element te' of Te' and vice versa differing only in the negation of the one-time costs and the gradient. We have $I_{te'} = I_{te}$, $cw_{te'} = -cw_{te}$ and $G_{\hat{\theta}'} = -G_{\hat{\theta}}$.*

Proof: It is obvious that the negation of a test list can be done by the negation of each relevant parameter.   ■

We can write $Te_C = Te_A + (-Te_B)$.

6.2   Shift Operation $(\uparrow, \downarrow)$

The shift operation can be realized by adding or subtracting the shift-value from each interval of all test list elements.

Definition 8. *($\uparrow$ shift-operation) Let Te be a test list that is shifted right by the value t resulting in the test list $Te' = Te \uparrow t$. The event bound functions have the following relationship:*

$$\Upsilon(I, Te') = \begin{cases} \Upsilon(I - t, Te) & I \geq t \\ 0 & else \end{cases}$$

Lemma 6. *$\Upsilon(I, Te) \uparrow t = \Upsilon(I, Te')$ if Te' contains and only contains for each element te of Te an element $te' \in Te'$ having the following relations to te: $I_{te'} = I_{te} + t$, $c_{te'} = c_{te}$, $G_{te'} = G_{te}$*

Proof: It is a simple shift operation on functions.   ■

The operation to shift a value left by the value t $(Te \downarrow t)$ can be defined in an equal way.

6.3   Scaling with a Cost Value

Another operation on test lists is to scale the total stream by a cost value. This is for example necessary for the integration of the worst-case execution times into the analysis.

Definition 9. *Let Te′ be the test list Te scaled by the cost value cw (Te′ = Te × cw). Then for each interval I:*

$$\Upsilon(I, Te') = \Upsilon(I, Te)cw$$

Lemma 7. $\Upsilon(I, Te') = \Upsilon(I, Te) \times cw$ if Te' contains and only contains for each test lists element θ of the child set of Te an element $te' \in Te'$ having the following relations to Te: $I_{te'} = I_{Te}$, $c_{te'} = c_{Te} \times cw$, $G_{te'} = G_{Te} \times cw$

Proof: All parts of the test list elements related to the amount of events are scaled by the variable cw. ∎

6.4   Operations of the Real-Time Calculus

A scheduling network is a system consisting of several chains of tasks and a set of resources. Each task τ of the task chain is mapped to one resource ρ. Tasks mapped on the same resource are scheduled with fixed priority scheduling. Different tasks of a chain can be mapped on different resources. In the figure 1 the tasks τ_1, τ_4, τ_6 form a task chain and the tasks τ_1, τ_4, τ_7 form another task chain. Each task τ is triggered by an upper and lower arrival curve $R_\tau^u(I)$ and $R_\tau^l(I)$ and the available computational effort for this task is described by an upper and lower service curve $\beta_\tau^u(I)$ and $\beta_\tau^l(I)$.

Figure 4 gives a closer look at one single task τ and their curves.

For each task we have an incoming (upper and lower) arrival curve $R_\tau^u(I)$ and $R_\tau^l(I)$ modeling the workload for τ. It includes and is based on the arrival times of those events generating workload for τ. We also have an (upper and lower) service curve $\beta_\tau^u(I)$ and $\beta_\tau^l(I)$ modeling the amount of workload that can be handled by the task.

The analysis of a task generates outgoing (upper and lower) arrival $(R_\tau^u(I)'$ and $R_\tau^l(I)')$ and service curves $(\beta_\tau^u(I)'$ and $\beta_\tau^l(I)')$. The outgoing arrival curve is a modification of the incoming arrival curves and is also the incoming arrival curve of the following task in the chain. The outgoing service curve is the incoming service curve reduced by the workload handled by the task. It is the incoming service curve for the task with the next lower priority on the same resource.

The real-time calculus provides the equations to describe the relationships between the incoming and outgoing curves [1]. For the calculation the functions sup and inf are needed providing upper and lower bounds. Their value can be reachable, but does not need to be.

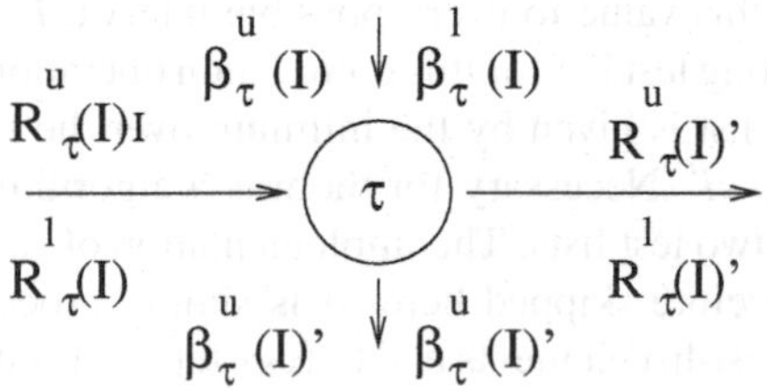

Fig. 4. Real-Time Calculus of single task

Algorithm 2. inf-split

```
Algorithm inf-split //  inf  (R(I') + β(I - I'))
                      0≤I'≤I
testlist R, β; testlist S = ∅
for all te ∈ R and all te ∈ β
  S := min(S, subAddOneList(R, Iₜₑ, β))
  S := min(S, subAddOneList(β, Iₜₑ, R))
end for
return S
Algorithm subAddOneList Te, I, Te'
testlist tmp := ∅
tmp := Te + I
c :=  Σ  [cₜₑ' + (I - Iₜₑ')Gₜₑ']
    ∀ₜₑ'∈Te'
    Iₜₑ'<Iₜₑ
tmp := tmp ∪ {(I, c, 0)}
return tmp;
```

The outgoing service curves, giving the available capacity for the task with the next lower priority on the same processor, can be calculated by:

$$\beta_\tau^l(I)' = \min(\sup_{0 \le I' \le I} \{\beta_\tau^l(I') - R_\tau^u(I)\}, 0)$$

$$\beta_\tau^u(I)' = \sup_{0 \le I' \le I} \{\beta_\tau^u(I') - R_\tau^l(I')\}$$

For our model we have already provided equations for calculating the remining capacity based on the exceeding costs function. They can be used in the real-time calculus:

$$\mathscr{C}^l(I, \tau_i) = \mathscr{C}^l(I, \tau_{i-1}) - \Phi^u(I, \tau_{i-1}) + \Upsilon^u(I, \tau_{i-1})$$

$$\mathscr{C}^u(I, \tau_i) = \mathscr{C}^u(I, \tau_{i-1}) - \Phi^l(I, \tau_{i-1}) + \Upsilon^l(I, \tau_{i-1})$$

We can set $\beta_\tau^x(I) = \mathscr{C}^x(I, \tau)$ and $R_\tau^x(I) = \Phi^x(I, \tau)$.
The outgoing lower arrival curve is given by:

$$R_\tau^l(I)' = \inf_{0 \le I' \le I} \{R_\tau^l(I') + \beta_\tau^l(I - I')\}$$

Algorithm 2 gives a concrete implementation for this operation based on test lists. The idea is to keep either I' or $I - I'$ fixed, calculate the fixed value for either $R_\tau^l(I')$ or $\beta_\tau^l(I - I')$ and complete this value to every possible interval I with the test list of the other function. The resulting test list for this completion operation can be calculated and the overall resulting test list is given by the infimum over the test lists of all possible fixed values for I' and $I - I'$. Necessary for them is a algorithm to find the step-wise minimum or infimum of two test lists. The implementation of such an algorithm is very straight forward and therefore skipped here. It is simply processing both lists in the ascending order of their test-list elements and to register always the dominating element (the element leading to the lower overall cost value). In case of different gradients of the corresponding elements the domination can change at an interval I' between two intervals. The calculation of I' is simply the calculation of the crossing point of two lines. The outgoing upper arrival curve is given by:

$$R_\tau^u(I)' = \min(\inf_{0 \le I' \le I} \{\sup_{0 \le v \le \infty} [R_\tau^u(I' + v) - \beta_\tau^l(v)] + \beta_\tau^u(I - I')\}, \beta_\tau^u(I))$$

Algorithm 3. sup-add

```
Algorithm sup-add // sup_{0≤v<∞}(R(I+v) − β(v))
TestList R,β
testList S = ∅
for all te ∈ R and all te ∈ β
   // I_te = v
   diff = Σ_{te'∈R, I_te'≤I_te} [cw_te' + (I_te − I_te')G_te'] − Σ_{te'∈β, I_te'<I_te} [cw_te' + (I_te − I_te')G_te']
   //diff = R(I_te) − lim_{I'→I_te, I'<I_te} β(I')

   // Hold the point of β
   G_R = Σ_{∀te'∈R, I_te'≤I_te} G_te'
   Te_tmp := {te'|te' ∈ R ∧ I_te' > I_te}
   Te_tmp := Te_tmp − I_te
   Te_tmp := Te_tmp + {(0, diff, G_R)}
   S := sup(S, Te_tmp)

   // Hold the point of R, Needed inverse β
   G_β = Σ_{∀te'∈β, I_te'<I_te} G_te'
   Te_tmp := {te'|te' ∈ R ∧ I_te' < I_te}
   Te_tmp2 := {(0, diff, G_β)}
   for each te_i ∈ Te_tmp
      Te_tmp2 := Te_tmp2 ∪ {(I_te − I_te_i, c_te_i', G_te_{i−1})}
   end for
   S := sup(S, Te_tmp2)
end for
return S
```

We define the sup-add operation handling the inner part of the equation

$$\sup_{0 \le v \le \infty} [R_\tau^u(I' + v) - \beta_\tau^l(v)]$$

Its implementation for test lists is given in algorithm 3. The idea is similar as for the inf-split operation, we also hold an interval and build a test list for all possible completions. But we use v here always as a fixed value. The implemetation of the sup or maximum operation is similar to the inf or minimum operation.

7   Conclusion

In this paper we propose an efficient approximative model to describe stimulations of tasks in a distributed real-time system. It was shown that this model integrates many other models describing stimulation in a system and delivers due to a chooseable degree of approximation a general description of stimulation. In the next step we described how an efficient real-time analysis for the model can be done for static and dynamic priorities. In order to show the relevant impact of our model and methods we use the real-time calculus. We give an efficient way to integrate the real-time calculus in our model. Thereby we show how the abstractly described functions can be implemented in a concrete manner. In future we will use this model for further applications in order to improve methods for the real-time analysis.

References

1. Chakraborty, S., Künzli, S., Thiele, L.: Performance evaluation of network processor architectures: Combining simulation with analytical estimations. Computer Networks 41(5), 641–665 (2003)
2. Thiele, L., Chakraborty, S., Gries, M., Künzli, S.: Design space exploration for the network processor architectures. In: 1st Workshop on Network Processors at the 8th International Symposium for High Performance Computer Architectures (2002)
3. Cruz, R.: A calculus for network delay. IEEE Transactions on Information Theory 37, 114–141 (1991)
4. Parekh, A., Gallager, R.G.: A generalized processor sharing approach to flow control in integrated service networks. IEEE/ACM Transactions on Networking (3), 344–357 (1993)
5. Künzli, S.: Efficient Design Space Exploration for Embedded Systems. PhD thesis, ETH Zürich No. 16589 (2006)
6. Albers, K., Slomka, F.: Efficient feasibility analysis for real-time systems with edf-scheduling. In: Proceedings of the Design Automation and Test Conference in Europa (DATE 2005), pp. 492–497 (2005)
7. Richter, K.: Compositional Scheduling Analysis Using Standart Event Models. Dissertation, TU Braunschweig (2005)
8. Richter, K., Ernst, R.: Event model interfaces for heterogeneous system analysis. In: Proceedings of the Design Automation and Test Conference in Europe, DATE 2002 (2002)
9. Gresser, K.: An event model for deadline verification of hard real-time systems. In: Proceedings of the 5th Euromicro Workshop on Real-Time Systems (1993)
10. Albers, K., Bodmann, F., Slomka, F.: Hierachical event streams and event dependency graphs. In: Proceedings of the 18th Euromicro Conference on Real-Time Systems (ECRTS 2006), pp. 97–106 (2006)
11. Albers, K., Slomka, F.: An event stream driven approximation for the analysis of real-time systems. In: IEEE Proceedings of the 16th Euromicro Conference on Real-Time Systems, Catania, pp. 187–195 (2004)
12. Baruah, S.: Dynamic- and static-priority scheduling of recurring real-time tasks. International Journal of Real-Time Systems 24, 98–128 (2003)
13. Baruah, S., Mok, A., Rosier, L.: Preemptive scheduling hard-real-time sporadic tasks on one processor. In: Proceedings of the Real-Time Systems Symposium, pp. 182–190 (1990)
14. Albers, K., Bodmann, F., Slomka, F.: Run-time efficient feasibility analysis of uni-processor systems with static priorities. In: Poceedings of the International Embedded Systems Symposium, IESS 2007 (2007)

Real-Time Scheduling in Heterogeneous Systems Considering Cache Reload Time Using Genetic Algorithms

Mohammad Reza Miryani and Mahmoud Naghibzadeh

Department of Computer Engineering, Ferdowsi University of Mashhad,
Mashhad, Iran
miryani@stu-mail.um.ac.ir, naghibzadeh@um.ac.ir

Abstract. Since optimal assignment of tasks in a multiprocessor system is, in almost all practical cases, an NP-hard problem, in recent years some algorithms based on genetic algorithms have been proposed. Some of these algorithms have considered real-time applications with multiple objectives, total tardiness, completion time, etc. Here, we propose a suboptimal static scheduler of nonpreemptable tasks in hard real-time heterogeneous multiprocessor systems considering time constraints and cache reload time. The approach makes use of genetic algorithm to minimize total completion time and number of processors used, simultaneously. One important issue which makes this research different from previous ones is cache reload time. The method is implemented and the results are compared against a similar method.

Keywords: Hard real-time systems, Heterogeneous multiprocessor systems, Cache reload time, Genetic algorithms, Multi-objective scheduling, Adaptive weight approach.

1 Introduction

Computational activities and their responses should be performed within a specified time-frame in real-time systems. A task τ_i requested at time t_i needs c_i units of time for execution and this time shall be allocate to it before its deadline $t_i + d_i$. Otherwise, problems may arise in the system. Real-time systems are classified into two categories with respect to the severity of missing a deadline to Hard Real-Time and Soft Real-Time systems [1]. All deadlines shall meet, in hard real-time systems.

Some optimal schedulers of real-time tasks, on single processor systems to meet deadlines are already developed considering the task characteristics. Scheduling algorithm of EDF and RM are optimal. However, in multiprocessor systems there is no known optimal scheduler [1], [2]. To be optimal for a scheduler means the schedules satisfies one or more criteria of optimality [1], [2]. Generally, it means each task was allocated to a processor such that the overall system is optimal based on predefined criteria. In real-time systems, these criteria can be total tardiness, completion time, throughput, utilization, waiting time, etc. Finding an efficient optimal scheduler for multiprocessor systems is an open problem [3] - [5]. Reference [3] has shown that just

A. Rettberg et al. (Eds.): IESS 2009, IFIP AICT 310, pp. 115–126, 2009.
© IFIP International Federation for Information Processing 2009

minimizing total tardiness for N independent task on one machine is an NP-hard problem and in majority of cases, the solution is an NP-hard one. Therefore, developing heuristic algorithms is useable in many applications. Genetic Algorithms is one such algorithm with reasonable efficiency, in many cases [4]-[6]. In recent years, several genetic approaches have been proposed for multiprocessor environments. Reference [6] proposes a scheduler with genetic algorithm for non-preemptive tasks with precedence and deadline constraints but it does not have suitable performance necessarily. Reference [7] presents a hybrid genetic algorithm, in which different operators are applied at different stages of the lifetime, for scheduling partially ordered non-preemptive tasks in a multiprocessor environment. Reference [8] proposes a genetic algorithm implementation to solve a scheduling problem for real-time non-preemptive tasks.

These algorithms minimize only one objective such as completion time, total tardiness, or cost. Reference [5] presents a multiobjective genetic algorithm for scheduling non-preemptive tasks in a soft real-time system with symmetric processors. Nevertheless, some extra local improvement heuristics has been used to find the smallest number of processors. In addition, this work has not considered cache reload time. Other works are in [9], [10] for tasks without timing constraints, but [4] considers to a multiobjective scheduling problem for non-preemptive soft real–time tasks with conflicting objectives, total tardiness and completion time without considering cache reload time. With respect to processor affinity one way to decrease the execution time is to try to assign processors to execute tasks so that two related tasks that share their code and data segments be executed on same processor. Therefore second task does not need to fetch all its data from main memory or auxiliary memories and it can use the already fetched data. In this paper, we propose a new static scheduling algorithm for non-preemptive tasks with precedence constraints on heterogeneous multiprocessor systems, with cache reload time (CRT) and other timing constrains. CRT is important because in practical systems, all timing constrains should be considered otherwise the system may crash. The criteria are completion time and number of processors in a way that all of deadlines are met. Trying to minimize both criteria is done simultaneously. Since there is a conflict between objectives, we use Adaptive Weight Approach [4], [11]. Adaptive Weight Approach uses some useful current population's information in order to justify weights and to move searching in answer space towards positive answers. The rest of the paper is organized as follows. In section 2, scheduling problem for hard real-time tasks on heterogonous multiprocessors will be defined mathematically. Section 3 describes the proposed genetic algorithm, applied procedures, genetic operators, and stopping condition. Section 4 and Section 5 explain validation and the experience results, respectively. Finally, conclusion and future works are in section 6.

2 Mathematical Model for Hard Real-Time Scheduling Problem

In this research, we consider the offline scheduling of a set of hard real-time tasks with precedence constraint with task graph on a set of heterogeneous processors in which completion time (f_1) and number of processors (f_2) are to be minimized under the following conditions:

- All tasks are non-preemptive
- Every task is processed on only one processor at a time

Every processor processes only one task at a given time

- All deadlines must be met.

In addition, there are these assumptions:

- A time unit is an artificial time unit
- Execution time of all tasks on each processor is given
- Precedence relationship or task graph is given prior to scheduling
- Cache reload time with respect to task graph and run time is computable.

Therefore, mathematical statements formulate problem as follows. Presented formulations are developed in [4]-[6] and we have done proper modifications based on new requirements, objectives and limitations of defined problem:

$$\min f_1 = \max\{t_i^F\} \tag{1}$$

$$\min f_2 = \text{Number of Processors} \tag{2}$$

$$s.t. \quad t_i^E \leq t_i^S \quad \forall i \tag{3}$$

$$t_i^E \geq \max_{\tau_j \in \text{pre}(\tau_i)} \{ t_j^F \} \tag{4}$$

$$\sum_{m=1}^{M} x_{im} = 1 \quad \forall i, \tag{5}$$

$$x_{im} \in \{0,1\} \quad \forall i, m \quad x_i = [x_{im}]_{1 \times M} \tag{6}$$

Equations (1) and (2) are fitness functions in this scheduling problem. Equation (1) defines minimizing completion time of tasks because minimization of finish time of each task (t_i^F) means that the completion time of the set of tasks is minimized, and (2) expresses minimizing number of processors. Constraint conditions have been shown in (3) to (6). Equation (3) means a task can be started after its own earliest start time begins [4] (t_i^S: real start time of τ_i). Equation (4) shows earliest start time (t_i^E) of the task which is based on its precedence in task graph. In the other word, each task can execute on a processor after its precedence tasks is finished. Equation (5) means that each processor process only one task at a time. Equation (6) is a decision variable because the system is heterogeneous. Note it is required to meet deadlines in hard real-time systems. Thus, there is a default objective formulated as follows:

$$\min f_3 = \sum_{i=1}^{N} \max\{0, \sum_{m=1}^{M} (t_i^S + c_{im} - \max\{crt_{ji} x_i x_j^T : \tau_j \in pre(\tau_i)\} - d_i) x_{im}\} \tag{7}$$

Equation (7) shows that when completion time of task is carried out after the relevant deadline, the system would have tardiness. Otherwise, tardiness will be equal to zero. Tardiness is not acceptable in the hard real-time systems. It is unacceptable because it has deadly effects. So it has to be equal to zero in our study. However, if child task τ_i executed on a processor which processed its precedence, $\max\{crt_{ji} x_i x_j^T : \tau_j \in pre(\tau_i)\}$ is time will be saved in completion time of τ_i.

Following and developing definitions on [4], [5] the following notations are used for the above equations:

- Indices:
  - i, j: task index, $i, j=1, 2, \dots, N$
  - m: processor index, $m=1, 2, \dots, M$
- Parameters:
  - N: Total number of tasks
  - M: Total number of processors
  - $G(T, E, K)$: task graph
  - $T = \{ \tau_1, \tau_2, \dots, \tau_n \}$:   a set of N tasks
  - $E = \{e_{ij}\}$: $i, j = 1, 2, \dots, N$, a directed acyclic graph representing precedence relationship
  - $K = \{k_{ij}\}$: $\forall\ eij\ \exists\ k_{ij}$:is a random value in$\in [10^3, 10^6]$
  - e_{ij}: precedence relationship between task τ_i and task τ_j
  - c_{im}: computation time of task τ_i on m^{th} processor
  - $crt_{ij} = \begin{cases} \gamma k_{ij}\ accessTime & \text{if a same processor processes } \tau_i \text{ and} \tau_j \\ 0 & \text{otherwise} \end{cases}$ (8)
  - γ :is a random value in $[0,1]$, $accessTime$ is average time to access main memory and auxiliary memory. $\gamma k_{ij}\ accessTime$ is not more than $0.05 \times c_{im}$.
  - d_i: deadline of task τ_i
  - $\text{pre}^*(\tau_i)$: set of all predecessors of task τ_i
  - $\text{suc}^*(\tau_i)$: set of all successors of task τ_i
  - $\text{pre}(\tau_i)$: set of immediate predecessors of task τ_i
  - $\text{suc}(\tau_i)$: set of immediate successors of task τ_i
  - t_i^E: earliest start time of task τ_i
  - $$t_i^E = \begin{cases} 0 & \text{if } pre(\tau_i) = \varnothing \\ \max_{\tau_j \in pre^*(\tau_i)} \left\{ t_j^E + \sum_{m=1}^{M} \left(c_{jm} x_{jm} - \max\{ crt_{kj} \times x_k x_j^T \mid \tau_k \in pre(\tau_j) \} \right) \right\} & \text{otherwise} \end{cases}$$ (9)
  - t_i^F: finish time of task τ_i
  - $t_i^F = \min\{ t_i^s + c_{im} x_{im} - \max\{ crt_{ji} \times x_i x_j^T \mid \tau_j \in pre(\tau_i) \}, d_i \} \forall i,$ (10)
- Decision variables:
  - t_i^S : real start time of task τ_i
  - $x_{im} = \begin{cases} 1 & \text{if processor } p_m \text{ is selected for task } \tau_i, \\ 0 & \text{otherwise.} \end{cases}$ (11)

3   The Proposed Genetic Algorithm

In this paper, our proposed scheduler is based on genetic algorithm. In genetic algorithm, an initial population of feasible answers is shown by a set of chromosomes. Then, a new population of chromosomes is produced by applying operations, such as selection, crossover, mutation, etc. The process of producing new generation continues until a stopping criterion is satisfied. Encoding acts as a mapping of feasible answers space of the problem to initial population and decoding evaluates chromosomes towards an ideal answer. For scheduling problem, several methods and versions for genetic's operators and procedures have been proposed and some of them can be found in [4]-[6]. In this paper, we propose a new encoding procedure. In addition, we have used the proposed decoding procedure in [4], and have extended it to be useful for our problem.

3.1 Encoding

A chromosome $ch_k = 1, 2, \ldots,$ *populationSize* is a feasible map from set of tasks to set of processors, in which the *populationSize* is the total number of chromosomes. A chromosome has two parts: $u(.)$ and $v(.)$. $u(.)$ shows scheduling order and $v(.)$ means allocation information [4]. The length of each chromosome is equal to the number of tasks, because all of the tasks must be executed. Scheduling order must satisfy a 'Topologic order' result [12] with respect to task graph. Allocation information determines that each processor shall execute which task. References [4], [5] propose an encoding procedure, while considering topological order but [5] has not implemented topological order. We noticed some errors in the implemented of [4]. In every next level of scheduling, we not only can schedule a task's children but also tasks without precedence. By doing this, we are able to produce more scheduling orders, and it will have positive effect on meeting deadlines. The proposed encoding procedure is shown in Fig. 1. Line 16 is designed to satisfy topological order.

In addition, for initial state, total number of processors is assumed to be equal to the total number of tasks (in worst case). In other hand, in order to meet deadlines, each task must execute on a separate processor, in the worst case. Therefore, in line 13 of Fig.1 M can be equal to N.

```
1     procedure: Encoding for Scheduling Problem for Hard Real-Time
2     input: task graph data set, total number of processors M
3     output: u(.),v(.)
4     begin
5         l ← 1 , W ← ∅;
6         while T ≠ ∅
7             W ← {τ_i | pre*(τ_i) = ∅ ∀i}
8             T ← T - W
9             j ← random(W);
10            u(l) ← j;
11            W ← W - { j }
12            pre*(τ_i) ← pre*(τ_i) -{τ_j} ∀i;
13            m ← random[1: M]
14            v(l) ← m;
15            l ← l + 1;
16            T ← T ∪ {τ_i, i ∈ W};
17        endwhile;
18        output u(.),v(.);
19    end;
```

Fig. 1. Encoding procedure

3.2 Decoding

Decoding procedure is shown in Fig. 2 that is the same decoding in [4]. Total tardiness of each task is computed in line 14, completion time of all tasks is determined in line 18 and number of applied processors is calculated in line 19.

```
1    procedure: Decoding for Scheduling Problem for Hard Real- Time
2    input: task graph data set, chromosome ch_k
3    output: schedule set S, completion time f₁, number of  processors f₂, total tardiness
         of tasks f₃
4    begin
5       l ← 1, S ← ∅;
6       while l ≤ N
7          i ← u(l)
8          m ← v(l)
9          if (exist suitable idle time) then
10            insert(i);
11         endif;
12         start(i);
13         update_idle();
14         f₃ ← f₃ + max {0 , tᵢˢ + cᵢₘ - max{crtⱼᵢ xᵢxⱼᵀ : τⱼ∈ pre(τᵢ)}- dᵢ } ;
15         S ← S ∪ { i, m : tᵢˢ - tᵢᶠ };
16         l ← l + 1;
17      endwhile;
18      f₁ ← max { tᵢᶠ };
19      f₂ ← Different Numbers in v(.);
20      output S, f₁, f₂, f₃;
21   end;
```

Fig. 2. Decoding procedure

3.3 Evolution Function and Competitive Selection

We use Adaptive Weighted Approach (AWA) to dominate conflict between objectives ([4], [11]). In AWA, maximum and minimum values are obtained among all the values of fitness functions of chromosomes by (12). Next, adaptive weight of each fitness function is calculated by (14). Since third objective (minimizing total tardiness) is very essential in hard real-time systems, so we considered priority for each weight. it means for each w_p (p=1,2,3) there is a w'_p which $w'_1=0.01$, $w'_2=1$, and $w'_3=1000$, .Then, the weighted-sum objective function for each chromosome is computed by (16). Finally, evaluated function for each chromosome is obtained as shown in (17).

For competitive selection we have used of Roulette Wheel Selection [11].

$$f_i^y = \begin{cases} \max\{f_i(ch_k)\} & \text{for y = max} \\ \min\{f_i(ch_k)\} & \text{for y = min} \end{cases} \qquad (12)$$

$$\text{where} \quad i=1,2,3; \; k=1, \ldots, populationSize \tag{13}$$

$$w_p = \frac{1}{f_p^{max} - f_p^{min}}, \quad p = 1,2,3 \tag{14}$$

$$w'_1 = 0.01, \; w'_2 = 1, \; w'_3 = 1000 \tag{15}$$

$$F(ch_k) = \sum_{p=1}^{3} w'_p w_p f_p(ch_k) = \sum_{p=1}^{3} \left(w'_p f_p(ch_k) \middle/ f_p^{max} - f_p^{min} \right) \tag{16}$$

$$eval(ch_k) = 1/F(ch_k) \tag{17}$$

3.4 Genetic Operators

We have used modified one-cut crossover and standard mutation ([4], [11]) in this research as shown in Fig. 3.a and 3.b respectively. Procedures of them operate on the $v(.)$ part of chromosomes. Because, if they operate on the $u(.)$ part, scheduling order might be changed. Therefore, it will not agree with task graph. So, our modified operators operate only on the $v(.)$ part of the chromosomes.

1 *procedure: Crossover*	
2 *input: parent chromosomes ch_k, h_k.*	1 *procedure: Mutation*
3 *output: proto-offspring chromosomes ch_k, $ch_{k'}$*	2 *input: chromosome ch_k,*
	3 *output: offspring chromosomes ch_k*
4 *begin*	4 *begin*
5 $r \leftarrow random[1:N]$;	5 $r \leftarrow random[1:N]$;
6 $temp \leftarrow v([r+1:N])$;	6 $v(r) \leftarrow random[1:M]$;
7 $v([r+1:N]) \leftarrow v'([r+1:N])$;	7 *output ch_k;*
8 $v'([r+1:N]) \leftarrow temp$;	8 *end;*
9 *output ch_k, $ch_{k'}$;*	
10 *end;*	
(a)	**(b)**

Fig. 3. Genetic Operators: (a) Crossover procedure, (b) Mutation procedure

3.5 The Proposed Genetic Algorithm

Proposed genetic algorithm has been presented in Fig. 4. Algorithm terminates when main loop in line 7 reaches a default value. In the other hand, it is iterated for a fix number of times.

4 Validation

For evaluation of the proposed genetic algorithm several numeral experiments were preformed. Numeral experiments are done with a random precedence task graph.

We used P-Method [13] to produce the random precedence task graph. P-Method is based on an adjacency matrix of a task graph. If there is a precedence relation between tasks τ_i and τ_j then element a_{ij} of adjacency matrix will be one, otherwise it will be zero. An adjacency matrix is made with all its lower triangular and diagonal elements equal to zero. Each of the remaining upper triangular elements of the matrix is examined independently as part of a Bernoulli process with factor ε, which represents the probability of a success [13], [4], [5]. For the tasks' computation time, deadline and cache reload time between them, we use random numbers based on exponential distribution and normal distribution as same as [4]. However, about value of cache reload time, we assumed it cannot be more than $0.05 \times \max\{c_{im}^{Exponential} \ or \ c_{im}^{Normal}\}$.

To have suitable compare with reported results in [4] we chose the parameters of genetic algorithm 0.7 for crossover and 0.3 for mutation.

1   ***procedure:*** *Proposed_Genetic_Algorithm*
2   ***input:*** *task graph data set*
3   ***output:*** *best schedule set S*
4   **begin**
5   *numberOfGeneration* $\leftarrow$ 0;
6   initialize *population(numberOfGeneration)* by*Encoding* procedure;
7   **while** (*NumberOfGeneration* $\leq$ *maxGeneration*) **do**
8   Evaluate f_1, f_2, f_3 by *Decoding* procedure;
9   *eval(population);*   /**eavl(ch_k): k=1,...,populationSize* (15)
10   **if** (**not** *NumberOfGeneration* $\leq$ *maxGeneration*) **then**
11   creating *new_population* by *roulette wheel selection*;
12   *new_population* $\leftarrow$ *crossover(new_population);*
13   *new_population* $\leftarrow$ *Mutation(new_population);*
14   *population* $\leftarrow$ *new_population;*
15   *numberOfGeneration* $\leftarrow$ *numberOfGeneration* +1;
16   **endif;**
17   **endwhile;**
18   **output** *best schedule set S;*
19   **end;**

Fig. 4. The proposed Genetic Algorithm

5   Experiments

Here, we have designed some experiments based on previous sections. We compared our proposed algorithm with the proposed algorithm in [4] because it acceded better answers in comparison the others.

5.1   Experiment 1

The first experiment is taken from [4]. In this experiment we have some information as well as it is shown in Table 1 that has been created by the P-Method.

Table 1. Data set of experiment 1

i	$pre^*(\tau_i)$	$\dfrac{c_{im}}{}$			d_i
		c_{i1}	c_{i2}	c_{i3}	
1	8	5	3	10	13
2	6	3	7	12	17
3	4, 5	3	4	1	12
4	6, 7, 8	2	16	6	12
5	6, 10	12	2	4	27
6	9	2	4	7	24
7	-	2	15	4	13
8	-	3	5	4	18
9	10	5	5	8	27
10	-	1	5	6	29

Table 2. Data set of experiment 2

i	$pre^*(\tau_i)$	$\dfrac{c_{im}}{}$				d_i
		c_{i1}	c_{i2}	c_{i3}	c_{i4}	
1	8	5	3	11	8	19
2	6	6	5	4	13	9
3	4, 5	11	8	6	7	18
4	6, 7, 8	10	13	5	6	37
5	6, 10	10	13	8	11	38
6	9	2	11	11	3	37
7	-	3	10	11	8	44
8	-	4	12	10	5	30
9	10	6	9	7	10	37
10	-	11	12	6	4	58

We divided this experiment into two parts. In first part we scheduled it without considering cache reload time. In our method, the best answer as the completion time (f_1) is 13, total tardiness (f_3) is 0, and number of applied processors (f_2) is 3 where asreport of this experiment in [4] is as completion time; 15, total tardiness is 6 and minimizing of number of processors is not their objective (Fig. 5-A). In addition, our proposed algorithm could schedule this task graph with 2 processors as is shown in Fig. 5-B. In the second part with respect to cache reload time, two suboptimal schedulers are shown in Fig. 6. In addition, some obtained results are shown in Fig. 7 and Fig. 8. In Fig. 7 has been shown a comparison between our proposed method and the proposed method in [4]. In Fig. 8 we computed average of completion time of best obtained scheduler in 50 iterations of experience with considering and nonconsidering cache reload time when population size increases.

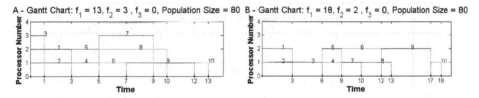

A - Gantt Chart: $f_1 = 13$, $f_2 = 3$, $f_3 = 0$, Population Size = 80   B - Gantt Chart: $f_1 = 18$, $f_2 = 2$, $f_3 = 0$, Population Size = 80

Fig. 5. Experiment 1 without cache reload time

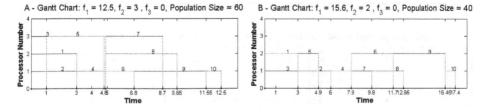

A - Gantt Chart: $f_1 = 12.5$, $f_2 = 3$, $f_3 = 0$, Population Size = 60   B - Gantt Chart: $f_1 = 15.6$, $f_2 = 2$, $f_3 = 0$, Population Size = 40

Fig. 6. Experiment 1 with cache reload time

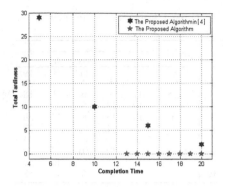
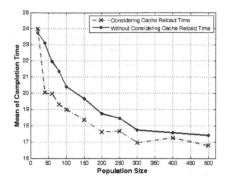

Fig. 7. A comparison between our proposed method and the proposed method in [4]

Fig. 8. A comparison of completion time considering and nonconsidering cache reload time

5.2 Experiment 2

Second experiment was taken from [4] too. Execution time of each task on processers is given in Table 2. Fig. 9 shows three instances of the best output answers that they describe the best answer of our proposed method according to Table 2 without considering cache reload time. In Fig. 10 has been shown two schedulers considering cache reload time. It is obvious scheduler with 3 processors has a lower completion time than scheduler with 4 processors. In fact this Comparison shows importance of considering cache reload time. An overall result has been presented in Fig. 11.

Table 3. Data set of experiment 2 with duplicated processors

i	$pre^*(\tau_i)$	c_{im}								d_i
		c_{i1}	c_{i2}	c_{i3}	c_{i4}	c_{i5}	c_{i6}	c_{i7}	c_{i8}	
1	8	5	3	11	8	5	3	11	8	19
2	6	6	5	4	13	6	5	4	13	9
3	4, 5	11	8	6	7	11	8	6	7	18
4	6, 7, 8	10	13	5	6	10	13	5	6	37
5	6, 10	10	13	8	11	10	13	8	11	38
6	9	2	11	11	3	2	11	11	3	37
7	-	3	10	11	8	3	10	11	8	44
8	-	4	12	10	5	4	12	10	5	30
9	10	6	9	7	10	6	9	7	10	37
10	-	11	12	6	4	11	12	6	4	58

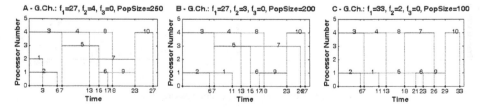

Fig. 9. Schedulers for experiment 2 considering Table 5 and without considering cache reload time

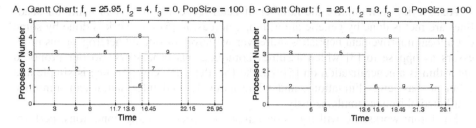

Fig. 10. Two best schedulers considering cache reload time

5.3 Experiment 3

In this part for testing of processors redundancy of proposed algorithm, we duplicated the assumed processors from Table 2 to Table 3 Overall results has been shown in Fig. 11 which this figure declares not only considering cache reload time in scheduling can cause using lower processor and decreases completion time simultaneously but also our proposed algorithm could gain obtained results when we use data set Table 2 without duplication. Fig. 12 shows always increasing number of processors does not lead to better answer for completion time where there is not tardiness.

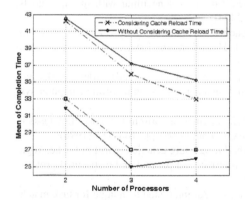

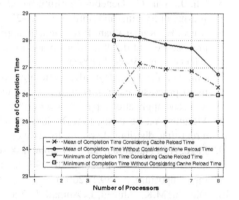

Fig. 11. Comparisons between obtained completion time considering and nonconsidering cache reload time

Fig. 12. Comparisons between obtained completion time considering and nonconsidering cache reload time

6 Conclusion and Future Works

In this paper we have tried generalization on latest works ([4] – [6]) and covered their shortcomings. Paying attention to cache reload time in heterogeneous real-time systems is one of the aspects of this work.

Improving the encoding procedure which has large influence on the proposed scheduler is part of this paper. For this part, we designed a suitable encoding procedure based on topological sort. Same chromosome like [4] has been used to be able for comparing the proposed algorithm and the proposed algorithms in [4].

Also, trying to minimize the number of heterogeneous processors while all deadlines are met is done by genetic algorithm, whereas, in [5] this work is done by some extra local improvement heuristics moreover we have considered heterogeneous processors as oppose to [5] which assumes homogeneous processors. So our proposed algorithm is a generalization on [5]. Unlike [6], designed chromosome is simple and efficient, has fewer limitations, and while using limited information can minimize conflicted objective simultaneously.

For future works, we will try to design some better stopping conditions, perform some improvements on convergent conditions, and compare with PSO method.

References

1. Krishna, C.M., Kang, G.S.: Real-time systems. McGraw-Hill, New York (1997)
2. Marwedel, P.: Embedded System Design. Springer, Netherland (2006)
3. Du, J., Leung, J.Y.T.: Minimizing total tardiness on one machine is NP-hard. Mathematics of Operational Research 15, 483–495 (1990)
4. Yoo, M., Gen, M.: Scheduling algorithm for real-time tasks using multiobjective hybrid genetic algorithm in heterogeneous multiprocessors system. Journal of Computers & Operations Research 34, 3084–3098 (2007)
5. Oh, J., Wu, C.: Genetic-algorithm-based real-time task scheduling with multiple goals. Journal of Systems and Software, 245–258 (2004)
6. Mitra, H., Ramanathan, P.A.: Genetic approach for scheduling non-preemptive tasks with precedence and deadline constraints. In: 26th Hawaii international conference on system sciences, pp. 556–564 (1993)
7. Lin, M., Yang, L.: Hybrid genetic algorithms for scheduling partially ordered tasks in a multi-processor environment. In: Sixth international conference on real-time computer systems and applications, pp. 382–387 (1999)
8. Monnier, Y., Beauvais, J.P., Deplanche, A.M.: A genetic algorithm for scheduling tasks in a real-time distributed system. In: 24th euromicro conference, pp. 708–714 (1998)
9. Page, A.J., Naughton, T.J.: Dynamic task scheduling using genetic algorithm for heterogeneous distributed computing. In: 19th IEEE international parallel and distributed processing symposium, p. 189.1 (2005)
10. Dhodhi, M.K., Ahmad, I., Ahmad, I., Yatama, A.: An integrated technique for task matching and scheduling onto distributed heterogeneous computing systems. Journal of Parallel and Distributed Computing 62, 1338–1361 (2002)
11. Gen, M., Cheng, R.: Genetic Algorithm and Optimization Engineering. John Wiley and Sons, INC., New York (2000)
12. Cormen, T.H., Leiserson, C.E., Rivest, R.L., Stein, C.: Introduction to Algorithms, 2nd edn. McGraw-Hill, New York (2001)
13. Al-Sharaeh, S., Wells, B.E.: A comparison of heuristics for list schedules using the box-method and P-method for random digraph generation. In: 28th Southeastern symposium on system theory, pp. 467–471 (1996)
14. Cosnard, M., Marrakchi, M., Robert, Y., Trystram, D.: Parallel Gaussian elimination on an MIMD computer. Journal of Parallel Computing 6(3), 275–296 (1998)
15. Wu, M.Y., Gajski, D.D.: Hypertool: A programming aid for message-passing system. IEEE Trans. Parallel and Distributed Systems 1(3), 330–343 (1990)

Task-Dependent Processor Shutdown for Hard Real-Time Systems

Henrik Lipskoch[1] and Frank Slomka[2]

[1] C.v.Ossietzky University Oldenburg, Department for Computer Science, Germany
[2] Ulm University, Institute for Embedded Systems, Germany

Abstract. Mobile devices relying on batteries can save energy by using low-power modes of their processors. In a hard real-time environment, one has to prove the real-time feasibility and thereby to guarantee that energy saving methods do not violate real-time constraints. Besides the processor's unavailability during low-power mode, the transition to and from the mode consumes energy and time.

This work introduces a task-dependent policy for mode switching and compares it to procrastination techniques from the literature. The low-power interval is placed between occurrences of one task of the task set such that low-power mode and instances of this task do not overlap.

Optimisation of task to depend on, duration of low-power, and shutdown rate is done with the help of a hard real-time test to provide feasible results. The used test provides analysis for preemptible, deadline scheduled task sets. Tasks are allowed to have periodic, periodic with jitter, sporadic, or other behaviour regarding their occurrence.

Thus, this work extends the applicability of processor shutdown to such environments. And since parameters are determined off-line, apart form a programmable real-time clock, no power consuming extra circuitry is needed. However, the method comes with a slight modification of the task set.

1 Introduction

Portable or hand-held devices rely on batteries, which's capacity determines the operating time of the system. Thus, minimising power consumption will increase the time of operation. Often these devices are subject to hard real-time constraints, e.g. for communication. In order to make them use the energy delivered from the battery more efficient, several energy saving options exist. Additional to dynamic voltage scaling, there exists the possibility to make use of low-power modes, e.g. sleep states or deep-sleep. Here, the devices have parts switched off (eg. no V_{cc} for an unused FFT) or frozen (processor clock stopped) or even the complete system is shut down by stopping the system clock or switching it into standby state.

Low-power modes provide an efficient way to save power during idle periods, even without loosing information stored in processor registers.

Almost every microprocessor can be woken up by an interrupt of its real-time clock (RTC), even out of the deepest mode. Because the timer has to be programmed beforehand, the task system has to be analysed beforehand. The analysis has to determine how

A. Rettberg et al. (Eds.): IESS 2009, IFIP AICT 310, pp. 127–138, 2009.

long at least the processor can stay disabled and when it is to be woken up, subject to retaining deadlines, i.e. to calculate only spare time is not enough.

Mobile applications, like mobile data loggers, are likely to have communication for data exchange that must not be interrupted. The point in time when to initiate communication can be chosen manually (sporadic) as well as periodically. In either case the system has to function properly to provide reliable data. Sensors may use interrupt based communication to a central plant, or time slotted data transmission. These communication systems cause jitters.

Thus, we want to minimise power consumption for devices having low-power modes with non-negligible switching overhead and hard real-time tasks running on them, scheduled with earliest deadline first scheduling. Whereby the tasks occurring behaviour is described by an event stream and may include periodic behaviour, jitters, be sporadic, or other, e.g. aroused by drifting clocks. Additional, to avoid extra control circuitry, we want to determine off-line, when and for how long to transit into low-power mode.

The content of this work is organised as follows. First, we give an overview on and discuss works dealing with power saving in hard real-time environments. Second, we briefly introduce the used feasibility test, after which we model and analyse our processor shutdown method. Experiments include comparisons to optimal shutdown, with and without procrastination, and LC-EDF procrastination technique. A concluding section summarises the results.

2 Related Work

We regard works exploring dynamic voltage scaling and power management guaranteeing hard real-time feasibility in worst-case situations, i.e. works providing feasibility for all possible schedules.

2.1 Dynamic Voltage Scaling

Works addressing voltage scaling for hard real-time task sets are [1] and [2], [3], and [4], whereof the former two works consider periodic task sets only, and the latter two are able to optimise for other occurrence behaviour as well. Nevertheless, all four works neglect transition costs for mode switching.

Works considering switching overhead are [5] and [6]. Both works apply to periodic task sets, where the tasks can have dependencies and individual deadlines. The period is identical in either case for the whole task set. Since both works have their task sets scheduled without preemption and calculate a complete schedule, i.e. determining jobs to execute, assigning execution start and end, and processor mode, either proves the exponential complexity of the energy saving problem.

2.2 Processor Shutdown

Dynamic power management is about to explore low-power modes for processors and peripherals at run-time. A lot of research in this area has taken place, for overview and comparison consider [7] or [8]. All authors categorise works on dynamic power management into time-out policies, predictive policies, and stochastic policies. The first shuts down the processor after it has been idle for a certain amount of time. The second addresses the wake-up penalty, it tries to predict the next time the processor has to be ready for processing. Stochastic policies use task set information in form of probability distributions on their occurrence, and try to fit time-outs and wake-up predictions for these minimising wake-up penalty and maximising time spent in low-power mode. None of the works mentioned in both surveys addresses hard real-time constraints, though most are aware of a latency caused by back transition from low-power mode to run mode.

The following works are online algorithms, providing deadline retention. Each needs extra control circuitry monitoring incoming tasks and maintaining data for forecasting next probable shutdown durations.

Power management for devices is used in [9]. The authors' approach makes use of a resource request list obtained by jobs in the schedulers run-queue. Their algorithm needs the list for a look ahead to ensure deadlines are met; The authors neglect the appliance of their approach to hard real-time systems, because of the latency due shut down devices an incoming job will have.

The authors of [10] extend the previously mentioned work by processor voltage scaling to stretch job execution and thus to cluster device usage with the aim of extended idle intervals. If there is no job requesting a device, the device is shut down; the next incoming job requesting this device will be confronted with a delay to switch the device on. The authors solve this drawback by requiring an extra maximal blocking time in their task model, but their power saving and real-time testing algorithm can only deal with periodic tasks.

A static schedule allowing estimation of switching costs is created in [11]. The work considers periodic and sporadic tasks. Periodic tasks are scheduled statically. For sporadic tasks, slots are inserted, which may be moved during run-time to further improve the schedule. Task jitters are not taken into account. Reduction of power dissipation is achieved by using dynamic power management and voltage scaling. The latter is preferred, based on an early argument, that neglects leakage power ([12]).

Task procrastination may extend idle periods, an algorithm exploiting this was presented in [13], known as LC-EDF. Only periodic tasks with deadlines equal to their periods are considered. The procrastination time δ_ω for a task ω is calculated via

$$\sum_{\tau \in \text{Tasks} \setminus \{\omega\}} \frac{c_\tau}{T_\tau} + \frac{c_\omega + \delta_\omega}{T_\omega} = 1, \tag{1}$$

with c, T being worst-case execution time and period. The Equation targets to keep utilisation below 100%. Deadlines shorter than periods may be handled by dividing by deadlines instead of periods, but the result will be very pessimistic and in cases with small deadlines compared to periods, the sum will grow beyond 1 and no procrastination will take place. Further, the authors assume external circuitry, e.g. special purpose device, to shut down and switch on the processor.

The previous work is extended by global processor slowdown in [14], with the same drawback regarding short deadlines, and their still requires extra circuitry monitoring job queues.

The work presented in [15] provides lower energy consumption, than the previous two. The authors relax the problem of periodic tasks to have their deadlines lower than the periods, but not higher. The approach works on a job set, which is said to contain a number of jobs with their release times, deadlines, and execution times. It considers individual job slow down, and procrastinates idle intervals to merge scattered frames of idle time. For every occurring jitter or other non-periodic behaviour, the job set monitoring device has to perform a re-calculation.

3   Test on Real-Time Feasibility

As motivated in the introductory section, we do not want to limit us to periodic only task systems. Instead, task jitters, sporadic tasks, and other behaviour are included as well. A worst-case execution time is assumed to obtain upper bounds on worst-case demand. We further assume the task set to be scheduled earliest deadline first. We assume a fixed relative deadline for each task, the deadline may be arbitrary.

A real-time feasibility test using the hyper-period will have a high complexity as the hyper-period can grow very large, e.g. if some periods contain large prime numbers. We reduce complexity by using a feasibility test which is based on an abstraction.

An upper bound of the execution demand to calculate a lower bound on available idle time is achieved via the demand bound function, introduced in [16], together with the event stream model. We use here the same event stream based calculation of the demand bound function and its approximation as given in [4] (and refer to that work for a more detailed introduction):

Let Γ be a set of tasks scheduled under earliest deadline first policy. For a task $\tau \in \Gamma$, let c_τ and d_τ be its worst-case execution time and deadline. Let each event stream be denoted by a sequence $\left(a_\tau^{(n)}\right)_{n \in \mathbb{N}}$, it is $a_\tau^{(n)}$ denotes the minimal time to pass for n tasks of type τ to be instantiated. Note, that an event stream is not a schedule, it is an abstraction. Then

$$D(\Delta) := \sum_{\tau \in \Gamma} \max\left\{i \in \mathbb{N}_0 : a_\tau^{(i)} + d_\tau \leq \Delta\right\} \cdot c_\tau \tag{2}$$

is an upper bound on the processing demand to be fulfilled in a time span of length Δ.

Then a system is hard real-time feasible if

$$\text{for all } \Delta \in \mathbb{R} : \quad D(\Delta) \leq \Delta. \tag{3}$$

By approximation (replacing the max-terms in (2) by linearisations, see [4]) and by testing only those time points at which a deadline is to be met, the complexity of the test is reduced to be polynomial, e.g. if all event streams are approximated after the second element, it is reduced to be twice the number of tasks.

For abbreviation, we define

$$m(\tau, x, \Delta) := \max\{i \in \mathbb{N}_0 : a_\tau^{(i)} + x \leq \Delta\}. \tag{4}$$

The Case of Two Never Overlapping Consecutive Executed Tasks: Suppose there are two tasks ρ, λ in the task set Γ, ρ to trigger λ, the latter to finish before the former has to be finished next, thus never overlapping (remember: earliest deadline first scheduling). Suppose too, that a job of task λ, if running, has always highest priority.

For better understanding the situation, we introduce a third task into the task graph, σ, which's purpose is to represent the trigger of λ, thus σ consumes no execution time, but is assigned a deadline: the latest time to trigger λ. The latter then is assigned a deadline equal to its execution time yielding highest priority. This situation is depicted in Fig. 1. The latest time to finish an instance of λ must not be later than right before the latest start time of the next instance of ρ, which is equal to $d_\rho - c_\rho + a_\rho^{(2)}$, with $a_\rho^{(2)} \in \left(a_\rho^{(n)}\right)_{n \in \mathbb{N}}$.

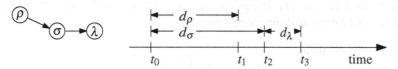

Fig. 1. Task graph of three consecutive tasks, it is $d_\lambda := c_\lambda, d_\sigma + d_\lambda \leq d_\rho + a_\rho^{(2)} - c_\rho$, and $d_\rho \leq d_\sigma$

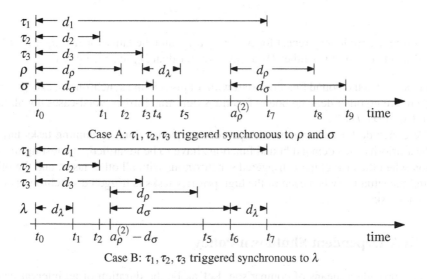

Case A: τ_1, τ_2, τ_3 triggered synchronous to ρ and σ

Case B: τ_1, τ_2, τ_3 triggered synchronous to λ

Fig. 2. Two worst-case situations in dealing with a task graph

Now two situations denote a worst-case, each depicted in Fig. 2. Either task ρ is triggered synchronous with all other tasks, task σ triggers task λ the latest at d_σ (Case A), or d_σ time units later than the last task ρ was triggered, an instance of λ starts running, blocking the processor for every other task triggered at the same instant (Case B). In Case B the next instance of task ρ is to be finished no later than $d_\rho + a_\rho^{(2)} - d_\sigma$. Then in Case A, the demand is denoted by

$$D_A(\Delta) = \sum_{\tau \in \Gamma \setminus \{\lambda\}} m(\tau, d_\tau, \Delta) c_\tau$$
$$+ m(\rho, d_\sigma + d_\lambda, \Delta) c_\lambda, \tag{5}$$

whereas in Case B the demand is denoted by

$$D_B(\Delta) = \sum_{\tau \in \Gamma \setminus \{\rho, \lambda\}} m(\tau, d_\tau, \Delta) c_\tau$$
$$+ m(\rho, c_\lambda, \Delta) c_\lambda$$
$$+ m(\rho, d_\rho + a_\rho^{(2)} - d_\sigma, \Delta) c_\rho. \tag{6}$$

We cannot decide which of the two cases dominates the other:

Lemma 1. *Both D_A and D_B denote a worst-case not included in the other, thus both have to be used for the real-time feasibility test.*

Proof. Let $\Delta = c_\lambda$, then
$$D_A(\Delta) - D_B(\Delta) = -c_\lambda.$$

Let now $\Delta = d_\rho = a_\rho^{(2)}$, then

$$D_A(\Delta) - D_B(\Delta) = c_\rho.$$

The former example may repeat for $\Delta = c_\lambda + a_\rho^{(2)}$, and the latter for $\Delta = d_\rho + n \cdot a_\rho^{(2)} - d_\sigma$. Thus in general it is neither D_A always greater than D_B nor vice versa.

Since both demand bound functions start with all tasks being synchronous, except ρ and λ, there are no other demand bound functions denoting further worst-cases not already included in D_A, D_B.

We conclude for task graphs with precedence constraints, containing tasks having highest priority, two demand bound functions have to be identified, one testing the situation when the task graph is triggered synchronous with all other tasks, and the other testing the situation when each of the high priority tasks is triggered synchronous with the other tasks.

4   Task-Dependent Shutdown Policy

We first provide a means of comparison. Let t_{lp} be the duration of an interval where switching to and from low-power mode is applied. Then, the actual time spent in low-power mode, t_{low}, depends on the time needed for transition, t_{switch}; it is $t_{low} = t_{lp} - t_{switch}$. The duration t_{lp} results in saved energy if and only if the reduced amount of energy consumed within t_{low} weighs up the energy cost for the transition and is longer than t_{switch}. Therefore, t_{lp} has to exceed the break-even time, t_{BE}, which is

$$t_{BE} = \max \left\{ t_{switch}, \frac{E_{switch} + P_{low} t_{switch}}{P_{run}} \right\}. \tag{7}$$

If a processor has multiple low-power modes, one has to determine which mode to use. According to the time available, the solution falls on the mode yielding a maximal difference $t_{lp} - t_{BE}$, which denotes the maximal energy saved.

Let $t_{lp}(\Delta)$ denote the least time reserved for low-power mode within an interval of length Δ, and let #transitions(Δ) be the maximal number of transitions into and out of low-power mode, occurring within an interval of length Δ. Then we define effectiveness of a shutdown method as the fraction of time spent in low-power mode:

$$\text{Eff}(\Delta) := \frac{1}{\Delta} \left(t_{lp}(\Delta) - \#\text{transitions}(\Delta) \cdot t_{BE} \right). \tag{8}$$

4.1   Shutdown in between Two Jobs of the Same Task

Our main idea is to exploit the case of *two never overlapping consecutive executed tasks* (see paragraph in Section 3). Processor shutdown is modelled as a task, and by depending on another task, the rate of shutdown is inherited from the task's instantiation rate.

Method: Append each job of a certain task ρ with an interval of duration c_l at low-power mode. Finish the low-power interval before the next job of ρ has to be begun. Determine a latest start d_l of the low-power interval.

This has the effect that these two participants will neither occur at the same time nor will they intersect each other.

Subject to real-time constraints are the duration of low-power, the deadline for its invocation, and the task to append.

This method has to be implemented in a task itself. As an advantage, if a job at run-time finds it will need less processing time than predicted for the worst-case, it could increase the duration of the low-power task by an amount yet to be determined.

According to (8), for a task ρ and duration c_l the efficiency of the method is

$$\text{Eff}(\Delta) = \frac{m(\rho, d_\rho, \Delta) \cdot (c_l - t_{BE})}{\Delta} \tag{9}$$

or with avg being the average number of jobs per time unit

$$\text{Eff} = \text{avg}(\rho) \cdot (c_l - t_{BE}). \tag{10}$$

Algorithm 1 determines the parameters ρ, d_l, and c_l. The if-conditions in lines 13 and 14 ensure real-time feasibility of the solution.

The used feasibility tests are those from (5), (6), in the approximated form.

For each task in the task set, the algorithm explores the design space by interval bisection over possible execution times c of the low-power task (outer while loop), and tries to determine a feasible deadline by interval bisection over a range of deadlines (inner while loop). If no deadline is found for c, this defines the new maximum c_{max}, and in the opposite case, it defines the new minimum c_{min}.

The decisions in lines 17 and 19 are based on two properties of D_A and D_B. Referring to Fig. 1 and (5),(6), increasing deadline d_σ leads for D_A to a more relaxed problem, and decreasing d_σ will do the same for D_B. Thus, if a deadline d_σ leads to an infeasible system according to D_A, then increasing the deadline will relax the problem and might yield a feasible system. On the other hand, if d_σ leads to an infeasible system according to D_B, then decreasing it will probably lead to a feasible system.

Algorithm 1. Determination of parameters for task-dependent shutdown

---

Input: Task set Γ, break-even time t_{BE}

Output: Task ρ, to be followed by time c_l in low-power mode, the latest d_l time units past instantiation of ρ, efficiency $best_{eff}$

1 $best_{eff} := 0$;
2 **for** $\tau \in \Gamma$ **do**
3 $\quad c_{max} := \min\{\Delta - d(\Delta, \Gamma \setminus \{\tau\}) : \Delta > 0\}$;
4 $\quad c_{min} := t_{BE} + best_{eff}/avg(\tau)$;
5 $\quad$**while** $c_{max} - c_{min} < \varepsilon_c$ **do**
6 $\quad\quad c = c_{min} - (c_{max} - c_{min})/2$;
7 $\quad\quad d_{min} := d_\tau$;
8 $\quad\quad d_{max} := a_\tau^{(2)} + d_\tau - c_\tau - c$;
9 $\quad\quad$solution_found:=false;
10 $\quad\quad$**if** $d_{min} < d_{max}$ and feasible_CASE_A $(\Gamma, \tau, (c, d_{max}))$ and feasible_CASE_B $(\Gamma, \tau, (c, d_{min}))$ **then**
11 $\quad\quad\quad$**while** $d_{max} - d_{min} > \varepsilon_d$ and not solution_found **do**
12 $\quad\quad\quad\quad d := d_{min} - (d_{max} - d_{min})/2$;
13 $\quad\quad\quad\quad$**if** feasible_CASE_A $(\Gamma, \tau, (c, d))$ **then**
14 $\quad\quad\quad\quad\quad$**if** feasible_CASE_B $(\Gamma, \tau, (c, d))$ **then**
$\quad\quad\quad\quad\quad\quad$/* CASES A and B successful   */
15 $\quad\quad\quad\quad\quad\quad$solution_found:=true;
16 $\quad\quad\quad\quad\quad$**else**
$\quad\quad\quad\quad\quad\quad$/* CASE B failed, increase d   */
17 $\quad\quad\quad\quad\quad\quad d_{max} := d$;
18 $\quad\quad\quad\quad$**else**
$\quad\quad\quad\quad\quad$/* CASE A failed, decrease d   */
19 $\quad\quad\quad\quad\quad d_{min} := d$;
20 $\quad\quad\quad$**if** solution_found **then**
21 $\quad\quad\quad\quad eff_\tau := avg(\tau) \cdot (c - t_{BE})$;
22 $\quad\quad\quad\quad$**if** $best_{eff} < eff_\tau$ **then**
23 $\quad\quad\quad\quad\quad (\rho, c_l, d_l) := (\tau, c, d)$;
24 $\quad\quad\quad\quad\quad best_{eff} := eff_\tau$;
25 $\quad\quad\quad\quad c_{min} := c$;
26 $\quad\quad\quad$**else**
27 $\quad\quad\quad\quad c_{max} := c$;

4.2 Shutdown in between n Jobs of the Same Task

Following the same argumentation as in the subsection before, it can also be thought of to wait for a number of instances, say n, then to apply shutdown, and then again wait for the same number of instances before the next shutdown. This can lead to longer low-power durations. And since the number of shutdowns depends on the task's instantiation rate, this modification may reduce the number of switches and may increase the efficiency.

The critical situations are the same as for the method in the previous subsection, because each shutdown transition is again placed between two consecutive task instances.

The efficiency formula in line 21 is replaced by "$\text{eff}_\tau := \frac{avg(\tau)}{n} \cdot (c - t_{\text{BE}})$".

With this modification, the Algorithm 1 gets an extra loop for each task, where it is to cycle through possible factorisations, $n = 1, \ldots$, of the task period, stopping cycling, when no further improvement is likely, that is $c_{\min} > c_{\max}$ (Note, in line 4, "$avg(\tau)$" is replaced by "$\frac{avg(\tau)}{n}$", thus becomes less by the number of task instances to wait for, this becomes eventually the source of overlapping bounds before entering the loop in line 5).

We refer to this modification as "Alg. 1 + mod." in the following section.

5 Experiments

We have investigated the effectiveness of each method by applying them on two different task sets, of which one is a periodic task set, and the other contains jitters and deadlines not equal to periods. For each task set we computed the effectiveness of either method along a range of break-even times and compared them to the best possible power saving, which we computed for a range of sample schedules. We applied best power saving with ("Opt. w/ p.") and without procrastination ("Opt. w/o p.").

Best possible power saving is hereby understood as optimisation by inserting shutdown intervals where the optimisation makes use of a beforehand computed occurrence schedule, i.e. knows for certain all occurrences, and thus can globally optimise over the complete schedule.

As our optimisations yield static results designed for the worst-case of processor demand, they will not vary for individual schedules. On the other hand, variations will occur for each of the online-methods. Therefore, we created random schedules for each of our experiments and calculated the mean, a 5% minimal bound, and a 95% maximal bound, thus both together depict a 90% confidence interval around the mean value, and to illustrate the variations, our figures depict efficiency as bands.

We did not explicitly calculate values for the online method of [15], but since it performs better than the LC-EDF method, we believe their results to be between LC-EDF and the optimal with procrastination.

Figures 3 and 4 show the cost dependent effective energy savings obtained by each method for our examples. On the y-axis it is shown the achieved portion of time spent in low-power mode, the rest of the time the system spends processing tasks or transiting from and into low-power modes. The x-axis gives the minimal duration for one mode transition, the break-even time.

The first experiment is on a task set given in [17]. It consists of seven periodic tasks, periods ranging from 20 to 150 ms, having their deadline equal to their periods. The tasks are to be run on a Palm-Pilot. The processor utilisation is 86.17% leaving 13.83% spare time for power saving.

Figure 3 shows the results. The figure also depicts the range of obtained efficiency values along our sample schedules for the LC-EDF method, since it is applicable here

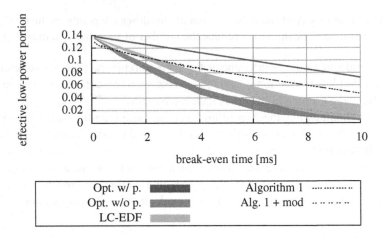

Fig. 3. Experiment Palm-pilot Original

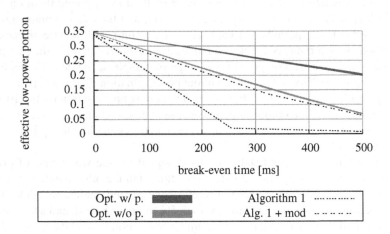

Fig. 4. Experiment Aircraft Control

("LC-EDF"). It consists of a band, depicting the range of the efficiencies of 90% obtained for the sample schedules, 5% lie above, 5% lie below the band. We observe the results of our optimisations overlapping, our modification seems not to have an effect. For a break-even time of 1 ms our methods intersect the ideal optimisation without procrastination, and for a break-even time of 2 ms, our methods intersect the LC-EDF, and supersedes it for a break-even time of 4 ms.

The next task set is taken from [18]. It represents software for an aircraft controller. It consists of 17 tasks, with 9 having jitters. Periods are in the range of 1 s to 800μs. Processor utilisation is 65.2%, leaving a slack of 34.8% available for power saving. Experimental results are depicted in Fig. 4.

We observe, that the policy to append shutdown after each job of a task does not perform well. The reason is it cannot trade off rate against duration of shutdown, which the modification is able to do. The latter is close to the optimal shutdown without procrastination, although our method lacks the advantage of online knowledge.

Procrastination estimation via (1) yields a delay of -0.1816 s per second, disabling LC-EDF, because this is an example with some tasks having deadlines shorter than their periods.

Additional, this example contains tasks with deadlines higher than their periods. Therefore, the work of [15] is not applicable here as well.

That is, our method is the only applicable in this case.

Note that for the feasibility test, we have limited the number of test points to be 10 for every task in both examples, which made the computations very fast (in both cases results were obtained in the order of seconds on a common computer with a 2 GHz CPU).

6 Conclusion

In this work, we have presented our method of task-dependent processor shutdown, where the transition into low-power mode inherits its activation rate from a certain task in a given task set. We have compared the method with optimal shutdown and with the LC-EDF method. Our examples show that our method performs better than LC-EDF for higher break-even times.

We used a fast real-time feasibility test allowing us to model periodic, jittering, or sporadic tasks. This enables guaranteed real-time feasible power optimisations with low complexity, and extends the applicability of processor shutdown to these kinds of occurring behaviour. Further, we can allow task deadlines to be greater than task periods.

Our optimisations are done off-line, yield predictable shutdown intervals, and thus be of use by an embedded software programmer in programming real-time clocks beforehand to use also deep sleep processor states.

The off-line prediction can also be understood as guarantee on maximal energy consumption a task set may yield, helping the designer to take right decisions if there is more than one implementation of the embedded software available.

Our solution needs a slight modification of task implementation, but does not require extra circuitry.

References

1. Ishihara, T., Yasuura, H.: Voltage scheduling problem for dynamically variable voltage processors. In: ISLPED, pp. 197–202 (1998)
2. Jejurika, R., Gupta, R.: Optmized slowdown in real-time task systems. In: Euromicro Conference on Real-Time Systems, pp. 155–164 (2004)
3. Racu, R., Hamann, A., Ernst, R., Mochocki, B., Hu, X.: Methods for power optimization in distributed embedded systems with real-time requirements. In: International Conference on Compilers, Architecture and Synthesis for Embedded Systems, pp. 379–388 (2006)
4. Lipskoch, H., Albers, K., Slomka, F.: Fast calculation of permissable slowdown factors for hard real-time systems. In: Azémard, N., Svensson, L. (eds.) PATMOS 2007. LNCS, vol. 4644, pp. 495–504. Springer, Heidelberg (2007)

5. Andrei, A., Schmitz, M., Eles, P., Peng, Z., Al-Hashimi, B.: Overhead conscious voltage selection for dynamic and leakage energy reduction of time-constrained systems. In: DATE (2004)
6. Rong, P., Pedram, M.: Power-aware scheduling and dynamic voltage setting for tasks running on a hard real-time system. In: Asia and South Pacific Design Automation Conference (2006)
7. Gupta, R.K., Irani, S., Shukla, S.K.: Formal methods for dynamic power management. In: ICCAD, p. 874 (2003)
8. Lu, Y.H., Micheli, G.D.: Comparing system-level power management policies. IEEE Design & Test of Computers 18(2), 10–19 (2001)
9. Swaminathan, V., Chakrabarty, K., Iyengar, S.S.: Dynamic i/o power management for hard real-time systems. In: International Symposium on Hardware/Software Codesign (CODES), pp. 237–242 (2001)
10. Cheng, H., Goddard, S.: Integrated device scheduling and processor voltage scaling for system-wide energy conservation. In: Workshop On Power-Aware Real-Time Computing, PARC (2005)
11. Luo, J., Jha, N.K.: Power-conscious joint scheduling of periodic task graphs and aperiodic tasks in distributed real-time embedded systems. In: ICCAD (2000)
12. Hong, I., Kirovski, D., Qu, G., Potkonjak, M., Srivastava, M.B.: Power optimization of variable voltage core-based systems. In: DAC, pp. 176–181 (1998)
13. Lee, Y.H., Reddy, K., Krishna, C.: Scheduling techniques for reducing leakage power in hard real-time systems. In: Euromicro Conference on Real-Time Systems, pp. 105–112 (2003)
14. Jejurika, R., Pereira, C., Gupta, R.: Leakage aware dynamic voltage scaling for real-time embedded systems. In: DAC, pp. 275–280 (2004)
15. Niu, L., Quan, G.: Reducing both dynamic and leakage energy consumption for hard real-time systems. In: Conference on Compilers, architecture, and synthesis for embedded systems (2004)
16. Baruah, S., Chen, D., Gorinsky, S., Mok, A.: Generalized multiframe tasks. Real-Time Systems 17(1), 5–22 (1999)
17. Lee, T.M., Henkel, J., Wolf, W.: Dynamic runtime re-scheduling allowing multiple implementations of a task for platform-based designs. In: DATE (2002)
18. Tindell, K., Clark, J.: Holistic schedulability analysis for distributed hard real-time systems. Microprocessing and Microprogramming - Euromicro Journal (Special Issue on Parallel Embedded Real-Time Systems) 40(2-3), 117–134 (1994)

Experimental Evaluation of a Hybrid Approach for Deriving Service-Time Bounds of Methods in Real-Time Distributed Computing Objects

Juan A. Colmenares[1], K.H. (Kane) Kim[1], and Doo-Hyun Kim[2]

[1] DREAM Laboratory, EECS Department, University of California, Irvine, USA
jcolmena@uci.edu, khkim@uci.edu
[2] School of Internet and Multimedia Engineering, Konkuk University, Korea
doohyun@konkuk.ac.kr

Abstract. Use of hybrid approaches that symbiotically combine analysis and measurements for deriving high-confidence tight service-time bounds (STBs) in real-time distributed computing (RTDC) applications represents a promising research area. A hybrid approach of this type was recently proposed for deriving STBs for methods in object-oriented RTDC applications. The approach combines analytical and measurement-based techniques to find a tight STB falling between the maximum measured service time and an analytically derived loose STB. A curve-fitting technique is applied to relate the measured data to the loose bound and also enables the estimation of the probability of the chosen STB not being exceeded at run time. Experimental research for checking the feasibility and potential problems of this type of hybrid approaches has been scarce. In this paper we report on the results of one case study aimed for validating the curve-fitting based hybrid approach mentioned above. The RTDC application dealt with in this experimental work is a relatively simple distributed video streaming application, called Televideo.

Keywords: service-time bound analysis, hybrid approach, curve fitting, time-triggered message-triggered objects.

1 Introduction

An essential requirement in real-time distributed computing (RTDC) is to obtain a high degree of assurance on the timeliness of critical actions taken by the systems. Previous research work on timing analysis has mostly covered single-node real-time programs involving no operating system (OS) or middleware service calls (e.g., [1]). But the timing analysis of RTDC applications involving substantial OS overhead and communication functions has not been sufficiently attempted.

A timely research issue is to derive *service-time bounds* (STBs) (or equivalently, guaranteed response times) for methods in object-oriented RTDC applications. When we use the term STB of an object-method M_i, we consider preemption-allowed executions of M_i and factor in both the actual execution times of M_i and the waiting times while M_i is in the active state.

A. Rettberg et al. (Eds.): IESS 2009, IFIP AICT 310, pp. 139–148, 2009.

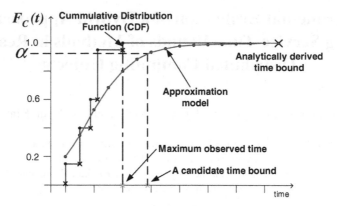

Fig. 1. Curve-fitting technique for deriving reasonably safe and tight time bounds (adapted from [2])

We focus on a hybrid approach for deriving tight STBs for methods in object-oriented RTDC applications. In our approach, analysis as well as testing and measurements are important parts. The central idea in our hybrid approach is to find a STB falling between the maximum measured service time and an analytically derived loose but safe bound. Specifically, service-time measurements and an analytically derived STB of a given object-method are used together for: 1) determining the safety margin to be added to the maximum observed service time in order to produce an acceptably tight and safe STB for the method, and 2) estimating the probability of this chosen STB not being exceeded at runtime.

A *curve-fitting technique* [2], illustrated in Fig. 1, plays a key role in relating the measured data to the analytically derived STB. This technique produces smooth approximation models that allow us to systematically determine tight and reasonably safe STBs. Note that time bounds produced analytically are considered *hard bounds* with a practically negligible probability of being violated at runtime. The reason is that methods for time bound analysis are frequently based on conservative assumptions and the derived bounds tend to have large error margins.

Conceptually, the approach presented in this paper can be seen as an extension of the segment-level hybrid approach in [2, 3] for deriving tight execution-time bounds (ETBs) for *program-segments* (i.e., non-interruptible code sequences not including OS and middleware calls) [4]. However, the analysis of service times of object-methods is a subject multiple times more complex than that of execution times of program-segments. In the analytical derivation of STBs for object-methods, we need to consider additional factors (e.g., concurrent method-executions, resource sharing, and communication activities) that influence the service times of methods.

As shown in Fig. 2, our approach works at the method level but it relies on the program-segment-level hybrid approach for obtaining tight ETBs for basic code elements (i.e., program-segments, local service calls, and non-blocking communication service calls) contained in the methods under analysis. The tight ETBs obtained for the basic code elements of the subject object-methods are integrated during the analytical derivation of safe STBs for the methods.

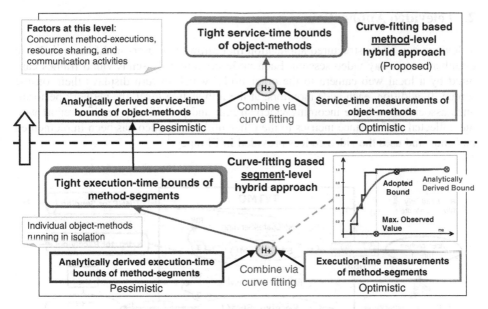

Fig. 2. General view of the proposed approach for deriving bounds for the service times of TMO-methods

Experimental work on deriving STBs of object-oriented RTDC applications has been scarce. This means that conceivable approaches for deriving STBs for object-methods in RTDC applications have not been much validated. In this paper we report on the results of one case study aimed for such validation. The RTDC application dealt with in this experimental research is a relatively simple distributed video streaming application, called *Televideo*. Deriving tight STBs of RTDC systems is, in general, a very complex problem. Thus, through this work we wanted to obtain better insight into the fundamental problem.

The Televideo application is structured as a network of *time-triggered message-triggered objects* (TMOs) and was developed according to the *TMO programming model* [5, 6]. The TMO model is a component-based programming scheme that relieves RTDC developers of the burden of dealing with low-level computing and communication abstractions. The TMO, the central element of this programming scheme, is a syntactically simple and natural but semantically major extension of the conventional object structure. The autonomous-action capability of TMO stems from the *time-triggered methods*, which are clearly separated from the *message-triggered methods* whose executions are activated by service request messages from clients. TMO allows developers to explicitly specify timing requirements in terms of global time in natural forms. The *TMO Support Middleware* (TMOSM) [7] is a middleware model that supports the execution of TMO-based applications.

The rest of the paper is structured as follows. Section 2 describes the Televideo application. The experimental setup is presented in Section 3. Section 4 presents the adopted ETBs for the object-methods in Televideo when each method runs in isolation; these time bounds are called *non-preemptive execution-time bounds* (NPETBs). Then, Section 5 discusses the derivation of STBs for the object-methods in Televideo. Section 6 provides a conclusion.

2   Televideo Application

Televideo is a TMO-structured application that allows two users in different nodes to establish a two-way video session. Each node continuously sends video frames captured by a local web camera to the other node, which in turn displays them on the screen. In addition, each node monitors, at the application level, the network performance associated with the incoming video stream and periodically sends a report with the collected performance metrics to the other node. Televideo has been implemented on Linux and uses the video codecs provided in FFmpeg.[1]

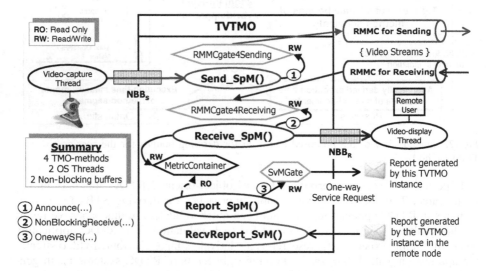

Fig. 3. Structure of the Televideo program running in each node

Fig. 3 presents the structure of the Televideo program running in each node. The Televideo program consists of: 1) a TMO (called **TVTMO**), 2) two OS native threads (the *video-capture thread* and the *video-display thread*), and 3) two non-blocking buffers (NBB$_S$ and NBB$_R$) [8, 9]. **TVTMO** is the central element of Televideo and contains three *time-triggered* or *spontaneous methods* (*SpMs*), and one *message-triggered* or *service method* (*SvM*).

SpMs and SvMs are collectively termed TMO-methods [5, 6]. Executions of SpMs are initiated during specified time windows. All time references in TMOs are global-time references and the SpM executions are thus triggered when the global time reaches specific values specified at design time. For example, the triggering times of an SpM may be specified as: {FOR t = FROM 8:00am TO 11:55pm;EVERY 100ms; START-DURING (t, t+30ms); FINISH-BY (t+80ms)}. This specification of the execution-time windows of an SpM is called the *Autonomous Activation Condition* (AAC) of the SpM.

---

[1] Available at http://ffmpeg.mplayerhq.hu

Executions of SvMs, on the other hand, are activated by service-request messages from local or remote clients (e.g., other TMOs). For each SvM, system designers specify: 1) a guaranteed execution-duration bound (GEDB); 2) the maximum invocation rate (MIR), in terms of the maximum number of service requests (`MaxInvocations`) that will lead to the activation of the subject SvM per basic period (`BasicPeriod`); and 3) the maximum number of instances of the SvM that can execute concurrently (`PipelineDegree`).

As shown in Fig. 3, the TMO-methods of TVTMO are:

- `Send_SpM()`: Each execution-instance of this method reads from NBB_S a video frame captured by the local web camera, encodes it, and then sends the encoded frame to the TVTMO in the other node via a logical multicast channel, called *Real-time Multicast and Memory-replication Channel* (RMMC) [6].

- `Receive_SpM()`: Each execution-instance of this method reads from an RMMC an encoded video frame sent by the other node, decodes it, and inserts the decoded frame into NBB_R. It also collects the network performance metrics associated with the incoming frames and stores them in `MetricContainer`.

- `Report_SpM()`: Each execution-instance of this method reads the performance metrics from `MetricContainer`, creates a report, and sends the report via a one-way service-request message to the `RecvReport_SvM()` in the other node.

- `RecvReport_SvM()`: Each instance of this method reads the report contained as a parameter in the SvM-call, i.e., the service-request message that activated its execution, and displays the content on the console.

The `MetricContainer` is a group of data members shared by `Receive_SpM()` and `Report_SpM()`. Such a group of data members in a TMO is called an *object-data-store segment* (ODSS) [5, 6]. An ODSS is a data-container unit that can be *automatically* locked to allow a TMO-method execution to have exclusive access. The TMO programming scheme defines several fundamental rules to orchestrate executions of TMO-method instances that have data-conflicts among themselves requiring exclusive access to ODSSs. The reader is referred to [10, 11] for a discussion on ODSSs and the concurrency rules in the TMO scheme.

TVTMO also contains *gate objects* [6] that provide call-paths to RMMCs and SvMs. The gate objects are treated as ODSSs with read-write access mode. TVTMO uses the gate objects to make *non-blocking communication service calls* only. These non-blocking calls return quickly without waiting for the completion of the activities of other TMOs and communication networks involved.

3 Experimental Setup

The experimental setup consists of two multi-core computers connected to an isolated 100-Mbps Ethernet switch. Both run Linux 2.6.25. One of the computers is equipped with a 2.4-GHz Intel Core 2 Quad CPU and 3GB of RAM. The results presented in this paper correspond to the Televideo program running in this computer, which is called the *test node*.

In each node, the *TMO Support Middleware* (TMOSM) [7] was configured to dedicate a core for the execution of TMO-methods. Moreover, a round-robin algorithm was incorporated into TMOSM to schedule the executions of the TMO-methods and the length of the round-robin time-slice was 3 ms in both nodes. Communication among TMOSM instantiations running in the two distributed computing nodes was performed in a TDMA manner.

Televideo was configured with the following parameters: 1) frame size: 320 pixels × 240 pixels, 2) frame rate: 10 fps, 3) color depth: 24 bits, and 4) encoding format: MPEG4.

4 Adopted NPETBs for the TMO-Methods in Televideo

As described in Section 2, the SpMs and SvM of TVTMO are *blocking-communication-call-free* (BCCF) methods. The most basic contribution of a BCCF TMO-method to its service time is the time the method takes to execute when it is neither affected by background activities nor subject to preemption. An ETB for a BCCF TMO-method M_i obtained under such execution conditions is called a *non-preemptive execution-time bound* (NPETB) for M_i.

Tight and reasonably safe NPETBs for the TMO-methods of TVTMO were obtained by applying the curve-fitting based hybrid approach originally proposed in [2] and using the measurement techniques discussed in [3]. This hybrid approach was slightly extended in order to consider, in addition to program-segments, the local service calls, non-blocking communication service calls, and application library calls present in the TMO-methods of TVTMO.

The adopted NPETBs for the TMO-methods of the Televideo program are the following: 11 ms for `Send_SpM()`, 2 ms for `Receive_SpM()`, 16 ms for `Report_SpM()`, and 19.1 ms for `RecvReport_SvM()`. The NPETBs for `Send_SpM()` and `Receive_SpM()` were the time values at which $F_c(t)$ values of the approximation models for the two SpMs became practically 1.0. For `Report_SpM()` and `RecvReport_SvM()` which executed less frequently than other TMO methods, we decided that it was sufficient to adopt NPETBs with estimated probabilities of not being exceeded at runtime equal to 90%.

Due to space limitation we do not discuss the derivation of the NPETBs and we refer the reader to [11] for the complete derivation analysis.

5 Derivation of GEDBs for the TMO-Methods in Televideo

During the design of a TMO-based application, the part that requires the biggest care is the specification of the *guaranteed execution-duration bounds* (GEDBs) and other timing parameters for the TMO-methods. Often, in practice, the selection of those parameters may be achieved via iterative cycles. Table 1 contains the timing parameters for the TMO-methods of TVTMO that resulted from this iterative process.

To avoid buffer overflow, the periods of `Send_SpM()` and `Receive_SpM()` are shorter than the interval at which the video frames are produced (i.e., 1 frame every 100 ms or equivalently, 10 fps). Additionally, we assume that a network performance report needs to be generated every 700 ms; this interval ensures that multiple execution-instances of `RecvReport_SvM()` never run concurrently. For this

Table 1. Timing parameters for the TMO-methods of TVTMO

SpM	FROM	UNTIL	EVERY	EST	LST	BY
Send_SpM()	3 s	24 h	70 ms	0	6 ms	39 ms
Receive_SpM()	3 s	24 h	70 ms	54 ms	61 ms	66 ms
Report_SpM()	3 s	24 h	700 ms	0	6 ms	54 ms

EVERY: period, EST: earliest start time, LST: latest start time, BY: relative deadline

SvM	BasicPeriod	MaxInv.	PipelineDegree	GEDB
RecvReport_SvM()	650 ms	1	1	58 ms

GEDB: guaranteed execution duration bound and relative deadline

reason, we configured RecvReport_SvM() with the parameters PipelineDe-gree, BasicPeriod, and MaxInvocations shown in Table 1. The rest of the timing parameters, in particular BY (= LST + GEDB) of the SpMs and GEDB of the SvM, were selected based on and validated using the present iterative STB analysis illustrated below.

We use a simple technique to analytically obtain loose GEDB candidates for the TMO-methods of TVTMO. We first determine the maximum number of TMO-method instances that can execute simultaneously during a certain interval; this quantity is denoted as *MaxIns*. This means that the CPU (which the TMO-methods were assigned to) may need to be multiplexed among the executions of *MaxIns* TMO-method instances. Since the round-robin scheduler is adopted and if we assume that the length of the round-robin time-slice is sufficiently small, then a loose GEDB candidate of a given TMO-method SxM_i can be obtained as follows:

$$GEDB\_Cand(\ SxM_i\ ) = MaxIns \times NPETB(\ SxM_i\ )\qquad(1)$$

In general, this GEDB calculation is rather conservative and the produced GEDBs tend to be pessimistic. System designers can, however, tighten those bounds by using the curve-fitting based hybrid approach, as will be shown later in this section.

Given the timing parameters of Table 1, at most 3 TMO-method instances, one of Send_SpM(), one of Report_SpM(), and one of RecvReport_SvM(), can be in execution at the same time (see Fig. 4). Hence, a loose GEDB candidate for each of those 3 TMO-methods can be obtained by multiplying its NPETB by 3. In the case of Receive_SpM(), however, its EST value makes its execution to be overlapped with none but for a possible instance of RecvReport_SvM(). Thus, a GEDB candidate for Receive_SpM() could be initially obtained as $2 \times NPETB$(Receive_SpM). Fig. 4 presents the preliminary GEDB candidates for the TMO-methods of TVTMO.

Note that the analytically derived GEDB candidate for Receive_SpM() (4 ms) needs to be verified because it is comparable with the length of the round-robin time-slice (3 ms). In other words, the assumption of having a round-robin time-slice sufficiently small does not hold for Receive_SpM(). The effect of time-slicing can cause an instance of Receive_SpM() to be delayed by 3 ms when the SpM becomes ready right after the time-slice taken by RecvReport_SvM() starts. Therefore, the tentative GEDB candidate obtained in Fig. 4 is not valid. Since

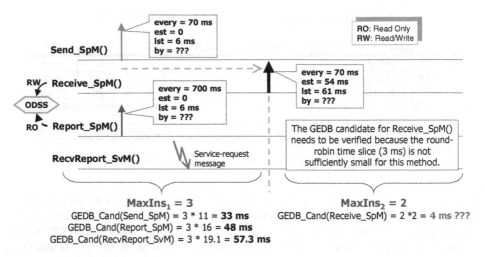

Fig. 4. Initiation times and preliminary analytically derived GEDB candidates for the TMO-methods of TVTMO. **MaxIns** is the maximum number of TMO-method instances that can execute simultaneously at a give time.

Table 2. Analytically derived GEDB candidates and maximum observed execution durations for the TMO-methods of TVTMO

TMO-method	GEDB Candidate	MMV	Ratio
Send_SpM()	33 ms	21.50 ms	1.53
Receive_SpM()	5 ms	3.47 ms	1.44
Report_SpM()	48 ms	25.19 ms	1.90
RecvReport_SvM()	57.3 ms	24.78 ms	2.31

MMV: Maximum Measured Value ∴ Ratio = (GEDB Candidate) / MMV.

NPETB($\mathtt{Receive\_SpM}$) = 2 ms, then a valid GEDB candidate for $\mathtt{Receive\_SpM()}$ is Max (2*2ms, 2ms + 3ms) = 5 ms. We also analyzed the consequences of a tick miss on the service time of $\mathtt{Send\_SpM()}$ and confirmed that the corresponding GEDB candidate shown in Fig. 4 is valid. Table 2 contains the verified analytically derived GEDB candidates for the TMO-method of TVTMO.

We measured the execution durations of the TMO-methods of TVTMO in the node under test to validate the analytically derived GEDB candidates and explore the possibility of tightening those bounds using the curve-fitting technique. We collected 6000 execution-duration measurements for $\mathtt{Send\_SpM()}$ and the same number for $\mathtt{Receive\_SpM()}$. In the case of $\mathtt{Report\_SpM()}$ and $\mathtt{RecvReport\_SvM()}$, we collected 750 measurements for each of them. Table 2 presents the maximum observed execution durations of the TMO-methods of TVTMO.

The ratios in Table 2 clearly suggest that we can obtain tighter GEDB candidates using the curve-fitting technique for $\mathtt{Report\_SpM()}$ and $\mathtt{RecvReport\_SvM()}$. Fig. 5 shows: 1) the *cumulative distribution function* (CDF) of the measured execution-duration times, 2) the analytically derived GEDB candidate, 3) the approximation

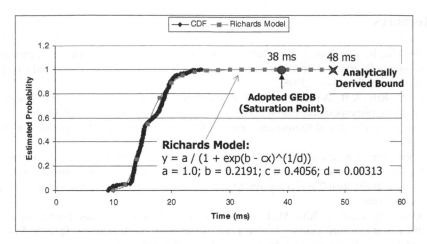

Fig. 5. Obtaining a tighter GEDB candidate for `Report_SpM()` via curve fitting

model that best fits the CDF among a collection of smooth models, and 4) the newly adopted GEDB for `Report_SpM()`, which is equal to 38 ms (ratio = 1.51). Using the same technique we also obtained a GEDB equal to 34 ms (ratio = 1.37) for `RecvReport_SvM()`. Thus, the hybrid approach produced tighter yet reasonably safe GEDBs for both TMO-methods.

6 Conclusion

In this paper we reported an experimental evaluation of a curve-fitting based hybrid approach for deriving service-time bounds of object-methods in RTDC applications. The hybrid approach was applied to a relatively simple TMO-structured multimedia application, called Televideo. In this case study, the approach turned out to be effective in tightening the service-time bounds for the object-methods in the subject application. The effectiveness of the hybrid approach must, however, be further evaluated under more complex application scenarios. This is the subject of our ongoing and future research efforts.

Acknowledgments

The research reported here is supported in part by the NSF under Grant Numbers 03-26606 (ITR) & 05-24050 (CNS), by the ETRI, Korea, by the Ministry of Knowledge Economy, Korea, under the ITRC support program supervised by the IITA (IITA-2008-C1090-0804-0015), and by the Konkuk Univ WCU project, No, R33-2008-000-10068-0 sponsored by the MEST, Korea. Juan A. Colmenares also thanks the Univ of Zulia (Venezuela) for supporting his participation. No part of this paper represents the views and opinions of the sponsors mentioned above.

References

1. Wilhelm, R., Engblom, J., Ermedahl, A., Holsti, N., et al.: The worst-case execution time problem - Overview of methods and survey of tools. ACM Trans. on Embedded Computing Systems 7(3), 1–53 (2008)
2. Im, C., Kim, K.H.: A hybrid approach in TADE for derivation of execution time bounds of program-segments in distributed real-time embedded computing. In: 9th IEEE Int'l. Symposium on Object and Component-Oriented Real-Time Distributed Computing, pp. 408–418 (2006)
3. Colmenares, J.A., Im, C., Kim, K.H., et al.: Measurement techniques in a hybrid approach for deriving tight execution-time bounds of program segments in fully-featured processors. In: 14th IEEE Real-Time and Embedded Technology and Applications Symposium, pp. 68–79 (2008)
4. Kim, K.H., Choi, L., Kim, M.H.: Issues in realization of an execution time analyzer for distributed real-time objects. In: 3rd IEEE Symposium on Application-Specific Systems and Software Engineering Technology, pp. 171–178 (2000)
5. Kim, K.H.: Object structures for real-time systems and simulators. IEEE Computer 30(8), 62–70 (1997)
6. Kim, K.H.: APIs for real-time distributed object programming. IEEE Computer 33(6), 72–80 (2000)
7. Jenks, S.F., Kim, K., et al.: A middleware model supporting time-triggered message-triggered objects for standard Linux systems. Real-Time Systems 36(1), 75–99 (2007)
8. Kim, K.H.: A non-blocking buffer mechanism for real-time event message communication. Real-Time Systems 32(3), 197–211 (2006)
9. Kim, K.H., Colmenares, J.A., Rim, K.-W.: Efficient adaptations of the non blocking buffer for event message communication between real-time threads. In: 10th IEEE Int'l. Symposium on Object/Component/Service-Oriented Real-time Distributed Computing, pp. 29–40 (2007)
10. Kim, K.H., Colmenares, J.A.: Maximizing concurrency and analyzable timing behavior in component-oriented real-time distributed computing application systems. J. Computing Science and Engineering 1(1), 56–73 (2007)
11. Colmenares, J.A.: Derivation of service-time bounds of methods in time-triggered message-triggered objects. PhD thesis, University of California, Irvine (2009)

Efficient Parallel Transaction Level Simulation by Exploiting Temporal Decoupling

Rauf Salimi Khaligh and Martin Radetzki

Embedded Systems Engineering Group
Institute of Computer Architecture and Computer Engineering (ITI)
Universität Stuttgart
Pfaffenwaldring 47, D-70569 Stuttgart, Germany
{salimi,radetzki}@informatik.uni-stuttgart.de

Abstract. In recent years, transaction level modeling (TLM) has enabled designers to simulate complex embedded systems and SoCs, orders of magnitude faster than simulation at the RTL. The increasing complexity of the systems on one hand, and availability of low cost parallel processing resources on the other hand have motivated the development of parallel simulation environments for TLMs. The existing simulation environments used for parallel simulation of TLMs are intended for general discrete event models and do not take advantage of the specific properties of TLMs. The fine-grain synchronization and communication between simulators in these environments can become a major impediment to the efficiency of the simulation environment. In this work, we exploit the properties of temporally decoupled TLMs to increase the efficiency of parallel simulation. Our approach does not require a special simulation kernel. We have implemented a parallel TLM simulation framework based on the publicly available OSCI SystemC simulator. The framework is based on the communication interfaces proposed in the recent OSCI TLM 2 standard. Our experimental results show the reduced synchronization overhead and improved simulation performance.

Keywords: Transaction-Level Modeling, Parallel Simulation, SystemC, Temporal Decoupling.

1 Introduction

A transaction level model is a network of *modules* representing logical or physical entities. In TLM terminology, modules may be *active* or *passive*. Active modules contain processes, the fundamental unit of behavior and concurrency. Active modules perform computations and initiate communication (i.e. transactions) with other modules. Passive modules on the other hand do not contain processes and the functionality provided by them is executed by, and in the context of the processes of the active modules. Several factors contribute to the total time required for simulation of a given transaction level model: The **computation** performed by processes, the **communication** between modules (e.g. via interface method calls), the **synchronization** between processes (e.g.

A. Rettberg et al. (Eds.): IESS 2009, IFIP AICT 310, pp. 149–158, 2009.

wait()-notify()) and the **synchronization** of the processes with the simulation time (e.g. *wait(delay)*).

For parallel simulation of a TLM on N simulators, the set of all modules in the TLM is partitioned into disjoint sets, with each set being assigned to a single simulator. The total amount of processor time consumed by the computations in the modules can be considered the same in parallel and sequential simulations. The amount of time consumed by inter-module communication depends on whether the communicating modules are assigned to the same or different simulators. Inter-simulator communication can be orders of magnitude slower than communication between modules in the same simulator. The overhead of inter-simulator communication can be reduced by analysis of inter-module communication patterns and appropriate assignment of modules to simulators. For example, by assignment of modules with high communication requirements to the same simulator. This issue has not been in the scope of this work. We have focused on the overhead incurred by the synchronization between the simulators which is described in the following paragraphs.

Existing frameworks available for parallel simulation of TLMs are in intended for simulation of general, discrete event models such as signal-based, RTL models written in SystemC. In terminology of parallel discrete event simulation these simulation frameworks are all *conservative*. That is, they guarantee that the causality relationships are never violated. For example it is guaranteed that no process will ever be notified of an event which belongs to the past. To ensure this, the progress of individual simulators in simulation time must be synchronized globally.

Let $S_1, \ldots, S_N$ be N simulators and T be the current global simulation time. In summary, at T, in each simulator S_i all processes sensitive to the events belonging to T are executed. Each simulator then reports the time of its next event t_i to a global synchronization process and waits. After collecting all t_i, the synchronization process then determines the next global simulation time $T' = min\{t_1, \ldots, t_N\}$, such that the causality relationships are not violated (conservatism). It then broadcasts T' as the next global simulation time to all simulators and they proceed to T', executing any process sensitive to events at T'. This process is repeated until a global simulation termination condition is satisfied. Especially in timed TLMs, this will require frequent communication between the simulators and the resulting overhead will negatively affect the efficiency of the simulation.

In our approach, synchronization between simulators is performed only at fixed, globally known points in the simulation time. This results in a simplified synchronization algorithm which can be implemented using efficient collective synchronization operations (e.g. barriers on SMP machines). We achieve this by exploiting a special, strict form of temporal decoupling (allowing the processes to run ahead of the simulation time). We will elaborate on this in the next sections.

This paper is organized as follows: In section 2 we give an overview of closely related work. Section 3 summarizes the main ideas behind our approach. In section 4 details of a SystemC-based and OSCI TLM 2 inspired implementation are presented. Section 5 shows the results of our experiments and section 6 summarizes the results and provides some direction for future work.

2   Related Work

Transaction level modeling [17, 4, 3, 9] is an already established and increasingly popular, simulation-centric modeling paradigm for embedded systems and systems-on-chip and is enabled by modeling languages such as SystemC [11], SpecC [7] and SystemVerilog [1]. Except for some special cases such as cycle-driven TLM simulators (e.g. [2]), currently most TLMs are simulated using sequential discrete event simulators (DES) such as the publicly available SystemC simulator from OSCI. Some researchers see the performance of such general simulation kernels insufficient for many applications. For example, some propose alternative simulation kernels (e.g. heterogeneous simulation kernel [18]) while others address this issue at the modeling level (e.g. adaptive models [12]). In the recent OSCI TLM 2 standard [17] communication interfaces, modeling guidelines and techniques such as temporal decoupling are proposed. The OSCI TLM 2 standard targets sequential TLM simulation, and temporal decoupling is recommended for reduction of the overhead of context switches caused by the synchronization of the processes with the simulation time (*wait(time)*).

Currently most of the parallel simulation environments for transaction level simulation are based on SystemC. These simulators are meant for general SystemC models and hence deal with low level synchronization and communication constructs such as signals and evaluate/update channels. One of the first works in this area is [5], where simulation kernels are synchronized at the end of every delta cycle to ensure causality and the evaluate/update channels are synchronized at the end of every update phase to ensure correctness of the communication. This simulation environment requires a modified SystemC kernel. The high overhead of this fine-grain synchronization and communication has been addressed by the authors in their recent work [6]. Another environment for parallel SystemC simulation is introduced in [10]. The simulation time synchronization in this environment is similar to [5, 6], with the difference that no specialized simulation kernel is required. In [14], authors present a distributed SystemC simulation environment for simulations involving geographically distributed intellectual property. Their main focus has been on geographical distribution and not on the simulation performance.

The current research in parallel simulation of TLMs is based on the well-established parallel/distributed discrete event simulation (PDES/DDES) concepts (e.g. [15, 8]). In addition to conservative PDES, there exist *optimistic* approaches (e.g. TimeWarp [13]) where the causality conditions are allowed to be violated. In case of a violation, the simulation must be rolled back in time to ensure correct results. Implementation complexity, and memory and performance costs of such roll-back mechanisms for large system-level models have prohibited their use in parallel TLM simulation. The idea of temporal decoupling can be traced back to early works in optimistic PDES/DDES. In [19] conservative

PDES principles are used to increase the speed of transaction level simulation by avoiding synchronization with the SystemC simulation time as much as possible. The simulation itself however is purely sequential and is performed in a single simulation process. The recent version of the commercial distributed simulation environment Simics [20] claims to utilize temporal decoupling for simulation acceleration. This environment is based on a proprietary simulation kernel and a custom modeling language, with a possibility for integration with SystemC models. However, at the time of this writing, the details of the simulation kernel and SystemC integration are not published to the best of our knowledge.

3   Exploiting Temporal Decoupling for Efficient Parallel Simulation

Similar to [5, 6, 14], we use an application and model dependent number of sequential discrete event simulator processes in parallel. Each simulator is assigned a subset of the modules of a given TLM. The most significant difference of our approach with existing approaches is the synchronization of processes with the simulation time and synchronization of the simulators with each other.

In timed TLMs, timing information is annotated in the processes, for example using a *wait(time)* statement which synchronizes the process with the global simulation time. In sequential DES frameworks, this will result in a process context switch and has a negative effect on the simulation performance. Temporal decoupling is a technique recommended by the recent OSCI TLM 2 standard to reduce the effects of these context switches. In temporally decoupled models, processes have a local time which is allowed to "run ahead" of the global simulation time for a maximum amount of time called a *quantum*, after which the process must synchronize with the global simulation time. In the form proposed by OSCI TLM 2 and implemented in the accompanying library, the deviation between the local time of the process and the global simulation time can become larger than the quantum as the synchronization is left to the processes and no enforcing mechanism exists. This can be seen in the following pseudocode which shows timing annotation portions of a temporally decoupled process:

$$\ldots$$
$$t_l = t_l + d_1$$
$$\ldots$$
$$t_l = t_l + d_2$$
if $t_l > q$ **then**
  $wait(t_l)$
end if
$$\ldots$$

Here t_l represents the local time offset, q the time quantum and d_1 and d_2 arbitrary time intervals. The local time offset can be incremented beyond a quantum boundary without synchronizing with the simulation time. At some point, the process decides to check the local offset and synchronize with the simulation time ($wait(t_l)$). Upon this synchronization, the local time offset becomes zero and the simulation time may or may not be on the quantum boundary. Our version of temporal decoupling is more strict in the sense that we enforce the processes to synchronize with the global simulation time exactly on *quantum boundaries*. That is, the local time offset of a process is never allowed to get larger than a quantum. For this, a specialized *wait* function is required which is to be used by all processes for timing annotations. The body of this function, which we call *decoupled_wait* is shown below. Here t_l is the local time offset of the process, q is the quantum, n_q is the number of complete quanta to elapse and o_q is the remainder offset.

function *decoupled_wait(d)*
begin
$n_q = \lfloor \frac{(t_l+d)}{q} \rfloor$
$o_q = (t_l + d) - n_q \times q$
if $n_q > 0$ **then**
    $wait(n_q \times q)$
    $t_l = 0$
end if
$t_l = t_l + o_q$
end

Using this function, the timing annotations shown in the previous example will require the following two calls:

. . .
decoupled_wait(d_1)
. . .
decoupled_wait(d_2)
. . .

Assuming that all processes in the model use this function for timing annotation, progress of simulation time in each simulator will be in multiples of the quantum q at all times. This can be exploited to simplify the synchronization of the simulators compared to existing methods (section 2).

There is no need for a central simulation synchronization process. Similarly, collection of local times from individual simulators and broadcasting back their minimum is not necessary. Figure 1 shows how the simulators can be synchronized using collective barrier synchronization. Each simulator executes the processes assigned to it for the duration of a quantum and then waits on a barrier shared by all simulators. After all simulators have reached the barrier, they either proceed to the next quantum boundary or terminate.

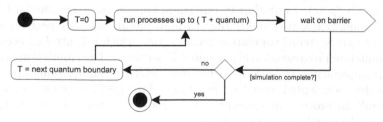

Fig. 1. Simulation progress in each sequential simulator

4   Implementation

As a proof of concept we have developed a parallel TLM simulation framework based on the ideas presented in section 3. The framework is intended for SystemC models and follows the communication interfaces introduced in the OSCI TLM 2 standard [17].

The framework provides a root module class *sc_ dist_ module* from which all modules in a TLM must be derived. This class has an attribute which identifies the simulator to which the module is assigned. This attribute is set upon construction and is specified as a constructor argument. This is used to simplify the task of assigning modules to simulators, and to avoid having different program sources for different simulators. The OSCI TLM 2 standard and the accompanying library are intended for sequential simulation and are not directly usable for parallel simulation. For example, the communication between OSCI TLM 2 modules is performed using *transport* methods which carry a payload, timing and phase information. To enable communication between modules in different simulation processes we have implemented a simple protocol based on a commercial Message Passing Interface (MPI [16]) implementation. The framework provides *stub* modules which handle the translation between the transport calls and MPI calls. For example, to communicate with a remote target *T1* (i.e. target residing in another simulator process), initiator *I1* calls the transport methods of the *initiator-side stub* of that target (*ISS*). This stub translates each transport call to a series of point-to-point MPI communication calls, which are received in the target simulator. Based on the information received in the target simulator, a *target-side stub* of the initiator (*TSS*) calls the transport method of the actual target (*T1*). The return values are transported back to *ISS* and finally to the initiator *I1*. Instantiation and interconnection of stubs are completely hidden from the user by a *binder* component, which handles the details in elaboration time whenever initiator and target sockets are bound.

The root module class *sc_ dist_ module* also provides the *decoupled_ wait* functionality discussed in section 3 in form of an overridden *wait* function. Additionally, it handles the local time offset of the processes. Another motivation for having the root module class was simplifying the migration of existing OSCI TLM 2 models to our parallel simulation framework. Ideally, the migration would require modifying a model to inherit from *sc_ dist_ module* instead of *sc_ module*. The communication between the simulators required for synchronization is also implemented using MPI, based on collective barrier synchronization.

It should be pointed out that in our framework we use the standard OSCI SystemC simulation kernel and library without modification. In each simulator process, a single SystemC simulation kernel is run, which is controlled according to the simulation progress control presented in section 3. The simulation progress control is implemented as a loop in the user-level *sc_ main()* function, and is based on the documented, user-level functions of the OSCI SystemC kernel [11]. For example to proceed in simulation time for a quantum Q, *sc_ start(Q)* is called from the simulation control loop.

5   Experimental Results

To evaluate our framework and the proposed parallel simulation approach we
have performed several experiments. It should be noted that application and
model-dependent factors can greatly affect the degree of speedup achieved when
using parallel simulation. The communication pattern between modules assigned
to different simulators and the degree of concurrency of computations in the
modules are two examples. These application and model specific issues have not
been in the scope of this work.

All following experiments were performed on a Linux-based, quad-core Intel
SMP simulation host. In the first experiment, we compared the performance of
the barrier-based synchronization of the simulators which we proposed in section
3, with the performance of synchronization based on the collection of local times
and broadcast of the next global time (section 1). Each simulator was assigned
a single active module, which only performed $wait(t)$ in a loop. The experiment
was performed with 2, 3 and 4 simulators on 2, 3 and 4 cores respectively,
with each core running a single simulator. The reduction in the synchronization
overhead using our proposed synchronization algorithm was approximately 52%
for 2 simulators and 35% for 3 and 4 simulators.

In the second experiment our objective was to determine the maximum achievable speedup in our framework when using 2, 3 and 4 cores. We simulated

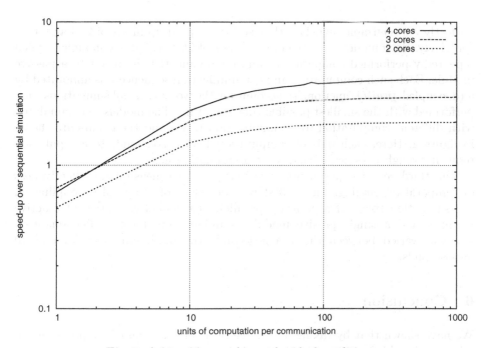

Fig. 2. Achievable speedup under ideal conditions

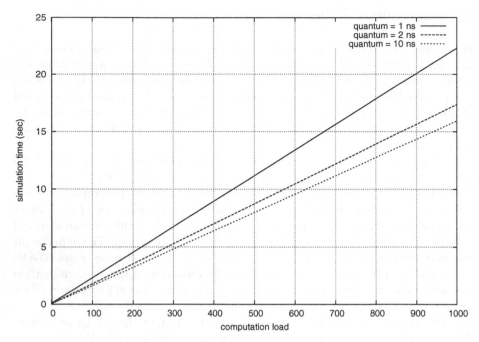

Fig. 3. Effect of temporal decoupling

perfectly parallelizable models with theoretical speed-up limits of 2, 3 and 4 respectively. Each model consisted of a number of identical active modules, which
repeatedly performed computations and communicated the result to a passive
module. Each such computation and communication sequence was annotated by
a (decoupled-)*wait()* function. To account for the worst case, all simulations were
performed with the smallest possible time quantum. The models were simulated
with different computation to communication ratios and the results are shown
in figure 2. Here, each unit of computation load corresponds to computation
requiring roughly 5 microseconds on our simulation host.

The third set of experiments were performed to measure the effectiveness
of temporal decoupling. Figure 3 shows the effect of temporal decoupling on
the simulation speed of a perfectly parallelizable model consisting of 2 active
modules and a single passive module, simulated on 3 cores. The quantum
size was varied between the 1 nanosecond (the minimum possible) and 10
nanoseconds.

6   Conclusion

We have shown that by taking advantage of a certain form of temporal decoupling we are able to reduce the overhead of synchronization between simulators,
resulting in a more efficient parallel simulation for a subclass of transaction

level models. With a suitable quantum size and with increasing computation-to-communication and synchronization ratio, the theoretical maximum speedup of N can be approached in a simulation on N cores. The current version of the framework can be easily modified to run on clusters of SMP hosts. Optimization of the framework for clusters, automatic analysis of the models for efficient module-simulator assignment and simulation frameworks for massively parallel MPSoCs and NoC-based systems are our planned future work in this direction.

References

[1] Accellera Organization, Inc. SystemVerilog 3.1a Language Reference Manual (May 2004)

[2] ARM Limited. Cycle-Accurate Simulation Interface (CASI) Specification, version 1.1.0 (June 2006)

[3] Burton, M., Aldisy, J., Guenzel, R., Klingauf, W.: Transaction Level Modelling: A Reflection on What TLM is and How TLMs May be Classified. In: Proceedings of the Forum on Specification and Design Languages (FDL 2007) (September 2007)

[4] Cai, L., Gajski, D.: Transaction Level Modeling: An Overview. In: Proceedings of the 1st IEEE/ACM/IFIP International Conference on Hardware/Software Codesign and System Synthesis (CODES+ISSS 2003) (October 2003)

[5] Chopard, B., Combes, P., Zory, J.: A Conservative Approach to SystemC Parallelization. In: Proceedings of the International Conference on Computational Science (ICCS 2006) (May 2006)

[6] Combes, P., Caron, E., Desprez, F., Chopard, B., Zory, J.: Relaxing Synchronization in a Parallel SystemC Kernel. In: Proceedings of the International Symposium on Parallel and Distributed Processing with Applications (ISPA 2008) (December 2008)

[7] Doemer, R., Gerstlauer, A., Gajski, D.: The SpecC Language Reference Manual, Version 2.0. SpecC Technology Open Consortium (December 2002),
http://www.specc.org

[8] Fujimoto, R.M.: Parallel and distributed simulation. In: Proceedings of the 31st Winter simulation conference, WSC 1999 (1999)

[9] Ghenassia, F.: Transaction-Level Modeling with SystemC: TLM Concepts and Applications for Embedded Systems. Springer-Verlag New York, Inc., Heidelberg (2006)

[10] Huang, K., Bacivarov, I., Hugelshofer, F., Thiele, L.: Scalably distributed SystemC simulation for embedded applications. In: Proceedings of the International Symposium on Industrial Embedded Systems (SIES 2008) (June 2008)

[11] IEEE Computer Society. Standard SystemC Language Reference Manual, Standard 1666-2005 (March 2006)

[12] Salimi Khaligh, R., Radetzki, M.: Adaptive Interconnect Models for Transaction-Level Simulation. In: LNEE 36, Languages for Embedded Systems and their Applications (2009)

[13] Lin, Y.-B., Lazowska, E.D.: A study of time warp rollback mechanisms. ACM Transactions on Modeling and Computer Simulation, TOMACS (1991)

[14] Meftali, S., Dziri, A., Charest, L., Marquet, P., Deskeyser, J.: SOAP Based Distributed Simulation Environment for SoC Design. In: Proceedings of the Forum on Specification and Design Languages (FDL 2005) (September 2005)

[15] Misra, J.: Distributed Discrete-Event Simulation. Computing Surveys (March 1986)
[16] MPI Forum. MPI: A Message-Passing Interface Standard, http://www.mpi-forum.org/
[17] Open SystemC Initiative (OSCI) TLM Working Group. Transaction Level Modeling Standard 2 (OSCI TLM 2) (June 2008), http://www.systemc.org
[18] Patel, H.D., Shukla, S.K.: Towards a Heterogeneous Simulation Kernel for System Level Models: A SystemC Kernel for Synchronous Data Flow Models. In: Proceedings of the 14th ACM Great Lakes symposium onVLSI (GLSVLSI 2004) (April 2004)
[19] Viaud, E., Pêcheux, F., Greiner, A.: An Efficient TLM/T Modeling and Simulation Environment Based on Conservative Parallel Discrete Event Principles. In: Proceedings of the Conference on Design, Automation and Test in Europe (DATE 2006) (March 2006)
[20] Virtutech. Virtutech Simics, http://www.virtutech.com/

Formal Verification for Embedded Systems Design Based on MDE

Francisco Assis Moreira do Nascimento[1], Marcio Ferreira da Silva Oliveira[2],
and Flávio Rech Wagner[1]

[1] Institute of Informatics - Federal University of Rio Grande do Sul - UFRGS
Av. Bento Gonçalves, 9500, Porto Alegre/RS, Brazil
`fanascimento@inf.ufrgs.br, flavio@inf.ufrgs.br`
[2] C-Lab, University of Paderborn
Fürstenallee, 11, Paderborn/NRW, Germany
`marcio@c-lab.de`

Abstract. This work presents a Model Driven Engineering (MDE) approach for the automatic generation of a network of timed automata from the functional specification of an embedded application described using UML class and sequence diagrams. By means of transformations on the UML model of the embedded system, a MOF-based representation for the network of timed automata is automatically obtained, which can be used as input to formal verification tools, as the Uppaal model checker, in order to validate desired functional and temporal properties of the embedded system specification. Since the network of timed automata is automatically generated, the methodology can be very useful for the designer, making easier the debugging and formal validation of the system specification. The paper describes the defined transformations between models, which generate the network of timed automata as well as the textual input to the Uppaal model checker, and illustrates the use of the methodology with a case study to show the effectiveness of the approach.

1 Introduction

Due mainly to severe design constraints and time-to-market urgency, embedded software applications are usually much more difficult to design than other types of applications. Furthermore, the complexity of embedded systems is increasing very fast. For example, in the automotive industry, nowdays 90 percent of the new features in recent models were related to electronics, making software be the main aspect in a car. In many recent car models, there are more than 200 functions the user interacts with, deployed over more than 60 independent embedded ECU (Electronic Control Unit).

One of the important aspects in the embedded system design is to ensure that a given system really does what it is intended to do. Nowadays, with the growing complexity of embedded systems, an exhaustive test of all possible system executions, or of at least a set of representative ones, is an impractical or even impossible approach. An alternative to testing is mathematically proving

A. Rettberg et al. (Eds.): IESS 2009, IFIP AICT 310, pp. 159–170, 2009.

correctness, by specifying precise models of the embedded system and formally verifying logical properties over these models.

1.1 Model Driven Engineering

To cope with the growing complexity of embedded systems design, several approaches based on MDE (Model Driven Engineering) have been proposed [1]. In MDE the main artifacts to be constructed and maintained are models, which are represented using a common modeling language. In the MDE context, software development consists of transforming a model into another one until a final model is obtained that is ready to be executed.

One variant of MDE is the Model Driven Architecture (MDA) ([2]), which is a framework proposed by OMG (Object Management Group) for the software development, driven by models at different abstraction levels and specified using UML ([3]). UML adopts the object oriented paradigm and includes different diagrams for the modeling of structure and behavior. In order to be used as input representation for formal verification and co-synthesis tools ([4]), a UML model must be translated into some formalism that can expose the control and data flow of the specified application in a concise and efficient way, since this information is essential to the algorithms used in the existing design automation tools.

In a UML model one can use Activity diagrams to specify such kind of information, but the internal representation defined in conformance to OMG's MOF (Meta Object Facility) ([5]) is not adequate to implement formal verification and co-synthesis algorithms, since the information is dispersed in different parts of the MOF based internal representation for UML. This makes very difficult to perform some basic operations on this representation, which are necessary for the design automation algorithms ([4]).

1.2 Formal Verification Approach Based on MDE

Differently from all other approaches oriented to MDE for embedded system design, which translate UML models to some specific internal representation format, we use only MOF concepts to define our internal design representation metamodel, and so, as a MOF-based metamodel, our internal design representation can take advantage of the concept of transformation between models to implement formal verification and co-synthesis tasks. This paper presents a formal verification methodology which adopts concepts from MDE for the automatic generation of a network of timed automata ([6]) from the functional specification of an embedded application described using UML class and sequence diagrams.

By means of transformations on the UML model of the embedded system, a MOF-based representation for the network of timed automata is automatically obtained, which can be used as input to model checking tools, as, for example, UPPAAL ([7]), in order to validate desired functional and temporal properties of the embedded system specification. Since the network of timed automata is automatically generated, the methodology can be very useful for the designers, making easier the debugging and formal validation of the system specification. Moreover, the formal verification methodology is part of a complete MDE-based co-synthesis approach, and thus, after the formal validation of the desired properties, this same validated system specification can be directly used as input to a set of MDE-based co-synthesis tools.

1.3   Outline

The paper is organized as follows. A comparison of our methodology with other related MDE-based approaches to design validaton is given in Section 2. Section 3 introduces our MDE-based approach for formal verification, Section 4 presents the Internal Application Meta-Model, Section 5 describes the Labeled Timed Automata Meta-Model, and Section 6 presents the transformations between models that generate a Labeled Timed Automata model from our Internal Application model. Section 7 describes a case study, which illustrates our approach. Section 8 presents main conclusions and future research dirctions.

2   Related Work

There are many recent research efforts on embedded systems design based on MDE. The adoption of platform-independent design and executable UML has been vastly investigated. For example, xtUML ([8]) defines an executable and translatable UML subset for embedded real-time systems, allowing the simulation of UML models and the code generation for C oriented to different microcontroller platforms. However, there is no support to formal verification tools in xtUML.

The model checking based approach to formal verification of an executable UML subset, described in ([9]), can generate a S/R model for the COSPAN model checking tool. But differently from our approach, the supported UML subset does not include sequence diagrams.

The Internal Format (IF) from the OMEGA project ([10]) associates a process to each class and captures the behavior as state machines that represent the interactions between these processes. There is no concept of module to group processes and so to take into account the different forms of communications according to the partitioning of the processes. This missing information would be essential for the functional validation and co-synthesis tasks.

In the approach presented in ([11]), UML Sequence Diagrams are translated into a communication dependency graph in order to implement a specific performance analysis technique. This approach does not consider the structure and hierarchy of a UML model, as our approach does.

The co-synthesis tool POLIS [12] has an internal design representation, called CFSM (Co-Design Finite State Machine), which allows the implementation of efficient co-synthesis and formal verification strategies. However, it is not possible to use UML as input modeling language for POLIS, neither to implement the co-synthesis and formal verification tasks using MDE concepts.

3   ModSyn and Its Formal Verification Approach

Our MDE-based approach to embedded systems design automation [13][14] adopts meta-models to represent *applications*, capturing functionality by means of processes communicating by ports and channels; *platforms*, indicating available hardware/software resources; *mappings* from application into platform; and *implementations*, oriented to code generation and hardware synthesis. Figure 1 shows our MDE-based design flow, called ModSyn (Model-driven co-Synthesis for embedded systems design). In our approach, the *application* is specified independently from the *platform*, using UML as modeling language, but any other DSL (Domain Specific Language) ([1]) could also be used. A *mapping* defines how application functionality is partitioned among architectural components in order to produce an *implementation* for the specified system. Accordingly, four internal meta-models allow the independent application and platform modeling: Internal Application Meta-model (IAMM), Internal Platform Meta-Model (IPMM), Mapping Meta-model (MMM), and Implementation Meta-Model (IMM). Each meta-model provides the abstract syntax for the adopted design concepts in ModSyn. These meta-models are described in ([14]) and will not be detailed here. This paper will present the generation of a MOF-based internal design representation model conforming to IAMM from UML class and sequence diagrams and, from this internal representation, the generation of a network of timed automata. This task is performed by the Application Manager and System Designer, respectively, which are shown in Figure 1.

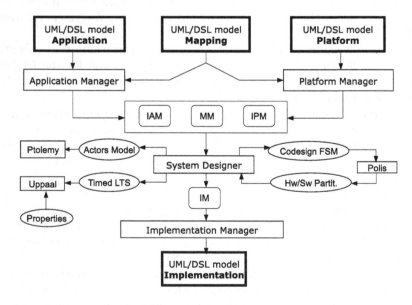

Fig. 1. ModSyn Design Flow

The ModSyn framework provides transformations between models that can generate a timed Labeled Transition System (LTS) ([6]) from IAM, which can be used in the Uppaal model checker ([7]), and also provides the generation of Co-Design Finite State Machines (CFSM) to be used by the Polis framework ([12]) in the Hardware/Software partitioning task, and an actor-based model for functional simulation using Ptolemy ([15]).

4   Internal Application Meta-model

In ModSyn, for the system structure, UML class diagrams indicate the components of the system under design, and the system behavior can be specified using UML Sequence diagrams that indicate the allowed execution scenarios. In order to represent an application in a standard way, a model that is captured using UML is translated into a common application model defined by the Internal Application Meta-model (IAMM) (illustrated by Figure 2 and Figure 3). This translation is implemented in ModSyn by means of transformations between models. As shown in Figure 2, in an application model conforming to IAMM, a system specification captures the functionality of the application in terms of a set of modules (`Module` class). Each module has module declarations (`Module Declaration class`) and a module body (`ModuleBody` class).

The control and data flow of an application model is represented by an `InteractionGraph`, presented in Figure 3. In the definition of our `Interaction Graph`, we adopt an approach similar to the proposed in ([16]), which takes MOF concepts from the UML Activity diagram meta-model. As illustrated in Figure 3, an `InteractionGraph` consists of a set of nodes (`IGNode` class) and edges (`IGEdge` class). Each node can represent different kinds of control

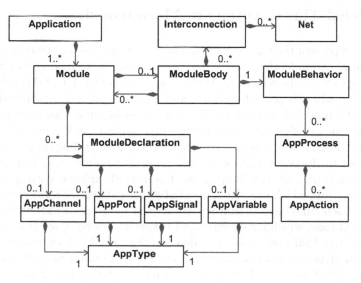

Fig. 2. Internal Application Meta-model (part 1)

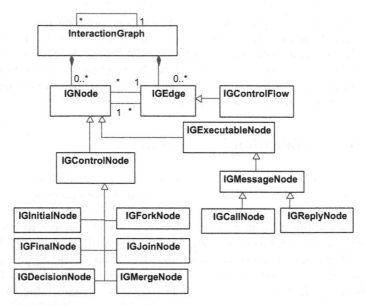

Fig. 3. Internal Application Meta-model (part 2)

flow (`IGInitialNode`, `IGFinalNode`, `IGForkNode`, `IGJoinNode`, `IGMergeNode`, `IGDecisionNode` classes) and two kinds of executable nodes (`IG CallNode` and `IGReplyNode`, sub-classes of the `IGMessageNode` class), which represent the possible actions of sending and replying messages in the UML Sequence diagram.

5   Labeled Timed Automata Meta-model

In order to represent the functional behavior of a UML model, the corresponding Internal Application Model is translated into a network of timed automata model conforming to the Labeled Timed Automata Meta-model (LTAMM) (illustrated by Figure 4), which is part of our IAM and captures all concepts introduced by the UPPAAL model checking tool ([7]). This translation is also implemented in ModSyn by means of transformations between models. As Figure 4 shows, conforming to the LTA Meta-Model, a system consists of `ltaDeclarations`, which can be used to declare variables, functions, and channels, and `ltaProcesses`, which are instances of `lta Templates`. Each `ltaTemplate` corresponds to a timed automaton, which can also have `ltaDecla rations` of local variables and functions. Each timed automaton is represented by a set of `ltaLocations` and `lta Transitions`, which have source and target locations. Each transition may have attributes: `ltaSelections` (non-deterministically bind a given identifier to a value in a given range when transition is taken), `ltaGuards` (transition is enabled in a state if and only if the guard evaluates to true), `ltaSyncronizations` (transitions labelled with complementary synchronization actions - send and

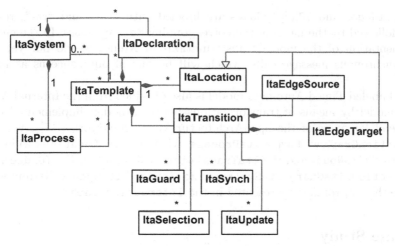

Fig. 4. LTA Meta-model

receive - over a common channel synchronise), and ltaUpdates (when transition is taken, its update expression is evaluated and the side effect of this expression changes the state of the system).

6 Generating the LTA Model from UML

The transformation from a UML model into our Internal Application Model consists of a set of transformations between models, which are implemented using the Xtend language from the OpenArchitectureWare framework ([17]). The main transformation consists of traversing the UML model, where the sub-modules are identified, according to the aggregation and composition between the classes; the processes are built from the Sequence diagrams, one process for each sequence diagram; and, finally, the InteractionGraphs are also built from the Sequence diagrams. Each Package in the UML model is traversed recursively and each existing UML Class in a package is transformed into a Module class. Each UML Attribute of each UML class is transformed into a Module Declaration class. The associations between the UML classes will determine the sub-modules of each module: Each UML Class, which is part of an aggregation or composition of another UML Class, will be transformed into a Submodule. Derived classes are transformed into modules, and all the inherited attributes are replicated inside each such module.

In the UML/MOF, each Lifeline in a UML Sequence diagram is transformed into a process, which has its actions determined by the Message classes covered by the corresponding Lifeline class. For each sequence diagram, a model transformation rule in Xtend initializes and creates an IGInitialNode and an IGFinalNode for a corresponding InteractionGraph. After that, for each synchronous message call or signal call in the Sequence diagram a IGCallNode is created, and for each reply message a IGReplyNode is created.

IGCallNodes and IGReplyNodes are labeled with "cn-" and "rn-", respectively, followed by the name of the corresponding Message class. In the current implementation of the model transformations in Xtend, we do not yet handle asynchronous message calls, which will be one of our concerns as future work.

The Labeled Timed Automata model is also obtained from the Internal Application model by means of transformations between models implemented using the Xtend language of the openArchitectureWare framework ([17]). For each InteractionGraph we have a ltaProcess, where the ltaLocations will correspond to the IGNodes and the ltaTransitions will represent the IGEdges. The ltaSelection, ltaGuard, ltaSynchronization, and ltaUpdate attributes will capture the control flow represented in the InteractionGraph.

7   Case Study

The case study consists of a real-time embedded system dedicated to the automation and control of an intelligent wheelchair, which has several functions, such as movement control, collision avoidance, navigation, target pursuit, battery control, system supervision, task scheduling, and automatic movement. In order to illustrate the generation of an internal application model from a UML model, we focus only on the wheelchair movement control, whose simplified UML class diagram is shown in Figure 5. The UML class diagram in Figure 5 shows the MoveCtrl class, which represents the wheelchair movement controller with sensor and actuator drivers (represented by the Driver class), and a navigation mechanism (represented by the Navigator class with a Joystick component). There are two types of movement controllers (represented by MoveS and MoveC classes) that have different functions to determine each move for the wheelchair. In Figure 6(a), the UML sequence diagram defines how the possible execution scenarios for the application are composed. As shown in Figure 6(a), we have a parallel composition of the UML sequence diagrams, which are shown in Figure 6(b), and Figures 7(a), and (b). In Figure 8(a), we have a graphical representation of the CDFG corresponding to the generated InteractionGraph

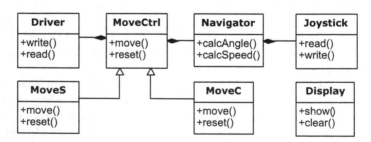

Fig. 5. Application Model: UML class diagram

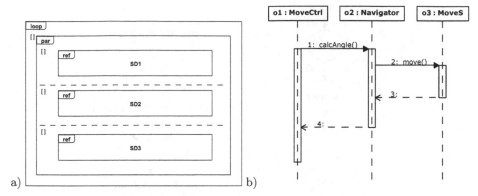

Fig. 6. UML Sequence Diagrams: a) Main b) SD1

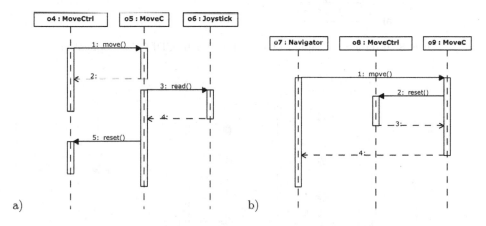

Fig. 7. UML Sequence Diagrams: a) SD2 b) SD3

for the Sequence diagram $SD1$ from Figure 6(a). The IGCallNodes cn-m1 and cn-m2 represent the message calls for calc Angle() and move() in the $SD1$, respectively. The IGReplyNodes rn-m1 and rn-m2 represent the corresponding reply messages for calcAngle() and move() in the same $SD1$, respectively. The InteractionGraph for the entire application is shown in Figure 8(b), where we have three IGExecutableNodes cn-ig1, cn-ig2, and cn-ig3, which are associated by the relation L to the corresponding InteractionGraphs of the sequence diagrams $SD1$, $SD2$, and $SD3$, respectively.

From the InteractionGraph in Figure 8, we obtain the network of timed automata shown in Figure 9. For the sequence diagram SD1, we have a ltaProcess PSD1 with six Locations (corresponding to the IGnodes labeled Start-IG-SD1, cn-m1, cn-m2, rn-m1, rn-m2, and cn-Final-IG-SD1) and five ltaTransitions (corresponding to the IG Edges labeled e1, e2, e3, e4, and e5). We also have a lpqProcess PWheelchair for the entire application. By using the Xpand

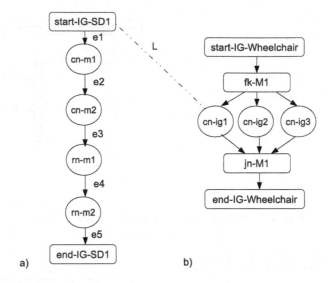

Fig. 8. InteractionGraph: a) CDFG for SD1 b) CDFG for application

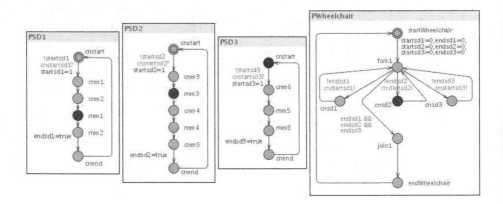

Fig. 9. Network of LTA in Uppaal for InteractionGraph

language of the openArchitectureWare framework ([17]), we implemented model-to-code transformations that generate, from the LTA model, the textual input for the Uppaal model checker. At this point, the designer can specify logical properties using CTL formulae and use Uppaal to verify them, as illustrated by Figure 10.

As shown in Figure 10, we have specified a property to check if the application model is deadlock-free (using the Uppaal macro A[] not deadlock) and if eventually the processes corresponding to the sequence diagrams will be executed all in parallel (using the CTL formula E<> startsd1 and startsd2 and startsd3).

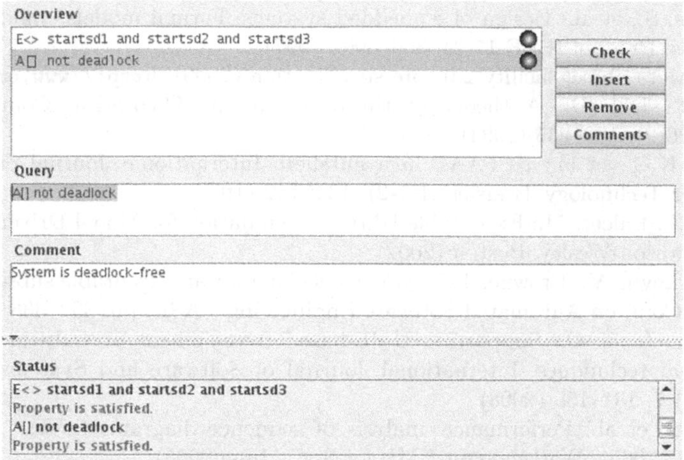

Fig. 10. Proving properties in Uppaal

8   Conclusions and Future Work

In this paper, the MDE fundamental notion of transformation between models is used to generate an internal representation model to be used by formal verification and co-synthesis tools, from a UML model of an application consisting of Class and Sequence diagrams. The obtained model captures structural aspects of an application model by using a hierarchy of modules and processes, as well as behavioral aspects by means of a control/data flow graph model.

We are currently implementing co-synthesis algorithms based on this internal representation model conforming to the Internal Application Meta-Model (IAMM) and using the concept of transformations between models from MDE to perform the co-synthesis tasks, as, for example, the task of hardware/software partitioning applied on the processes represented by the InteractionGraphs of an application. Some types of message calls and combined fragments in the sequence diagrams of UML 2.0 are not yet handled by our current implementation and will be one of our topics for future work.

Acknowledgements

This work described herein was partly supported by the German Ministry for Education and Research (BMBF) through the ITEA2 project TIMMO (01IS07002).

References

1. Schmidt, D.C.: Model driven engineering. IEEE Computer 23(2), 25–31 (2004)
2. OMG: MDA guide version 1.0.1 (2003), http://www.omg.org
3. OMG: UML - unified modeling language (2009), http://www.omg.org

4. Edwards, S., et al.: Design of embedded systems: Formal models, validation, and synthesis. Proc. of IEEE 15(3), 366–390 (1997)
5. OMG: Meta object facility 2.0 core specification (2009), http://www.omg.org
6. Alur, R., Dill, D.: A theory of timed automata. Theoretical Computer Sciences 126(2), 183–235 (1994)
7. Larsen, K.G., et al.: UPPAAL in a nutshell. International Journal on Software Tools for Technology Transfers 1(1-2), 134–152 (1997)
8. Mellor, S., Balcer, M.: Executable UML: A foundation for Model Driven Architecture. Addison-Wesley, Boston (2002)
9. Xie, F., Levin, V., Browne, J.C.: Model checking for an executable subset of UML. In: Int. Conf. on Automated Software Engineering - ASE, pp. 333–336 (2001)
10. Hooman, J., et al.: Supporting UML-based development of embedded systems by formal techniques. International Journal of Software and Systems Modeling (SoSym) 7, 131–155 (2008)
11. Viehl, A., et al.: Performance analysis of sequence diagrams for soc design. In: UMLSoC 2005 - Workshop on UML for SoC (June 2005)
12. Balarin, F., et al.: Hardware-Software Co-Design of Embedded Systems: The Polis Approach. Kluwer Academic Publishers, Boston (1997)
13. do Nascimento, F.A.M., da Oliveira, M.F.S., Wehrmeister, M.A., Pereira, C.E., Wagner, F.R.: MDA-based approach for embedded software generation from a UML/MOF repository. In: Brazilian Symposium on Integrated Circuits (SBCCI), pp. 143–148 (2006)
14. do Nascimento, F.A.M., Oliveira, M.F.S., Wagner, F.R.: ModES: Embedded systems design methodology and tools based on MDE. In: International Workshop on Model-Based Methodologies for Pervasive and Embedded Software (MOMPES), pp. 67–76 (2007)
15. Lee, E.A.: Overview of the ptolemy project - technical memorandum UCB/ERL m03/25. Technical report, University of California, Berkeley, CA, USA (July 2003)
16. Garousi, V., et al.: Control flow analysis of UML 2.0 sequence diagrams. In: Hartman, A., Kreische, D. (eds.) ECMDA-FA 2005. LNCS, vol. 3748, pp. 160–174. Springer, Heidelberg (2005)
17. openArchitectureWare: openarchitectureware portal (2009), http://www.openarchitectureware.org

Systematic Model-in-the-Loop Test of Embedded Control Systems

Alexander Krupp and Wolfgang Müller

Paderborn University/C-LAB, Fuerstenallee 11, 33102 Paderborn, Germany
alexander.krupp@c-lab.de, wolfgang.mueller@c-lab.de

Abstract. Current model-based development processes offer new opportunities for verification automation, e.g., in automotive development. The duty of functional verification is the detection of design flaws. Current functional verification approaches exhibit a major gap between requirement definition and formal property definition, especially when analog signals are involved. Besides lack of methodical support for natural language formalization, there does not exist a standardized and accepted means for formal property definition as a target for verification planning. This article addresses several shortcomings of embedded system verification. An Enhanced Classification Tree Method is developed based on the established *Classification Tree Method for Embeded Systems* CTM/ES which applies a hardware verification language to define a verification environment.

1 Introduction

Verification cost has become a major cost factor in mechatronic systems development and in electronic design. Verification cost mitigation has become a priority, and any efficiency increase in verification contributes substantially to overall development efficiency.

This article describes an approach which supports the definition of a functional verification plan for mechatronic systems with full support for testbench automation, traceability, visibility, and repeatability. We introduce a methodology to close the gap between requirements and test definition by means of an enhanced classification tree method (CTM). It supports functional stimulus patterns, acceptance criteria which are compatible to the stimulus definition, and test quality criteria. The latter relate to requirements and they enable requirements coverage. Horizontal and vertical reuse is facilitated by the unified notation of the enhanced CTM. A concept for automation of the testbench execution is presented to reduce cost- and time -intensive manual human intervention in the verification process. Ideally, this leads to higher throughput of test cases due to reduced setup times for faster or more intense testing.

1.1 Mechatronic vs. Electronic Systems Design

Todays mechatronic systems development processes are increasingly dealing with a formal model of the mechatronic system, which enables code generation as well

A. Rettberg et al. (Eds.): IESS 2009, IFIP AICT 310, pp. 171–184, 2009.

as early verification of system features. Currently, model-based development is an accepted methodology in mechatronics systems design, which is being established in industry. The use of models and associated code generation replaces traditional manual coding for electronic control units. The increasing development productivity enables the creation of models of increasing complexity. While code generation removes many sources of coding errors, it cannot remove flaws in the models themselves. However, the use of models in mechatronic systems development opens up additional opportunities for verification. E.g., the automotive industry applies test and simulation environments at several levels of abstraction. Model-In-The-Loop (MIL) environments are applied to tests at model level with, e.g., MATLAB/Simulink. The integration of hardware and software on an embedded control unit (ECU) is being tested by means of a Hardware-In-The-Loop (HIL) environment. Sometimes additional abstraction levels, such as Software-In-The-Loop (SIL) and Processor-In-The-Loop (PIL) technologies are applied. Recently, with increasing computation power, the construction of virtual prototypes, i.e., a combination of behavioral and geometrical models, has become feasible. The focus of existing technology is on efficiency gains in the development and in the integration of models and hardware rather than extensive verification. The existence of a formal mechatronic model, however, paves the way towards extensive verification beyond the capabilities of a physical prototype. With formal verification for mechatronic systems being introduced mostly at research level, the most widespread mode of verification remains simulation and testing. Existing test tools by, e.g., National Instruments, dSPACE, Etas, Vector, and MBtech are rather specialized and apply proprietary languages and proprietary concepts.

Todays test patterns for mechatronic systems are either defined manually as fixed waveforms, or generated automatically from models. Automatic test pattern generation for mechatronic systems either derives test patterns from the model-under-test itself, or it requires the redundant creation of a reference model at the same level of abstraction [22]. The drawback of the first approach is that it does not support the generation of test patterns to detect missing functionality. The drawback of the second approach is that it requires the development of another model of similar complexity as the model-under-test. Both approaches derive their test patterns from models instead of from requirements. The relation of requirements to a model and, consequentially, to generated test patterns, remains unspecified.

Classification Tree Method CTM and CTM/ES. *Classification Trees* were introduced during the early 90s by Grimm and Grochtmann for the structured representation of test cases [10, 11]. The construction of classification trees and their associated combination tables is supported by the Classification-Tree Method (CTM), which is derived from the category-partition method [19]. In its basic form, a classification tree and the accompanying combination table describe abstract high-level test cases in a graphical manner without an explicit notion of time. Since 1999, the method and notion has been enhanced by Conrad and Fey to accommodate the description of time-dependent test scenarios termed test sequences [5, 4]. These extensions are known as the Classification-Tree Method for Embedded Systems CTM/ES. The CTM/ES has recently been successfully employed in different control software development projects [17]. One of the main application areas is the testing of in-vehicle software developed in a model-based way [21]. Strengths of the CTM/ES approach are the description of time-continuous test patterns [6], it may also be applied as a front-end to Time Partition Testing [18].

The CTM/ES is mainly applied in the automotive domain. Several tools exist for editing classification trees (CTE/XL, Razorcat CTE) and for test data derivation support (MTest). The syntax of classification trees is a simple graphical notation. Its main advantage is the combination of discrete and continuous elements by means of interpolation for stimuli generation. Randomized stimuli instantiation is supported. However, it does not provide a gradual path towards directed test data definition.

Functional Verification. In the domain of electronic design the concept of model-based engineering across several levels of abstraction has been employed for several decades. Formal verification, simulation and testing are employed on a regular basis. The increasing demand for verification at an early abstraction level, like system level, has led to the creation and introduction of methods and languages for *functional verification*. Functional verification is a methodology, which encompasses formal verification as well as simulation approaches. It builds on the declarative formulation of design properties as formal requirements, which provide a redundant path from natural language and semi-formal requirements to the design to enable consistency checks. Once defined, the formal properties can be applied for formal verification as well as for verification by simulation. Meanwhile, libraries and methodological guidelines have become available to supplement the tooling and standardization efforts, such as the *Verification Methodology Manual for SystemVerilog* and the *Open Verification Methodology*. Today, the domain of electronic design is able to apply a rather complete methodology for functional verification of digital designs [2].

2   Shortcomings of Mechatronic System Verification

Model-based development requires a thorough verification approach at modeling level before any code generation and implementation on an execution platform is performed. Generally, for verification purposes a requirements document in model-based development has to be accompanied by a verification document, the so-called *verification plan*. This document captures information, which does not belong into the requirements document, but is yet essential for successful implementation of a substantial verification task. As shown in figure 1, requirements guide the development of a mechatronic system model, whereas the verification plan determines verification goals, which are derived from the requirements as well. For testing purposes, the verification plan also needs to determine the actual system interfaces from the actual model-under-test. On application to

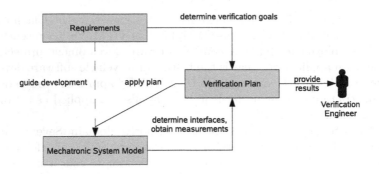

Fig. 1. Verification Plan, Requirements and Mechatronic Model

the model-under-test, execution of the verification plan connects a testbench to the model interfaces, which then provides stimuli to the model-under-test, obtains measurements from it and provides verification results to the verification engineer.

In comparison to the electronic design verification approach, we observe several methodical shortcomings in mechatronic system verification.

1. Support for traceability and visibility is limited.
2. A methodical gap exists between requirements and testbench definition for mechatronic systems. This is due to
   (a) missing methodical support for the derivation of test descriptions from natural language requirements,
   (b) missing stimulus patterns which describe requirements,
   (c) missing requirements-based acceptance criteria,
   (d) missing test quality criteria for requirements coverage, which are easily derived,
3. Missing horizontal and vertical re-use of test definitions.

The limited support for traceability and visibility is due to the lack of functional coverage definitions, which can provide an independent means of requirement coverage measurement for tracing tested requirements, and for visibility of the current state of verification. The methodical gap from requirements exists for several reasons: a methodical support for derivation of test descriptions requires a suitable target. As most requirements allow an infinite number of possible stimuli, a directed stimulus definition cannot capture such a requirement, as it represents a single instance of stimulus only. However, the CTM/ES provides a first step for the definition of functional stimulus patterns. The definition of requirements based acceptance criteria for automatic acceptance evaluation is only possible usually by definition of accepting predicates. Existing predicate languages do not cover the definition of characteristic acceptance criteria for continuous systems. Existing proposals for test quality criteria are usually based on structural coverage criteria, which do not easily relate to requirements. Moreover, the re-use of test descriptions is only possible with high effort. Similar drawbacks have been described for mixed-signal verification in [3].

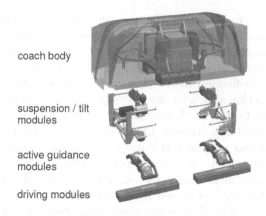

coach body

suspension / tilt
modules

active guidance
modules

driving modules

Fig. 2. Modules of the RailCab Shuttle

3   Example System: RailCab Suspension-Tilt Module

RailCab is a linear motor driven train system developed by the University of
Paderborn [23]. RailCab is based on shuttles, which are composed of modules, which are arranged as shown in figure 2. The coach body is mounted on
two suspension-tilt modules, which are used for active suspension and tilting.
The suspension-tilt modules are coupled to the active guidance modules via air
springs. The active guidance modules can actively rotate the axles relative to
the rails to avoid striking the flange against the rail head, they also facilitate the
driving through passive shunting switches. The rotors of the linear motor form
the driving modules which provide propulsion and braking force. The active suspension system of the shuttle does without passive dampers in order to avoid
the propagation of high-frequency disturbance into the coach body. The forces
necessary for the damping are computed by the control and transferred to the
body by displacing the spring bases via hydraulic cylinders [9].

The suspension-tilt module is the sub-system which links the active guidance modules and the coach body of the shuttle. A model of the system exists
as a MATLAB/Simulink model. The model captures the functionality of one
suspension-tilt module. It also contains a model of the coach body, and a model
of the hydraulic system. The model controls the body position relative to the
guidance modules. The elevation, the lateral position of the body, and its angle
relative to the longitudinal axis is controlled. The controller and plant is influ-
enced by the hydraulic pressure, and by disturbing forces. The coach body is to
be controlled to provide maximum comfort for the passengers.

4   Concept for Systematic Testing of Mechatronic
Systems

Main goal of this new approach to systematic testing of mechatronic
systems is to narrow the methodical gap between requirements and testbenches.

Existing methods for functional verification and testing of mechatronic systems lack in expressiveness and do not cover all areas of functional verification. Moreover, there is no accepted and standardized test definition language for control systems. An important precondition for a clean verification process is a plan. The concept of a verification plan is not new, however, current concepts and tools for testing mechatronic systems do only support a limited subset of the aspects of a verification plan. A verification plan has to support traceability, visibility, and repeatability. Traceability of the verification plan is provided by links between requirements and verification plan artifacts, namely stimulus definitions, test quality criteria and acceptance criteria. As the purpose of testing is bug hunting, requirement violations are traced from violated acceptance criteria. Test "completeness" is traced from test quality criteria, which describe covered requirements. Visibility of the state of verification is provided by such requirements coverage. Repeatability in model-based development is maintained through a deterministic simulation and test environment.

Similar to the functional requirements document as a design specification, the verification plan assumes the role of the verification specification. This document captures information, which does not belong into the requirements document, but is yet essential for successful implementation of a substantial verification task. While the requirements are being implemented, concurrently the verification plan has to be implemented. The implementation of a verification plan frequently consumes resources in the order of the design and model implementation. Increased efficiency in the process of verification plan generation and execution therefore results in substantial savings in the overall development process.

Figure 3 gives an overview of the new concept for systematic testing of mechatronic systems. The verification plan is based on the requirements and a so-called *principle solution*, which is a first step in requirements formalization [1]. For increased flexibility and precision of stimulus definition, constraints are applied for declarative stimulus definition, supported by a graphical notation similar to the CTM/ES. A new approach to acceptance criteria definition is introduced, which

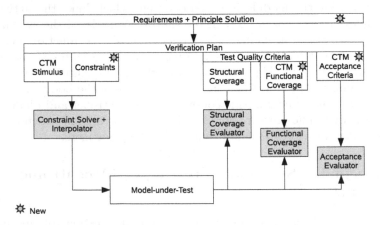

Fig. 3. Verification Plan for Systematic Testing

applies a graphical notation similar to CTM/ES. A new CTM/ES-like notation is applied for functional coverage definition.

Stimulus definition with *constraints* allows requirement based *stimulus pattern* definitions, which can be more accurately targeted for improved test quality: The declarative nature of the constraint-based stimulus patterns enables automatic generation of a wide range of stimuli. As more implementation details become available, the declarative stimulus patterns can be adapted in a straightforward manner. The new notation for *acceptance criteria* complements the stimulus pattern definition and it enables automatic acceptance criteria generation together with stimuli generation for fully automatic testbench execution. Moreover, the level of abstraction of the acceptance criteria definition is different from that of the model-under-test. The expensive creation of a reference model at the same level of abstraction can therefore be avoided for automatic acceptance evaluation. *Test quality criteria* define verification goals. These criteria encompass structural coverage metrics, usually. Structural coverage metrics, however, do not enable the derivation of requirements coverage. Recently, in the domain of electronic design, additional test quality criteria have been introduced by means of *functional coverage*. There are no approaches to functional coverage definition for mechatronic systems, which seamlessly fit into a verification process. A new approach to functional coverage definition for mechatronic systems is defined, which relates to requirements and enables requirements coverage derivation.

The definition of a unified CTM/ES notation for stimulus, acceptance criteria, and test quality criteria immediately enables exchange and re-use of information between, e.g., the stimulus and functional coverage aspects of the notation. Functional coverage definition is a tedious process usually, which can be alleviated by the derivation from previous stimulus pattern definitions.

The test control is described by means of the verification languages for execution of the testbench elements. Current industrial approaches to automatic testbench generation and execution are able to extract a subsystem from a simulation model for, e.g., MATLAB/Simulink. The extracted subsystem interfaces are then mapped into a testbench for automatic execution. One example of such a system is AutomationDesk from dSPACE. The automotive testbench features lack in expressivity though in comparison to state-of-the-art "intelligent testbenches" as exist for electronic design [2, 14].

4.1   Enhanced CTM for Constraint-Based Stimulus Patterns

The original CTM/ES stimuli generation process is rather monolithic and inflexible. It takes a classification tree, instantiates it by means of certain heuristics, interpolates between synchronization points and discretizes the stimulus for test input as illustrated in figure 4. The enhanced CTM provides a new syntax for the constraint based definition of synchronization points, which allows an the definition of constraints between synchronization point timing and value instantiation.

The new and enhanced stimuli generation process is based on a verification language (VL). The classification tree and constraints are mapped to the

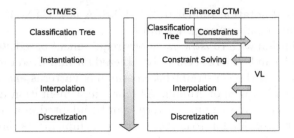

Fig. 4. CTM/ES vs. Enhanced CTM Stimuli Generation Process

Table 1. Stimulus pattern definition with enhanced CTM

	CTM/ES	Enhanced CTM
Randomized instantiation	+	+
Constraint based randomized instantiation	-	+
Synchronization Points with fixed time	+	+
Synchronization Points with constraint based time	-	+
Integration with Verification Language	-	+

+ : supported.
- : unsupported.

verification language, which controls the further generation process of constraint solving, interpolation, and discretization. A randomized constraint solver replaces the former instantiation step. Then, interpolation and discretization are performed under control of the verification language. The mapping and integration of the CTM syntax to a verification language allows to use verification language elements such as additional constraints with the classification tree. This provides a higher control over the value instantiation, as it enables the definition of dependencies between classifications and synchronization point times. The enhancements over CTM/ES are summarized in table 1.

Stimulus Patterns. This section illustrates the definition of stimulus patterns. First, the interface definitions are captured by a classification tree. Based on the interface definition, a raw classification tree is partly automatically derived as described for the CTM/ES, where interfaces become combinations, signals become classifications and classes are setup heuristically for the signal range described for the interface. The tree is then manually readjusted to the feature descriptions of the interface. The resulting tree is shown in figure 5. It shows four classifications related to the input signals of the interface *stim1_if*. For the three signals *z_Anr*, *y_Anr*, and *phi_Anr* the tree shows the automatically derived classes. They cover the signal range as defined for the interface. Three corner cases are generated by the CTM/ES heuristics: the two corner cases of the range, and the value 0. The fourth classification for the hydraulics pressure, *p_Versorgung*, has been modified according to the requirements. In addition to the two standard corner cases, it defines, e.g., the nominal pressure of 120 bar. The nominal pressure range

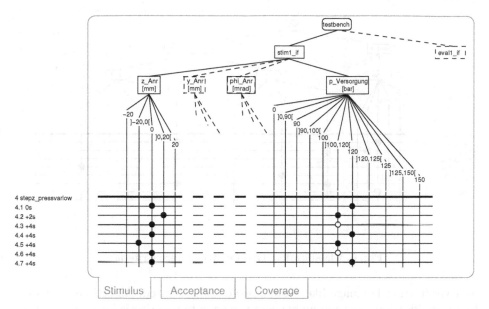

Fig. 5. Classification Tree for Stimulus

generates two more corner cases at 100 bar, and at 125 bar. Another corner case is determined by a low pressure emergency shutdown at 90 bar.

Figure 5 shows a classification tree with one stimulus pattern on the stimulus interface *stim1_if*. The test sequence performs step transitions on a single axis (*z_Anr*), while the hydraulic pressure drops with each movement. The test sequences are translated to SystemVerilog constraints as input to a stimulus generator with constraint solver. Multiple test runs are constraint-randomly generated from a single stimulus pattern with different value instantiations. Additional constraints formulated in SystemVerilog can be inserted for increased control over the stimuli generation. This provides a seamless transition from constraint-randomized to directed stimuli generation.

4.2   Enhanced CTM for Acceptance Criteria

Automatic acceptance evaluation is performed by correlation to a reference model or by predicate evaluation [12, 13]. The definition of continuous, interpolated behavioral boundaries is not covered by current assertion languages, therefore a reference model is required for correlation purposes. The new acceptance criteria based on an enhanced CTM notation can provide such a reference model at the same level of abstraction as the stimulus pattern definition with enhanced CTM. This replaces the effort of redundant creation of a reference model at the same abstraction level as the model-under-test. The acceptance criteria do not attempt to capture the exact behavior of the complete model-under-test, they rather set acceptable *behavioral boundaries* for a certain operational range of the model-under-test. From the CTM representation an acceptance evaluator

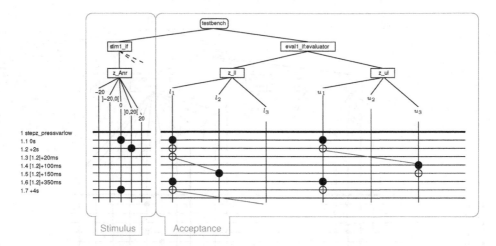

Fig. 6. Classification Tree for Acceptance Criteria

in a verification language like SystemVerilog is generated. Assertions provided by the verification language supplement the acceptance criteria for reporting test results. They provide the link to the testbench evaluation infrastructure of the underlying execution environment.

This section illustrates the definition of acceptance criteria, which fit the stimulus defined in figure 5. The acceptance criteria define a functional relation between stimulus and response. They are defined by an additional classification tree synchronized to the stimulus classification tree for automatic generation of an evaluator (cf. figure 6). The acceptance tree is associated to the response interface *eval1_if* of the testbench. The acceptance aspect of the tree is derived from the interface such that for each signal, a supremum- and an infimum signal is defined as a class. Waveforms generated for these signals enable the formulation of control theoretic system response criteria, such as rise times, transient overshoot, and stabilization time as described in [8, 7].

The acceptance classification tree in figure 6 starts from a root node which represents the *testbench*. On the left hand side, the next lower node represents the stimulus interface *stim1_if*, and, on the right hand side, the next lower node represents the evaluation interface *eval1_if* for the evaluator. The *evaluator* annotation announces the different syntax and semantics of this part of the tree for generation of the evaluator. In the example tree, for the input interface *stim1_if* only the signal *z_Anr* is shown for brevity. Below this node the combination table shows the test sequence *stepz_pressvarlow*. The response signal *aufbauZ* of the interface *eval1_if* is to be evaluated. The signal itself is not present in the classification tree, visually. Instead, the limits for *aufbauZ* are defined below the combination node *eval1_if:evaluator*. A lower limit of *aufbauZ* is defined as classification *z_ll* in the classification tree, and an upper limit is defined as classification *z_ul*.

In classes, functions are specified (l_1, l_2, ...) instead of intervals. They describe the expected functional input-output relation of the model-under-test for a specific operational range. At each acceptance criteria synchronization point, a functional relation is selected, which is then evaluated in relation to the synchronization points of the stimulus. The acceptance criteria represent properties derived from the requirements and from control-theoretic quality criteria, such as transient overshoot, and stabilization time. The definition of a functional relation to certain stimuli definitions enables an exact and automatic evaluation of the system behavior for automatically generated stimuli.

4.3   Enhanced CTM for Functional Coverage

The concept of functional coverage definition [20] has been transferred to classification trees [15, 16] for the definition of functional coverage criteria for mechatronic systems. A classification tree with its value ranges and associated combination table provides the basis for the definition of relevant functional coverage criteria. The concept encompasses the coverage definition for value intervals on specific signals, the cross-coverage of value intervals on several signals, and the (cross-) coverage of transition sequences between the value intervals. The benefit of using classification trees for this purpose is twofold: they alleviate the task of initial formulation of functional coverage criteria and they enable hierarchical reuse of classification tree based stimuli definitions, e.g., from previous test definitions for sub-systems. The operational ranges of mechatronic controls can be captured as test quality criteria, without dependency on a concrete implementation of the system. In short, the CTM stimulus aspect *controls* the operational ranges of a system, whereas the CTM functional coverage aspect *observes* the activated operational ranges of a system for independent test quality evaluation.

The new CTM notation for functional coverage definition builds on the concept of coverpoints employed by the major hardware verification languages in electronic design. Coverpoints are associated to one or more signals and measure the occurrence of several ranges of values, or sequences thereof. Cross

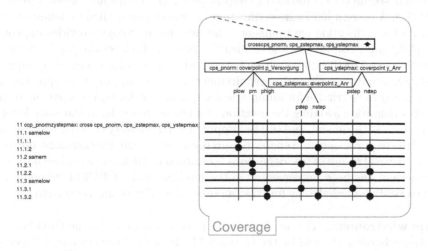

Fig. 7. Classification Tree for Sequence Cross Coverage

coverpoints deal with multiple signals and their value combinations. Figure 7 shows a cross coverpoint definition in classification tree notation as a sub-tree. The top node defines a cross coverpoint over three coverpoints associated to signals *p_Versorgung, y_Anr, z_Anr*. These coverpoints with their value sequences *plow,pm,phigh,pstep,nstep* have been defined elsewhere in the classification tree in the usual CTM notation for sequences. The combination table then describes a coverage of pairwise disturbance of the suspension-tilt platform axes *y* and *z* in the same direction. The pairwise movement is also crossed with the three nominal pressure classes. For the cross coverpoint *ccp_pnormzystepmax* in line 11, the coverpoints to be crossed are duplicated as nodes beneath an additional classification tree node (*cross cps_pnorm, cps_zstepmax, cps_ystepmax*) which selects the crossed signals. On line 11.1, the bin *samelow* captures disturbance movement in the same direction for the low nominal pressure range by selecting `<plow, pstep, pstep>`, or `<plow, nstep, nstep>` on the next two lines. The pattern is repeated for the next two bins *samem*, and *samehigh* for the two pressure ranges *pm*, and *phigh*. Similar patterns define functional coverage for opposite movement of the suspension-tilt platform. By means of measurements defined by this functional coverage metric, it can be determined, whether movement of the platform has been stimulated in selected directions with 3 different ranges of hydraulic pressure. Stimulus definitions can be used as a basis for such metric definitions, as the syntax of the combination table remains identical.

5 Conclusion

This article introduced a new methodology and formalism for the systematic verification of embedded control systems. The formalism enables the definition of formal behavioral properties for a model-based functional verification approach. The formalism applies the new Enhanced Classification Tree Method, which was developed based on the established *Classification Tree Method for Embeded Systems* CTM/ES. A current hardware verification language was applied to definition and control of a verification environment. The new methodology provides improved traceability and visibility for the verification process. It closes the gap between requirements and testbench definition for embedded control systems (i) by support for stimulus patterns capturing requirements, (ii) by support for requirements-based acceptance criteria for automatic acceptance evaluation compatible to the stimulus definition avoiding the creation of a reference model at the same level of abstraction as the model, and (iii) by support for test quality criteria, which relate to specific requirements and enable requirements coverage. Furthermore, horizontal and vertical re-use of test definitions is enabled by means of a unified notation. The method has been implemented in the context of the CRC614, where it was used to verify a mechatronic function module of a railway shuttle system.

Acknowledgement. This work has been partly supported by the DFG Sonderforschungsbereich 614 and by the German Ministry for Education and Research (BMBF) through the ITEA2 project TIMMO (01IS07002).

References

[1] Adelt, P., Donoth, J., Gausemeier, J., Geisler, J., Henkler, S., Kahl, S., Klöpper, B., Krupp, A., Münch, E., Oberthür, S., Paiz, C., Podlogar, H., Porrmann, M., Radkowski, R., Romaus, C., Schmidt, A., Schulz, B., Vöcking, H., Witkowski, U., Witting, K., Znamenshchykov, O.: Selbstoptimierende Systeme des Maschinenbaus – Definitionen, Anwendungen, Konzepte, vol. Band 234. HNI-Verlagsschriftenreihe, Paderborn (2008)

[2] Bailey, B., Martin, G., Piziali, A.: ESL Design and Verification: A prescription for electronic system-level methodology. Morgan Kaufmann series in systems on silicon. Elsevier, San Francisco (2007)

[3] Carter, H.B., Hemmady, S.G.: Metric Driven Design Verification. Springer, Heidelberg (2007)

[4] Conrad, M., Dörr, H., Fey, I., Yap, A.: Model-based Generation and Structured Representation of Test Scenarios. In: Workshop on Software-Embedded Systems Testing (WSEST), Gaithersburg, USA (November 1999)

[5] Conrad, M.: The Classification-Tree Method for Embedded Systems. In: Dagstuhl Seminar Proceedings 04371 (2005)

[6] Conrad, M., Krupp, A.: An Extension of the Classification-Tree Method for Embedded Systems for the Description of Events. In: Second Workshop on Model Based Testing, MBT 2006, Vienna, Austria (March 2006)

[7] Dörrscheidt, F., Latzel, W.: Grundlagen der Regelungstechnik, 2nd edn. Leitfaden der Elektrotechnik. B.G. Teubner, Stuttgart (1993)

[8] Föllinger, O.: Nichtlineare Regelungen II, 7th edn. R. Oldenbourg, Wien (1993)

[9] Geisler, J.: Auslegung und Implementierung der verteilten Aktor- und Aufbauregelung für ein aktiv gefedertes Schienenfahrzeug. Master's thesis, University of Paderborn, Germany (2006)

[10] Grimm, K.: Systematisches Testen von Software – Eine neue Methode und eine effektive Teststrategie (Systematic Software Testing – A new method and an effective test strategy). GMD-Report, vol. 251. GMD, Oldenbourg (1995)

[11] Grochtmann, M., Grimm, K.: Classification Trees for Partition Testing. Software Testing, Verification and Reliability 3(2), 63–82 (1993)

[12] Grossmann, J., Conrad, M., Fey, I., Krupp, A., Lamberg, K., Wewetzer, C.: TestML – A Test Exchange Language for Model-based Testing of Embedded Software. In: Automotive Software Workshop 2006, San Diego (March 2006)

[13] Grossmann, J., Mueller, W.: A Formal Behavioral Semantics for TestML. In: Proc. of IEEE ISoLA 2006, Paphos Cyprus, pp. 453–460 (2006)

[14] ITRS. International technology roadmap for semiconductors 2008 UPDATE (December 2008),
http://www.itrs.net/Links/2008ITRS/Update/2008_Update.pdf

[15] Krupp, A., Müller, W.: Classification Trees for Random Test and Functional Coverage. In: Design, Automation and Test in Europe (DATE 2006), Munich, Germany (March 2006)

[16] Krupp, A., Müller, W.: Systematic Testbench Specification for Constrained Randomized Test and Functional Coverage. In: 21st European Conference on Modelling and Simulation ECMS 2007, Prague, Czech Republic (June 2007)

[17] Lamberg, K., Beine, M., Eschmann, M., Otterbach, R., Conrad, M., Fey, I.: Model-based Testing of Embedded Automotive Software using MTest. SAE 2004 Transactions, Journal of Passenger Cars - Electronic and Electrical Systems 7, 132–140 (2005)

[18] Lehmann, E.: Time partition testing: A method for testing dynamic functional behaviour. In: Proceedings of TEST 2000, London, UK (May 2000)
[19] Ostrand, T.J., Balcer, M.J.: The category-partition method for specifying and generating fuctional tests. Commun. ACM 31(6), 676–686 (1988)
[20] Piziali, A.: Functional Verification Coverage Measurement and Analysis. Springer, New York (2004)
[21] Rau, A.: Model-Based Development of Embedded Automotive Control Systems. PhD thesis, Dept. of Computer Science, University of Tübingen, Germany (2002)
[22] Schäuffele, J., Zurawka, T.: Automotive Software Engineering, 3rd edn. Vieweg, Wiesbaden (2006)
[23] Trächtler, A., Münch, E., Vöcking, H.: Iterative learning and self-optimization techniques for the innovative railcab-system. In: 32nd Annual Conference of the IEEE Industrial Electronics Society — IECON 2006, Paris, France (2006)

Proteus, a Hybrid Virtualization Platform for Embedded Systems

Daniel Baldin and Timo Kerstan

Heinz-Nixdorf-Institute
University of Paderborn
33102 Paderborn, Germany
dbaldin@uni-paderborn.de,
timo.kerstan@uni-paderborn.de

Abstract. By the use of virtualization the security of a system can be significantly increased and performance can be improved by sharing hardware resources while reducing the overall costs of the whole system. Nowadays virtualization also finds approval within the field of embedded systems. However, the currently available virtualization platforms designed for embedded systems only support para-virtualization trying to provide reasonable performance and support realtime applications only by the use of dedicated resources. Our approach introduces a hybrid configurable hypervisor architecture designed to support real-time applications. We do not restrict the set of applications which can be run virtualized on top of our hypervisor to para-virtualized applications but also allow applications to run unmodified or even partly para-virtualized while using state of the art methodologies to obtain high performance.

Introduction

In the last decade, embedded systems tended to become increasingly complex systems while retaining the requirements of security and robustness. This inherent problem has usually been faced by the use of redundancy in which the whole hardware and software system is replicated multiple times to compensate a broken system. Additionally, embedded systems applications also often serve completely unrelated purposes which raises the need of being isolated from each other. Virtualization offers a solution to all of these problems, allowing the coexistence of multiple virtual machines on one hardware platform. By the use of virtual resources, the security of a system can be significantly increased [Heiser, 2008] [Chen and Noble, 2001] [Smith and Nair, 2005] and performance can be gained by sharing hardware resources while reducing the overall costs of the whole system [Chen and Noble, 2001]. The rapid increasing performance of embedded system hardware and the increasing availability of memory protection mechanisms inside embedded system processors make virtualization inside embedded systems more and more attractive.

A. Rettberg et al. (Eds.): IESS 2009, IFIP AICT 310, pp. 185–194, 2009.

1   Related Work

There already exist a few commercial virtualization platforms or hypervisors for a range of embedded processors with nearly all of them being proprietary systems. Trango [VmWare, 2009] and VirtualLogix [VirtualLogix, 2009] are two of those hypervisors allowing virtualization for a range of ARM and MIPS processors. Greenhills Integrity [Hills, 2009] and LynxSecure [LynuxWorks, 2009] are using virtualization to implement high security systems targeted for the military market and have been certified to fulfill the EAL7 standard. All of these available products only use para-virtualization trying to provide reasonable performance and support realtime applications only by the use of dedicated resources. Naturally, this limits the applicability of virtualization using these products to a subset of all possible scenarios. Especially, whenever there are applications that can not be para-virtualized since the source code is not available these applications can not be virtualized using the currently available virtualization products as this would require a binary analysis of the whole application which most often is not completely possible [Laune C. Harris, 2006] [Saumya Debray, 1998].

Our approach overcomes this problem by introducing a hybrid configurable hypervisor architecture designed and implemented for the PowerPC405 processor which allows the virtualization of unmodified applications as well as para-virtualized applications or a combination of both. Support for realtime applications was a major goal of our design which allows the integration of any kind of scheduling mechanism for virtual machines while being completely deterministic. Additionally, the high configurability allows the system to be optimized explicitly for the intended field of use.

2   Hybrid Architecture

The basic requirements which the design of this virtualization platform faces are:

- Security
- Real-time capabilities
- High performance
- Configurability
- Minimal demand on memory and energy consumption

In order to meet the requirements of high performance and configurability, the virtualization platform uses a hybrid architecture as depicted in figure 1. Therefore, it represents a hybrid hypervisor which uses full-virtualization as the basic virtualization technique with additional support for para-virtualization. Partially para-virtualized applications or self modifying applications are also supported by the use of a fallback feature which ensures the consistency while executing in and switching between both kind of states. The configurability of the hypervisor and the para-virtualization interface allows the system designer to create a system which is tailored for the particular field of application and saves as much memory as possible.

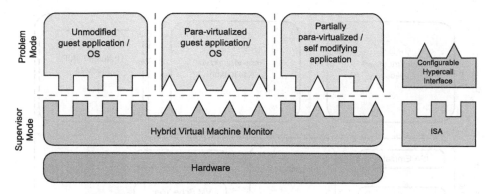

Fig. 1. The virtual machine monitor allows the virtualized execution of any kind of guest application. Left: a unmodified application. Middle: a completely para-virtualized application. Right: a partially modified application.

In general, the design is based on the multiple independent levels of security (MILS) architecture [Systems, 2008]. As illustrated in figure 2, only the minimal set of components which are needed to implement the secure partitioning, scheduling and communication between virtual machines are part of the hypervisor running in privileged mode. All other components called "Untrusted VMP Modules" are placed inside a separate partition and are executed in user mode as this is one of the fundamental concepts of the MILS architecture. The communication between partitions is controlled by the Inter Partition Communication Manager (IPCM) who, on request, creates shared memory tunnels between two partitions which can be used for virtual machines to ease the communication between each other. Especially this feature allows formerly physically spread systems which had to use real-time capable bus systems (e.g. a CAN-bus) for communication to enhance the security, robustness and performance of the information flow between each other if they are virtualized and placed on top of the same hypervisor.

The fundamental components of the whole system form the interrupt handler as seen in figure 2. Since the hypervisor executes the guest application in user mode, any interrupt occurring is first delegated to the hypervisor which then has to analyze the interrupt and forward it to the appropriate component or the virtual machine itself. Program interrupts raised amongst others by privileged instructions inside the guest application are forwarded to the emulation routine dispatcher which will determine the corresponding ISA emulation routine. Whenever the virtualization platform has been configured to support para-virtualization, applications running inside a virtual machine can use hypercalls to emulate privileged instructions, call the IPCM, use para-virtualized I/O drivers or call scheduler related functions. Especially the last component offers methods to set scheduler related parameters at runtime or the possibility to yield the cpu directly in order to allow system designers to incorporate special scheduling mechanisms.

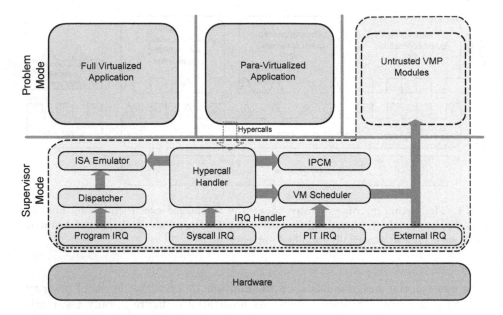

Fig. 2. Information and control flow of the components used inside the virtualization platform

3   Concepts

3.1   Configurability

Achieving only a small overhead as needed for the intended field of use was one of the major design goals of this system. This goal is met by the high flexibility offered through the possibility to configure a wide range of system components. Using the provided configuration files, the system designer is able to enable or disable features of the virtual machine monitor or specify which parts of the hypercall interface shall be supported. The principle workflow of the configuration is depicted in figure 3. The whole configuration workflow is based on the extensive usage of preprocessor statements. Based on the configuration files the preprocessor eliminates, adds or changes code segments inside the implementation files to create a source code which does not suffer from unneeded code parts any more. This is a very valuable feature if the platform is about to be deployed inside a very memory-limited environment.

Our virtualization platform allows the system designer to explicitly define whether there is the need for full-virtualization or para-virtualization or even both. It is even possible to configure the support for special parts of the host ISA as e.g. support for virtual memory. The hypercall interface may explicitly be configured by defining whether para-virtualized drivers are supported, inter partition communication is needed and which scheduler has to be used. Each of the components can then be configured as well to allow the platform to match the needs of the target system to a maximum amount.

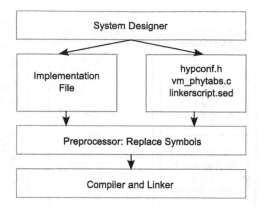

Fig. 3. Configuration flow of the virtualization platform

3.2 Innocuous Register File Mapping

Virtualizing the processor is one of the main tasks of the virtual machine monitor. Every virtual machine gets its own set of virtual registers stored inside the Register File as depicted in figure 4a. Whenever the virtual machine is activated, the registers are copied into the registers of the physical processor. During the execution the virtual machine has unrestricted access to the user space registers of the processor. Registers that need to be accessed by the use of privileged instructions will trap to the virtual machine monitor which then emulates the behaviour of that instruction on the virtual register inside the register file. However, there exist registers which can be accessed without having immediate influence on the state or behaviour of the virtual machine. An example is given by the Save Restore Registers (SRR) of the PowerPC Processor. The value of these registers will only be used whenever the processor executes the privileged "recover from interrupt" (rfi) instruction. In order to speed up the access to this kind of registers, Proteus uses a technique we call Innocuous Register File Mapping (IRFM) which allows virtual registers to be mapped to memory pages inside the virtual machines accessible memory area as illustrated in figure 4b. Virtual registers, which may be read directly without the need of any emulation, are mapped into a read-only memory page. Registers, that can be either read or written without immediate influence, are made accessible inside a readable and writable memory page whose address can be configured to conform to the systems memory map. Therefore, access to these registers is possible by using load and store commands instead of trapping to the virtual machine monitor which speeds up the virtualized execution of a program dramatically. A similar approach has been used inside the ia64 port of the Xen hypervisor [Barham et al., 2003] for desktop systems to speedup the information flow between the hypervisor and the virtual machines. However, the approach has not been applied completely to all possible registers of the ISA as this virtualization platform does.

Since the IRFM feature can only be used by para-virtualized applications, partially modified applications may still use privileged instructions to access the virtual registers. In order to ensure the consistency of the mapped registers and

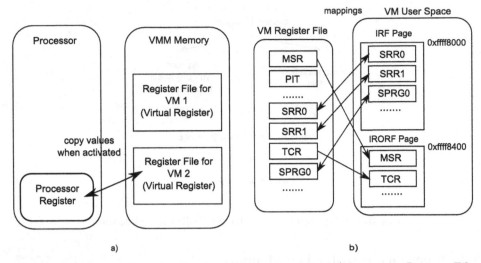

Fig. 4. a) Processor Virtualization by using Register Files. b) Innocuous Register File Mapping. Temporarily innocuous register are mapped into pages inside the VM memory space.

the virtual registers inside the register file, the virtual machine monitor updates the mapped registers whenever a value is written to the register file. This feature is called the Innocuous Register File Mapping Fallback Feature and may be enabled if the system designer is unsure whether all privileged instructions are para-virtualized or not. Especially for systems using third party libraries without access to the source code this is a very valuable feature.

3.3   Pre-virtualization Support

As some features like the IRFM are only accessible for para-virtualized applications, our virtualization platform supports a technique called Pre-Virtualization [LeVasseur et al., 2006] which is based on the principle of binary replacement. The technique is based on the idea to append "no operation" (nop) instructions to every privileged instruction inside the guests' applications source code in order to create space for a later replacement of these instructions by hypercall instructions to the virtual machine monitor. The overall process is illustrated exemplarily in figure 5. We developed a python script which first parses the source code of an application for privileged instructions. Whenever a privileged instruction is found, its address is stored inside a pre-virtualization table together with the binary code of the hypercall instructions. The code itself is only modified by appending nop instructions to the privileged instructions found. Therefore the intermediate pre-virtualized code can still be executed natively. At loadtime, the virtual machine monitor finally para-virtualizes the pre-virtualized applications by the use of the pre-virtualization table which is stored within the applications data area.

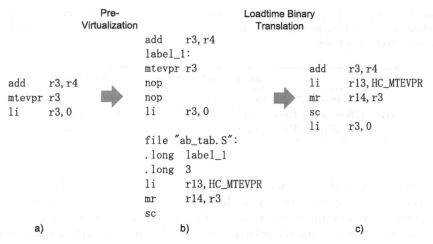

Fig. 5. Pre-Virtualization illustrated. a) Base source code. b) Pre-Virtualized source code and Pre-Virtualization table. c) The final para-virtualized code.

3.4   Programming Concept

A substantial part of the virtual machine monitor is comprised of the interrupt handler. Since a significant amount of time is spent inside these routines, most of the components called by the handlers and the handler themselves are directly written in assembly language. By using this methodology it was possible to create source code without the usual overhead induced by higher level languages like C oder C++ and EABI overheads like saving/restoring stack frames. Actually the implemented virtual machine monitor operates without using a stack as often as possible. The amount of registers used by the interrupt handler and emulation routines has been minimized as well to reduce the amount of time needed for a context switch between the virtual machine and the emulation software. Only if higher level activities are processed as e.g. calling the VM scheduler or triggering a driver, the whole context of the virtual machine needs to be saved. Additionally every operation of the virtual machine monitor has been implemented to behave deterministically in order to allow the calculation of an upper bound for the execution time of these operations.

4   Performance Figures

The performance overhead introduced by the virtualization software has been measured for a set of application scenarios. We used the real-time operating system ORCOS [University of Paderborn, 2009] running on a PowerPC405 processor to measure the overhead for two application scenarios. The first scenario used a simple periodic real-time task with the only purpose to count a variable to a specific value. The execution time was measured for an interval of two hundred repetitions to get a reasonable measurement. The overhead produced here was

Table 1. Execution in ms measured for a set of application scenarios and the corresponding percental lengthening of the execution time for the best case compared to the native execution time

	native	full-virt	para-virt	Overhead
ORCOS + CTask	10,7342	26,5085	17,1618	59,88%
ORCOS + FFTTask	5094,97	5123,382	5117,936	0,45%
SimpleFFT	294,564	294,564	294,564	0,00%

about 60% compared to the native execution time. The high overhead in this scenario can be easily explained by the fact that the amount of time spent inside the operating system compared to the amount of time spent inside the real-time task was really high. Thus the relative amount of privileged instructions used by the operating system which needed to be emulated was high as well leading to this kind of overhead.

A more realistic scenario was given by another real-time task which had to calculate a Fast Fourier Transformation for a set of input values for a fixed amount of repetitions. Since the relative amount of time spent for this calculation was much higher compared to the amount of emulation routines called the overhead reduced to less then one percent if the application was executed para-virtualized. It is also possible to see that running the unmodified application in full-virtualization mode is only slightly slower. The overhead increased by 0.56% in that case. Considering embedded control systems, which often consist of a comparable amount of calculations, this makes the usage of full-virtualization extremely interesting. Additionally, this observation gives reason to believe that the execution time of applications that could not be para-virtualized completely, since e.g. a part of the application has been linked against static libraries, will not suffer much by running inside our virtual machine.

Applications using only the user ISA, as given by the third example application SimpleFFT which calculated a Fast Fourier Transformation without using the support of an operating system, can be executed with native performance because no instruction needs to be emulated by the virtual machine monitor.

5   Footprint

In order to be deployed on small scale nodes, the memory overhead introduced by the virtual machine monitor needs to be as small as possible. Since Proteus is completely configurable, the amount of binary and memory footprint occupied by the virtual machine monitor strongly depends on the features used by the target system. The basis system, which already supports full-virtualization of the ISA and which is able to emulate a fairly complete set of privileged instructions needs about 4.4 Kb for the binary and about 2.5 Kb for the data structures whereas about 2.4 Kb of the data area, together with the whole text area, may be placed inside the ROM of the host platform. The biggest fraction of the data

Table 2. Binary and memory footprint of the virtualization platform in bytes for a set of configurable components for the PowerPC405 processor (32 Bit Architecture)

	.text	.data
Basis System	4348	2444
Para-Virtualization Support	252	144
IRFM Support	516	0
IRFM Fallback Support	572	0
Pre-Virtualization Support	192	0
TLB Virtualization Support	960	0
Driver Support	504	44
IPCM Support	460	4

area is used for dispatching purposes of the ISA emulation dispatcher. Adding Para-Virtualization support, including the whole IRFM feature set, increases the footprint by additional 1.5 Kb. The whole system (with all its features) has a footprint of under 11 Kb with 10 Kb being read-only data or executable code respectively which could be placed inside the ROM memory area of the platform.

The sizes listed above do not include the required space for the register files of the virtual machines. Depending on how many virtual machines the hypervisor shall support, additional 304 bytes need to be reserved for every virtual machine for our target processor the PowerPC405. If the TLB needs to be virtualized as well, in order to allow the virtual machines to use virtual memory, the reserved bytes per virtual machine increases by 956.

6   Conclusion and Future Work

In this work we presented the first hybrid configurable virtualization platform which supports full-virtualization and para-virtualization as well as a mixture of both as needed. The high configurability allows the system designer to adapt the platform for its dedicated field of use. This feature allows the system to be very small and efficient as the maximum memory overhead induced by the virtual machine monitor is below 11Kb which lets Proteus compete with current State of the Art virtualization platforms like Trango or VirtualLogix.

The system combines state of the art features like the IRFM feature and Pre-Virtualization while being implemented directly in assembler to minimize the overhead. Our newly introduced IRFM Fallback feature ensures the consistency while switching between full and para-virtualization. It is designed and implemented to support real-time applications and offers an interface to add deterministic real-time capable hierarchical scheduling mechanisms as e.g. described in [Lipari and Bini, 2005] in the future.

We are currently working on further measurements demonstrating the real-time capabilities of the system. Additionally we are working on dynamic self-optimizing features that shall be integrated into the system in the future.

References

[Barham et al., 2003] Barham, P., Dragovic, B., Fraser, K., Hand, S., Harris, T., Ho, A., Neugebauery, R., Pratt, I., Warfield, A.: Xen and the Art of Virtualization. ACM, New York (2003)

[Chen and Noble, 2001] Chen, P.M., Noble, B.D.: When virtual is better than real. In: HOTOS 2001: Proceedings of the Eighth Workshop on Hot Topics in Operating Systems, Washington, DC, USA, p. 133. IEEE Computer Society, Los Alamitos (2001)

[Heiser, 2008] Heiser, G.: The role of virtualization in embedded systems. In: IIES 2008: Proceedings of the 1st workshop on Isolation and integration in embedded systems, pp. 11–16. ACM, New York (2008)

[Hills, 2009] Hills, G.: Real-Time Operating Systems (RTOS), Embedded Development Tools, Optimizing Compilers, IDE tools, Debuggers - Green Hills Software (2009), http://www.ghs.com/

[Laune C. Harris, 2006] Laune, C., Harris, B.P.M.: Practical Analysis of Stripped Binary Code. Technical report, Computer Sciences Department, University of Wisconsin (2006)

[LeVasseur et al., 2006] LeVasseur, J., Uhlig, V., Chapman, M., Chubb, P., Leslie, B., Heiser, G.: Pre-virtualization: soft layering for virtual machines. Technical Report 2006-15, Fakultät für Informatik, Universität Karlsruhe, TH (2006)

[Lipari and Bini, 2005] Lipari, G., Bini, E.: A methodology for designing hierarchical scheduling systems. J. Embedded Comput. 1(2), 257–269 (2005)

[LynuxWorks, 2009] LynuxWorks, Embedded Hypervisor and Separation Kernel for Operating-system Virtualization: LynxSecure (2009), http://www.lynuxworks.com/virtualization/hypervisor.php

[Saumya Debray, 1998] Debray, S., Muth, R., Weippert, M.: Alias Analysis of Executable Code. Technical report, Department of Computer Science, University of Arizona (1998)

[Smith and Nair, 2005] Smith, J., Nair, R.: The architecture of virtual machines. Computer 38(5), 32–38 (2005)

[Systems, 2008] Systems, O.I.: MILS Technical Primer (2008), http://www.ois.com/Products/MILS-Technical-Primer.html

[University of Paderborn, 2009] University of Paderborn, ORCOS (2009), https://orcos.cs.uni-paderborn.de/orcos/

[VirtualLogix, 2009] VirtualLogix, VirtualLogix - Real-time Virtualization for Connected Devices: Products - VLX for Embedded Systems (2009), http://www.virtuallogix.com/

[VmWare, 2009] VmWare, TRANGO Virtual Prozessors: Scalable security for embedded devices (2009), http://www.trango-vp.com/

Constructing a Multi-OS Platform with Minimal Engineering Cost

Yuki Kinebuchi[1], Takushi Morita[1], Kazuo Makijima[1],
Midori Sugaya[2], and Tatsuo Nakajima[1]

[1] Department of Computer Science, Waseda University
{yukikine,morita_t,makijima,tatsuo}@dcl.info.waseda.ac.jp
[2] Dependable Embedded OS Center, Japan Science and Technology Agency (JST)
doly@dependable-os.net

Abstract. Constructing an embedded device with a real-time and a general-purpose operating system has attracted attention as a promising approach to let the device balance real-time responsiveness and rich functionalities. This paper introduces our methodology for constructing such multi-OS platform with minimal engineering cost by assuming asymmetric OS combinations unique to embedded systems. Our methodology consists of two parts. One is a simple hypervisor for multiplexing resources to be shared between operating systems. The other is modifying operating systems to allow them to be aware of each other. We constructed an experimental system executing TOPPERS and Linux simultaneously on a hardware equipped with an SH-4A processor. The modification to each operating system kernel limited to a few dozen lines of code and do not introduce any overhead that would compromise real-time responsiveness or system throughput.

1 Introduction

Software for embedded systems used to be small and simple, but nowadays it is dominating a large part of the system implementation for providing rich functionalities. For instance, modern cell-phones consist of control software (such as a radio transmitter device controller) and rich applications (such as a web browser, a video player, a mailer, etc.). Thus, development with traditional embedded real-time OSes (RTOSes) are unsuited for modern devices. Those traditional RTOSes are only equipped with minimal functionalities, therefore it is hard to meet the strict time-to-market requirements while implementing considerable applications and middleware on top of such RTOSes to provide rich functionalities. This motivated manufacturers to use general-purpose OSes (GPOSes), instead of traditional RTOSes, as the platforms of embedded system software.

However, because GPOSes are unsuited for supporting real-time properties required by embedded systems, some efforts are made to modify them to achieve sufficient real-time responsiveness. The modification to a GPOS kernel requires deep insights into the kernel internal architecture and also requires significant engineering cost. For instance, adding preemption points into a large monolithic

A. Rettberg et al. (Eds.): IESS 2009, IFIP AICT 310, pp. 195–206, 2009.

kernel requires redesigning various parts of the kernel and could introduce complex timing bugs.

To balance real-time responsiveness and rich functionalities, some approaches constructing an embedded device with both an RTOS and a GPOS have been proposed. One of the approaches is the hybrid system[1,2]. It is a method to link an RTOS kernel and a functional GPOS kernel together. This approach achieves constructing a system supporting the high real-time responsiveness of an RTOS together with the rich functionalities of a GPOS. However even though this solution is capable of executing real-time applications, the engineering cost of porting existing real-time applications to the real-time layer is problematic for manufacturers. This can be mitigated by using an existing RTOS for a hard-real-time layer like Linux on ITRON[3]. Linux on ITRON has a capability to execute applications developed for the μITRON specification[4].

Typically embedded device manufacturers leverage diverse RTOSes depending on the real-time constraints, the applications set, the software properties they require, etc. Considering various combinations of RTOSes and GPOSes, even though the engineering cost of constructing a single hybrid system is claimed to be small enough, the engineering cost for supporting various combinations of RTOSes and GPOSes would still introduce a great engineering effort.

In this paper, we propose an approach for constructing an embedded device with an RTOS and a GPOS while introducing minimal modifications to both OS kernels by assuming asymmetric OS combinations unique to embedded systems. Our approach is based on a simple hypervisor and paravirtualization like technique. By leveraging the hypervisor, our approach is free to combine various RTOSes and GPOSes. The contributions of this paper are proposing the methodology, and showing its validity by implementing and evaluating it against real-world software and hardware. We developed the hypervisor from scratch, paravirtualized the TOPPERS RTOS and the Linux kernel, and executed them on top of the SH-4A architecture processor. The resulting implementation is simple and efficient enough to accommodate multiple OSes together with a few dozen lines of modifications to both OS kernels while maintaining the real-time responsiveness of the RTOS.

2   Related Work

Various approaches are proposed to balance real-time responsiveness and rich functionalities on a single platform. One of the approaches is modifying a GPOS to support real-time responsiveness. The real-time patch is a modification to a plain Linux kernel to support kernel preemption[5]. It achieves a few hundred μseconds latency[6], but still the result is slower by a factor of ten comparing to typical RTOSes. Even though the mechanism is potentially capable of achieving real-time responsiveness, it could be easily spoiled by a bad-mannered device driver, which holds a lock for a long period. Porting software from an RTOS to Linux would increase the risk of implementing such drivers, because of the difference of programming models between the RTOS and Linux or the developers being unfamiliar with programming on Linux. In addition, porting all the software from the RTOS to Linux would impose substantial engineering cost.

Another approach, known as the hybrid system, is to link an RTOS with a GPOS. RTLinux and RTAI replace the Linux hardware abstraction layer with their own version of RTOSes[1,2]. Those RTOSes would be executed in privileged mode together with the Linux kernel. The interrupt response time would only be a few μseconds, which is comparable to typical RTOSes. However those microkernels only support their original programming interfaces, which prevents the straight-forward reuse of some real-time software developed for traditional RTOSes. Linux on ITRON is an alternative method to RTLinux and RTAI, which replaces the Linux hardware abstraction layer with an existing RTOS, μITRON[3]. This architecture enables the system to reuse both the software developed for Linux and μITRON. The hybrid system provides high real-time responsiveness comparable with an RTOS with reasonable engineering cost by reusing existing GPOSes. However considering another combination of an RTOS and a GPOS would impose redesigning the hybrid system again from scratch. Because it is usual for manufacturers to leverage diverse OSes, this engineering cost would be problematic.

A virtual machine monitor (VMM) is another technology focusing on accommodating an RTOS and a GPOS into a single embedded device without modifications or with just minimal modifications to the OS kernels[7]. A VMM provides a virtual hardware interface which is identical (or almost identical) to some real hardware and isolation between virtualized guest OSes. To leverage a VMM on embedded systems, developers should consider three trade-offs. First is the trade-off between system throughput and real-time responsiveness, which is a well-known trade-off on system design. Traditional VMMs focus on how to increase the total throughput of workloads provided by guest OSes, because their main targets are enterprise systems or high-performance computing[8,9]. Thus, they are unsuited for handling real-time properties or supporting embedded system processor architectures. Some VMMs for embedded systems have been developed to meet these real-time requirements on embedded systems. L4 is one of them, and is capable of executing Linux on top of it[10]. Second is the trade-off between full virtualization and paravirtualization. A VMM supporting full virtualization exposes a virtual hardware interface identical to a real hardware interface. OSes can be executed without any modification on full virtualization. However, implementing full virtualization complexifies the design of the VMM itself or requires hardware support for virtualization. Unfortunately hardware support for virtualization is still an unfamiliar feature for embedded system processors. This motivates embedded system VMMs to use paravirtualization for their system design, like L4 did. Third is the trade-off between providing isolation among OSes or not. Strong isolation among guest OSes is an attractive feature for constructing a secure and reliable system. However unlike the VMMs used in the area of enterprise systems, most embedded systems consist of a fixed number of OSes. In addition, as the guest OSes are statically decided by the hardware manufacturer, they can be 'trusted'. This removes the necessity of strong isolation. Without isolation, the design of VMMs would be simpler and their overhead would be smaller.

The previous contributions take a good balance of performance and engineering cost. However their propositions only focus on the combinations of specific RTOSes and GPOSes, and do not consider neither the portability of applications developed for various OSes nor the portability of OSes themselves. From the aspect of accommodating diverse combinations of RTOSes and GPOSes together into a single embedded device, portability should be the primary concern of manufacturers. The advantage of minimizing modifications to OS kernels reduces the possibility of introducing new bugs into virtualized systems. Furthermore, it helps updating the virtualized OSes for bug fixes and security patches.

In order to achieve this requirement while not penalizing performance, our virtualization layer executes guest OS kernels and itself in privileged mode. The virtualization layer multiplexes only minimal hardware resources, while other resources are exclusively assigned to each OS by simply modifying each OS kernel not to access the same devices. Relocating OS kernels in privileged mode degrades the reliability of the system. However, in a multi-OS platform, even though the failure of real-time applications are not propagated to other part of the system, it is a fatal error for the system to continue its service. Recovering from such a real-time application failure with seamless execution is a topic beyond this paper.

3   Design and Implementation

This section introduces our methodology for constructing an embedded device with multiple OSes. The methodology is based on a simple hypervisor called SPUMONE and some modifications to guest OS kernels.

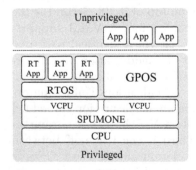

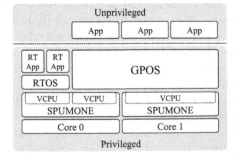

Fig. 1. SPUMONE based system on a single-core processor

Fig. 2. SPUMONE based system on a multi-core processor

3.1   SPUMONE

SPUMONE (Software Processing Unit, Multiplexing ONE into two or more) is a thin software layer for multiplexing a single physical processor into multiple virtual ones. Unlike traditional hypervisors, SPUMONE itself and guest OSes are executed in privileged mode as shown in Fig.1, in order to simplify the system design and to eliminate the overhead of trapping between privileged and non-privileged mode for system-calls and hypercalls. If an OS does not support user land, its applications would be executed in privileged mode altogether.

This contributes to minimize the overhead and the amount of modifications to the guest OS kernels. Furthermore it makes the implementation of SPUMONE itself simple. Executing OS kernels in non-privileged mode complicates the implementation of the hypervisor, because various privileged instructions have to be emulated. The majority of the kernel and application instructions, including the privileged instructions, are executed directly by the real processor, and only the minimal instructions are emulated by SPUMONE. These emulated instructions are invoked from the OS kernels using a simple function call. Since the interface has no binary compatibility with the original processor interface, we simply modify the source code of guest OS kernels, a method known as the paravirtualization[11,8]. Thus we assume we have access to the source code of the guest OS kernels. The modifications required to the guest OS kernels are described in details in Sec.3.2.

Virtual Processor Scheduling. A processor is multiplexed by scheduling the execution of guest OSes. The execution states of the guest OSes are managed by a data structure that we call a virtual processor. When switching the execution of the virtual processors, all the hardware registers are stored into the corresponding virtual processor's register table, and then loaded from the table of the next executing virtual processor. The mechanism is similar to the process paradigm of a classical OS, however the virtual processor saves the entire processor state, including the privileged control registers.

The scheduling algorithm of virtual processors is a fixed priority preemptive scheduling. A virtual processor bound to the RTOS would gain a higher priority than a virtual processor bound to the GPOS in order to maintain the real-time responsiveness. This means the GPOS is executed only when the virtual processor for the RTOS is in an idle state and has no task to execute. The process or task scheduling is left up to guest OS so the scheduling model for each OS is maintained as is. The idle RTOS resumes its execution when it receives an interrupt. The interrupt for RTOS preempts the GPOS immediately, even if the GPOS is disabling interrupts.

Interrupt/Trap Delivery. Interrupt virtualization is a key feature of SPUMONE. Interrupts are investigated by SPUMONE before they are delivered to each OS. SPUMONE receives an interrupt, then looks up the interrupt destination table to see which OS should receive it. The destination virtual processor is statically defined for each interrupt. Traps are also sent to SPUMONE first, then are directly forwarded to the currently executing OS.

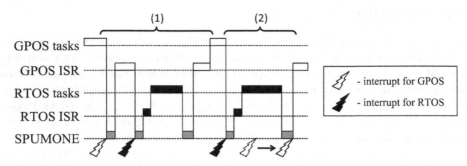

Fig. 3. Interrupt Delivery Mechanism

To let SPUMONE receive interrupts before the guest OSes, we modified the entry point of the interrupts to SPUMONE's vector table. The entry point of each OS is notified to SPUMONE via a virtual instruction for registering their vector table. An interrupt is first handled by SPUMONE interrupt handler in which the destination virtual processor is decided and the corresponding scheduler is invoked. When the interrupt triggers an OS switch, all the registers of the current OS are saved into the register stack, then the register stack for the other OS is loaded. Finally the execution branches into the entry point of the destination OS. The processor registers are setup just as the real interrupt occurred, so the code of the guest OS entry points does not need to be modified.

The interrupt enable and disable instructions are also replaced with the virtual instruction interface. A typical OS disables all interrupt sources when disabling interrupts for atomic execution. In our approach, by leveraging the interrupt mechanism of the processor, we assign the higher half of the interrupt priority levels to the RTOS and the lower half to the GPOS. When the GPOS tries to block the interrupts, it modifies its interrupt mask to the middle priority. The RTOS may therefore preempt the GPOS even if it is disabling the interrupts (Fig.3 (1)). On the other hand when the RTOS is running, the interrupts are blocked by the processor (Fig.3 (2)). These blocked interrupts could be sent immediately when the GPOS is dispatched.

Multi-core Support. SPUMONE also runs on multi-core processors. The design of multi-core SPUMONE is basically the same as the single-core version. As shown in Fig.2, each core is managed by a dedicated SPUMONE instance. Interrupts are handled by the instance bound to each core, then forwarded to the guest OS. Each instance communicates using inter-core interrupt (ICI) and shared memory area. The original processor mechanism of resetting a core is replaced with SPUMONE's function. The development of multi-core SPUMONE is still in progress, so we would not go in details in this paper.

3.2   Modifying OS Kernels

Each OS is modified to be aware of the existence of the other OS, because hardware resources other than the processor are not multiplexed by SPUMONE.

Thus those are exclusively assigned to each OS by modifying their kernels. The following describes the points of the OSes to be modified in order to run on top of SPUMONE.

Interrupt Vector Table Register Instruction. The instruction registering the address of a vector table is modified to notify the address to SPUMONE's interrupt manager. Typically this instruction is invoked once during the OS initialization.

Interrupt Enable and Disable Instruction. The instructions enabling and disabling interrupts are typically provided as kernel internal APIs. They are typically coded as inline functions or macros in the kernel source code. For the GPOS, we replace those APIs with the instructions enabling the entire level of interrupts and disabling only low priorities interrupts. For the RTOS, we replace those APIs with the instructions enabling only high priority interrupts and disabling the entire level of interrupts. Therefore, interrupts assigned to the RTOS are immediately delivered to the RTOS, and the interrupts assigned to the GPOS are blocked during the RTOS execution.

Figure 4 shows the interrupt priority levels assignment for each OS, which we used in the evaluation environment.

Physical Memory. A fixed physical memory area is assigned to each OS. The physical address for the guest OSes can be simply changed by modifying the configuration file or their source code. Virtualizing the physical memory would impose a large code into the virtualization layer and substantial performance overhead. In addition, unlike the virtual machine monitor for enterprise systems, embedded systems have a fixed number of OSes. From these reasons we assigned fixed physical memory area for each OS.

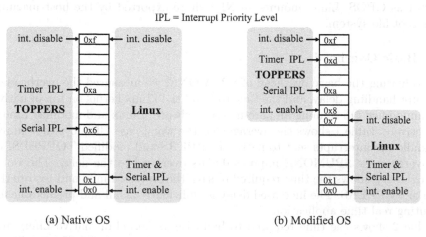

Fig. 4. The interrupt priority levels assignment

Idle Instruction. On a real processor, the `idle` instruction suspends a processor till it receives an interrupt. On a virtualized environment, this is used to yield the use of real processor to another guest OS. We prevent the execution of this instruction by replacing it with the SPUMONE API. Typically this instruction is embedded in a specific part of kernel, which is fairly easy to find.

Peripheral Devices. Peripheral devices are assigned by SPUMONE to each OS exclusively. This is done by modifying the configuration of each OS not to share the same peripherals. We assume that most of devices are assigned exclusively to each OS. This assumption is reasonable because embedded system multi-OS platforms have asymmetric OS combinations unlike a symmetric multi-OS platform for enterprise systems. It consists of different kinds of OSes, usually an RTOS and a GPOS. For instance, an RTOS is used for controlling specific peripherals such as a radio transmitter and some digital signal processors, and a GPOS for controlling a display and buttons.

However some devices cannot be assigned exclusively to each OS because both systems need to use them. For instance, only one interrupt controller is provided by the experimental processor we used. Usually the OS clears some of its registers during its initialization. In the case of running on SPUMONE, the OS booting after the first one should be careful not to clear or overwrite the settings of the OS executed first. We modified the Linux initialization code to preserve the settings done by TOPPERS.

4   Evaluation

We evaluated the basic overhead, the engineering cost of modifying the guest OS kernels, and the real-time responsiveness of an RTOS running on SPUMONE. The evaluation is done on the SH-2007 reference board, with the SH-4A 400 MHz processor and 128MB memory. We use TOPPERS/JSP 1.3 as RTOS and Linux 2.6.20.1 as GPOS. Linux mounts an NFS share exported by the host machine as its root file system.

4.1   Basic Overhead

For evaluating the basic overhead of SPUMONE, we measured the overhead of interrupt handling delay, and the time to build the Linux kernel on top of native (an unmodified OS running on bare-metal hardware) Linux and modified Linux, respectively. Table 1 shows the average and the worst case CPU cycles required to handle the interrupts sent to native TOPPERS and modified TOPPERS. In the average case SPUMONE imposes $0.67\mu s$ overhead to the delay. The worst case overhead shows the time required to save the state of Linux and restore the state of TOPPERS. The increased delay is sufficiently small and predictable for executing real-time applications.

Table 2 shows the time required to build Linux kernel on native Linux and modified Linux executed on top of SPUMONE together with TOPPERS. TOPPERS only receives the timer interrupts each 1ms, and executes no other tasks.

Table 1. The delay of handling the timer interrupts in TOPPERS. Over 20,000 interrupts were measured to obtained the average and the worst case time.

Configuration		CPU Clocks	Time (μs)	Overhead (μs)
TOPPERS	average	102	0.25	-
(native)	worst	102	0.26	-
TOPPERS	average	367	0.92	0.67
on SPUMONE	worst	1582	3.96	3.70

Table 2. Linux kernel build time

Configuration	Time	Overhead
Linux only	68m5.898s	-
Linux and TOPPERS on SPUMONE	69m3.091s	1.4%

Table 3. A list of the modifications to the Linux kernel

File	Function/Variable	Description
.config	`CONFIG_MEMORY_START` `CONFIG_MEMORY_SIZE`	Modified to use the upper half (64MB) of the main memory
setup.c	`sh2007_setup(char **cmdline_p)`	Modified not to overwrite the value in the interrupt controller register set by TOPPERS
setup-sh7780.c	`intc2_irq_table`	The interrupt source table. Removed one of the serial devices which is used by TOPPERS
head.S	Flag register initial value	Modified IPL, not to block the interrupts for TOPPERS
traps.c	`per_cpu_trap_init(void)`	Replaced the vector table register instruction with SPUMONE API
irqflags.h	`raw_local_irq_disable(void)` `__raw_local_irq_disable(void)` `raw_local_irq_restore(void)`	Modified not to mask the interrupts assigned to TOPPERS
processor.h	`cpu_sleep()`	Replaced the idle instruction with the SPUMONE API

The result shows that SPUMONE and TOPPERS impose overhead of 1.4% to Linux performance. Note that the overhead includes the cycles consumed by TOPPERS. The result shows that the overhead of the virtualization to the system throughput is sufficiently small.

4.2   Engineering Cost

We evaluated the engineering cost of reusing the RTOS and the GPOS by comparing the number of modified lines of code (LOC) in each guest OS kernel. Table 3 is a list of the modified files in Linux. Table 4 shows the amount of

Table 4. The total number of modified LOC in *.c, *.S, *.h, Makefiles

OS	Added LOC	Removed LOC
Linux on SPUMONE (Linux 2.6.20.1)	56	17
RTLinux 3.2 (Linux 2.6.9)	2798	1131
RTAI 3.6.2 (Linux 2.6.19)	5920	163
OK Linux (Linux 2.6.24)	28149	-

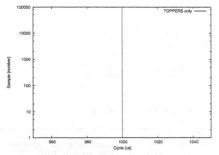

Fig. 5. The frequency distribution of the periodic task execution intervals. TOPPERS only. Only the periodic task running.

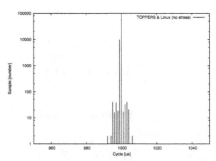

Fig. 6. The frequency distribution of the periodic task execution intervals. TOPPERS and Linux with no load on SPUMONE.

code added and removed from the original OS kernels. Since we could not find RTLinux, RTAI, OK Linux for the SH-4A processor architecture, we evaluated them developed for the x86 architecture. OK Linux is a Linux kernel virtualized to run on the L4 microkernel. For OK Linux, we only counted the code added to the architecture dependent directory `arch/l4` and `include/asm-l4`. The comparison would not be fair in a precise sense, however as the table shows, it is clear that our approach requires significantly small modifications to the Linux kernel. This result is achieved because we are executing guest OS in privileged mode.

4.3   Effect of Linux Load to TOPPERS Real-Time Properties

We measured the effect of Linux load to TOPPERS periodic task execution intervals. Only the periodic task is executed on TOPPERS. Figure 5, 6, 7, 8 shows the frequency distribution of the intervals of the 1ms periodic task running on TOPPERS. Figure 7 and 8 are measured with running the `stress` command on Linux to show the effect of the CPU load and the I/O load. CPU load repeat invoking `sqrt()`. I/O load repeats invoking `sync()`, which triggers flushing data to the file system. The intervals are sampled 100,000 times each. Note that the y-axis is showed in log scale. The overhead of switching from Linux to TOPPERS and execution inside SPUMONE would delay the start-up of the periodic task, which could be the cause of jitters. The maximum error for delay was $20\mu s$

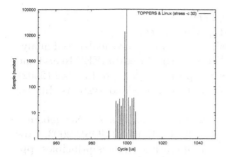

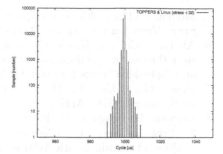

Fig. 7. The frequency distribution of the periodic task execution intervals. TOPPERS and Linux with CPU load on SPUMONE.

Fig. 8. The frequency distribution of the periodic task execution intervals. TOPPERS and Linux with I/O load on SPUMONE.

showed in Fig.8. The results show the jitters are small, however we need further investigations to explain the cause of the jitters.

5   Conclusion

One of the primary requirements for constructing a hybrid system for embedded system is engineering cost. Existing research only focused on the engineering cost of a specific combination of RTOSes and GPOSes, however those approaches did not consider diverse combinations of OSes. This paper introduced our approach to construct an embedded device with an RTOS and a GPOS with minimal engineering cost, which can be adapted to various OS kernels in the similar way. The approach is based on utilizing the thin SPUMONE virtualization layer and modifying a few parts of the guest OS kernels, a method known as paravirtualization. Our approach executes the virtualization layer and the guest OS kernels in privileged mode altogether in order to reduce the performance over head engineering cost of virtualization. The evaluation shows our approach requires significantly small modifications with introducing reasonable overhead to the real-time responsiveness of the guest RTOS, which allows the freedom of combining various RTOSes and GPOSes to run on top of embedded devices.

References

1. Yodaiken, V.: The RTLinux Manifesto. In: Proc. of The 5th Linux Expo. (1999)
2. Mantegazza, P., Dozio, E., Papacharalambous, S.: RTAI: Real Time Application Interface, vol. 2000. Specialized Systems Consultants, Inc., Seattle (2000)
3. Takada, H., Kindaichi, T., Hachiya, S.: Linux on ITRON: A Hybrid Operating System Architecture for Embedded Systems. In: Proceedings of the 2002 Symposium on Applications and the Internet (SAINT) Workshops, Washington DC, USA. IEEE Computer Society, Los Alamitos (2002)
4. ITRON Project: μitron4.0 specification, http://www.ertl.jp/ITRON/

5. Molnar, I.: The realtime preemption patch (2009),
   http://www.kernel.org/pub/linux/kernel/projects/rt/
6. Abeni, L., Goel, A., Krasic, C., Snow, J., Walpole, J.: A measurement-based analysis of the real-time performance of linux. In: Proceedings of Eighth IEEE Real-Time and Embedded Technology and Applications Symposium, 2002, pp. 133–142 (2002)
7. Heiser, G., Sydney, A.: The role of virtualization in embedded systems. In: 1st IIES, Glasgow, UK (April 2008)
8. Barham, P., Dragovic, B., Fraser, K., Hand, S., Harris, T., Ho, A., Neugebauer, R., Pratt, I., Warfield, A.: Xen and the art of virtualization. In: SOSP 2003: Proceedings of the nineteenth ACM symposium on Operating systems principles, pp. 164–177. ACM Press, New York (2003)
9. Sugerman, J., Venkitachalam, G., Lim, B.H.: Virtualizing I/O devices on VMware workstation's hosted virtual machine monitor. In: Proceedings of the General Track: 2002 USENIX Annual Technical Conference, Berkeley, CA, USA, USENIX Association, pp. 1–14 (2001)
10. Leslie, B., van Schaik, C., Heiser, G.: Wombat: A portable user-mode Linux for embedded systems. In: Proceedings of the 6th Linux. Conf. Au (2005)
11. Whitaker, A., Shaw, M., Gribble, S.: Denali: Lightweight virtual machines for distributed and networked applications. In: Proceedings of the USENIX Annual Technical Conference, pp. 195–209 (2002)

A Synchronization Method for Register Traces of Pipelined Processors

Ralf Dreesen[1], Thorsten Jungeblut[2], Michael Thies[1], Mario Porrmann[2],
Uwe Kastens[1], and Ulrich Rückert[2]

[1] University of Paderborn, Department of Computer Science
{rdreesen,mthies,uwe}@upb.de
Fürstenallee 11, 33102 Paderborn, Germany
[2] University of Paderborn, Heinz Nixdorf Institute,
Fürstenallee 11, 33102 Paderborn, Germany
{tj,porrmann,rueckert}@hni.upb.de

Abstract. During a typical development process of an embedded application specific processor (ASIP), the architecture is implemented multiple times on different levels of abstractions. As a result of this redundant specification, certain inconsistencies may show up. For example, the implementation of an instruction in the simulator may differ from the HDL implementation. To detect such inconsistencies, we use register trace comparison. Our key contribution is a generic method for systematic trace synchronization. Therefore, we convert a micro-architectural trace into an architectural trace. This method considers pipeline hazards and non-uniform write latencies. To simplify the validation of a processor, we further have implemented an automatic validation environment that includes a tool which points the developer directly to erroneous instructions. The flow has been validated during the development of our CoreVA architecture for mobile applications.

1 Introduction

Our *processor design flow* is divided into the development of a compiler tool chain and the development of the hardware description (see Figure 1). The compiler tool chain consists of a compiler, an assembler, a linker, various debugging tools and an instruction set simulator (ISS).

All these tools are generated from a central processor specification (UPSLA [7] — Unified Processor Specification Language). This allows the rapid generation of a complete and consistent toolchain, which can be used to perform a *design space exploration* of the processor. Using this approach, we can easily add application specific instructions, re-generate the toolchain and evaluate the processor using the ISS. The consistency within the toolchain is guaranteed by the use of a central processor specification. All aspects (e.g., machine format, write latencies) of an instruction are specified once in this specification and then re-used throughout the assembler, linker, simulator, and disassembler. For the *hardware development* we describe the processor in VHDL and use the standard design flow to obtain an FPGA prototype or the final ASIC implementation of the processor.

A. Rettberg et al. (Eds.): IESS 2009, IFIP AICT 310, pp. 207–217, 2009.

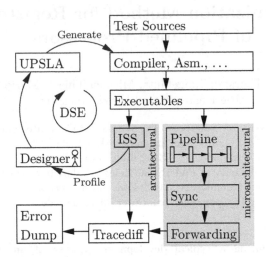

Fig. 1. Overview of our design flow and validation environment

The usability of the toolchain has been proven in multiple industry related projects, in which very long instruction word (VLIW), multiprocessor system-on-chip (MPSoC), or other non-orthogonal processor architectures were developed. The toolchain covers the complete instruction set.

Due to the *separate specification* of the tool chain and the hardware description, inconsistencies may result. Therefore, we need to check the equivalence of the ISS and the synthesized processor. To validate the consistency, we apply a non-formal co-verification approach. Basically, we compare the traces of executing a program on the ISS with the hardware implementation. If the traces diverge, an error in the specification has been detected.

Of course a *non-formal validation by simulation* approach does not guarantee the correctness of the implementation. The effectiveness of the validation heavily depends on the set of *test programs*. The generation of such tests is covered in [5] and is not subject of this paper.

The abstraction level of the ISS implementation differs from the micro-architectural implementation. For example, the micro-architectural implementation executes instructions pipelined, whereas the ISS simulates each instruction as a whole. As a result, the micro-architectural trace differs from the ISS trace and hence *synchronization* is required (Section 3).

As an extension to existing approaches, we do not only perform a *multi-domain validation* of the ISS and the RTL simulation, but also of the processor emulation. Therefore, we have added a trace interface to the processor, which is used to emit the state sequence (Section 4). The ISS is available in an early design stage and essential for a design space exploration. The RTL implementation is more detailed but therefore also more expensive to simulate. The hardware emulation approximates the final ASIC implementation most accurately and is even faster than the ISS and RTL simulation. Some timing issues manifest themselves at the stage of processor development. The system can also be integrated in real world systems (due to its real time ability). However, the implementation effort for the emulation is high. In addition, the observation of the internal processor state is limited and therefore debugging is cumbersome.

We also attach importance to locating an error, in case that an inconsistency between both traces is detected. Therefore, we have implemented a *specialized comparison tool*, which processes two execution traces and dumps a meaningful description of any detected inconsistency (Section 5).

2 Related Work

A formal verification approach for processor control is presented in [2,8]. Both papers regard a processor model with out-of-order-execution. They conceptually flush the pipeline to synchronize the micro-architectural and the ISA model. We extend this approach by considering pipelining effects caused by forwarding circuits. In addition we also validate the datapath of the processor.

In [3] the trace of an ISS is compared with a Verilog simulator. The Verilog simulator captures the state at the write-back stage at the expense of additional hardware resources. The approach does not consider non-uniform write latencies.

The generation of test cases with coverage feedback is discussed in [5]. For validation a co-simulation approach is used, where the RTL trace is converted into an ISA trace. The authors mention this conversion to be a challenge beyond the scope of their paper. The approach in [10] performs a co-simulation of an ISS and an RTL simulator, both manually written in C. The authors also identified the problem of trace conversion, but do not present a systematic solution. In Section 3 we present a solution to this conversion problem.

The architecture description language "ArchC" to generate an ISS is presented in [1]. To validate the consistency of this simulator and a hardware description language (HDL) implementation, a validation approach which compares memory-transactions is used. We have extended this method by a cycle accurate comparison of registers, including the effects of a forwarding circuit.

The Tensilica tools [4] offer the generation of a toolchain and a hardware description from a single processor specification. Their approach allows the extension of a predefined processor architecture by application specific instructions. However, the core of the processor remains fixed and certain design parameters like instruction format or pipeline depth are not exposed to the developer.

In [9] the authors describe the functional verification of a POWER5 processor. They use a coarse grained memory-trace mechanism that is well suited for system-level verification. The tracing mechanism is tailored to the POWER5 architecture. In contrast, our fine-grained trace-mechanism is generic and focuses on core-level verification.

In summary, trace comparison is a widely accepted approach for processor validation. Prior work has focused on specific architectures and does not offer a *generic method* for synchronization of traces.

3 A Generic Tracing Approach for Pipelined Processors

In this Section we describe a general method for adding a trace interface to a processor. Our method can cope with common processor architectures and pipelining effects like stalls, flushes and non-uniform write latencies. We do also consider forwarding of instruction results. Our approach does not require the trace information to be emitted in a specific pipeline stage. Instead, each signal can be captured at the most convenient stage to avoid additional hardware overhead (Section 3.1). To incorporate the effects of forwarding, we introduce a method to derive the *publication cycle* of an instruction result from its final write-back cycle (Section 3.2). The *publication cycle* is defined as the clock cycle, in which the result becomes visible to other instructions, i.e. when it is fed into the forwarding circuit.

3.1 Synchronization of Traced Signals

A simple implementation for tracing in a pipelined processor would collect all information at the last stage, which is typically the write-back stage. This may introduce additional hardware overhead to pipeline signals that are otherwise not needed in the last stage. Examples include the program counter and the memory write ports. Instead, we capture the signals to be traced immediately in the originating stage.

However, this introduces the problem of *synchronizing* the data, which has been captured at different stages. For example stalls may defer the execution of some instructions in the pipeline or a flush may invalidate an instruction. To synchronize the information we use a *virtual pipeline*, which emulates the hardware pipeline. The virtual pipeline is implemented in software and runs on the computer that monitors the device under test (DUT). Therefore, it does not require additional hardware resources. The virtual pipeline also receives the stall and flush signals from the hardware pipeline, to accurately emulate its behavior.

The example in Figure 2 juxtaposes the operation of the hardware pipeline and the virtual pipeline. In this example, stages 0 and 2 of the hardware pipeline emit trace information which is passed to the respective stage of the virtual pipeline. The trace information A_i represents a set of signals that were emitted in stage i.

In cycle 0 instruction A is executed in stage 0 and emits information A_0. In cycle 1, instruction A is passed to the next stage, just like the information A_0 in the

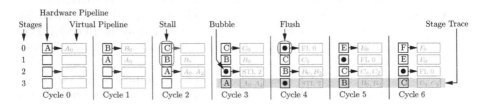

Fig. 2. Example of virtual pipelining

virtual pipeline. In cycle 2 the stages 0 and 1 are stalled. Stage 0 does therefore not emit information and a *bubble* is inserted in stage 2 of the hardware pipeline. The *bubble* floats through the pipeline like a normal instruction without carrying any useful work. The virtual pipeline labels its bubble with the originating stage (STL 2). This allows us to reconstruct the stall and flush events. In cycle 4 stage 0 of the hardware pipeline is flushed and the virtual pipeline records the number of the flushed stage (FL 0). In cycle 5 and 6 execution advances normally.

The final synchronous trace information is collected at the last stage of the virtual pipeline. We will call this trace the *stage trace* in the following. However, this trace does not reflect forwarding effects, which are covered in the next Section.

3.2   Incorporating Forwarding Effects

In this Section we present a method to derive a *storage trace* from a stage trace. The storage trace lists every instruction result, when it is published and therefore visible to other instructions.

This publication cycle of an instruction result can not directly be derived from the stage trace. It is not possible to calculate the publication cycle by simply subtracting a constant from the stage trace cycle. There are two reasons that prevent such an easy computation, namely *non-uniform latencies* and *stalls*.

In a processor architecture with *non-uniform latencies*, results are published in different pipeline stages. Assume that instruction D in Figure 3 publishes its result in stage 2 and E in stage 3. Hence, the result of D appears in cycle 7 and the result of E in cycle 9, whereas D and E show up at cycle 10 and 11 in the stage trace. The cycle difference between the publication cycle and the stage trace cycle is not constant, but depends on the instruction. We therefore need to know the *publication stage* of each instruction. This information can be extracted from our processor specification.

To accurately handle *stalls*, information about pipelined execution is required. Assume that instruction A and B (see Figure 3) publish their results both in stage 2. The difference between publication cycle and stage trace cycle is 3 for

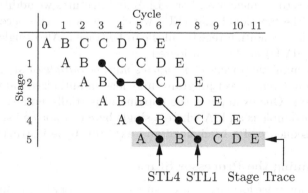

Fig. 3. Pipeline diagram illustrating the instruction execution

instruction A, but 4 for instruction B. If A and B would instead publish their results in stage 4, the difference would be equal. To derive the storage trace from the stage trace, we need to know for every cycle, which instruction is contained in a given stage. Therefore, we need to reconstruct the pipeline execution from the stage trace.

We can *reconstruct the instruction execution* shown in Figure 3 from the stage trace, i.e. the last line of the pipeline diagram. We construct the diagram during a single right to left pass, i.e. from cycle 11 towards cycle 0. The instruction of a given stage s and cycle c can be derived from the next cycle as follows:

$$\text{instr}(c, s) := \begin{cases} \text{instr}(c + 1, s) & \text{stalled}(c + 1, s) \\ \text{instr}(c + 1, s + 1) & \text{else} \end{cases}$$

where the predicate stalled is defined as

$$\text{stalled}(c, s) := \exists s' > s : \text{isBubbleOrigin}(c, s')$$

This means that an instruction in a given stage and cycle is equal to the instruction in the next cycle and the next stage, unless there is a stall. In the example in Figure 3 the instruction in cycle 7 at stage 2 is the same as the instruction in cycle 8 at stage 3, as there is no bubble in cycle 8 at stage 4 or 5. The instruction in cycle 4 at stage 0 however is taken from cycle 5 at stage 0, as there is a bubble originating in cycle 5 at stage 4.

The pipeline execution reconstruction gives us the information in which cycle an instruction was executed in a given stage. Together with the information in which *stage* an instruction publishes its result, the pipeline reconstruction allows us to compute the cycle in which the result is published.

4   Emitting Traces

Our multi-domain consistency check is based on the comparison of states. We define the *processor state* as the content of all memory elements in the architecture. These are typically the register files and the data memories. The current state of the processor can be derived from its initial state by continuously tracing all write accesses to its memories. For VLIW architectures we additionally trace the number of the functional unit (FU) which causes a write access. For conditional execution, condition register files can be traced. Also single instruction multiple data (SIMD) mode is considered.

To get a deterministic trace, the *memories must be initialized* at the beginning of the simulation. Even correct programs may load uninitialized data from memory into registers. One example is the copying of partially uninitialized unions in C. Another example is an ISA where a single byte can not be loaded directly, but only by a sequence of a `load word` and `extract byte` instruction.

4.1   Determining the Processor State

To emit a common trace format, we use a single trace library for all three domains. The processor state is passed to a central `trace_cycle` function of this library.

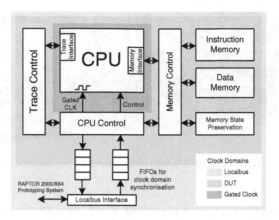

Fig. 4. CPU Control Unit (CCU)

For the ISS the current processor trace can be directly constructed from the memories. To compensate the pipelined execution of instructions in the hardware implementation, we apply our synchronization method as described in Section 3. Results that are written back to the register file are captured in the write-back stage, which is usually the last stage. Memory signals and the program counter are captured at earlier stages, thus requiring synchronization by virtual pipelining.

Branches to unaligned instruction groups (VLIW architecture), accesses to external memory (e.g., cache misses), as well as data or control hazards, can stall pipeline stages of the processor core. These stall signals are forwarded to the virtual pipeline to enable an accurate pipeline emulation.

In the *RTL simulation* we can access the internal signals of the design using the ModelSim Foreign Language Interface (FLI). Just the signal names have to be known by the trace mechanism. The processor core itself is not altered.

To trace processor states from the *hardware emulation*, we offer the designer a generic wrapper (CPU Control Unit, CCU, see Figure 4) to embed the processor core. Only slight changes have to be made to the processor core, by making the signals aforementioned available to the top entity. All signals are connected to register inputs, no additional combinatorial logic is added. As we retrieve most of the signals directly from pipeline registers, tracing has a negligible impact on the timing.

The CCU is mapped to an FPGA and emulated in our rapid prototyping environment RAPTOR2000/X64 (see Figure 5, [6]) This modular system allows the use of a large selection of FPGA daughter boards or physical interfaces (e.g., Ethernet), which enable the use in real environments. Also, the CCU is suitable for ASIC realizations to assist testing. As our prototyping environment features a modular design, the FPGA module can easily be replaced by the ASIC realization after verification. Identical control and test software is used, thus reducing developing time.

Fig. 5. RAPTOR2000/X64 rapid prototyping environment

To gather all information of a processor state, multiple accesses have to be made to the CCU. This requires clock gating for a cycle-by-cycle execution of the processor core. As the latency of synchronous SRAM or caches is usually at least one clock cycle, some additional considerations have to be made. If the processor core performs a read access to instruction or data memory, it applies address and control signals to the memory. For example, if the output of the memory is registered, the requested data is valid one clock cycle later. As we perform a cycle-by-cycle-based execution, this data cannot be stored in the processor pipeline registers in the following clock cycle, so it has to be preserved in the control unit. Between two steps of the processor core, unrelated memory accesses can occur, disturbing the CPU state. Hence, before the next step the state of the memory has to be restored by applying the preserved memory address before the next CPU step.

4.2 Output of Traces

There are two possible ways of passing trace output to the consistency check: by a trace file or online. A trace file enables offline regression tests between the current and a former revision of each domain but has the disadvantage of very large files to be stored and transfered. Even if considering a standard single core as a lower bound, at least the program counter, one register or memory write access (data and address) and some control signals have to be traced, which adds up to about 10 Bytes per clock cycle. For just one simulated second of a 300 MHz CPU, 3 GB of data are generated. Considering more complex architectures, like VLIW or SIMD, multiplies this data. Compression could reduce the size by an order of magnitude but would not completely eliminate the problem of large data size. Another solution is an online consistency check, as used in our approach.

5   Validation Tools

To automate the execution of a large set of test cases, we implemented a *validation environment* as outlined in Figure 1. The environment allows the distributed simulation on multiple systems.

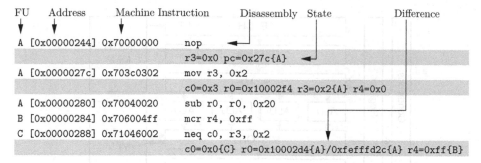

Fig. 6. Example of a tracediff dump

The register traces from the simulators are compared state-by-state using our `tracediff` tool. If states differ, the tool aborts with a meaningful error description which points the developer directly to the location of the error.

The description is a *backtrace* of the last n processor states interleaved with a disassembly of the respective executed instructions as shown in Figure 6. Only those registers that are relevant for debugging are listed. Accesses to the main memory are treated the same way. If the register was written, the respective functional unit is appended in curly braces. If the register value differs in the traces, both values are printed. The disassembly between two states lists one or more instructions that were executed in parallel. Each line is prefixed with the identifier of the functional unit (`A,B,...`).

In Figure 6 the value of register `r0` which was written by functional unit `A` differs. Considering the `sub` instruction and its input value `0x10002f4`, the result in the right-hand trace is obviously wrong.

6   Evaluation

We have evaluated our system with our CoreVA architecture developed in our research groups. This VLIW processor is a six stage pipelined harvard architecture with non-uniform latencies (see Figure 7). Common features like branch prediction, conditional execution, pipeline forwarding have been implemented. Two load store units access a dual ported memory. 30 general purpose registers (32 bit) can be accessed by ten read and six write ports. Two condition register files (8 bit each) can be accessed by four write ports each. The processor core has been integrated in the CPU Control Unit (CCU). The resource consumption, including 32 kBytes instruction and data memory each, is described in Table 1. The CCU occupies about 6 % of slices of the total system. The FPGA on-chip memory is used as instruction and data memory. The critical path of the processor core is not affected by the connection to the CCU and the trace unit.

For Co-Simulation we use the following setup: On one machine a graphical user interface controls the processor core, and reads out the processor states. On another machine the ISS runs in a Linux environment. Both, emulation

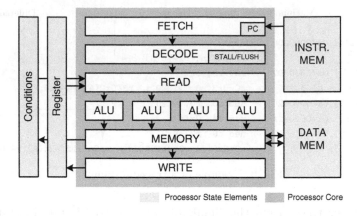

Fig. 7. VLIW architecture

Table 1. Resource consumption of the design mapped on a Xilinx Virtex-II 6000 FPGA

Instance	Registers	LUTS	Slices
RAPTOR Interface	142	36	268
CCU	460	1408	1340
VLIW Core	4875	43063	22344
Total	5477	44507	23952

and simulation, transfer their traces to a third machine, where the validation environment is executed as described in Section 5. Our test repository ranges from microbenchmarks and synthetic benchmarks (e.g., EEMBC, Dhrystone) to real world applications (e.g., 802.11b). Using this setup, we have successfully tracked down an inconsistency due to an ambiguous specification. The error was located in the decoder of the processor's RTL description.

Certainly, tracing of every processor state has an impact on simulation and emulation speed. The ISS and the RTL simulation have to invoke the `trace_cycle()` function. Simulation speed of the RTL implementation reduces by 6% (1.92 kHz vs. 1.83 kHz). For the ISS the execution speed is reduced from 4 MHz to 2 MHz. The hardware emulation has to run the CPU cycle-by-cycle and read out the processor state in between.

7   Conclusion

We have presented a generic validation method for processors to perform consistency checks across multiple simulation and emulation domains. We have developed a generic method for systematic tracing of pipelined processors. The method minimizes hardware overhead, by applying virtual pipelining for the synchronization of traced signals. Processor states are derived from ISS, RTL simulation, and FPGA emulation. It is possible to apply this method to final

ASIC implementations for improved testing. We have implemented a generic framework in which a processor core can be embedded. The framework employs our approach to perform tracing.

A validation environment is used to emit meaningful error descriptions and to point the developer to the location of the error that caused the inconsistency.

Current work focuses on the cycle accurate integration of internal states of hardware accelerators into our consistency check.

Acknowledgement

Substantial parts of the research described in this paper were funded by the Federal Ministry of Education and Research (Bundesministerium für Bildung und Forschung — BMBF) registered there under grant numbers 01BU0661 (MxMobile) and 01BU0643 (Easy-C).

References

1. Azevedo, R., Rigo, S., Bartholomeu, M., Araujo, G., Araujo, C., Barros, E.: The ArchC architecture description language and tools. Int. J. Parallel Program. 33, 453–484 (2005)
2. Burch, J., Dill, D.: Automatic verification of Pipelined Microprocessor Control. In: Dill, D.L. (ed.) CAV 1994. LNCS, vol. 818, pp. 68–80. Springer, Heidelberg (1994)
3. Chang, Y., Lee, S., Park, I., Kyung, C.: Verification of a microprocessor using real world applications. In: DAC 1999, pp. 181–184 (1999)
4. Gonzalez, R.: Xtensa: A Configurable and Extensible Processor. IEEE Micro., 60–70 (2000)
5. Hosseini, A., Mavroidis, D., Konas, P.: Code generation and analysis for the functional verification of micro processors. In: DAC 1996, pp. 305–310 (1996)
6. Kalte, H., Porrmann, M., Rückert, U.: A Prototyping Platform for Dynamically Reconfigurable System on Chip Designs. In: Proc. of the IEEE Workshop Heterogeneous reconfigurable Systems on Chip, SoC (2002)
7. Kastens, U., Le, D., Slowik, A., Thies, M.: Feedback Driven Instruction-Set Extension. In: LCTES 2004 (2004)
8. Sawada, J., Hunt, W.: Trace Table Based Approach for Pipeline Microprocessor Verification. In: Grumberg, O. (ed.) CAV 1997. LNCS, vol. 1254, Springer, Heidelberg (1997)
9. Victor, D., Ludden, J., Peterson, R., Nelson, B., Sharp, W., Hsu, J., Chu, B., Behm, M., Gott, R., Romonosky, A., Farago, A.: Functional verification of the POWER5 microprocessor and POWER5 multiprocessor systems. IBM J. Res. Dev. 49, 541–553 (2005)
10. Yim, J., Hwang, Y., Park, C., Choi, H., Yang, W., Oh, H., Park, I., Kyung, C.-M.: A C-based RTL Design Verification Methodology For Complex Microprocessor. In: DAC 1997, pp. 83–88 (1997)

Development of Automotive Communication Based Real-Time Systems - A Steer-by-Wire Case Study

Kay Klobedanz, Christoph Kuznik, Ahmed Elfeky, and Wolfgang Müller

University of Paderborn/C-LAB
Faculty of Electrical Engineering,
Computer Science and Mathematics,
33102 Paderborn, Germany
{kay.klobedanz,christoph.kuznik,ahmed.elfeky,wolfgang.mueller}@c-lab.de

Abstract. Safety-critical automotive systems must fulfill hard real-time constraints to guarantee their reliability and safety requirements. In the context of network-based electronics systems, high-level timing requirements have to be carefully mastered and traced throughout the whole development process. In this paper, we outline the management of scheduling-specific timing information by the application of a steer-by-wire design example. We apply the principles of the AUTOSAR-compliant Timing Augmented Description Language (TADL) following the methodology introduced by the TIMMO project[2]. Focus of the example will be the identification of end-to-end timing constraints and their refinement by means of stimuli-response event chains.

1 Introduction

The development of embedded automotive electronic systems is at a turning point. Modern cars incorporate multiple embedded electronics systems and contain complex distributed heterogeneous bus networks like FlexRay™and CAN. For example, in the year 2004 the embedded electronic system of a Volkswagen Phaeton was composed of hundreds of electrical devices like sensors and actuators, 61 microprocessors, three controller area networks (CAN) and several subnetworks [1]. It is estimated that the average vehicle electronic and software part will rise continuously from its current level of 13 percent of the car's value up to 14.8 percent in 2012 [8]. Despite the first automotive electronics were mainly targeted in the power train domain, recent activities aim to replace traditional mechanical components by their electronic counterparts within the chassis domain. Developing electronics in these safety-critical domains like power train (i.e., control of engine and transmission) and chassis (i.e., control of suspension, steering, and braking) puts many constraints on reliability and predictability onto these components. Especially worst-case timing behavior is becoming more and more relevant to comply with European safety norms like IEC EN 61508 and the automotive focussed version ISO 26262 [10]. For example, a brake-by-wire

A. Rettberg et al. (Eds.): IESS 2009, IFIP AICT 310, pp. 218–225, 2009.

system should react as fast as possible. The designed technical solutions must ensure that the system is dependable (i.e., able to deliver a service that can be justifiably trusted) while being cost-effective at the same time [1].

An example is the Steer-by-Wire concept, whereas all driving commands are propagated electrically. Therefore, the steering wheel is no longer mechanically linked to the front wheels of the car but a system of sensors and actuators perform that way. As additional challenge a typical design process consists of one or more OEMs and several TIER-1 suppliers, which may again have sub contractors. Within in this complex product chain the responsibility for fulfilling end-to-end timing requirements is split between the involved partners [9]. This design trend demands methodologies augmented with timing and verification information in order to avoid costly iterations due to the fact that the actual integration of all distinct developed components takes place as recently as within the last design stages.

Within the TIMing MOdel (TIMMO) ITEA2 project[2] an EAST-ADL[6] based meta model was developed to capture timing requirements right from the most abstract levels of the design process to enable right by design timing behavior. We will show how the TIMMO concepts and the modeling of event chains can be used to gain extensive knowledge and coverage of the intended system timing behavior right from the first design decisions. Therefore, we will describe how the TIMMO concepts are efficiently used for the development of a steer-by-wire validator. Moreover, we will place comments on usability and effectiveness of the proposed workflow.

In Section 2 we will introduce the developed concepts and abilities of the TIMMO project. Thereby, we will focus on the Timing Augmented Description Language (TADL) event chain descriptions of TIMMO. Section 3 will describe how we made use of the TIMMO concepts for the steer-by-wire validator development. Finally, section 4 will draw conclusions with consideration of the designers and end-users' perspectives.

2   Methods and Concepts

Nowadays many different manufacturers and suppliers are involved in the development of modern automotive hardware and software components. Therefore, a standardization of the development process and the corresponding ex-change-formats among the manufacturers is desirable. This standardization is mainly accomplished by model-driven approaches like AUTOSAR and EAST-ADL2. AUTOSAR focuses on implementation relevant aspects, e.g. separation of software development and underlying hardware architecture. EAST-ADL2 addresses the description and refinement of vehicle features on higher abstraction levels [9]. Although a combination of both approaches enables a detailed modeling and implementation of automotive components, a comprehensive formalization of timing constraints throughout the whole development process is still missing. The TIMMO project introduces a methodology and workflow with the desired coupling of AUTOSAR and EAST-ADL2 (see figure 1). Moreover this

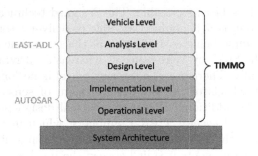

Fig. 1. Coupling of different design levels within the TIMMO project

approach allows the description of timing constrains using the stimuli-response event chains of the Timing Augmented Description Language (TADL). In general, timing information can be distinguished into timing requirements (what is demanded), timing properties (what is offered) and timing contracts (what is negotiated between stakeholders) [9]. In the following we will give a detailed overview of the syntactically and semantically properties of the TADL event chains.

The timing constraints of automotive systems, which are very often register-based multi-rate sampling systems, can be formalized well by the introduced event chains. The element of an event chain with an input register r is further specified by several attributes. These parameters are:

- **Period T**
  Specifies the period of the element, e.g. period of a task execution.

- **Sampling Period T_r**
  Describes the period at which the element reads data. T_r does not have to be equal to T.

- **Writing Period T_w**
  Describes the period at which the element writes data. T_w does not have to be equal to T_r or Tr.

- **Delay d**
  Specifies the time which is needed by the element internally between the stimulus and response, e.g. task execution time.

If there are no detailed information about the internal behavior of a component available, it can be modeled as so-called "black box"-element with the available timing properties (see figure 2). This allows complete verification on higher level of abstraction without having all implementation details on lower levels of abstraction present, for example if suppliers are not willing to share too much data among each other [9].

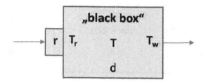

Fig. 2. Model of a "black-box"

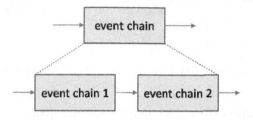

Fig. 3. Example for event chain refinement

TADL allows refinement and composability steps to represent timing on different abstraction levels with event chains. An event chain can be further refined until the actual existing architecture is defined, as shown conceptional in figure 3.

With the principles introduced by the TADL notation it is possible to describe and analyze the system for different end-to-end timing constraints. The most important variants of end-to-end timings in the context of typically automotive systems with sensors and actuators are:

- **Reaction**
  Represents the delay from a certain (sensor) input value until a corresponding (actuator) output value is available. This is essential for fast-response systems like x-by-wire.
- **Age**
  Represents the delay until a certain output (actuator) value is available from a corresponding (sensor) input value. The age of data has a great impact on the quality of control algorithms.

In the next chapter we will describe how we used the presented TADL event chains for the development process of a Steer-By-Wire system.

3   Design and Implementation

In the previous chapter we described concepts and methods proposed by the TIMMO project for the design of real-time automotive systems. Thereby we focused on the stimuli-response event chains as a valuable instrument for the definition and formalization of timing constraints throughout the whole development process. Here we will present how we applied the described approach for the design and implementation of a steer-by-wire-system validator from scratch to evaluate its capabilities.

Fig. 4. "Black box"-element for steer-by-wire system

Fig. 5. First refinement step of the event chain with timing properties

At higher abstraction levels the requirements of a steer-by-wire system can be generally formulated for the whole system, e.g.: The reaction of the steering axle and wheel as well as the resulting feedback has to be "instantly". This means that the end-to-end reaction delay is constraint and must not be bigger than a few milliseconds. Based on the information of this abstraction level, we model the whole system as a single "black box"-element within a first abstract event chain (see figure 4).

Like common in the development of industrial automotive systems we use predetermined sensor/actuator components from third party manufacturers. As steering wheel we utilize an existing device from the manufacturer TRW Automotive [3]. This component is equipped with a CAN Interface over which messages with measured sensor values like torque, position and rotational velocity are send with a writing period of $T_W = 2,3ms$. Apart from that, little about the internal behavior is known. Therefore, we will model it as a "black box"-element in the upcoming event chains.

The second major component is a specially designed setup of a steering and damping test bed constructed by the department for control engineering and mechatronics from the University of Paderborn. It is composed of a steering axle with a standard tire and a wheel suspension equipped with active damping. The assembled electric actuating motors are connected to the system via CAN interfaces. The steering testbed is also modeled as a "black box"-element.

A first refinement step of the previous abstract event chain is shown in figure 5 and includes the combination of steering wheel, the steering and a communication & control "black box" element.

On this abstraction level the timing properties of the components of the event chain already allow to conclude properties for other elements of further refinement steps. For example, the given writing period T_w of the steering wheel imposes requirements for the sampling periods T_r of subsequent elements. Here, $T_r \leq T_w$ must hold for the avoidance of undersampling effects, e.g. message loss. The delay of the communication and control "black box" is composed of several subcomponent delays. Hence, an additional refinement step to the functional component level is necessary, to realize a detailed description of the timing

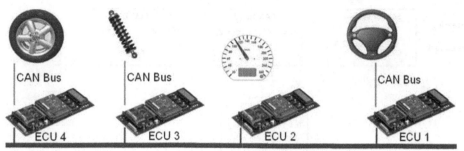

Fig. 6. System Architecture of the Steer-By-Wire Validator

constraints of the system. To allow a detailed definition and analysis of the timing requirements on this abstraction level an identification of the used components and their temporal properties is essential. In the following we give an overview of the functional architecture and components of the communication & control part of our steer-by-wire system.

Architecture. The functionality of our validator is implemented by a distributed communication based system. It consists of the already mentioned actuator and sensor units as well as several electronic control units (ECUs) communicating over a heterogeneous network infrastructure with CAN and FlexRay interfaces (see architecture in figure 6).

Hardware (ECUs). As ECUs we use Universal FlexRay Control Units from TT-Tech Computertechnik AG[4] with a TriCore TC1796 CPU and integrated CAN interface. The connection between the ECUs and the sensors/actuators is realized via CAN. The Units are also equipped with a FlexRay controller for the communication between the ECUs. Due to the CAN and FlexRay interfaces the ECUs can also act as gateway between these two communication protocols. Like common in distributed automotive systems every ECU is dedicated to a specific sensor/actuator and running a single control task. The implementation of control and communication tasks is based on a cluster design and node configuration realized with a toolchain from TTTech which generates COM-Stacks confirm to AUTOSAR [5].

The previous described complex system and communication architecture in combination with the given hard real-time constraints result in a big challenge for the design and the definition of appropriate schedules for tasks and messages. Based on the information from our defined event chains (writing period of the steering wheel $T_w = 2, 3ms$) we set the period T of the FlexRay cycle to $2ms$, which results in an according sampling period T_r and writing period T_w. Additionally the control and communication tasks as well as the other necessary CAN Bus are synchronized to the FlexRay cycle to minimize the end-to-end delays throughout the whole system. The timing constraints of the elements on the functional component level can now be described by the event chain in figure 7 with its significant properties.

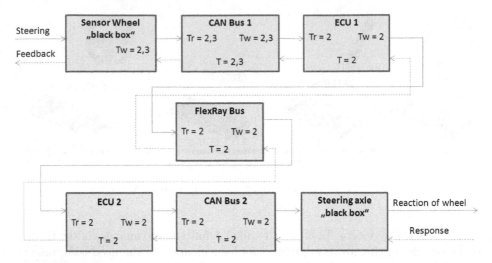

Fig. 7. Event chain of steer-by-wire system on functional component level

The event chain in figure 7 represents the system architecture in a sufficient level of detail for our scope. Therefore, we perform the implementation on this level of abstraction. The implemented communication tasks including the protocol translations for the gated-network components do work correctly regarding the specified reaction end-to-end timing constraints. Experiments with the validator prove that the desired timing requirement of sensed instant reaction between steering wheel and the steering axle, as defined on feature level, is fulfilled. Additionally we made use of worst-case execution time analysis tools, as proposed by the TIMMO methodology. Based on assumptions for the WCETs of the control and communication tasks we get results for the steering path worst-case end-to-end delays which show that our system will react in a few milliseconds, as intended. The worst case-reaction delay for the implementation is estimated to be $\sim 8ms$.

4   Evaluation and Outlook

With help of the TIMMO TADL language and the usage of formal scheduling analysis as proposed by the TIMMO workflow, an issue for the response path (feedback) could be identified. In the worst case the scheduling delays the actuator response to the steering wheel so much that the data age is getting to big. In general, this affects the quality of control. Within the Steer-by-Wire validator the controlling algorithm could show abnormal behavior.

In order to avoid this case, an ideal combination of task schedule and offsets was calculated with help of SymTA/S from Symtavision GmbH [7]. Moreover, we decided to further separate SWC functions into smaller modules, resulting in the chance of a tighter schedule. In general, the application of the principles of the Timing Augmented Description Language (TADL) gives great benefit to network-based electronic systems design. Timing properties (and later scheduling properties) can be annotated to features within early design phases and can be verified prior the actual implementation. The measured timings coincides with the estimated timing behavior, assumed an accurate architecture event chain model is specified. The event chain based evaluation of system behavior reveals possible design flaws and is a good starting point for design partitioning and revision.

On applying the TIMMO methodology the challenge for the user will be to perform accurate and consistent functional decomposition and refinement of top-level functions from Analysis Level down to SWC component level. Moreover, the segmentation for end-to-end delays into single timing chain segments has to be considered at the same time [9].

With help of this "timing is right-by-design" approach the implementation caused no trouble. The avoidance of costly iterations can save high amounts of money within large industry projects. Moreover, the possibility of WCET and scheduling analysis can avoid over-provisioning within electronic systems design, resulting in lower overall costs.

It is planned to validate additional timing related concepts within the steer-by-wire validator in the near future. Ideas range from the estimation of hardware execution time based on a SystemC library as well as usage of static program analysis tools to estimate the necessary ECU cycles of the software. Combining all these concepts the TIMMO workflow will further advance the accuracy of right-by-design timing behavior modeling of complex HW/SW systems.

Acknowledgements

This work described herein was partly supported by the DFG Sonderforschungs-bereich 614 and by the German Ministry for Education and Research (BMBF) through the ITEA2 project TIMMO (01IS07002).

References

1. Navet, N., Simonot-Lion, F.: Automotive Embedded Systems Handbook. CRC Press, Boca Raton (2008)
2. TIMing MOdel (TIMMO) project: (2009), http://www.timmo.org/
3. TRW Automotive Inc. (2009), http://www.trwauto.com/
4. TTTech Computertechnik AG: (2009), http://www.tttech.com/
5. Janouch, S.: FlexRay and AUTOSAR get it right, Elektronik automotive (2009), http://www.elektroniknet.de/
6. Advanced Traffic Efficiency and Safety through Software Technology (ATESST2) project (2008), http://www.atesst.org/
7. Symtavision GmbH: (2009), http://www.symtavision.com/
8. Hammerschmidt, C.: Automotive electronics to recover slowly after deep dip, EE-Times (2009)
9. Cuenot, P., Frey, P., Johansson, R., et al.: Developing Automotive Products Using the EAST-ADL2, an AUTOSAR Compliant Architecture Description Language, Mentor Graphics Techpub (2009)
10. Reif, K.: Automobilelektronik, Eine Einführung für Ingenieure. Vieweg-Verlag, Wiesbaden, 3. Auflage (2008)

Automatic Transformation of System Models in Automotive Electronics

Ralph Görgen[1], Jan-Hendrik Oetjens[2], Jan Freuer[2], and Wolfgang Nebel[3]

[1] OFFIS Institute for Information Technology Oldenburg, Germany
Ralph.Goergen@offis.de
[2] Robert Bosch GmbH Reutlingen, Germany
{Jan-Hendrik.Oetjens,Jan.Freuer}@de.bosch.com
[3] Carl von Ossietzky University Oldenburg, Germany
Wolfgang.Nebel@informatik.uni-oldenburg.de

Abstract. Evaluation and refinement of system models often require modifications in the model that follow concrete rules. In this work, a method for a flexible automation of such transformation steps will be presented. It allows savings in development time and reduces the error proneness. Therefore, a tool for rule based manipulation of VHDL design descriptions has been extended to enable its use with system models in C++ and SystemC. An automotive electronics application, the integration of SystemC modules into a MATLAB/Simulink simulation by automatic wrapper generation, will show its use in the design process.

Introduction

While electronic components in cars become more and more complex to optimize comfort, security, and environmental impact, the increasing pressure in the automobile market permanently involves cost reductions. A further increase of complexity comes with the special demands of automotive electronics, e. g. reliability and robustness over long periods of time in a harmful environment regarding to vibrations, temperature changes, and electro-magnetic interference. Design and verification of such systems are exceeding challenges that need support by appropriate methods and tools.

Often, the V-Model is the basis of hardware/software development processes. After the specification, an abstract model is created to perform first analyses. MATLAB/Simulink [15] and SystemC [14] are common in this context. Then, a stepwise refinement follows until a final implementation is found. The way from a system model to a final implementation requires lots of code transformations, either as a step to a lower level of abstraction, or to realize several design decisions. Some transformations need the creativity of a designer. Others follow concrete rules, they rather laborious work and a possible source of needless errors.

A cooperation of Robert Bosch GmbH and OFFIS has developed a framework for rule based design transformations[1]. It includes an easy way to define

---

[1] This work has been partially founded by the German Bundesministerium für Bildung und Forschung (BMBF) in the VISION project (01M3078D).

A. Rettberg et al. (Eds.): IESS 2009, IFIP AICT 310, pp. 226–237, 2009.

transformation rules and to apply them automatically to a design description in the hardware description languages VHDL and VHDL-AMS [13]. In this contribution, an extension of the framework for C++ and SystemC is presented. Hence, the designer is able to use the same tool at higher levels of abstraction too. Furthermore, inter-language transformations become possible.

Section 1 explains the underlying design flow. In Section 2 the transformation framework is presented in detail. Section 3 deals with related work and shows the problems in the present case. In Section 4, the C++/SystemC frontend is described, and in Section 5, an automotive electronics example shows how the new possibilities can be used in the design process. Finally, in Section 6, the results are summed up and a short outlook on future work is given.

1   Transformations in a System Design Flow

Regarding to the V-Model (Figure 1), a system development process contains a number of more or less complex changes in the system description. Step by step, the final implementation develops from an abstract system specification. Some refinement steps require creativity of a designer or specific knowledge about the application. Automation of these steps is often impossible. Others offer very little degrees of freedom or follow concrete rules because they are defined by requirements or process standards or because they follow common laws. In general, performing them automatically is less error-prone and saves time and costs. Lots of these design steps can be realized with common tool chains but there are others that are not covered by available tools. Each application domain, company, or even particular designer knows individual design steps that are either too specific to be provided by commercial tools or based on confidential knowledge.

The method presented here allows the automation of individual design steps by creating a particular transformation rule. Whenever a design step is not covered by the available tools, the designer can decide whether its automation

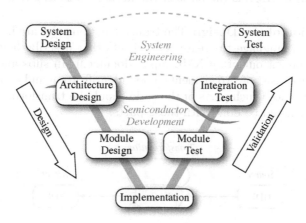

Fig. 1. V-Model

makes sense, depending on how often a transformation rule can be used and how complex its implementation is by contrast with the manual transformation. An important detail is that the design can be written out in a human readable and recognizable form. Hence, it is possible to perform pursuing steps by hand or by any other tool. The tool to create and apply the transformation rules is already in use and successful in the lower regions of the V-Model (VHDL). Currently existing applications are the insertion of clock gating cells to reduce power consumption, code obfuscation, insertion of hamming codes into busses, and many more. Now, it has been extended for its use at higher levels of abstraction.

2   Transformation Framework

The transformation framework allows the flexible transformation of design descriptions based on user-defined rules. Figure 2 shows the general transformation flow. At first, the design is read by a frontend and an XML based description is generated. Then, this XML tree can be transformed using XSLT [18]. When all transformations are finished, the result tree can be written out in the original description language. The tool is implemented in Java to allow its usage on every common platform. Furthermore, it is prepared for the integration into development environments, e. g. Eclipse [3].

Reading the Design Accordant with the flow mentioned above, firstly, it is necessary to create an XML representation of the design. This is done by a parser, which is generated with ANTLR [2], an open-source tool for parser and lexer generation. Its input is an EBNF like syntax definition extended by semantic attributes. The generated parser reads text in the particular language and builds an abstract syntax tree. Besides syntax elements, comments and formatting characters are included in that tree to allow its use in later processing steps. A tree generated like that, supplemented with some semantic information, and written out as XML is the basis of the actual transformations.

Transformation of the Design The transformation rules are implemented in XSLT. This is a language to create style sheets that describe how to generate an output document out of an XML input document. In substance, the transformation rules consist of two elements, code identification and code generation. The first determines which parts of the code should be transformed, the second which changes should be done with those parts.

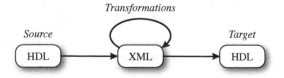

Fig. 2. Transformation Approach

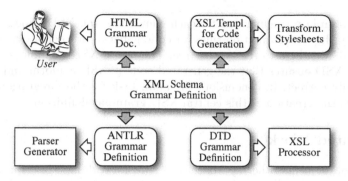

Fig. 3. Grammar definition as central document

Output of the Transformed Source Text To write out the tree in its original description language after the transformation, XSLT is used again. A style sheet outputs the syntax tree elements as text. The original appearance of the code can be restored by considering formatting characters and comments as well. Hence, the designer is able to recognize the code and to continue to work with it.

Frontend Requirements

Some specific requirements result from the mentioned application scheme.

1. It must be able to create an XML tree.
2. In order to facilitate the implementation of transformation rules, the XML syntax tree has to meet the formal syntax definition as stated in the particular language standards as near as possible.
3. Besides the syntactical elements, the XML tree must contain comments and formatting characters. Their recovery has to be possible when transforming the design back to source code to preserve its readability.
4. The frontend should be maintainable and easy to extend; many description languages are permanently refined and the language standards are regularly adapted to new challenges too.

Extensions to Support Various Languages

The maintainability of the transformation tool's language support extensions is guaranteed by the use of a single central document, the grammar definition in form of an XML Schema (abr. XSD) [17]. As shown in Figure 3, any other components of the environment are created out of it automatically. An ANTLR grammar definition is built to generate the parser. The used XSLT processor does not support XSD. Therefore, a grammar definition as a DTD is necessary to validate the XML trees and therewith the syntactical correctness of the corresponding code. Furthermore, the XSD is translated to an HTML grammar documentation to relieve the implementation of transformation rules. Finally, an XSLT template is generated for each element of the XSD. These templates are used by the transformation rules for code generation to create new XML elements and add them to the syntax tree. The use of XSLT templates generated out of the XSD ensures that the generated code is XSD conform and therewith syntactically correct. In conclusion, the main task for the integration of a new language is the creation of this central XSD grammar definition.

3   Related Work

This section presents other approaches to transform design descriptions and to parse C++ and SystemC and explains why they are inappropriate in our case.

Transforming Design Descriptions In industrial practice, it is common to use scripting languages like sed [4], AWK [1], and Perl [16] to modify design descriptions. They allow the definition of regular expressions to analyze the source code and perform changes to it. Languages like VHDL and SystemC are no regular languages and their analysis with such scripts is very limited. As a consequence, there are only local and not too complex changes possible.

In [10], another XML based representation of VHDL designs and the way to generate it is presented. Then, to the XML tree several transformations like the generation of HTML documentations can be applied. It is useful for VHDL but there is no support for any other language available.

Parsing C++ and SystemC One possible opportunity is the use of the frontend of a standard C++ compiler. Some of them offer a way to output their internal representation of the source code as XML trees [9]. That meets the first requirement but not the others. Conformance to the standard is not given. Only parts of the resulting trees correspond to the formal syntax definition on one hand, the here examined frontends add some compiler specific elements to the code on the other. Hence, requirement 2 is broken. But the crucial point is that requirement 3 cannot be fulfilled, the retrieval of the original source files is not possible. The problem arises from the two-stage strategy of common C++ frontends. At first, the source code is read by a preprocessor unit. Then, the pre-processed text is given to the actual C++ parser. The preprocessing contains the removal of comments as well as text replacements according to the preprocessor directives. The XML output of the compiler frontends solely contains the so prepared C++ code. Consequently, some information like the original file structure, comments and formatting characters are not included in the result tree and thus unrecoverable.

Furthermore, there are explicit SystemC parsers like KaSCPar [5] or Pinapa [11]. KaSCPar performs two phases. The first creates a syntax tree. Within the second, the generated tree is elaborated and supplemented with structural information. In contrast to C++ parsers, the KaSCPar frontend knows dedicated tokens for some of the SystemC specific Keywords. This facilitates recognizing SystemC constructs in the syntax tree but it complicates maintenance and adaption to changes in the language standard. That conflicts with requirement 4. The open-source solution Pinapa also provides a SystemC frontend that supplements the syntax tree with structural information in a second step. It uses a tree that is similar to the internal representation of the GNU GCC. The tool does not offer a possibility to output the tree in XML, and hence, requirement 1 is not met. Both of the two parsers break requirement 3. Since they both use the GNU GCC preprocessor, important information for the recovery of the source text is missing in the result trees.

Thus, to the best of our knowledge, none of the existing approaches is able to satisfy all of the key requirements identified in Section 1 for our specific application scenario.

4   C++/SystemC Extension

The C++/SystemC frontend developed by us works in three phases. In the first phase, a customized preprocessor is called, in the second the actual C++ parser. In the third phase, the generated C++ syntax tree is transformed to a modified syntax tree with XSLT. Figure 4 pictures this procedure that will be explained in detail in the following section. Due to the fact that the frontend is based on a regular C++ frontend, it is easy to extend it for other C++ based languages like SystemC-AMS [6] or OSSS [7]. One solely has to integrate the particular header files.

To reduce the effort for the development of the C++ parser and preprocessor, we modified existing implementations in ANTLR for our purpose. The preliminaries originate from Youngki Ku (preprocessor) and David Wigg (C++ parser). Their results are available for free at the ANTLR homepage [2].

Preprocessor

As described in Section 3, it is important in our application that code modifications done by the preprocessor are reconstructible to allow reassembling the code in its original appearance. Therefore, comments and formatting characters are

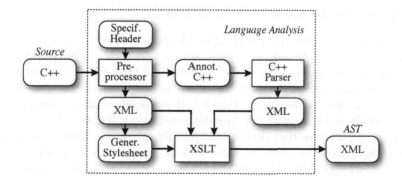

Fig. 4. Frontend work-flow

not removed by the preprocessor described here. But the preprocessor directives are processed as usual. That means in substance expanding macros, integrating include files and evaluation of conditional compilation directives. For this reason, a preprocessor syntax tree is created and then the prepared C++ code is generated out of it. In addition to these basic functionalities, every statement concerning the preprocessor is annotated with a unique ID. Meta-tokens that contain these IDs are inserted in the generated C++ code. They mark the parts of the code that arise from the corresponding preprocessor action. As a result, the output of the preprocessor is clearly associated with the original source code.

Finally, the preprocessor result and its syntax tree are passed to the downstream C++ parser.

C++ Parser

The C++ parser receives the preprocessor output and converts it to a C++ syntax tree. Therewith, comments and formatting characters are included in the tree. Since they do not have any syntactical meaning, no specific nodes are generated for them. They are added to the following terminal as attributes. The meta-tokens inserted by the preprocessor do not become nodes in the C++ syntax tree but attributes to terminals as well. Figure 5 shows schematically the connections between input text, preprocessor syntax tree, preprocessor output and C++ syntax tree. Macro definitions and macro calls can be seen in the preprocessor syntax tree. Each macro call is annotated with a unique ID and a reference to the corresponding macro definition. In addition, the ID of the macro call is inserted as a meta-token into the preprocessor output text. The C++ parser can use this ID as a reference to the macro call to annotate it to the terminals in the C++ syntax tree. Finally, the syntax trees of preprocessor and C++ parser are written together into a single file as XML trees. Now, this file contains all necessary information. The C++ syntax tree contains the actual relevant code as well as comments and formatting characters, the preprocessor tree contains the original source code. IDs and references describe the relations between the two trees.

Transformation to Modified Syntax Tree

In the third phase, the generated XML file is processed with XSLT. Here, a difference is made between the actual design and code parts that have been added by the integration of external header files. This differentiation is crucial because external code must not be modified on one hand and it does not need to be written out on the other. Usually, these headers are system files or in the case of SystemC part of the language definition. Those parts are allowed to be removed because they do not contain any relevant information. A further task in this phase is to undo the calls of those macros whose definitions are in one of the external files. This step facilitates the recognition of specific parts of the code because macros are often used as language elements, e. g. SC_MODULE or SC_METHOD. This procedure automatically works with any other library like

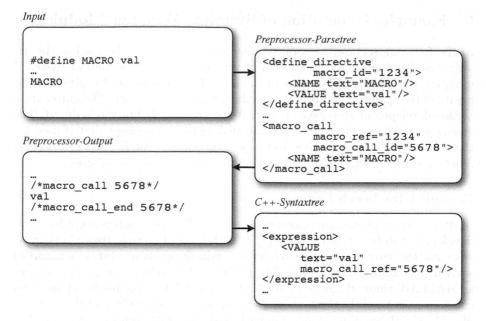

Fig. 5. IDs and references in the syntax tree

OSSS or SystemC-AMS as well. The result is a modified syntax tree and any transformation can be applied to it.

Output of the Transformed Source Text

To get back to the original source text, XSLT is used again. The XML tree is written to files as C++ code. The original formatting and directory structure is reconstructed as far as possible. The preprocessor logs the beginnings and ends of each file as well as include directives and file paths. With this, the reconstruction of files and directory structure is unproblematic. The retransformation of macro expansions and conditional compilation directives is more complex. If the code that came out of such a directive has been changed by a transformation and new or transformed code has been generated, the original code must not be written out. As a consequence, the original formatting and the particular preprocessor directive get lost. All parts of the code that has not been transformed are typed out exactly like the preprocessor read it. For newly generated parts that do not contain formatting information a standard formatting is used.

A special case of conditional compilation directives is the surrounding `#ifndef` – `#define` – `#endif` which is used in header files to prevent multiple compilations. When this instruction sequence cannot be reconstructed, a new one that surrounds the content of the file is generated automatically.

Now, the transformation flow is complete. Design descriptions in C++, and as a consequence in SystemC as well, can be read, transformed and typed out again as source text, and the frontend meets all requirements stated in Section 1.

5   Example: Generation of SystemC Wrapper Modules

In the following section, we want to show how the tool can be used in the design flow. The automatic generation of wrapper modules to connect SystemC modules to a MATLAB/Simulink model is used as an example. Despite the simplicity of the example, it involves a significant gain in efficiency. The automation of this development step saves time and the error probability is reduced. The generated wrappers are part of an extended testbench concept that is used for the development of automotive electronic components. The following subsection illustrates it in short, before the wrapper generation itself is explained.

Extended Testbench Concept

In support of verification by simulation, an extended testbench concept has been developed at Robert Bosch GmbH [8]. It is shown in Figure 6. Its main purpose is to use the same testbench modules at multiple levels of abstraction and in several simulation environments. The design under verification may be present as MATLAB/Simulink, SystemC, or VHDL model. The same testbench modules can be used in all of the three cases. We want to have a closer look at the coupling of a MATLAB/Simulink simulation with SystemC testbench modules now. Using MATLAB/Simulink and SystemC at the same time causes problems because the two simulation environments are based on two different simulation concepts. MATLAB/Simulink uses continuous simulation, SystemC discrete event simulation. It is required to synchronize the two environments in an appropriate way. Furthermore they use different data types so that conversions are necessary for data exchange. The data type conversion as well as the synchronization is done by a SystemC wrapper that encloses the actual testbench module. This wrapper is composed of two parts. Firstly, the wrapper module must be derived from an abstract wrapper class. It must provide one port for each port of the testbench module. Secondly, a so called `createModule` method must be implemented to bind

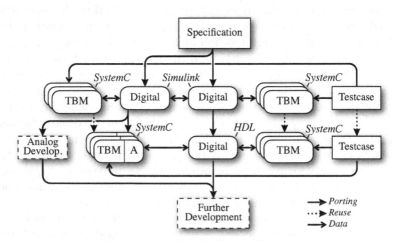

Fig. 6. Extended Testbench Concept

the ports. This method also registers the ports because the wrapper must know the number of ports and whether they are input or output ports.

Automatic Wrapper Generation

Now, the SystemC wrappers should be generated automatically by a transformation rule. At first, the frontend must read the testbench module and transfer it to an XML syntax tree. Then, the required parts are inserted. That is, the tool generates subtrees that correspond to the wrapper module and the `createModule` method. For each port of the testbench module the actual port declaration in the wrapper module and its binding and register statements in the `createModule` method are generated. Then, these subtrees are inserted into the syntax tree at the appropriate positions. Finally, the extended syntax can be written out as C++ code and the testbench module is ready to use it in a MATLAB/Simulink simulation. Since an example implementation of a wrapper was available in our case, the first step was to set up a transformation rule that generates exactly this source code. That is very easy because the transformation tool offers a feature to read a piece of source code and automatically create a rule that generates the same code in form of a syntax tree, which can be inserted in a design then. In this rule, those parts where the port declaration, binding, and register statements are generated had to be surrounded by loop statements to generate the required elements for all ports of any module. Furthermore, the static port names had to be changed to dynamic ones picked out of the testbench module.

Evaluation of the Results

By means of the transformation tool, its C++/SystemC extension, and the transformation rule, we are able to surround any SystemC testbench module with a wrapper to integrate it in a MATLAB/Simulink simulation. This can be done fully automated and many times faster as well as less error-prone than its manual implementation. Table 1 compares the durations for the manual and automatic wrapper generation to test of a sensor evaluation circuit used in an automotive controller IC. When the manual wrapper generation is used, the implementation of the wrappers can start immediately. Otherwise, it is necessary to implement the code for one wrapper at first. Then, the creation of the transformation rule can start as depicted above. After that, the generation of further wrappers is

Table 1. Comparison of wrapper generation

Task	manual	automatic
Implementation 1st wrapper	1 h	1 h
Transformation rule	–	2 h
Implementation 2nd wrapper	1 h	–
Generation 2nd wrapper	–	≈ 0 h
Total	2 h	3 h

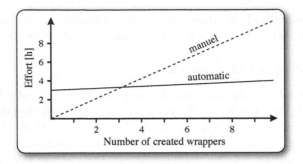

Fig. 7. Time needed for creation of the wrappers

possible in only a few seconds. The times used here had been worked out with a concrete example. Of course, the exact values heavily depend on the particular testbench module and designer. But, it is obvious that the automatic generation takes longer when only few wrappers are needed. However, the transformation rule must be implemented only once and can be used again and again. As shown in Figure 7, the time needed for the generation of several wrappers rises very little whereas the effort for the manual method increases much more. Since generally several testbench modules are used in one project, and with it, several wrappers are needed, and additionally, the same transformation rule can be used in more than one project, the automation of this design step is a good opportunity to improve the development process in terms of design effort and quality.

Besides transformations of SystemC models, the newly added grammar definition allows inter language transformations. An application that uses this functionality is a VHDL-to-SystemC translation that already has been published [12]. Additionally, this example shows the potential of our approach.

6   Conclusion and Outlook

This contribution presented an extension for a tool for design transformations. Apart from its use with design descriptions in VHDL, it can be applied to C++ and SystemC. As a result, the developer can use a tool he already knows in the context of VHDL as well at higher levels of abstraction. He is able to read descriptions in C++ and SystemC, transform them, and output them again. In substance, the extension consists of a C++ preprocessor and parser. They are based on existing implementations available for free. As a result, the effort for the adaption to our needs was very small. An example has shown how the new possibilities can be used in a design process. In order to do so, an automatic generation of SystemC wrappers has been implemented. It allows the integration of SystemC modules into a MATLAB/Simulink simulation. With the automation of that step, it is possible to achieve results faster and less error-prone.

In the future, we plan to use the tool for more complex transformations, e. g. optimization of design descriptions in SystemC. Additionally, we want to integrate Verilog as a further design language.

References

1. Aho, A.V., Kernighan, B.W., Weinberger, P.J.: The AWK Programming Language. Addison Wesley, Reading (1988)
2. ANTLR. ANother Tool for Language Recognition (2009), http://www.antlr.org
3. Eclipse Foundation (2009), http://www.eclipse.org
4. Free Software Foundation. ses, a stream editor (1999), http://www.gnu.org/software/sed/manual/sed.html
5. FZI Karlsruhe. KaSCPar - Karlsruher SystemC Parser Suite (2006), http://www.fzi.de/sim/kascpar.html
6. Grimm, C., Barnasconi, M., Vachoux, A., Einwich, K.: An Introduction to Modeling Embedded Analog/Mixed-Signal Systems using SystemC AMS Extensions. Whitepaper, Open SystemC Initiative (2008)
7. Grabbe, C., Grüttner, K., Kleen, H., Schubert, T.: OSSS - A Library for Synthesisable System Level Models in SystemC (2007), http://www.system-synthesis.org
8. Hylla, K., Oetjens, J.-H., Nebel, W.: Using SystemC for an extended MATLAB/Simulink verification flow. In: FDL 2008: Proceedings of the Forum on Specification and Design Languages (2008)
9. Kitware. GCC-XML - XML output for GCC (2007), http://www.gccxml.org
10. Karayiannis, T., Mades, J., Windisch, A., Schneider, T., Ecker, W.: Using XML in VHDL Analysis and Simulation. In: Proceedings of the Forum on Design Languages (FDL) (September 2000)
11. Moy, M.: Pinapa: An open-source SystemC front-end (2005), http://greensocs.sourceforge.net/pinapa/
12. Oetjens, J.-H., Görgen, R., Gerlach, J., Nebel, W.: An Automated Flow for Integration Hardware IP into the Automotive Systemc Engeneering Process. In: DATE 2009: Proceedings of the conference on Design, automation and test in Europe (2009)
13. Oetjens, J.-H., Gerlach, J., Rosenstiel, W.: Flexible specification and application of rule-based transformations in an automotive design flow. In: DATE 2006: Proceedings of the conference on Design, automation and test in Europe (2006)
14. OSCI. IEEE Std. 1666, SystemC Language Reference Manual (2005), http://www.systemc.org
15. The Mathworks Inc. (2009), http://www.mathworks.com
16. Wall, L., Christiansen, T., Orwant, J. (eds.): Programming Perl. O'Reilly Media, Inc., Sebastopol (2000)
17. World Wide Web Consortium. XML Schema 1.0 (2004), http://www.w3.org/XML/Schema
18. World Wide Web Consortium. XSL Transformtions (XSLT) Version 2.0 (2007), http://www.w3.org/TR/xslt20

Towards a Load Balancing Middleware for Automotive Infotainment Systems

Yara Khaluf[1] and Achim Rettberg[2]

[1] University of Paderborn, Warburger Str. 100, 33098 Paderborn, Germany
khaluf@googlemail.com
[2] Carl von Ossietzky University Oldenburg, Escherweg 2, D-26121 Oldenburg,
Germany
achim.rettberg@informatik.uni-oldenburg.de

Abstract. In this paper a middleware for distributed automotive systems is developed. The goal of this middleware is to support the load bal- ancing and service optimization in automotive infotainment and entertainment systems. These systems provide navigation, telecommunication, Internet, audio/video and many other services where a kind of dynamic load balancing mechanisms in addition to service quality optimization mechanisms will be applied by the developed middleware in order to improve the system performance and also at the same time improve the quality of services if possible.

Keywords: Load Balancing, Automotive Infotainment Systems, Service Migration, Service Quality, Service Availability.

1 Introduction

The last decade has seen a resurgence of advanced technologies being implemented in automobiles. Functions that were considered highly complex and difficult to be implemented are now being provided with various facilities.

When so many services are being embedded in a car on many devices, there might be mechanism which regulates the way of providing the services (tasks) in an optimal way with a high performance. The rest of this paper is organized as follows: section 2 describes the related work in the field of research where the developed middleware is located. Section 3 explains shortly the motivation of this work depending on some scenarios. The description of the middleware architecture and services provided by it are in section 4. Section 5 gives a look at the C-Simulation of the middleware and the conclusion and future work are then in section 6.

2 Related Work

Several publications regarding load balancing and extensive research has been done on static and dynamic strategies and algorithms [1]. Load balancing is

A. Rettberg et al. (Eds.): IESS 2009, IFIP AICT 310, pp. 238–249, 2009.

used in the domain of parallel and grid computing for optimization. Cybenko addresses the dynamic load balancing for distributed memory multiprocessors [2]. In [3] Hu et. al. regard an optimal dynamic algorithm and Azar discusses on-line load balancing. Diekmann et. al. present the difference between dynamic and static load balancing strategies for distributed memory machines [4]. Heiss and Schmitz introduce the Particle Approach for mapping tasks to processor nodes at runtime in multiprogrammed multicomputer systems solved by considering tasks as particles acted upon by forces. Furthermore the developed load balancing mechanisms are located on a separate middleware layer. Balasubramanian, Schmidt, Dowdy, and Othman consider in [5], and [6] middleware load balancing strategies and adaptive load balancing services. They introduce the Cygnus, an adaptive load balancing/ monitoring service based on CORBA middleware standard. The concept of dynamic reconfigurable automotive systems is also regarded in [7] and [8]

3 Motivation

Performance in automotive infotainment systems is a critical field of research. For many infotainment services like navigating and telecommunication ones, the performance is a question of service robustness and accurate response time of the system. For some other infotainment or entertainment systems the performance is a question of service quality more than other factors like by the audio and video services.

Overloaded ECUs, crashed ECU or new attached ECUs are cases to be faced in the domain of infotainment systems, this will make it important for the automotive industry to have some strategies which help to overcome such problems.

4 Middleware Architecture and Services

In this section, I will give an overview of the proposed architecture of the developed middleware in addition to a summary of the different services provided by it.

The design decision of embedding the developed load balancing and load optimization mechanisms on a separate middleware layer has the advantage to use this middleware later independent of the operating system running on the considered infotainment system 1. There are on the other hand middlewares which provide such load balancing techniques like CORBA [12] and Autosar [13], but they are not suitable to be used in the scenario of automotive infotainment systems we present in this work.

First of all, the developed automotive middleware has some design requirements to fulfill like fault tolerance, special communication model for automotive network, global time base and resource frugality. Such requirements are needed to satisfy the distributed, real-time and service criticality of automotive systems.

On the automotive infotainment systems there is a kind of real time behaviour with soft deadlines system needed. Like in the navigation system, where sometimes it is not more useful to get the direction where to drive after passing the

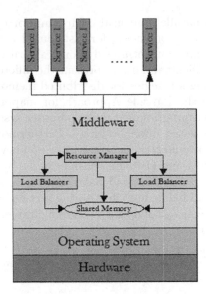

Fig. 1. Developed Middleware Layer

traffic crossing. Real time behaviour with hard deadlines is not needed on the infotainment systems yet, which does not give the possibility to discuss some concepts like automotive safety critical systems. Before explaining the main services provided by the developed middleware, I would like to give a short overview of the main components of the middleware 1.

4.1 Middleware Main Components

There are three main components of the developed middleware listed as followings:

Load Balancer: The load balancer is the component responsible of applying the different load balancing mechanisms supported by the middleware in addition to the performance optimization services.It is responsible of assigning first the tasks to the different vehicle ECUs and then balance and rebalance the different loads on the system ECUs in order to get optimal resource utilization and decrease the computing time of these tasks.

A kind of dynamic load balancing is needed here to be applied by the load balancer. There is always the ability to receive user requests and system tasks to perform on the system without expecting these a prior, in addition to the ECU crash and new attachment cases. for these reasons is the static load balancing not useful to be applied and a dynamic load balancing is the right solution. There maybe more than one load balancer on the system to guarantee the redundancy and reduce the communication costs.

Resource Manager: The resource manager supervises the different resources of the system and the ECUs. It is aware of the complete network resource situation at any point of time and can provide the load balancer with the information it needs at any time. There maybe more than one resource manager in the system and all the resource managers synchronize with each other.

Shared memory: The shared memory is needed to store some information which is required by the other middleware components like load balancer and resource manager. According to the relative small size of the ECU local memory, we will use the concept of distributed shared memory, distributed on some or all system ECUs.

4.2   Middleware Services

A summary of the different services provided by the developed middleware to improve the overall performance is in following:

– **Tasks Assignment service:** This service is provided to assign the different tasks arrive to the system to the different ECUs to be executed. A specific scheduling policy is applied on the different tasks to determine their priorities. EDF (Earliest Deadline First) is the scheduling policy used in this work.

  The automotive infotainment and entertainment systems are heterogeneous environments, where the different ECUs differ from each other in one or more property. The main difference between the ECUs is that they are not able to execute the same kind of tasks referred to as task categories. Each ECU is able to execute a set of tasks categories consists minimum of one, for example the navigating system can provide navigating, music and internet services. This heterogeneity of the system ECUs make it not possible to assign a specific task to any of the available ECUs. By assigning a specific task according to its priority to some ECU, it must be checked that the ECU can execute the selected task and that the new load of the ECU is hold within a predefined limit.

  This service will be provided by the load balancer periodically. At each time the load balancer applies this mechanism, it sends a request to the resource manager to get the necessary information about the available ECUs in the system and the different task categories they can execute 2. After that the load balancer select the tasks according to their priorities and for each one tries to find the suitable ECU which can execute it with keeping the load within the predefined limits. After that, the assigned task will be stored also on the shared memory in a special queue called Currently Executing Tasks queue which will be used later in the case of ECU crash. This information will also be stored on the resource manager, as the resource manager must have at each point of time the up-to-date information of the system.

– **Load Balancing Service:** This service is the core of the developed middleware. it aims to balance the different loads of the different ECUs in order to improve the performance of the system. Dynamic load balancing mechanisms are used and developed to be suitable on the heterogeneous systems. The two developed policies developed mainly are the sender and receiver policies. The

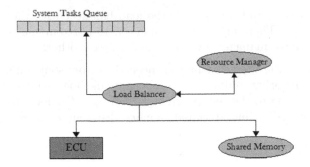

Fig. 2. Tasks Assignment Service

load balancing policies are applied also by the load balancer in aid of the information provided by the resource manager. At the beginning a threshold must be defined referred to as overload threshold. All ECUs with loads higher than the overload threshold are overloaded and all others are not overloaded in other words under-loaded. The resource manager performs checks of the system and ECUs periodically and depending on the overloaded and under-loaded number of ECUs it triggers the sender or the receiver load balancer policy on the load balancer. The development of the tradition sender and receiver policies for our special heterogeneous infotainment systems are in followings:

- **Sender Policy:** Like in the traditional sender policy, the load balancing mechanism will be triggered by the overloaded ECUs. So when the resource manager discovers in one of its periodic checks that there is a specific number of overloaded ECUs on the system, it will trigger the sender policy on some load balancer. The load balancer then will send back a request to the resource manager for getting some information necessary to apply the sender load balancing policy like the lists of overloaded and under-loaded ECUs and the different task categories they can execute 3. After this information is sent back to the load balancer it will then checks the tasks running on the overloaded ECUs according to their priorities and for each task search for the suitable destination ECU to migrate this task to in order to reduce the load of the handled overloaded ECU. Now the destination ECU must in the same time satisfy some condition to be suitable for the migration:

  * The destination ECU must be able of executing the task. In other word it must be able of executing the task category to which the task belongs.
  * The load of the destination ECU after the migration must not exceed the defined overload threshold. In other words the ECU must not become overloaded after the migration of the task.
  * The load of the destination ECU after the migration must be smaller than the load of the source ECU of the task to have benefit from this migration.

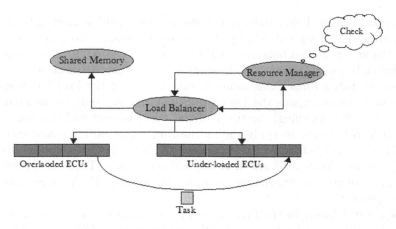

Fig. 3. Sender Load Balancing Policy

In case that only one ECU found which satisfies the previous conditions then the task will be migrated to this ECU. otherwise the task will be assigned to the ECU which execute it at a lower load. If all found ECUs can execute the task at the same load then the task will be assigned to the fastest ECU.

- **Receiver Policy:** This load balancing policy is triggered by the under-loaded ECUs of the system. This is the main difference between the sender and receiver policies. So when the resource manager discovers a specific number of under-loaded ECUs, it triggers the receiver policy on the load balancer. Then the load balancer in its turn sends a request back to the resource manager to get the required information to apply the policy and begin applying it in order to balance the loads overall the system.

If the defined overloaded threshold of the system is high then it is preferable to select the receiver load balancing policy. The reason is that there will be a few number of overloaded ECUs and some times no overloaded ECUs at all. And as the sender policy is triggered by the overloaded ECUs, this means that the sender policy will not be mostly triggered and no load balancing will be applied to handle the case of ECUs with high loads on the systems. On the other hand the receiver load balancing policy is triggered by the under-loaded ECUs and with a high overload threshold there will be always enough number of under-loaded ECUs to trigger this load balancing mechanism and improve the system performance.

In both sender and receiver load balancing policies, after a task is migrated, the information on the resource manager must be updated and the migrated task must be also stored on the shared memory in a queue called migrated tasks queue.

- **Related Loads Service:** This is a performance improvement Service developed with the goal of making the loads of the different ECUs on the infotainemnt system having similar loads which are related to a predefined threshold referred to as Balance threshold. This service is applied by the load balancer and triggered first by the resource manager. To determine which of the available load balancers will be responsible to apply the mechanism, a token is used. The token is generated by the resource manager which set also the token timer. This token is sent to one of the load balancers and when its timer expires the load balancer begin to apply the related loads service. After finishing, the timer of the token is reset and it is sent to the next load balancer to apply the mechanism again. So the token will travel from one load balancer to the another till finish applying the mechanism. The related loads mechanism is applied on rounds. There is a predefined number of rounds determined as a design decision. Each round consist of two phases:

- **First Phase:** In the first phase of the round the load balancer builds two lists of ECUs 4, source ECUs and destination ECUs lists. The list of the source ECUs contains the ECUs with loads higher than the defined balance threshold, where the list of the destination ECUs contains the other ECUs. After the ECUs in the destination ECUs lists will be checked one by one and for each destination ECU tasks running on the source ECUs will be tested and the ones which are suitable to be migrated to this specific destination ECU will be marked with The checked ECU ID. To determine if some task is suitable to be migrated later to some destination ECU, the following conditions must be satisfied:
  * The destination ECU must be able to execute the task category of the tested task
  * The load of the destination ECU after migration must be smaller than the load of the source ECU of this task to have benefit from this migration

  After finished selecting the task suitable to be migrated to the currently handled destination ECU, comes the next destination ECU to check and

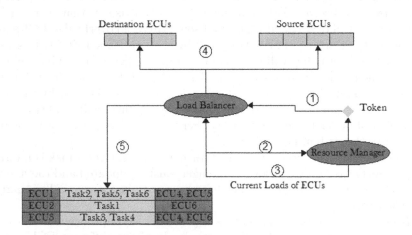

Fig. 4. Related Loads Mechanism-Round First Phase

so on till all destination ECUs are checked. At the end of this phase a table is built by the load balancer contains the destination ECUs and suitable tasks to be migrated to each of them in addition to the source ECUs of these tasks 4.

One rules of this mechanism is that: During the same round only one task is allowed to be migrated to a specific destination ECU. Migrating a task to some ECU represent an increment of the load of this ECU and to prevent a big increment jumps in load within one round, maximum one task is allowed to be migrated to a specific destination ECU.

At the end of the round first phase, we have noticed like in figure 4 that sometimes more than one task is suitable to be migrated to the same destination ECU. In such a case we need to select only one of these tasks and this is what will be done in the second phase of the round.

- **Second Phase:** The goal of this mechanism was to make the loads of the system different ECUs related to the predefined balance threshold as much as possible. In this phase we are going to choose at the maximum one task to be migrated to each of the destination ECUs. The best task to be chosen according to the goal of this mechanism, is the task which its migration makes the loads of its source and destination ECUs related to the defined balance threshold at the maximum. To determine which task, the calculations of the source and destination ECUs loads in case of migrating the tasks found in the first phase must be done.

Depending of these calculations at most one task will be selected to migrate to each of the destination ECUs. After the migrating the information of the resource manager will be updated and the migrated tasks will be stored on the shared memory again in the migrated tasks queue.

The mechanism is applied recursively in rounds till one or both of the two following conditions is satisfied:

- The predefined number of rounds is reached
- The loads of the system ECUs are related to the balance threshold with an acceptable defined failure limits

- **Handle ECU Crash Cases Service:** electronic control units are like any controlling system can experience a crash. The reasons of this crash is not the subject of this work, but we must know that there is two kinds of crashes.
  - Partly crash: where the ECU still able to perform some tasks or requests and can still provide some of the services it had provided.
  - Totally crash: in the case of totally crash the ECU become not more able to provide any service or execute any task more.

In both crash cases the philosophy followed by the developed middleware to handle such crash cases is to try migrating and tasks and services the ECU can not execute or provide any more to other available ECU which can do this. In the case of our automotive infotainment system,as we know that the resource manager performs periodic checks on the system. If it discovers in one of these periodic checks that there is a crashed ECU in the system, the resource manager sends the IDs of the tasks and services could not execute and provide any more on the crashed ECU to the load balancer 5. Some of

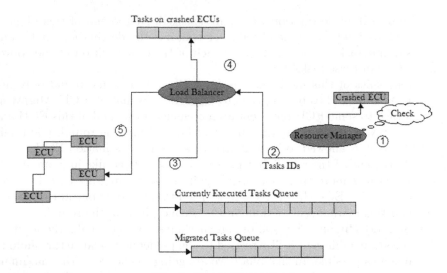

Fig. 5. Handle ECU Crash

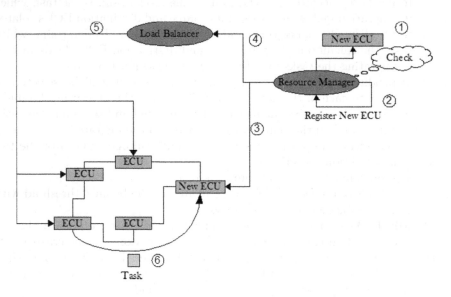

Fig. 6. Handle New ECU Attachment

these tasks were executing on the crashed ECU and other were migrated to it and not executed yet. The load balancer in its turn will access the shared memory the currently executing tasks queue and the migrated tasks queue and get the tasks were executing on or migrated to the crashed ECU. After that the load balancer will try to assign these tasks one by one according to their priorities to the available ECUs which can execute them and execute their categories.

- **Handle New ECU Attachment Service:** In the modern automotive infotainment systems there is the ability to attach new ECU to the system. The developed middleware then must be able to migrate tasks to the new ECU if it can execute them with a better quality. The resource manager discovers first the existence of a new ECU. After that it will register and integrate the new ECU in the system 6. The resource manager will also inform the load balancer that there is a new ECU attached to the system. The laod balancer access all the system ECUs and checks all the tasks and services running on them. If there is any of these tasks or services could be run with a better quality on the new attached ECU and with taking the ECUs loads into account. This task will be then migrated from its source ECU to the new attached ECU.

5   Middleware Simulation

A C-Simulation is also implemented within this work for the developed middleware including some of the main services it provides. Different scenarios were simulated with different parameters. One of the most important result to present here is the loads improvement after applying the sender load balancing policy. Figure 7 shows the loads improvement after applying the sender policy for only one time on five ECUs with twenty tasks. As we can notice in figure 7, ECU1 and ECU3 were the overloaded ECUs, where the other ECUs were not overloaded. After applying the load rebalancing mechanism for one time, the loads of ECU1 and ECU3 were reduced and the loads of ECU2, ECU4 and ECU5 were increased after becoming some tasks from the overloaded ECUs. But The new loads of ECU2, ECU4 and ECU5 are still under the predefined balancing threshold. so the result is an improvement in the overall performance of the system.

Usually many Parameters affect the performance improvement or load rebalancing on the system. Some of the most important ones are the size of the task categories the ECUs can perform and the load balancing threshold which is a predefined parameter. The size of the tasks categories the ECUs can execute

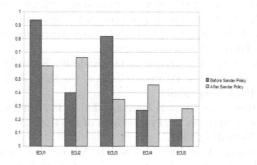

Fig. 7. Loads Improvement after applying Sender Policy one time

determines the level of migration flexibility by having the chance to migrate a service or task to more than one ECU, which lead to a better load rebalancing. on the other hand the predefined load balancing threshold is the parameter we depend on to determine the overload cases. It would improve the performance of the load balancing algorithm later if we can set the load balancing threshold dynamically at each time the algorithm is executed.

6   Summary and Future Work

We have presented in this work a middleware architecture for automotive info-tainment and entertainment systems. This middleware enables a dynamic load balancing on a heterogeneous environment. Several services are provided by it like tasks assignment service, load balancing, related loads mechanism and handling of the ECU crash cases and new ECU attachment. The integration of load balancing is a step towards a self-reconfiguration within the vehicle. The main parameter considered in this heterogeneity environment was the difference in task categories could be executed by each ECU. later other parameters could be taken into account like the speed and memory size of the ECUs. Also the selection of the overload threshold used in the load balancing mechanisms could be dynamically done each time the load balancing policy is applied, depending on the current loads of system ECUs.

References

1. Hui, C.-C., Chanson, S.T.: Improved strategies for dynamic load balancing. IEEE Concurrency (1999)
2. Cybenko, G.: Dynamic load balancing for distributed memory multiprocessors. In: Parallel and Distributed Computing (1989)
3. Hu, Y.F., Blake, R.J.: An optimal dynamic load balancing algorithm (1995), http://citeseer.ist.psu.edu/hu95optimal.htm
4. Diekmann, R., Monien, B., Preis, R.: Load balancing strategies for distributed memory machines. World Scientific, Singapore (1997)
5. Balasubramanian, J., Schmidt, D.C.: Evaluating the performance of middleware load balancing strategies (2004), http://citeseer.ist.psu.edu/635250.html
6. Othman, O., Schmidt, D.: Optimizing distributed system performance via adaptive middleware load balancing. In: ACM SIGPLAN Workshop on Optimization of Middleware and Distributed Systems (2001)
7. Anthony, R., Rettberg, A.: Towards a Dynamically Reconfigurable Automotive Control System Architecture. In: Proceedings of the IESS 2007, Irvine, California, USA. Springer, Heidelberg (2007)
8. Jahnich, I., Rettberg, A.: Towards Dynamic Load Balancing for Distributed Embedded Automotive Systems. In: Proceedings of the IESS 2007, Irvine, California, USA. Springer, Heidelberg (2007)
9. Podolski, I., Rettberg, A., Drüke, I.: Towards Autonomous Sensor Networks by a Self-Configurable Middleware. In: Proceedings of Workshop on Sensor Networks and Applications (WSeNA 2008), Gramado, Brazil (2008)

10. Drüke, I., Podolski, I., Rettberg, A.: Integrating Dynamic Load Balancing Strategies into the Car-Network. In: Proceedings of the IEEE International Workshop on Electronic Desing, Test and Applications (DELTA 2008), Hong Kong (2008)
11. Drüke, I., Podolski, I., Rettberg, A.: Towards a Middleware Approach for a Self-Configurable Automotive Embedded System. In: Brinkschulte, U., Givargis, T., Russo, S. (eds.) SEUS 2008. LNCS, vol. 5287, pp. 55–65. Springer, Heidelberg (2008)
12. Othman, O., Ryan, C.Ó., Schmidt, D.C.: The Design of an Adaptive CORBA Load Balancing Service. IEEE Distributed Systems Online (2001)
13. Othman, O., Ryan, C.Ó., Schmidt, D.C.: The Design and Performance of an Adaptive CORBA Load Balancing Service. IEEE Distributed Systems Online (2001)

Towards an Irritable Bowel Syndrome Control System Based on Artificial Neural Networks

Ina Podolski and Achim Rettberg

Carl von Ossietzky University Oldenburg, Germany, Eschwerg 2
26121 Oldenburg, Germany
{Ina.Podolski,Achim.Rettberg}@iess.org

Abstract. To solve health problems with medical applications that use complex algorithms is a trend nowadays. It could also be a chance to help patients with critical problems caused from nerve irritations to overcome them and provide a better living situation. In this paper a system for monitoring and controlling the nerves from the intestine is described on a theoretical basis. The presented system could be applied to the irritable bowel syndrome. For control a neural network is used. The advantages for using a neural network for the control of irritable bowel syndrome are the adaptation and learning. These two aspects are important because the syndrome behavior varies from patient to patient and have also concerning the time a lot of variations with respect to each patient. The developed neural network is implemented and can be simulated. Therefore, it can be shown how the network monitor and control the nerves for individual input parameters.

Keywords: Medical Applications, Irritable Bowel Syndrome, Artificial Neural Networks.

1 Introduction

Medical support for example to remote supervision and monitoring by automated devices for control medication and treatment is a new trend in medical systems. The development of nano-devices offers the freedom to realize monitoring and controlling of specific functionalities. Especially for human's, nano-devices can play an important role to support their life in the case of diseases, pain or illness. Complex tasks of the human body can be supported with nano-devices. They can be implanted into the body to observe internal functionalities. Besides measurement such devices can control and therefore help the human body to overcome the critical situations. For example, if a system is able to measure enzymes, hormones, and temperatures and to observe the nerves of the large intestine it is possible to control the irritable bowel syndrome (IBS). We assume the availability to observe those parameters. Then we are able to set up such a system by implant small nano-devices. On every device an algorithm based on an artificial neural network (ANN) is executed. These networks are able to learn and adapt themselves. This is necessary for IBS, because these symptoms differ for every patient and are changing over time.

A. Rettberg et al. (Eds.): IESS 2009, IFIP AICT 310, pp. 250–258, 2009.

The paper is structured as follows. In section 2 the IBS problem is briefly described. Afterwards, in section 3 the biological nerves system respectively the parts of the human nerves system involved in IBS is presented. This description is necessary to get a notion of the complexity of the nerves. Therefore, the different nerves and their correlation are shown. Section 4 discusses the control method based on an ANN. There the interaction with the human nerves and our system is given. The paper is closed by a summary and outlook given in section 5. This paper gives an overview of the possibilities for IBS control from a computer scientist perspective. We had a lot of discussions with doctors and medical scientist working in this area and they are highly interested in this idea.

2 Irritable Bowel Syndrome

The irritable bowel syndrome (IBS) is a dysfunction of the digestive tract with chronic medical conditions. In the last decades IBS has been dramatically growing. Meanwhile a fair intestine is an exception. In Germany an approximation shows that more than five million people have IBS or large intestine problems [7]. Symptoms vary and change from time to time. Between the intestine and the human brain exist a strong connection. A network of nerves interconnects the nerve plexus of the digestive tract with the central nervous system in the head. Information between the state of the intestine and the brain will permanently exchange. In the case of a fair intestine the human is not recognizing this information flow. Humans with IBS have problems with this information exchange from intestine to brain, because the nerves are seriously overestimated. Furthermore, the nerves threshold is decreasing with the effect of a really painful digestion. The autonomic nervous system, as well as hormones and enzymes in the intestine play an important role of this disorder [1][6]. This will be discussed in detail in the next section.

3 Human Nervous Systems

In this section the structure of the central nervous system (CNS) and the peripheral nervous system (PNS) is described. We call our system Intestine-Nano-Attack (INA). The human body has two nerves systems: the central and peripheral nervous system. Figure 1 gives an overview of the nervous systems involved in the context of this paper. The communication and the tasks of the nerves will be described in detail in this section.

The peripheral nervous system operates mainly autonomous and independent from the CNS, some decisions are controlled by the CNS and other ones are locally handled. It consists out of a congregation from nerve cells and quiet more compared with the spinal cord.

The PNS is responsible for the organ smooth muscles, the heart and the glands. Smooth muscles are inside the organs and are without arbitrary control like the stomach and intestine. The PNS consists out of three components: the sympathetic nervous system (responsible for the activation), the parasympathetic nervous system (responsible for the passive states) and the enteric nervous system (ENS). The ENS is known

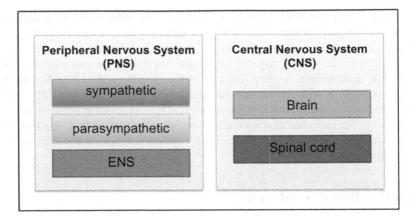

Fig. 1. Human nervous system.

as the second brain by researchers [3]. Therefore, to reduce IBS symptoms the monitoring and control of the PNS and all involved nervous systems are in the focus of this work.

There exist no direct connection between CNS and ENS. The ENS consists of vegetative nerve fiber in the wall of the intestine. The second brain consists on one hand out of a nerve fiber system between the muscles layers of the intestine and on the other hand of a nerve congregation underneath the intestine mucosa. The tasks of these nerves are: analysis of nutrition components, coordination of intestine motility, control of the glands, control of the liquid and food intake and finally the control of the immune system.

The second brain isn't only based on nerve impulse furthermore it produces intensively neuron transmitters. Every chemical messenger produced by the brain is also used inside the intestine and his second brain. There is about 97 % of the serotonin a hormone of the human body is produced by the intestine. The PNS is really fast with the production of the chemical messengers. Control cycles need only milliseconds for the activation. In opposite to this hormones have a longer reaction cycle and responsible for the global change of the intestine [3].

Usually ENS is a stable system, but nevertheless due to different causes vegetative dysfunction can appear. There are no structural changes, but functional interferences. Right now we will focus only on nerves with our system, later on we will extend our approach by measuring hormones and enzymes. In the following we will discuss the nervous system and characteristics of the involved neurons.

The ENS and spinal cord consists of different neuron types like motor neurons, inter and sensory neurons. Table 1 shows the differences between the neurons respectively their applications and properties. Additionally the neurons can be divided by their location in the spinal cord. The motor neuron is the neuron that could be easily detected. The cell bodies of the motor neuron connected with the body muscles are located in the spinal cord. They hand over the neuronal information to the muscles and influence the activity of the human body.

Table 1. Neuron types and their applications

Types of neurons	Property	Application
Inter neuron	Structure element	Structural filter
Sensory neuron	Stimulus receiver & filter	Signal absorption
Motor neuron	Stimulus sender & filter	Signal dispensary

An inter neuron is a nerve from the CNS, that connects two nerve cells. It is also known as switch neuron. The inter neuron is a sensory and activity neuron that modifies the information between nerve cells.

The dorsal horn is the part of the spinal cord that receives painful nerve impulse. The dorsal spinal cord handles different impulses like pain, temperature or mechanical pressure recognized by the sensory nerve cells. An important sensory neuron is the pain receptor, called nociceptor. They are specialized nerve endings located throughout the body in most body tissues. Once the nerve endings are stimulated they begin firing the nerves that are connected to them and send pain signals to the spinal cord and brain. [2].

Nociceptors of the intestine are activated by extension and contraction. If the impulse reaches a specific bound an action potential will be activated and directed by the nerves fibre to the spinal cord. Afterwards the information reaches the brain and the human recognizes the pain of the intestine. All levels of the CNS have pain blocking mechanism systems for modulation of the pain. In the case the CNS is confronted with steady pain signals, a lot of complex changes within the peripheral nerve system and CNS happens. Still inactive nociceptors are activated, new proteins are produced and tremendous changes on molecular biological level will take place. This often vividly changes in the CNS leads to a pain memory. The pain outlasts the damaging event for days, weeks, months or years. This leads to chronic pain that is typical for IBS patients.

Chronic pain occurs when the back part of the spinal cord has been bombarded by severe pain for a long time, see figure 2. The inter neuron adjusts and transforms to the wind-up nerve by adding fast pain receptors that amplify the pain signal and pass the amplified signal to the nerve tract that runs up to the brain. From there, the thinking and emotional centers of the brain receive a large pain signal and the mind perceives increasingly severe intractable pain. Modifier pathways in the brain attempt to tone down the pain, but are defeated at the back part of the spinal cord by the wind-up nerve. The brain keeps receiving amplified pain signals and the mind continues to perceive unrelenting and severe pain [2].

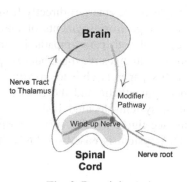

Fig. 2. Remaining pain

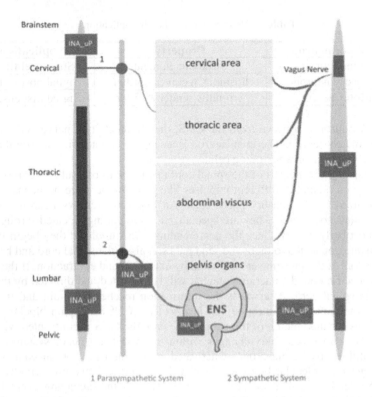

Fig. 3. Communication between nerves and organs and the monitoring and control with the INA system

Figure 3 shows the communication between nerves and organs. The composition of the nerve fibres to the organs will be explained in the following paragraph. Additionally we will show how the nerves influence the organs.

The sympathetic nervous system is richly connected to the thoracic and peripheral organs. Many levels of sympathetic nerves connect with cell bodies in the spinal cord. Pain can become coupled with the sympathetic nerves causing a dramatic central pain [2].

The cranial nerve called vagus nerve emerges directly from the brain stem in contrast to spinal nerves, which emerge from segments of the spinal cord. The vagus nerve serves the head and cervical with parasympathetic fibre and furthermore the thoracic organs as heart, stomach and digestive tract, but except the colon.

The system presented in this paper is able to measure, observe and stimulate parts of the sympathetic, parasympathetic and the ENS to reduce IBS based pain and convulsion. Several nano systems located inside the human body build the hardware part of the system (see figure 3). The software running on a nano-device or microprocessor for the INA system is based on ANN. This is described in the next section.

4   Control Method Based on Artificial Neural Nets

The proposed control method used inside the INA system is based on neural nets [8], [9] and [10]. As already known artificial neural nets (ANN) are a biological inspired model consisting of a graph with neurons as nodes and edges as connection elements. There exist different types of ANNs. Here Kohonen nets [11] are a perfect match for the application, because this net allows unsupervised learning, which is really important for the INA system control.

In figure 4 we see inputs in form of patterns for the ANN. Additionally, neurons in the figure correspond to circles, hormones are ellipses, enzymes are triangles and finally proteins are diamonds. The net may learn similar patterns to identify them and combine them to groups. Afterwards, the trained net is able to find patterns and have to ensure correct selection/learning of new and similar patterns. The learning of similar patterns is important for our approach, because as we discussed previously IBS patterns vary. To ensure the correct execution the knowledge of the training phase is stored within the neurons. We test the net with similar pattern of the same class that are similar but not equal to the training patterns. In figure 4 for example we can see that neurons corresponds to circles, but the size of the circle vary. Our net has to learn that a circle may have different sizes, which means an element may has different characteristics.

IBS control requires self-organization, so to learn new pain patterns and to react on it without an observation for each evaluation step. For safety reasons such a system can end up in a chaotic state, but this can be avoided by the error detection.

The Kohonen net support exactly this behavior the INA system needs. Unsupervised learning implies self-organization and the Kohonen net starts initially with a so-called self-organizing map.

In our case this map is constructed from typical pattern by measuring the nerves, hormones and enzymes. With a cluster analysis [10], [11] the net is pre-partitioned into clusters (see figure 5). The cluster will show regions consisting of different types of neurons. Regular neurons correspond to normal situation inside the human body

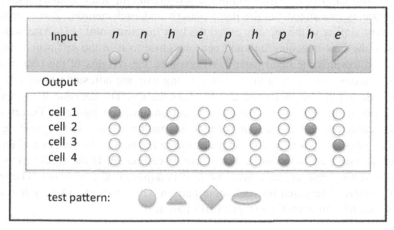

Fig. 4. Training pattern with neurons (n), hormones (h), enzymes (e) and proteins (p)

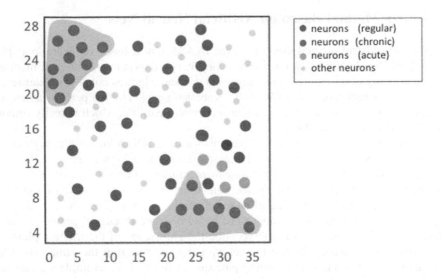

Fig. 5. Learning and finding patterns by recognizing cluster points

without IBS attacks. Acute pain from IBS are represented by acute or chronicle neurons. The difference between both is described in section 3. The other neurons in figure 5 are not related with IBS. The cluster analysis ensures that neurons with similar behavior built a region in the self-organizing map. For the initial clustering the weight of the neurons is calculated. The value of the weight inherits the measured nerves, enzymes and hormones.

Figure 6 shows an abstract implementation of the INA system. The clustered self-organizing map is the initial net of the neural network block. For each input pattern the system calculates the weight by the same calculation as for the neurons of the initial net. Afterwards the learning algorithm of the Kohonen net matches the input pattern by similarity to a neuron within the self-organizing map. Usually, the Euklidean distance is calculated for the input pattern and each neuron. The neuron with weight most similar to the input is called the best matching unit [11]. Afterwards, the weights of the best matching unit and neurons close to it in the self-organizing map are adjusted towards the input pattern. Afterwards, the weights of the best matching unit and neurons close to it in the self-organizing map are adjusted towards the input pattern, if the input is a good candidate to adapt the net. The decision if an input pattern is good or not is done by the error detection unit, see figure 6. Therefore, the error detection tries to ensure an optimal adaptation of the self-organizing map. Within the error detection the similarity according the nerves, hormones and enzymes between the best matching unit and the input is compared. If the similarity is given the best matching unit and neurons close to it is adjusted otherwise not. The process described above is repeated for each input pattern. Obviously the INA system is able to adapt over time to normal and typical IBS patterns.

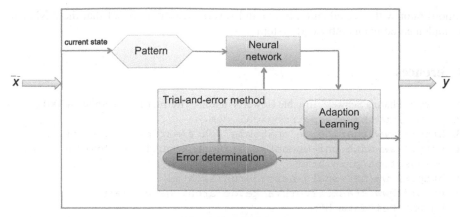

Fig. 6. The INA system

The ANN of the INA system consists of neurons that correspond to nerves of the nervous system. For every measured value and for all necessary outputs an input respectively output neuron is created. From the nerves (parasympathetic, sympathetic, vagus nerve), the temperature within the large intestine, the hormones and enzymes a feature vector (input) is built.

The error detection method is good to handle the complexity and correlation. The method helps to adjust an optimal adaptation of the net to the problem. The INA system finds optimal counteractions to avoid chronic pain of IBS patients. Counteractions may be a temperature adjustment in the large intestine, a hormones and enzymes control and nerves stimulation so that a typical IBS pattern is blocked. By blocking the IBS pattern the patient is not confronted with chronic pain from IBS. This was exactly the goal of the INA system.

5 Conclusion and Future Work

Within this paper we presented an embedded medical system to help patients with IBS. Several so-called nano-devices or microprocessors with INA system running could be used in the body to measure and influence the nerves involved in IBS. IBS is a complex problem and observing nerves it not sufficient enough, therefore, our system controls additionally the temperature, hormones and enzymes inside the large intestine. The control algorithm based on an ANN that offers the freedom of adaptation and learning of the control algorithm. By the artificial network our system is able to train especially for the detection of IBS typical patterns and not to touch other pain problems in the large intestine. Up to now, our approach is an idea and partly implemented. We contacted medical scientist and they are really interested. We set up the ANN and start with the training of the net and the simulation. Our approach is a real-time system that reacts efficiently by parallel execution on partial patterns. It is failure tolerant in the case of errors and besides this it can be interpreted as an early warning system.

Future work will be a complete software implementation of the ANN to make a deeply training of the network. Additionally, we plan to set up a hardware demonstrator with an evaluation board and several sensors to proof that the ANN can be implemented in an embedded system.

References

1. Novartis Pharma Schweiz, Irritable Bowel Syndrome (Reizdarm – Überblick) (2001)
2. http://www.bayareapainmedical.com/
3. http://www.charite.de/anatomie/lehre/skripte/vegetativ.htm
4. http://wwwmath.uni-muenster.de/SoftComputing/lehre/material/ wwwnnscript/prin.html
5. http://www.neuronalesnetz.de/units.html
6. http://www.krankerfuerkranke.de/archivgesundheit/ Rheuma_Reizdarm.htm
7. Weiß, T.: Fibromyalgie: Das erfolgreiche Ernährungsprogramm. Südwest-Verlag (2008)
8. Kratzer, K.P.: Neuronale Netze - Grundlagen und Anwendungen. Carl Hanser Verlag, München (1999)
9. Rey, G.D., Wender, K.F.: Neuronale Netze: Eine Einführung in die Grundlagen, Anwendungen und Datenauswertung. Huber Verlag, Bern (2008)
10. Yoshida, M., Sato, H.: New Research on Neuronal Networks, Nova Science Pub. Inc., Bombay (2008)
11. Kohonen, T.: Self-Organizing Maps. Springer, Berlin (1995)

A Hybrid Hardware and Software Component Architecture for Embedded System Design

Hugo Marcondes and Antônio Augusto Fröhlich

Laboratory for Software and Hardware Integration
Federal University of Santa Catarina
PO Box 476 - Florianópolis - Brazil
88040-900
{hugom,guto}@lisha.ufsc.br

Abstract. Embedded systems are increasing in complexity, while several metrics such as time-to-market, reliability, safety and performance should be considered during the design of such systems. A component-based design which enables the migration of its components between hardware and software can cope to achieve such metrics. To enable that, we define hybrid hardware and software components as a development artifact that can be deployed by different combinations of hardware and software elements. In this paper, we present an architecture for developing such components in order to construct a repository of components that can migrate between the hardware and software domains to meet the design system requirements.

1 Introduction

Several challenges arise on the design and implementation of current embedded systems. The applications themselves are becoming increasingly complex as the advances of the semiconductor industry enabled more sophisticated use of computational resources on a spread of market appliances. If by one way the applications are becoming more complex, on the other way the pressure of the market for rapid development of those systems makes the task of designing them a challenge.

The constraints imposed to such systems, in terms of functionality, performance, energy consumption, cost, reliability and time-to-market are getting tighter. Therefore, the task of designing such systems is becoming increasingly important and difficult at the same time [1]. Moreover, those systems could require an integrated hardware and software design that can be realized by a myriad of distinct computational architectures, ranging from simple 8-bit microcontrollers, digital signal processors (DSP), programmable logic devices (FPGA) to dedicated chips (ASIC) that provides the system functionality. In order to cope with these challenges, several methodologies were proposed by the hardware and software co-design community over the last decade. One approach to deal with these challenges is based on the concept of build a system based on the assembly of pre-validated components, like the *Platform-based design* [2].

A. Rettberg et al. (Eds.): IESS 2009, IFIP AICT 310, pp. 259–270, 2009.

However, designing such reusable artifacts to meet the requirements of several distinct applications should be as challenging as well [3]. The partition of the system between hardware and software also plays a key role in the design process. Usually, this mapping of system functionality into hardware implementation and software implementation is done in the initial phases of the specification of the system, enabling the development and implementation of the hardware and software occur concurrently. This approach however, is not ideal, as a mistake on this beginning phase of the project could lead to a re-engineering of the system, which can sometimes be too costly.

Our proposal to deal with these challenges is to use refined engineering techniques to build a repository of components that are flexible enough to provide an interface that is free of implementation domain. In this scenario, embedded systems could be built on such components that can be migrated to hardware or software domains without major redesigns to the system, according to the requirements of the application. To enable the construction of those flexible components, a set of engineering techniques was used. Domain Engineering was used to identify a set of representative entities within a domain. Such entities are modeled using Object-oriented design, Family-based design, and Aspect-orientation. A framework models the composition rules of such components, using advance techniques such as generative programming to ensure a low overhead to the composed system.

The next section will present the related work on hardware and software co-design. In section 3 the proposed architecture of hybrid hardware and software components is introduced. Three components built with this architecture are described and evaluated in section 4, followed by the conclusion of this paper.

2   Related Work

Several methodologies propose the integration of tools and design phases of embedded systems, to promote a rapid-prototyping and design of such systems. Metropolis [4] proposes the use of a unified framework, based on a metamodel with formal semantics that developers can use to capture designs, and an environment to support the simulation, formal analysis and synthesis of complex electronic systems, providing an adequate support to the design chain.

The Ptolemy project [5] focuses on the modeling design of heterogeneous systems, as mostly modern embedded computing systems are heterogeneous in the sense of being composed of subsystems with very different characteristics among their interactions as synchronous or asynchronous calls, buffered or unbuffered, etc. To deal with such heterogeneity, Ptolemy proposes a model structure and semantic framework that support several models of computations, such as *Communicating Sequential Processes*, *Continuous Time*, *Discrete Events*, *Process Network*, and *Synchronous Dataflow*.

While most of existent hardware-software co-design tools focus mainly on the hw-sw co-simulation to build a virtual prototyping environment for performing software design and system verification, PeaCE [6] appear as an extension to

Ptolemy to provide a full-fledged co-design environment from functional simulation to system synthesis. It is targeted for multimedia applications with real-time constraints, specifying the system behavior with a heterogeneous composition of three models of computations and exploiting features of formal models maximally during the design process.

The use of a component-based design approach for multiprocessor SoC platforms are presented by [7]. This work proposes a unified methodology for automatic integration of heterogeneous pre-designed components effectively. A design flow called ROSES [8], uses this methodology to generate hardware, software, and functional interface sub-systems automatically starting from a system architectural model.

Another approach to deal with the component communication on multiprocessors SoC is based on the distributed system paradigm to provide a unified abstraction for both hardware and software components [9] that is deeply inspired by the concepts of communication objects standards such as CORBA. This approach uses the generation of a proxy-skeleton scheme to provide transparent communication architecture of the components in both domains (hardware and software).

HThreads [10], focus on specifying and unifying the programming model for hybrid CPU/FPGA systems, under the umbrella of multithreading programming. In this sense, they provide what they call *hardware thread interface* (HWTI) which supports the generalized pthreads API semantics, allowing for the passing of abstract data types between hardware and software. This approach enabled the migration of threads to the hardware domain, to be implemented as hardware accelerators. The HWTI interface provides access to the same system calls available to software threads, a globally distributed memory to support pointers, a generalized function call model including recursion, local variable declaration, dynamic memory allocation, and a remote procedural call model that enables hardware threads access to any library function [10].

3   Hybrid Hw/Sw Components

Hybrid hw/sw components can be realized as a mixture of hardware and software implementation that can vary from a component that realizes all your functionality in hardware to an implementation fully realized in software. The Fig. 1 depicts this concept, illustrating a full hardware implementation (A), a full software implementation (C) and a mixture of both (B).

In this way, a system composed by such kind of components can adapt to its requirements according to the actual implementation selected to realize a specific interface, used by the application. For instance, a mobile application that requires an efficient use of energy could select an implementation that optimize such a metric to the detriment of others (i.e. cost), while applications that have an unlimited source of power could select implementations that benefit other metrics (i.e. performance, costs).

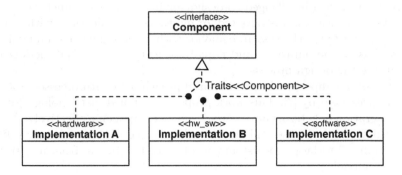

Fig. 1. Hybrid components

To illustrate such components, consider a very common component of most embedded system: a task scheduler. Such a component is mainly represented by a queue of elements that are ready to receive a resource from the system, usually the CPU, an ordering algorithm to establish the order in which the elements on the queue will receive the resource, and a timer responsible for managing the amount of time in which each element will receive of the resource (*quantum*). A hybrid hw/sw component could arise by pushing those elements to hardware or software domains in several combinations. As an example, the queue and the ordering algorithm could be realized in hardware to improve performance, in detriment of cost. The realization of the time management by the scheduler in hardware could also reduce the occurrence of interruptions of the CPU (to deal with time ticks that will not cause a rescheduling) that could lead to decreased energy consumption for instance.

Design Reusable Hybrid Hw/Sw Components

Most of the methodologies in the design of embedded systems focus the design of each system independently. Although most of them consider the use and selection of pre-existent components already in the initial phases of the design process, most of them do not address how to guide the system development process to yield components that can be effectively reused on further projects. In fact, the construction of components that can be extremely reusable is one of the most challenging issues in *Platform-based design* [3]. Our proposal rests on the foundation of refined software engineering techniques to overcome such challenges and bring not only a flexible interface of components that can freely migrate between hardware and software domains, but also foster the reuse of the captured knowledge from previous projects in the form of reusable components.

To achieve such a degree of flexibility, it is essential to use a domain engineering methodology that elaborates on the well-known domain decomposition strategies, allied with Family-Based Design (FBD) and Object-Orientation (OO). In such an approach, the use of *commonality* and *variability* analysis captures the usage variations of the elements of the domain, than can be further factored out as aspects. In

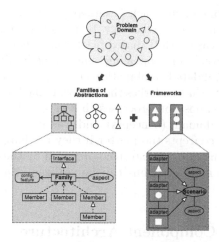

Fig. 2. Overview of domain decomposition

this sense, the use of such techniques guides the domain engineering towards families of components, of which execution scenario dependencies are factored out as "aspects" and external relationships are captured in a component framework, addressing consistently some of the most relevant issues in component-based design, such as reusability, complexity management and composability.

Figure 2 illustrate the main elements of domain decomposition, with domain entities being captured as abstractions that are organized in families and exported to users through comprehensive interfaces. Abstractions designate scenario independent components, since scenario dependencies are captured as aspects during design. Subsequent factorization captures configurable features as constructs that can be reused throughout the family. Relationships between families of abstractions delineate a component framework. Each of these elements is subsequently modeled according to the guidelines of Object-Oriented Design (OOD).

The portability of such components, and thus of applications that use them, across distinct hardware platforms is achieved by means of a construct called "*hardware mediator*", which defines a hardware/software interface contract between higher-level components and the hardware [11]. Hardware mediators are meant to be implemented using Generative Programming techniques and, instead of building an ordinary *Hardware Abstraction Layer* (HAL), implicitly adapt existing hardware components to match the required interface by adding software to client components. For example, the hardware mediator for a hardware component that already presents the desired interface would be eliminated totally during the system generation process; while the hardware mediator for a hardware component that does not provide all the desired functionality could exceed the role of interface and include software elements to complement the hardware functionality.

Indirectly, the concept of hardware mediator defines a kind of *hybrid hardware/software component*, since different mediator implementations can exist for the same hardware component, each designed around a particular set of goals such as performance and energy efficiency. If the hardware platform itself can be synthesized—as is the case with IP-based platforms—then the notion of a hybrid component becomes even more appealing, since some hardware mediators could exist in different pre-validated combinations of hardware and software.

In fact, the flexibility that underlies the hardware mediator concepts is yielded from the domain decomposition processes that established a model that represents elements of the domain (concepts) and was not driven by a specific implementation of these concepts (no matter if they are hardware or software). In other words, this means that the interface provided by these components is free of implementation domain, and thus can be realized either as hardware or as software.

Hybrid Hw/Sw Component Architecture

In order to provide the seamless migration of the components between both implementation domains, not only should the interface be able to be realized in both domains, but also behave equally in both domains, avoiding the refactoring of the clients that use them. Analyzing how client components interact with their providers, we observed three distinct behaviors patterns:

Synchronous: observed in components with sequential objects that only perform tasks when their methods are explicitly invoked; client components are blocked on the method call until service is completed. Such behavior is intrinsic to software components, and can be preserved in hardware by means of its hardware mediator that can block client requests until the service is completed. The Fig. 3 illustrates an UML activity diagram of such behavior when the component is implemented on the hardware domain. The client requests the service to the component, which is executed while the client stands polling a register to be notified upon the finish of the service (busy waiting), or suspend itself until the hardware interrupts the CPU to resume the suspended client (idle waiting).

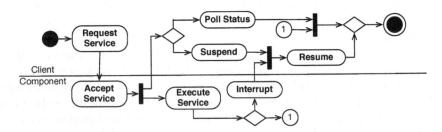

Fig. 3. UML activity diagram of Synchronous Components

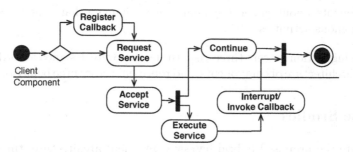

Fig. 4. UML activity diagram of Asynchronous Components

Asynchronous: observed in components around active objects that perform tasks when their methods are explicitly invoked, but do not block the execution of the client component; some sort of callback mechanism is used to notify the client about service completion. Typical examples for this class of hybrid components are I/O related subsystems, such as file systems and communication systems. The Fig. 4 illustrates an UML activity diagram of such behavior. The client register a callback function if this is not already set (i.e. at initialization of the component) and then requests the service. Once the service is accepted by the component (i.e. the component is not servicing another request) the client continues it execution, while the component executes the service. When the requested service is finished, the component will call the registered call back function, which can be achieved by a simple call if the component is implemented in software or through an interrupt if the component is in hardware.

Autonomous: components implemented as active objects that perform tasks independently of clients; the services provided by the component are either ubiquitous or generate events for clients. Its behavior is depicted in Fig. 5, by a loop of service execution and event generation activities that could be interrupted by external events. In this scenario, moving a hybrid component from software to hardware is feasible as long as the triggering events can be forward to the hardware component. The other way around this is usually accomplished by having the hardware to generate interrupts to notify other

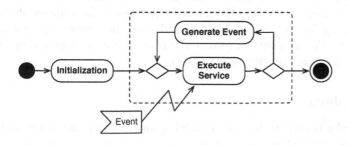

Fig. 5. UML activity diagram of Autonomous Components

components about general system status changes that might result from autonomous activities.

The following section present three case studies that were designed according to the proposed architecture of components, and represent these three behavior patterns.

4 Case Studies

To evaluate the proposed hybrid hw/sw component architecture, three components were developed in both implementation domains, each one representing a specific behavior. A *Semaphore* component, that behaves as a synchronous component, a *Scheduler* that behaves as an autonomous component and an *Alarm* component that behaves as an asynchronous component. The following sections describe the implementation of those components.

4.1 Semaphore

A semaphore is a synchronization tool represented by an integer variable that can be accessed only by two *atomic* operations: p (from the Dutch *proberen*, to test) and v (from Dutch *verhogen*, to increment). The software implementation of the component is realized by an object that aggregates the semaphore variable and a list of blocked threads that are waiting for the resource guarded by the semaphore abstraction. To guarantee the atomicity of its methods, the software implementation of the semaphore components uses the bus locking mechanisms of the underlying architecture, and when such a feature is not available, the atomicity is provided by masking the occurrence of interrupts.

The hardware implementation of the semaphore component, pushes each semaphore variable to a hardware implementation, and also manipulates the blocked threads queue on hardware. In this sense, four commands are implemented by the controller: `Create` and `Destroy`, responsible for allocation and deallocation of the internal resources (memory for the variable and the queue) and the other two traditional methods of semaphores P and V. For every P operation, the address of the caller of the method is passed through the input registers to the hardware, and if the caller has to be blocked its address is automatically inserted on the respective queue, and signalized by the status register. Once the resource becomes available (through a V operation) the address of the blocked thread waiting for the resource is removed from the queue, and put in the output registers. The necessity of resume the thread that is addressed on the output register is signalized by the status register.

4.2 Scheduler

The scheduler is responsible for organizing and defining the order that elements access a resource, when such a resource is shared among several elements. The most common use of a scheduler is to establish the order that tasks or process

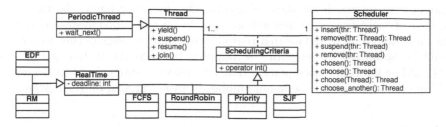

Fig. 6. Process Management family of components

(elements) gain access to use the CPU to run (resource). Figure 6 depict the design of the process management family of components, where the `Scheduler` hybrid hw/sw components arise.

The `Scheduler` provides the basic implementation of methods to manipulate the queue of elements that are ready to use the resource managed by the scheduler, such as `insert()`, `remove()`, `resume()` and `suspend()`. A deeper explanation around the whole *Process management* family of components is beyond the scope of this paper. Let's focus here only on the component `Scheduler` that was implemented as a hybrid component. Such a component implements the fundamental structure of a scheduler, which consists of a queue of ready elements and time management mechanisms.

The implementation of the software scheduler follows the traditional design of lists. Such a list implementation could be configured to be realized as a conventional ordering list of its elements, as well as a relative list, where each element stores its ordering parameter relative to its predecessor. In this sense each element will hold the difference of its ordering parameter from the previous element, and so and on. In such kinds of implementations, it is particularly interesting when the scheduling policy has dynamic priority increases over time, such as the EDF policy. In such a policy, as the absolute deadline is always a crescent value, the use of a conventional ordering, using the absolute deadline should lead to an overflow of the variable as the execution time is always growing (which can occur in a few hours on 8 bits microcontrollers). Instead of this, the use of a relative queue insures that the deadline is always stored relatively close to the current time, and in this way, the variable will not overflow.

The scheduler implemented in hardware realize an ordered list on its internal memory. It is worth highlight two aspects of this component implementation on hardware, especially for programmable logic devices. Both of these aspects are related to constraints in terms of the resources of such devices. Ideally, the hardware scheduler should exploit maximally the inherent parallelism of the hardware resources. However, such resources are very expensive, especially when the internal resources are used to implement several parallel bit comparators in order to search for elements in the queue, as well as, to find the insertion position of an element in queue.

Moreover, the use of 32 bits pointers, to reference the elements stored on the list (in this case `Threads`) becomes extremely costly, for implementing the comparators to search for those elements. On the other hand, the maximum number of tasks that a system will execute in an embedded system is usually known at design time, and for that reason, the resources usage of this component could be optimized implementing a mapping between the system pointer (32 bits) and an internal representation that uses only the number of bits necessary, taking into account, the maximum number of tasks running on the system.

4.3 Alarm

The `Alarm` component is responsible for providing the abstraction of an event generator to the system. This component behaves asynchronously, as its service (the event generation) occurs asynchronous from its request (Alarm instantiation). The Fig. 7 illustrate the design of the `Alarm` component. This component provides three types of event generation: call a function implemented by the user, resumes a blocked thread, or releases a semaphore (by calling it's `v()` operation). These events are supported by the `Handler` interface.

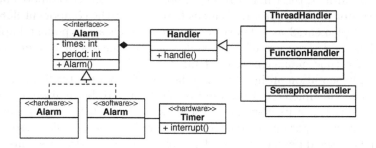

Fig. 7. Alarm component design

The software implementation of the `Alarm` component is implemented sharing a `Timer` used to manage the passage of time, and a relative queue of event requests. This queue is organized relative to the number of ticks missing for the occurrence of the event. At each interrupt of the `Timer`, the number of ticks is updated in the queue, and when this number is less than zero, the handler of the event is invoked. Its implementation on hardware is realized by dedicated counters for each supported `Alarm` instance, while the maximum number of concurrent instances are defined on design time. The internal memory of the component is used to store a reference for each `Alarm` handler that is passed to the interrupt routine of the component to generate the respective event.

4.4 Results

An experimentation platform was used to develop, debug, and evaluate those components. It was used the XILINX development board `ML-403`, which has a VIRTEX 4 FPGA (`XC4VFX12`), that enable the instantiation of the hardware

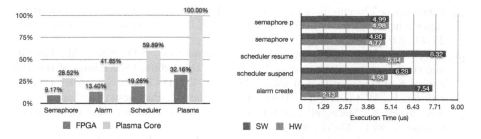

Fig. 8. Logic usage and performance of hybrid hw/sw components

components on the configurable logic, while running the software components on its embedded POWERPC.

In order to evaluate the hybrid component implementations, the "The Dining Philosophers" application was implemented using the three components. The alarm was used to wake-up the philosophers when their thinking period expired. The Fig. 8 shows the area consumed by the hardware implementation of the components, and the execution time of some methods of the components on both domains. The consumed logic of the hardware implementations is compared with the *Plasma* processor (MIPS), as a comparative of deploying a co-processor approach to handle hardware acceleration. The execution time shows a better performance of the hardware implementation of the Scheduler and the Alarm component, while the Semaphore component did not gain that much performance from its hardware implementation, mainly because the evaluated application did not push the usage of semaphores queues, whereas a hardware implementation could effectively bring benefits.

5   Conclusions

This paper presented an architecture of hybrid hw/sw components. It highlighted the importance of the use of an adequate engineering technique in order to design components that are flexible enough to migrate from hardware to software, and vice-versa. Three hybrid hw/sw components was developed and representing the possibles communication behaviors. Several experiments were done building a benchmark application using different combinations of hardware and software implementation of those components. Further research is directed to the migration of hybrid hw/sw components during runtime.

References

[1] Pop, P.: Embedded systems design: Optimization challenges. In: Barták, R., Milano, M. (eds.) CPAIOR 2005. LNCS, vol. 3524, pp. 16–16. Springer, Heidelberg (2005)

[2] Sangiovanni-Vincentelli, A.L., Martin, G.: Platform-based design and software design methodology for embedded systems. IEEE Design & Test of Computers 18(6), 23–33 (2001)

[3] Sangiovanni-Vincentelli, A., Carloni, L., Bernardinis, F.D., Sgroi, M.: Benefits and challenges for platform-based design. In: DAC 2004: Proceedings of the 41st annual conference on Design automation, pp. 409–414. ACM, New York (2004)

[4] Balarin, F., Watanabe, Y., Hsieh, H., Lavagno, L., Passerone, C., Sangiovanni-Vincentelli, A.: Metropolis: an integrated electronic system design environment. Computer 36(4), 45–52 (2003)

[5] Eker, J., Janneck, J., Lee, E., Liu, J., Liu, X., Ludvig, J., Neuendorffer, S., Sachs, S., Xiong, Y.: Taming heterogeneity - the ptolemy approach. Proceedings of the IEEE 91(1), 127–144 (2003)

[6] Ha, S., Kim, S., Lee, C., Yi, Y., Kwon, S., Joo, Y.P.: Peace: A hardware-software codesign environment for multimedia embedded systems. ACM Trans. Des. Autom. Electron. Syst. 12(3), 1–25 (2007)

[7] Cesario, W., Lyonnard, D., Nicolescu, G., Paviot, Y., Yoo, S., Jerraya, A., Gauthier, L., Diaz-Nava, M.: Multiprocessor soc platforms: a component-based design approach. IEEE Design & Test of Computers 19(6), 52–63 (2002)

[8] Dziri, M.A., Cesario, W., Wagner, F., Jerraya, A.: Unified component integration flow for multi-processor soc design and validation. In: Design, Automation and Test in Europe Conference and Exhibition, 2004. Proceedings, vol. 2, pp. 1132–1137 (2004)

[9] Rincon, F., Barba, J., Moya, F., Villanueva, F., Villa, D., Dondo, J., Lopez, J.: Unified inter-communication architecture for systems-on-chip, pp. 17–26 (May 2007)

[10] Anderson, E., Peck, W., Stevens, J., Agron, J., Baijot, F., Warn, S., Andrews, D.: Supporting high level language semantics within hardware resident threads. In: International Conference on Field Programmable Logic and Applications, 2007. FPL 2007, August 2007, pp. 98–103 (2007)

[11] Polpeta, F.V., Fröhlich, A.A.: Hardware mediators: A portability artifact for component-based systems. In: Yang, L.T., Guo, M., Gao, G.R., Jha, N.K. (eds.) EUC 2004. LNCS, vol. 3207, pp. 271–280. Springer, Heidelberg (2004)

Low–Level Space Optimization of an AES Implementation for a Bit–Serial Fully Pipelined Architecture

Raphael Weber[1] and Achim Rettberg[2]

[1] OFFIS, Escherweg 2, 26121 Oldenburg, Germany
[2] Carl von Ossietzky University Oldenburg, OFFIS, Escherweg 2, 26121 Oldenburg, Germany

Abstract. A previously developed AES (Advanced Encryption Standard) implementation is optimized and described in this paper. The special architecture for which this implementation is targeted comprises synchronous and systematic bit–serial processing without a central controlling instance. In order to shrink the design in terms of logic utilization we deeply analyzed the architecture and the AES implementation to identify the most costly logic elements. We propose to merge certain parts of the logic to achieve better area efficiency. The approach was integrated into an existing synthesis tool which we used to produce synthesizable VHDL code. For testing purposes, we simulated the generated VHDL code and ran tests on an FPGA board.

1 Introduction

People's demand to keep secrets, only accessible to chosen people, is as old as mankind. In order to keep something secret one has to make sure that only trustworthy people can understand the secret's contents. The most popular cipher algorithm is the Advanced Encryption Standard (AES) announced by the U.S. American National Institute of Standards and Technology (NIST) in late 2000.

In this paper we analyze the AES implementation for a special bit–serial, reconfigurable, fully pipelined, self–controlled architecture, covered in [11]. Our goal is to optimize the AES implementation targeted for resource restricted environments in terms of hardware usage.

Bit–serial architectures have the advantage of a low number of input and output lines leading to a low number of required pins. In synchronous design, however, the performance of these architectures is affected by the long wires, which are used to control the operators or the potential gated clocks. Nowadays, the wire delay in chip design is near to a break with the gate delay. Solutions to overcome this drawback are required. Basically, long control wires can be avoided by a local distribution of the control circuitry at the operator level. A similar approach is used for the architecture described in this work.

While the design of a fully interlocked asynchronous architecture is well understood, realizing a fully synchronous pipeline architecture still remains a difficult task. Through a one-hot implementation of the central control engine, its

A. Rettberg et al. (Eds.): IESS 2009, IFIP AICT 310, pp. 271–278, 2009.

folding into the data path, and the use of a shift register, we realized a synchronous fully self–timed bit–serial and fully interlocked pipeline architecture called MACT (MACT = Mauro, Achim, Christophe and Tom).

The paper is organized as follows. In Section 2 we will shortly explain the AES cipher algorithm and the basics of the MACT architecture. In Section 3 we analyze the MACT AES implementation and present our low–level space optimization including a description of our modifications. Finally, Section 4 states the optimization results, sums up with a conclusion and gives an outlook.

2   Basics

2.1   The Advanced Encryption Standard

AES is a block cipher algorithm which has a constant input/output block size of 128 bits. Data is encrypted in a differing number of loops in which four transformations are applied to the block, called *state*. The number of loops depends on the key size which can either be 128, 192, or 256 bits. In this work we will only consider the AES-128 with a 128-bit key and 10 loops (rounds).

Figure 1 displays how the cipher works, utilizing four transformations, described below. The roundKey is generated from the key and changes each round. This procedure is called key expansion.

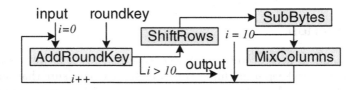

Fig. 1. AES-128 cipher

AddRoundKey XORs the state byte–wise with the current round key. The RoundKey applied before the loop is equal to the key. The byte–wise SubBytes transformation is the most costly operation in terms of hardware utilization. First, each byte is considered as an element in the Gallois Field ($GF(2^8)$) and the multiplicative inverse is calculated. Second, an affine transformation is applied to the byte. This results in a highly non linear mapping, which can be stored in a so called S-Box. SubBytes can be implemented using combinational logic only using simple bit–wise XOR and AND operators [5,9]. Other implementations use a look–up–table [2,10,1]. ShiftRows cyclically shifts the bytes of a row over a differing number of offsets. MixColumns considers the bytes in each column of the state as coefficients in $GF(2^8)$ and performs $GF(2^8)$ multiplication and XOR operations to the bytes of all four columns of the state. A multiplication in $GF(2^8)$ can be performed by a series of shift lefts with a conditional XOR with the irreducible polynomial $m(x) = x^8 + x^4 + x^3 + x + 1 = \{01\}\{1b\}$.

2.2   The MACT Architecture

MACT is an architecture that breaks with classical design paradigms. Its development came in combination with a design paradigm shift to adapt to market requirements. The architecture is based on small and distributed local control units instead of a global control instance. MACT is a synchronous, de-centralized and self-controlling architecture. Data and control information is combined into one packet which is shifted through a network of operators using one single wire only (refer to Figure 2). To our knowledge, this is the second approach to implement a fully interlocked synchronous architecture after that of [4] and the first one which does not rely on gated clocks to realize the local control of operators.

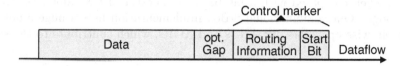

Fig. 2. Example data packet

The controlling operates locally, only based on arriving data. Thus, there are no long control wires, which would limit the operating speed due to wire delays [6]. This enables a high frequency. Yet, the architecture operates synchronously, thus enabling accurate estimation of the latency, etc. a priori. To overcome the increased latency of the bit–serial operation, MACT uses pipelining, i. e., there are no buffers, operators are placed following each other immediately. MACT implementations are based on data flow graphs. Nodes of these graphs are directly connected, similar to a shift register.

We consider the flow of data through the operator network as processing in waves, i. e., valid data alternates with gaps. Additionally, we have to ensure that the control marker is not modified by an operator. This can be achieved by the two additional signals *open bypass* and *close bypass*. If *open bypass* is true the control marker and the gap of the data packet are routed around the operating unit inside the operator. If *close bypass* is true the data of the data packet is directed to the operating unit.

MACT is characterized by short and local control wires and no necessity to implement costly parallel/serial decoders or encoders. Thus, it may run with high speed, compensating the drawbacks of bit–serial processing. Furthermore, the local control structure avoids complex controllers. Additionally, the fully interlocked pipeline allows the architecture to support multiple applications within one implementation. The architecture is described in more detail in [8,7].

In order to realize reconfiguration within our architecture a component called router was developed. The router offers path selection, which can be controlled by the extension of the control marker in the data packet. That means, the control marker contains the routing information, see Figure 2. The realization of loops can also be achieved with routers.

3   Low–Level Space Optimization of the Implementation

MACT is a data flow oriented architecture, logic circuits can be generated from a data flow graph specification by a high level synthesis tool. We used this tool to draw our data flow graphs for all AES components including the key expansion in order to get a working prototype [11]. This might have been a straight forward realization for the MACT architecture. However, while analyzing and testing the design, we discovered that it was not as space–saving as we had expected.

When dealing with bit–serial designs one might expect small operators and few input/output pins. While the latter applies for MACT, the first does not necessarily. Since each MACT operator contains not only the actual operator logic but also the control logic, it naturally results in a higher hardware utilization, when compared with a bit–parallel operator of the same size without control logic. Our combinational S-Box implementation uses a huge amount of simple bit–wise operators like ANDs and XORs, which contribute to the size.

3.1   Analyzing the Design

After we implemented and tested the combinational S-Box we synthesized it, utilizing a Spartan 3 FPGA evaluation board with the Software Xilinx ISE. The synthesis report stated a total of 467 occupied slices and 713 utilized 4–input–look–up–tables. To us, this seemed a rather high device utilization.

We discovered a high level of concurrently operating MACT operators, each of which receiving its own control signals, even if they arrive at the same time. Two operators run concurrently, if the packets they process have been synchronized at some point in the data flow graph and stay synchronized.

When taking a closer look at the operators, one can distinguish between the logic and the control part of the operator. The latter is based on basic principles of the MACT architecture. Special signals are a result of the design of the architecture, such as *close_bypass*, *open_bypass*, stall, reset and clock signals. Figure 3 displays an XOR operator on the register transfer level (RTL).

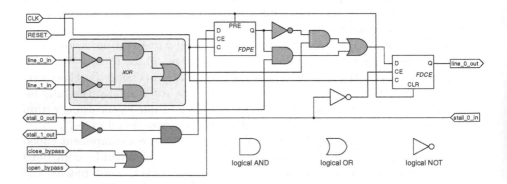

Fig. 3. Register transfer level design of the logical XOR operator

The framed brightened part in the figure denoted by XOR represents the logic operators for the logical XOR. The rest of the logic in Figure 3 is dedicated to control handling. The operator's logic is necessary, but when two or more operators receive similar control signals, which eventually result in the same control behaviour, it might be possible to reduce the number of control signals needed to get the same behaviour. We propose a new way to exploit similar control signals of concurrently processing operators.

3.2   Merging Operators

In order to use the same control logic for different operators we part the control signal processing from the operator logic. This was done via a new modified Finite State Machine (FSM) design (see Figure 4). The separation improves the code analysis and processing of the high level synthesis, which was modified to comply with the new FSM VHDL code of the MACT operators. Thus, we can replace the operator logic by any other logic without touching the control logic.

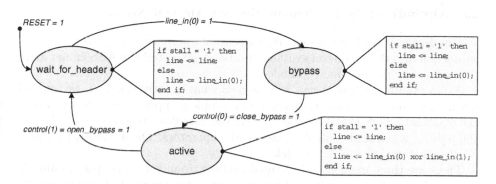

Fig. 4. Finite State Machine representation of the MACT XOR

With our new FSM design, it is possible to retrieve the relevant information of a new operator from the VHDL source file. This approach can not completely replace the old data flow graph nodes, it merely combines a category of operators to a more abstract representation. This categorization is done in order to collect similar nodes of the same category and unite them to a new *merged* MACT node. A merged node has multiple inputs and outputs from several operators, but receives and processes its control signals only once, since it contains only one logic unit to handle its control signals.

For the merging of nodes to work correctly, the data flow graph has to be analyzed, since this approach is only applicable under certain circumstances. Operators only receive similar control signals when they are synchronized and have the same packet layout and duration. This applies for large parts of the S-Box. First off, we assume that the targeted data flow graph has been analyzed so that the synchronization information is available, this includes synchronized classes as described in our previous work in [3]. Our approach can be decomposed into three steps:

- look for all synchronized operators in the same category and the same synchronized class, for example XORs, ANDs, ORs, etc.
- replace these sets of operators by a single new merged node with as many in- and outputs as the operators in the associated set, store the information in the merged node for code generation
- generate the merged nodes with the FSM VHDL interface as described above

"Information" in the second step can for example refer to the mathematical representation of the operator, or the way the routing information is handled. This information can be stored in comments. Later on, the generated interfaces can be parsed using the very same function as for parsing MACT operators to retrieve operator information. Thus, our approach is scalable and extensible for future reuse.

3.3   Optimizing the Implementation via Merged Nodes

We implemented and integrated the conceptual approach explained in the last subsection into the high level synthesis tool and generated the AES cipher algorithm utilizing the new merged nodes.

As an example, where it can be observed what exactly changed, we applied our merging nodes optimization to the isomorphic mapping δ, which is a part of the combinational S-Box. Figure 5 displays the data flow structure of δ including the reduced amount of control signals for the operators. The b_8 till b_{20} represent XOR operators, the D's denote delay elements.

There are three merged nodes (the dark backgrounded shapes) containing 5, 5, and 3 XORs. For example the lower merged node only needs 2 control signals instead of 6 which results in a smaller control logic. Applying the merging to the

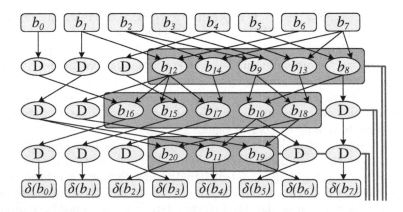

Fig. 5. Data flow graph of the optimized isomorphic mapping with merged nodes

other AES transformations resulted in less optimization possibilities. Nonetheless, the `AddRoundKey` and `MixColumns` transformations use some XORs, which have been merged. The next section will state the results of the prototype and the optimized implementation, compare them and draw a conclusion.

4   Results and Conclusion

We synthesized our implementation for an inexpensive Xilinx Spartan 3 board, running at 50 MHz. One AES round takes 62 cycles, capable of processing two blocks at once. The packets are 13 bits long, so the minimum loop duration is 26 cycles (the minimum gap between packets is also 13). The logic (including an RS232 interface) utilizes 4,745 of the 4-input LUTs.

With a 50 MHz clock frequency and encrypting 128 bit in a total of 626 clock cycles we calculate a throughput of 9.75 MBit per second. As we stated earlier, the S-Box has quite some parallelism in it. We minimized the number of control signals by merging logic nodes. Table 1 shows a direct comparison between the prototype and the optimized S-Box. The maximum clock frequency has improved by 38.3% from 141.824 MHz to 196.155 MHz.

Table 1. Comparison between the prototype and the optimized S-Box

Logic utilization	prototype	optimized	reduced perc.
No. of occupied Slices	467	327	30.0%
No. of Slice FF	646	543	15.9%
Total no. 4–input LUTs	713	491	31.1%

The table indicates an improvement of $\approx$ 30%. Occupied slices have been reduced by 30.0%. The number of occupied slice flip–flops has been reduced by only 15.9%. Table 2 shows the comparison between prototype and optimized AES-128. The maximum clock frequency shrunk by 24%.

Table 2. Comparison between the prototype and the optimized AES-128

Logic utilization	prototype	optimized	reduced perc.
No. of occupied Slices	3616	2960	18.1%
No. of Slice FF	5902	4663	21.0%
Total no. 4–input LUTs	4745	2905	38.8%

The space reduction is $\approx$ 25% on average. As can be seen, the reduction in percent is about the same for the S-Box and the complete AES-128. This is due to the fact that the S-Boxes in the AES-128 make up the most costly part.

Special data computation algorithms proved to offer high optimization potential for our space reduction algorithm. They produced excellent results for the

AES implementation, especially the combinational S-Box. Within the scope of this paper, we did not describe all optimization possibilities, we merely restricted the space reduction to the most important MACT parts. However, the proto-type and optimized AES-128 algorithm proved the MACT architecture and the MHLS tool being capable of implementing and handling very complex designs.

In our opinion, MACT has a high potential, but scheduling and optimizing remains a difficult task. Future work could focus on a deeper analysis of MACT's unique properties and possible applcations to give new research directions.

References

1. Atasu, K., Breveglieri, L., Macchetti, M.: Efficient AES implementations for ARM based platforms. In: SAC 2004: Proceedings of the 2004 ACM symposium on Applied computing, pp. 841–845. ACM, New York (2004)
2. Chodowiec, P., Gaj, K.: Very Compact FPGA Implementation of the AES Algorithm. In: Walter, C.D., Koç, Ç.K., Paar, C. (eds.) CHES 2003. LNCS, vol. 2779, pp. 319–333. Springer, Heidelberg (2003)
3. Dittmann, F., Rettberg, A., Weber, R.: Optimization techniques for a reconfigurable self-timed and bit-serial architecture. In: Proceedings of the SBCCI 2007, Rio de Janeiro, Brazil, September 3-6 (2007)
4. Jacobson, H.M., Kudva, P.N., Bose, P., Cook, P.W., Schuster, S.E., Mercer, E.G., Myers, C.J.: Synchronous interlocked pipelines. In: 8th Intern. Symposium on Asynchronous Circuits and Systems (April 2002)
5. Mui, E.N.: Practical Implementation of Rijndael S-Box Using Combinational Logic (2007), http://www.xess.com/projects/Rijndael_SBox.pdf
6. Renshaw, D., Denyer, P.: VLSI Signal Processing: A Bit Serial Approach. Addison-Wesley, Reading (1985)
7. Rettberg, A., Dittmann, F., Zanella, M.C., Lehmann, T.: Towards a high-level synthesis of reconfigurable bit-serial architectures. In: Proceedings of the 16th Symposium on Integrated Circuits and System Design (SBCCI), Sao Paulo, Brazil, September 8-11 (2003)
8. Rettberg, A., Zanella, M.C., Bobda, C., Lehmann, T.: A fully self-timed bit-serial pipeline architecture for embedded systems. In: Proceedings of the Design Automation and Test Conference (DATE), Messe Munich, Munich, Germany, March 3-7 (2003)
9. Satoh, A., Morioka, S., Takano, K., Munetoh, S.: A Compact Rijndael Hardware Architecture with S-Box Optimization. In: Boyd, C. (ed.) ASIACRYPT 2001. LNCS, vol. 2248, pp. 239–254. Springer, Heidelberg (2001)
10. Trichina, E., Korkishko, L.: Secure and Efficient AES Software Implementation for Smart Cards. In: Lim, C.H., Yung, M. (eds.) WISA 2004. LNCS, vol. 3325, pp. 425–439. Springer, Heidelberg (2005)
11. Weber, R., Rettberg, A.: Implementation of the AES Algorithm for a Reconfigurable, Bit Serial, Fully Pipelined Architecture. In: Reconfigurable Computing: Architectures, Tools and Applications, 5th International Workshop, ARC 2009. Proceedings, Karlsruhe, Germany, March 16-18, pp. 330–335 (2009)

The Case for Interpreted Languages in Sensor Networks

Leonardo Steinfeld[1] and Luigi Carro[2]

[1] Instituto de Ingeniería Eléctrica, Universidad de la República, Montevideo, Uruguay
leo@fing.edu.uy
[2] Instituto de Informática, Universidade Federal do Rio Grande do Sul, Porto Alegre, Brazil
luigi.carro@inf.ufrgs.br

Abstract. As sensor networks gain popularity and technology scaling allows further processing in each network node, the programming of these distributed computational structures becomes a serious bottleneck. Interpreted languages adoption may allow a smaller programming effort, and since they show a denser code representation than their directly executed counterpart, interpreted code exhibits smaller power dissipation during over-the-air reprogramming. As technology scales, the processing energy cost tends to reduce more than communication energy, which is bounded by the required irradiated radio power. By allowing the execution of more complex software WSN can be used for more refined applications, like image processing, compression and recognition. Also, interpretation can allow the use of object oriented technology software, allowing high productivity gains. However, the interpretation overhead cost and the extra memory required in Java, for example, argue against interpreted languages adoption in WSN. In this paper we show the design space for interpreted languages, and demonstrate that there is a large application domain where interpretation benefits can be used together with energy efficiency.

1 Introduction

Wireless sensor networks are a new computing platform that combines computation, sensing, and communication with a physical environment. The sensor node, a new class of networked embedded computer, is characterized by severe resource constraints, especially energy, since they are powered from batteries or harvest energy from the surrounding environment. As technology scales, the capacity of integrated processors increase and new applications can be devised where previously their cost in terms of price and energy were unacceptable. Sensor network applications used to be tightly close to the hardware and after deployment the sensors distribution and function remained unaltered. As a result, current applications are unlikely to change much during network lifetime, since they have not been designed for that at all. However, we envisage a new generation of nodes equipped with a more rich set of sensors, like the artificial retina [1], were costly local processing is mandatory. If more computational power is available at each node, the amount of possible applications tend to explode, enabling a broader utilization of a WSN, and an increased lifetime thanks to reprogramability of new applications on the same platform.

However, this increasing complexity of applications using wireless sensor networks soon becomes a barrier to the adoption of these networks. The currently

A. Rettberg et al. (Eds.): IESS 2009, IFIP AICT 310, pp. 279–289, 2009.

available wireless sensor network programming models do not scale well from simple data collection models to collaborative information processing ones. On a different scenario, complex distributed applications have been developed for powerful platforms (such PDA, laptops, etc.), but they are not appropriate for scarce resource platforms like the so-called Berkeley motes or even for more powerful but emerging ones, since the batteries would be drained too soon. New programming models are essential to develop complex distributed applications, and at the same time obtain a decent level of energy-efficiency.

Because of the large amounts of nodes present in a WSN, and since they usually are in an unreachable location, they are expected to run for years unattended. The necessity to perform software changes in deployed wireless sensor network is an important issue that increasingly calls the attention of the scientific community. Reprogramming the software of a running sensor network enables to correct software bugs, test new applications more easily and consequently helps to shorten the development time [2]. Moreover, application reconfiguration can be done by reprogramming the application software. Even though the application behavior adjustment could be performed by modifying operational parameters, a more profound modification, like algorithm changes or even completely updating the software application, cannot be achieved by simply adjusting a set of parameters. Since the new application needs to be transmitted though the network, the reprogramming has an associated energy cost. Moreover, the execution cost depends on the program representation level. An interpreted representation will have an execution overhead if compared to a direct executed program. On the other hand, an interpreted representation typically is smaller than its natively executed counterpart. Furthermore, application specific virtual machines could lead to dense program representation, thus reducing communication cost [3]. Therefore, a precise and more profound analysis is still required to build models for energy and its trade-offs with other system metrics [4].

In this paper we analyze the design space for interpreted languages, considering the different power modes of communication and processing components, and how these evolve with technology scaling.

The remainder of this paper is organized as follows. In Section 2, we survey related work. In Section 3 a first order analytical energy model is derived, considering the different power modes and the activity profiles of the communicating and the processing units. In Section 4 we present the results and delimit the actual space for interpretation in WSN. In Section 5 we discuss possible evolutions of the design space according to the foreseen technology evolution. Finally, Section 6 contains concluding remarks and future research directions.

2   Related Work

The reasons for adopting interpreted languages in WSN are mainly two: the appropriate programming model and the opportunity for energy optimization, and both are interrelated.

Programming models suitable for developing complex distributed applications and at the same time being energy-aware are essential to enable more sophisticated applications. The difficulty in programming sensor networks comes from their inherently distributed nature, and also from their harsh operating conditions, such as unreliable communications [5]. The extremely constrained resources prevent the adoption of proposed solutions like PIECES [6]. To cope with the energy limited budget, sensor network programmers must deal with too many implementation-level details besides the application logic that they normally focus on, and usually to design extremely efficient systems, break the traditional networking and systems layers, thus compromising reuse and other good software engineering principles. Early node-centric programming models are inadequate and unable to scale up. New service architectures, inter-operation protocols, programming models that are resource-aware and resource-efficient, even across heterogeneous devices, are needed [7].

There are several benefits in using virtual machines (VMs) in WSN. First, VMs allow applications to be developed uniformly across WSN platforms, platform-independent applications can be written using VM abstractions whose implementations are scaled to meet resource constraints. VMs provide a clean separation of system software and application software, which reduces the cost of reprogramming after deployment. Finally, VMs mask the variations among the WSN platforms through a common execution framework [8].

Several works had explored the energy trade-off between communication and processing cost, adopting different approaches: dynamic linking of native code, interpreted code execution instead of direct execution, or a hybrid between these two approaches.

A reprogramming mechanism via in-situ dynamic run-time linking and loading of native code to enable application reconfiguration was proposed in [2]. The energy cost of dynamic linking and execution of native code is measured, quantified and compared to the energy cost of transmission and execution of code for two virtual machines (Java and an optimised one). The obtained execution overhead varied from roughly 4 to 100 times, and code reduction size was about 1/15 in the optimised version. The break-even point between direct and interpreted execution ranges from 100 to 40,000 iterations, that is the number of execution completed by a program before a new version is distributed.

Maté [3] is a bytecode interpreter that runs on TinyOS [9], implemented as a single TinyOS component that sits on top of several system components, including sensors, the network stack, and non-volatile storage. Code is broken up into small capsules of 24 instructions, which can self-replicate through the network for code distribution. Larger programs can be composed of multiple capsules. Maté's high-level interface allows complex programs to be very short (under 100 bytes), and consequently reducing the energy cost of transmitting new programs. The execution overhead of some typical instruction was measured by the execution of tight loops: 33.5 times for a logical and on two words, and just 1.03 times to send a packet. The code reduction size obtained for some applications ranged from 1/100 to 1/400, approximately.

Many Java virtual machines implemented on bare metal microcontroller targeted for wireless sensor networks have been reported, like Squawk[10], and more recently Darjeeling [11] and Taka Tuka[12]. All of them perform some post processing, performing static linking within group of classes and optimising bytecodes to reduce code size. The achieved code reduction was up to 3-4 times w.r.t. the original Java classes.

A hybrid execution environment that enables the co-execution of platform-independent VM instructions with native instructions was proposed in [8]. Platform-independent byte code is interpreted by an interpretive execution engine, while a lightweight native interface is used to access natively implemented functionality. A proxy JIT-compilation on a powerful compilation server is used to compile the relevant bytecode for the node. The authors argue that the problems associated with purely native or purely virtual execution environments are addressed.

None of the previous reviewed works consider all the fundamental parameters involved in these new and complex WSNs, like execution and update rates. Some works establish some relations between those variables, but do not explore the whole space for the interpreted languages execution approach. In this work we develop an analysis of the usage of interpreted languages taking into account not only the ratio from interpreted to native code, but also some physical mote aspects that have been previously disregarded, and are shown to be very important.

3 Power Consumption Model

A precise analysis is required to build energy models, in order to analyze their trade-offs with other system metrics [4], in order to carefully design the system and extend its lifetime to the desired duration.

The total energy of the system node results from the sum of each sub-system module or component contribution, which in turn depends on the activity profile and the current consumption of the various operating modes, i.e. for a microcontroller: active, idle, sleep mode, among others. Longer time periods can be analysed based on a periodic behaviour of duration T.

Being T_i the time spent at the power level P_i, we define d_i as the ratio of T_i and the period T. For the rest of the time, the processor is in power P_0, the lowest possible power mode (power down or sleep). The average power can then be expressed as:

$$\overline{P} = \sum_{i=1} P_i \, d_i + P_0 \left(1 - \sum_{i=1} d_i\right) = \sum_{i=1} (P_i - P_0) d_i + P_0 \, . \tag{1}$$

Eq. (1) shows that the average power is the sum of the increment from the lowest power mode to the considered power consumption mode, weighted by the corresponding duty-cycle, plus the lowest power mode, which represents the minimum power consumption. Thus, the total minimum power dissipated per node is the sum of the minimum power level of all components. Low duty cycle operation is a common approach to minimize the energy drain of the higher power modes. As a result, the energy drain in the lowest possible power mode becomes significant, and must be carefully considered when the average power consumption is calculated.

Since a component could be used for several purposes or be shared by other modules, the time spent at each level must be evaluated. For example, the transceiver can be used to transfer acquired data from the node to a base, or to receive an update of the software application. These services can be considered independent and modeled separately.

Certainly, the energy waste for transitions between different operating modes must be considered. To simplify the derived equations these contributions will be take into consideration increasing the time spend in the higher power level.

The node is basically a reactive system that responds to external stimulus: a successful reception of a packet, a time trigger to initiate some measurement, data ready interruption, and so on. Apart from the active mode the microcontroller must remain at an operation level suitable for using the internal timer/counter to be able to wake-up from the timer expiration interruption. For example, this lowest power mode for microcontroller of a Telosb sensor node [13] - MSP430 microcontroller [14]- is the LPM3, and for the CC2420 radio [15] is the off power mode (oscillator and voltage regulator being off).

We developed a first order analytical energy model using Eq. (1), considering the previously mentioned power modes, and the activity profiles of the communicating and the processing units. Nevertheless, the same procedure can be followed to include any other subsystem. When analyzing the interpreted code and native execution trade-off, the break even iteration is normally derived [3][8].

3.1 Average Power for Native Code Distribution and Execution

The node computing activity can be modeled as a periodic processing system that process data with a period T_e. On average, the computation amount can be considered as a piece of code of size S that runs to completion. Furthermore, the program update size is also S. During computation time the microprocessor is in active mode dissipating power, P_e^{active}, executing bytes at a rate R_e. The rest of the time the microcontroller goes into low power mode with P_e^{sleep}.

The execution average power is calculated as a function of the duty cycle:

$$\overline{P_e^{native}} = P_e^{active} d_e + \left(1 - d_e\right)P_e^{sleep} = P_e d_e + P_e^{sleep}. \tag{2}$$

where:

$d_e = S/(R_e \cdot T_e)$ is the execution duty cycle, and
$P_e = P_e^{active} - P_e^{sleep}$ is power increase from the sleep power baseline.

The distribution of new code is performed via radio-frequency communication. The average time between each code upgrade is considered to be T_d. The radio is in active mode, consuming P_d^{active} power, during the time needed to transfer the code at a rate R_d. The final amount of bytes that goes through the radio is given by the multiplication of the code size by the protocol overhead, k_{mac}, and the overhead for relying packets through the network, k_{nwk}. The rest of the time the radio is in low power mode, draining power P_d^{sleep}.
The distribution average power is:

$$\overline{P_d^{native}} = P_d^{acitve} d_d + \left(1 - d_d\right)P_d^{sleep} = P_d d_d + P_d^{sleep}. \tag{3}$$

where:

$d_d = S_d/(R_d \cdot T_d)$ is the distribution duty cycle,
$S_d = k_{mac} \cdot k_{nwk} \cdot S$, the distribution effective size, and
$P_d = P_d^{active} - P_d^{sleep}$ is power increase from the sleep power baseline.

The total average power for distributing and executing native code is calculated, assuming that distribution and processing are independent task and just adding them:

$$\overline{P^{native}} = \overline{P_d^{native}} + \overline{P_e^{native}} = P_d \frac{k_{mac} k_{nwk} S}{R_d T_d} + P_e \frac{S}{R_e T_e} + P^{sleep} . \tag{4}$$

where:
$\quad P_d = P_d^{sleep} + P_d^{sleep}$ is the total sleep power.

Eq.(4) can be written in the following form:

$$\overline{P^{native}} = \frac{E_d S}{T_d} + \frac{E_e S}{T_e} + P^{sleep} . \tag{5}$$

where:
$\quad E_d = k_{mac} k_{nwk} P_d / R_d$ is the energy to distribute a byte of code and,
$\quad E_e = P_e / R_e$ is the energy to execute a byte of code.

3.2 Average Power for Interpreted Code Distribution and Execution

The average power for interpreted code is straightforward to compute, considering that the time to execute interpreted code is increased by the execution overhead of the virtual machine, k_e. In the same way, the time to distribute the interpreted code, corresponding to certain piece of native code, is affected by the distribution factor k_d. This factor is the reciprocal of the bloat factor, term used to denote the code size increment when interpreted code is compiled to native.

The average power for the interpreted case is:

$$\overline{P^{int\ erp}} = \left(k_d \frac{E_d}{T_d} + k_e \frac{E_e}{T_e} \right) S + P^{sleep} . \tag{6}$$

3.3 The Trade-Off Factor

The interpreted versus native average power rate is defined as κ, and a value less than the unit means that interpreted language is preferable of over native, that is, it executes with less power.

$$\kappa = \frac{\left(k_d \dfrac{E_d}{T_d} + k_e \dfrac{E_e}{T_e} \right) S + P^{sleep}}{\left(\dfrac{E_d}{T_d} + \dfrac{E_e}{T_e} \right) S + P^{sleep}} . \tag{7}$$

The trade-ff factor results from relation of the following values: T_e, T_d, and S, which are application dependant, E_d, E_e and P^{sleep}, which are technology parameters, and finally the interpreted language factors k_e and k_d, resulting from the virtual machine design.

For the case that P^{sleep} is much smaller than the average power of distribution and execution, the gain factor is simply the sum of each relative power weight multiplied by the corresponding factor.

$$\kappa = k_d \frac{\overline{P}_d}{\overline{P}_d + \overline{P}_e} + k_e \frac{\overline{P}_e}{\overline{P}_d + \overline{P}_e}. \tag{8}$$

where:

$\overline{P}_d = \dfrac{E_d S}{T_d}$ is the average power associated to native code distribution,

$\overline{P}_e = \dfrac{E_e S}{T_e}$ is the average power associated to native code execution.

3.4 Break Even Locus

The break even locus, where the trade-off factor equals the unity (κ=1), does not depend on the sleep power nor on the code size. The derived equation still has four degrees of freedom, but one can substitute the factor T_d/T_e by n, so the break even locus becomes a 3D surface. The parameter n represents the average number of iterations completed by a program before a new version is distributed.

The following expression must be satisfied,

$$(k_e - 1)\frac{E_e}{E_d} n + (k_d - 1) = 0. \tag{9}$$

and restricts the surface domains by:

$$0 < k_d \leq 1$$

$$0 < k_e \leq 1 - \frac{E_d}{E_e}\frac{T_e}{T_d} = 1 - \frac{\overline{P}_d}{\overline{P}_e}$$

The former expression limits the distribution factor to positives values less than the unit, since a reduction factor is considered. The last restriction comes simply by substituting the first one in the surface Eq. (9).

4   Results

4.1   Measurements of the Energy Parameters

We measured the total system current, radio plus microcontroller, of a Telosb mote powered by batteries (3.3 V) in steady state for the meaningful combination of operation modes. Then, the separated values were obtained subtracting different

Table 1. Telosb mote measured parameters

	CC2420		MSP430	Units
$P_d{}^{active}$	68.10	$P_e{}^{active}$	1.20	mW
R_d	31250	R_e	1000000	B/s
E_d	11360	E_e	1.20	nJ/B
$P_d{}^{sleep}$	0.001	$P_e{}^{sleep}$	0.015	mW

measurements. The protocol overhead k_{mac} is considered constant, and we have used an estimated value of 1.2 (range from about 1.1 to 1.3 for payload greater than 70 bytes). For the code diffusion we considered the Delunge protocol [16], thus the overhead factor, k_{nwk}, is about 3.35 times the number of received packets and one more time for retransmission. Table 1 shows the results.

Note that the energy values are considered for processing or communicating one byte of executed code and not per byte of information processed. The last one is usually used to analyse the trade-off between process-before-transmit information, while the first one is used to calculate the total energy when a certain amount code is executed or transmitted. The rate of distribution to processing energy is almost 10,000, stressing the huge advantage of locally processing information instead of transmitting it.

The radio oscillator startup time, i.e. transition from low to active power, is about 600 μs, and corresponds to the time used to transmit about 18 bytes, roughly the MAC protocol overhead. The time for the microcontroller to go into active mode is about a few clock cycles, considered negligible.

4.2 Code Size

Assuming the evolution of technology, and also using this evolution to integrate more powerful processors in a WSN node, we compared the code size for a 10-tap FIR filter written in C and compiled to native MSP430 code. Also, we implemented the filter in Java and counted class bytecodes, discarding some bytes not useful during execution. Table 2 shows the results.

Table 2. Code and data memory comparison for a FIR filter (MSP430)

	text	Data	bss	ROM	RAM
Native (MSP430)	442	32	40	474	72
Java	262	-	-	262	-
Java/Native	0.59			0.55	

This simple example shows that Java code is denser than native code. However, the code reduction obtained is still modest, since a low size class leads to high overhead and because the low complexity of the application prevents code reuse.

4.3 Simulation Results

The actual space for interpreted code can be obtained from the above equations and the corresponding hardware parameters of Table 1.

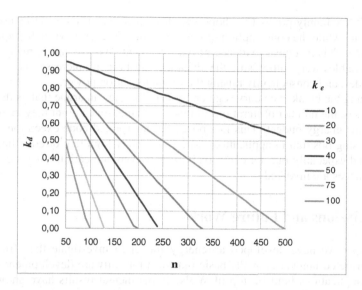

Fig. 1. Break-even locus

The break-even point triplets $\{n, k_e, k_d\}$ are plotted in the Fig. 1 as curves k_d (n, k_e). For example, considering a VM with a 30-fold execution time overhead and a distributing factor of 0.1, then the number of iterations (the number of times a program is executed before it is updated) required to have the same average power of interpreted and native code is about 300.

4.4 Discussion

The energy consumed by the radio can be separated in two components: electronic power and transmission radio power. The former is consumed by digital and analog processing circuits required for wireless communication or, in other words, digital and analog circuits that perform the necessary RF, baseband, and protocol processing. The last component, associated to the irradiated power, is consumed by the radio power amplifier that depends on the signal power required by the receiver and the path loss suffered by the signal. The path loss increases proportionally with receiver-transmitter separation distance, and depends on the environment condition, being a power of two in free space but up to four in real life channels[17]. As it is dictated by the Shannon's Information Theory and Maxwell's Laws, this power cannot be reduced.

In medium-to-large range communication the radio-power dominates (over the electronic-power), and in many cases the transmission power is orders of magnitude greater than reception power. However, in short range communication the electronic-power takes about the same radio power needed for successful reception at the desired short-distance, so it can get some benefit from technology progression, limited by the remainder component, waveform propagation power, which does not benefit from any technology progression.

Consequently, the communication energy cost tends to get less benefit from technology scaling than processing cost. The current consumption of the new

MSP430F5XX family product is about 30% less than the MSP430F1611 used in the Telosb mote, while the consumption of the new radio CC2520 is virtually equal to the old CC2420. This is a clear evidence of our argument. What is more, many environmental variables vary little with the distance, pushing to increase the separation among nodes, and consequently raising the communication power.

Analyzing the break even curves given by Eq. (8), one can argue that as the rate E_e /E_d decreases, the number of iterations to reach the break-even point may increase, not affecting the energy budget. This fact poses the interpreted code execution approach in a promising position in applications where relatively high rate of code updates are needed, and especially but not exclusively, where communication covering medium-range distances are involved.

5 Conclusions and Future Work

In this paper we have developed an energy model to investigate the efficiency of using interpreted languages as the basic platform for software development of future complex applications built on top of WSN. Experimental results have shown that a huge savings in code space and amount of transmitted information can be obtained when an interpreted language like Java is used. Moreover, following technology scaling, it is very likely that future applications will be able to use complex processors, and saving energy during the transmission of information or code will be the most effective optimization procedure.

Currently we are developing complex dynamic applications to validate the approach here proposed.

References

1. Mitsubishi's M64282FP CMOS image sensor,
   `http://www.seattlerobotics.org/Encoder/200205/downloads/`
   `M64282FP.pdf`
2. Dunkels, A., Finne, N., Eriksson, J., Voigt, T.: Run-time dynamic linking for reprogramming wireless sensor networks. In: Proceedings of the 4th international Conference on Embedded Networked Sensor Systems, SenSys 2006, Boulder, Colorado, USA, October 31 - November 03, pp. 15–28. ACM, New York (2006)
3. Levis, P., Culler, D.: Maté: a tiny virtual machine for sensor networks. SIGOPS Oper. Syst. Rev. 36(5), 85–95 (2002)
4. Zhao, F.: Technical Perspective: The physical side of computing. Commun. ACM 51(7), 98–98 (2008)
5. Sugihara, R., Gupta, R.K.: Programming models for sensor networks: A survey. ACM Trans. Sen. Netw. 4(2), 1–29 (2008)
6. Liu, J., Chu, M., Reich, J., Zhao, F.: State-centric programming for sensor-actuator network systems. IEEE Pervasive Computing 2(4), 50–62 (2003)
7. Zhao, F.: Challenges in Programming Sensor Networks. In: Prasanna, V.K., Iyengar, S.S., Spirakis, P.G., Welsh, M. (eds.) DCOSS 2005. LNCS, vol. 3560, pp. 3–3. Springer, Heidelberg (2005)

8. Koshy, J., Wirjawan, I., Pandey, R., Ramin, Y.: Balancing computation and communication costs: The case for hybrid execution in sensor networks. Ad Hoc Netw. 6(8), 1185–1200 (2008)
9. Hill, J., Szewczyk, R., Woo, A., Hollar, S., Culler, D., Pister, K.: System architecture directions for networked sensors. SIGPLAN Not. 35(11), 93–104 (2000)
10. Simon, D., et al.: Java on the bare metal of wireless sensor devices: the squawk Java virtual machine. In: Proceedings of the 2nd international Conference on Virtual Execution Environments, VEE 2006, Ottawa, Ontario, Canada, pp. 78–88. ACM, New York (2006)
11. Brouwers, N., Corke, P., Langendoen, K.: Darjeeling, a Java compatible virtual machine for microcontrollers. In: Proceedings of the ACM/IFIP/USENIX Middleware '08 Conference Companion, Companion 2008, Leuven, Belgium, pp. 18–23. ACM, New York (2008)
12. Aslam, F., Schindelhauer, C., Ernst, G., Spyra, D., Meyer, J., Zalloom, M.: Introducing TakaTuka: a Java virtualmachine for motes. In: Proceedings of the 6th ACM Conference on Embedded Network Sensor Systems, SenSys 2008, Raleigh, NC, USA, pp. 399–400. ACM, New York (2008)
13. Telosb Mote Platform (rev. B). Crossbow Technology, Inc.,
    http://www.xbow.com/Products/Product_pdf_files/Wireless_pdf/TelosB_Datasheet.pdf
14. Texas Instruments Inc., MSP430x15x, MSP430x16x, MSP430x161x Mixed Signal Microcontroller (Rev. E),
    http://focus.ti.com/docs/prod/folders/print/msp430f1611.html
15. 2.4 GHz IEEE 802.15. 4/ZigBee-Ready RF Transceiver (Rev. B),
    http://focus.ti.com/docs/prod/folders/print/cc2420.html
16. Hui, J.W., Culler, D.: The dynamic behavior of a data dissemination protocol for network programming at scale. In: Proc. SenSys 2004, Baltimore, Maryland, USA (November 2004)
17. Srivatsava, M.: Power-aware communication systems. In: Power Aware Design Methodologies. Kluwer, Norwell (2002)

Characterization of Inaccessibility in Wireless Networks: A Case Study on IEEE 802.15.4 Standard*

Jeferson L.R. Souza and José Rufino

University of Lisboa, LaSIGE
jsouza@lasige.di.fc.ul.pt, ruf@di.fc.ul.pt

Abstract. Wireless technology has been seen as the communication technology of the future. One of many challenges is the support for predictability and time-bounded communications over this technology. In this way, the control of temporary partitions, called inaccessibility, is of fundamental importance. For this reason, this paper makes a characterization of inaccessibility in wireless networks and describes an exhaustive study about it on IEEE 802.15.4 wireless standard. The knowledge of inaccessibility incidents and their duration is a first step to define means to control network partitioning and therefore to form a basis for supporting real-time communications over wireless technology.

1 Introduction

Industrial and aerospace applications has seen wireless technology as the network infrastructure of the future. The advantages of this technology are the mobility, and mainly the elimination of cables for communication among devices. For example, wireless technologies are seen as relevant communication infrastructure in many kinds of spacecrafts: satellites, and orbital vehicles, with respect to cabling issues; robotic vehicles for planetary exploration. Both applications have real-time constrains and need guarantees about transmission time bounds. The study of the provision of these guarantees in wireless technologies involves the analysis of low-level protocol components and of high-level software layers, present in the wireless network model, and involved in the communication process.

Different characteristics of wireless networks, e.g., bounded delay to transmission of a frame, to handling of omission faults and control of partitions in the network, must be addressed to support real-time communication. In this way, this paper presents a exhaustive study about temporary partitions in IEEE 802.15.4 standard. These partitions are called inaccessibility [1,2] and this study

---

* Faculdade de Ciências da Universidade de Lisboa, Bloco C6, Piso III, Campo Grande, 1749–016 Lisboa, Portugal. This work was partially motivated by our work within the scope of the ESA (European Space Agency) Innovation Triangular Initiative program, through ESTEC Project AIR-II (ARINC 653 in Space — Industrial Initiative), URL: http://air.di.fc.ul.pt. This work was partially supported by FCT through the Multiannual Funding and the CMU-Portugal Programs.

A. Rettberg et al. (Eds.): IESS 2009, IFIP AICT 310, pp. 290–301, 2009.
© IFIP International Federation for Information Processing 2009

is important to define means to control inaccessibility in IEEE 802.15.4 networks. A similar study was made successfully for other wired network technologies such as CAN [3,4], and Token-Bus [5], demonstrating the importance of the study for the support of real-time communication in wired networks. On a similar manner, the control of inaccessibility is one of some desired properties to achieve real-time communication in wireless networks.

The control of timeliness and predictability in input/output operations (wireless network interfaces included) is a fundamental condition in partitioned architectures, such as those we are addressing within the scope of AIR technology [6].

This paper is organized as follows: Section 2 presents the main concept of inaccessibility, explaining the observation of this concept in wireless networks. Section 3 presents an overview of IEEE 802.15.4 standard. Section 4 describes the study of inaccessibility in 802.15.4 networks and shows its impact in the network temporal behavior. Section 5 presents some related works. Finally, section 6 draws some conclusions.

2 What Is Inaccessibility ?

Disturbances induced in the operation of medium access control (MAC) protocols may create temporary partitions in the network, derived of the time required to detect and recover from these situations. These disturbances can be produced by external interferences or by some glitches in the operation of the MAC sublayer. A solution for controlling these partitions for LAN-based networks was presented in [7]. These temporary network partitions are called inaccessibility [1,2] and the definition of this concept is summarized here:

> *Certain kinds of components may temporarily refrain from providing service, without that having to be necessarily considered a failure. That state is called* **inaccessibility**. *It can be made known to the users of network components; limits are specified (duration, rate); violation of those limits implies permanent failure of the component.*

The same kind of problems present in wired networks also are present in wireless networks. However, while LAN-based networks may offer additional facilities to

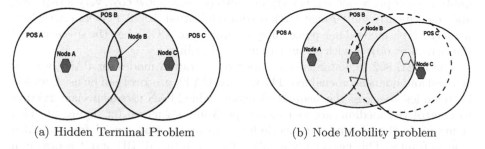

(a) Hidden Terminal Problem   (b) Node Mobility problem

Fig. 1. Some problems in Wireless networks

allow the transmitter to detect a problem (e.g. collision detection), in wireless networks these mechanisms do not exist in general. For example, in wireless networks, the transceiver of each node cannot receive and transmit data simultaneously. Consequently, the algorithms used in the MAC sublayer do not have means to detect a collision without the support of timeout-based mechanisms, or additional control channels.

These problems may be originated externally or derived of the proximity and position of a node, in relation to operating space of other nodes. The circles in figure 1(a) show the transmission and interference range of three different nodes. In the example presented in figure 1, the node A may overlap, total or partial, the frame transmission of node B and vice-versa. It may result in periods of inaccessibility for the two nodes. The RTS/CTS handshake used in IEEE 802.11 tries to solve the hidden node problem. However, this technique does not solve completely the problem and increase the overhead of a transmission, an unacceptable condition, for example, for wireless sensor networks [8].

The node mobility, provided by wireless technology, allows the change of a node location easily. This mobility may cause connection loss between nodes. Figure 1(b) shows that, after moves, node C is outside of node B Personal Operating Space (POS) and it may cause periods of inaccessibility in both nodes. An environment with a high level of node mobility may cause the occurrence of various periods of inaccessibility if the nodes will move their position to outside range of each other constantly.

The inaccessibility times, in both cases, are the time a node needs to reestablish normal operation of the MAC protocol. The knowledge of inaccessibility time bounds is important to achieve the support of real-time communication over the wireless networks.

This paper presents a study of the IEEE 802.15.4 standard concerning the evaluation of inaccessibility and its impact in a wireless network. For completeness, the next section presents an overview of this standard.

3   IEEE 802.15.4 - Overview

The IEEE 802.15.4 standard [9] was designed for Low-Rate Wireless Personal Area Networks (LR-WPANs). These networks were designed for being used with limited power processor and battery life devices, have a low-cost, very low-power, and consequently short-range wireless communication [10]. A Personal Area Network (PAN) is focused in a personal operating space (POS), i.e., the space around the person or object with some ten meters of radius.

The IEEE 802.15.4 standard defines two operation modes for PAN: beacon-enabled and nonbeacon-enabled. The CSMA/CA [9] protocol can be used, within both modes, to access the medium. Beacon-enabled PAN uses a special structure to control the medium access called superframe structure (cf. figure 2). This structure is time bounded by periodic transmissions of special frames called beacon frames. This periodicity is called Beacon Interval (BI) and it is drawn in figure 2.

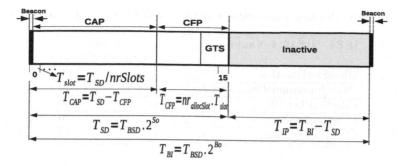

Fig. 2. Superframe Structure

In this paper, the analyses of the network inaccessibility are focused in a beacon-enabled PAN. The exhaustive study of inaccessibility periods based on IEEE 802.15.4 standard is presented. This study shows the best (^{bc}) and worst (^{wc}) case inaccessibility time bounds in a set of relevant scenarios.

4   Inaccessibility in IEEE 802.15.4

The IEEE 802.15.4 standard has been viewed as a potential technology by industrial, vehicular and aerospace applications. These applications have necessity of real-time communications, i.e., the temporal behavior must be well-defined and the communication infrastructure strongly reliable. One of many challenges of the study of hardware and software components, used within wireless networks, is to define a solution for reliable and real-time communication over this type of networks. The study of inaccessibility is one step in that direction.

The study present in this paper is focused in beacon-enabled PAN that use the superframe structure (Figure 2) to control medium access. Constants and variables used for IEEE 802.15.4 network configuration and parametrisation are the standard values, summarized in tables 1 and 2. The characterization of the inaccessibility scenarios in nonbeacon-enabled PAN was made as an extension of this work and is available in a technical report [11].

Next, we define a set of general equations describing frame transmission times. Equations 1 and 2 are used for unreliable (non acknowledged) frame transmission, and equations 3 and 4 for reliable (acknowledged) frame transmission.

$$T_{MAC}^{bc}(type) = T_{backoff} + T_{MAC-type}^{bc} \tag{1}$$

$$T_{MAC}^{wc}(type) = \sum_{j=1}^{maxBackoff} \left\{ T_{backoff} \cdot (2^{BE} + 1) \right\} + T_{MAC-type}^{wc} \tag{2}$$

$$T_{MAC\_ack}^{bc}(type) = T_{MAC}^{bc}(type) + T_{ackDelay}^{bc} + T_{ack} \tag{3}$$

$$T_{MAC\_ack}^{wc}(type) = \sum_{i=0}^{maxRetries} T_{MAC}^{wc}(type) + T_{ackDelay}^{wc} + T_{ack} \tag{4}$$

Table 1. Relevant time-related constants of IEEE 802.15.4 Standard

IEEE 802.15.4 Name	Abbr	Value (symbol times)
aBaseSlotDuration	$\mathcal{T}_{base}$	60
aBaseSuperframeDuration	$\mathcal{T}_{BSD}$	960
aMinCAPLength	$\mathcal{T}_{minCAP}$	440
aUnitBackoffPeriod	$\mathcal{T}_{backoff}$	20
aTurnaroundTime	$\mathcal{T}_{xvrcmd}$	12

where, $\mathcal{T}^{bc}_{ackDelay} = \mathcal{T}_{xvrcmd}$ and $\mathcal{T}^{wc}_{ackDelay} = \mathcal{T}_{xvrcmd} + \mathcal{T}_{backoff} + \mathcal{T}_{freq}$ are the times to wait the acknowledgment in reliable transmissions. $\mathcal{T}_{freq}$ depends of technology and to simplify we will consider an upper bound $\mathcal{T}_{freq} = 100$ symbols. The reference *type* in equations (1) to (4) identifies one specific type of MAC frames.

4.1 Single Beacon Frame Loss - No Tracking

Let us start our analysis considering that a subset of nodes (may have a single element) in a PAN does not track beacon frames. If a node in this set needs to transmit a frame it should enable the radio transceiver (receive mode) and start a wait period of at most $\mathcal{T}_{BSD} \cdot (2^{BO} + 1)$ symbols. If the beacon frame is received before the end of this search period, the frame shall be transmitted in the appropriate portion of the superframe. No inaccessibility event exists. Otherwise, the operation of the MAC protocol is disturbed by the lack of beacon frame synchronization and the network is inaccessible, as described by equation:

$$\mathcal{T}^{wc}_{ina \leftarrow sbfl} = \mathcal{T}_{xvrcmd} + \mathcal{T}_{BSD} \cdot (2^{BO} + 1) \qquad (5)$$

After the period of inaccessibility, the node may proceed with the transmission of the frame using the unslotted version of the CSMA/CA algorithm.

4.2 Multiple Beacon Frame Loss - Tracking

A beacon-enabled PAN uses the superframe structure for controlling medium access. Under normal operation, a node must receive the beacon frame before it is allowed to transmit data. If some nodes in the PAN do not receive the beacon frame, the network will be inaccessible for such nodes.

Based on the superframe structure of the last received beacon, the node can control the radio interface and track consecutive beacon transmissions. The tracking mechanism is also called beacon synchronization and allows all nodes to know the characteristics of the superframe structure (duration of active and inactive periods, number of allocated GTS slots, etc.).

For tracking a beacon frame, a node searches for beacons during at most $\mathcal{T}_{BSD} \cdot (2^{BO} + 1)$ symbol times. If a beacon frame with the current PAN identifier of the node is not received, this search is repeated from one to at most *nrLost*

Table 2. Relevant integer parameters of IEEE 802.15.4 Standard

IEEE 802.15.4 Name	Abbr	Range	Value
macBeaconOrder	BO	0 - 15	8
macSuperframeOrder	SO	0 - 15	5
macMinBE	$minBE$	0 - maxBE	3
macMaxBE	$maxBE$	3 - 8	5
macMaxCSMABackoffs	$maxBackoff$	0 - 5	4
macMaxFrameRetries	$maxRetries$	0 - 7	3
macResponseWaitTime	$nrWait$	2 - 64	32
aMaxLostBeacons	$nrLost$	-	4
aNumSuperframeSlots	$nrSlots$	-	16

times. The best and worst-case inaccessibility durations are therefore given by equations 6 and 7, respectively.

$$T^{bc}_{ina\leftarrow mbfl} = T_{BSD} \cdot \left(2^{BO} + 1\right) \tag{6}$$

$$T^{wc}_{ina\leftarrow mbfl} = \left(T_{BSD} \cdot \left(2^{BO} + 1\right)\right) \cdot nrLost \tag{7}$$

4.3   Synchronization Loss

If the search for the beacon frame does not succeed in any of the $nrLost$ tries, a node loses synchronization with its coordinator, being obliged to signal a **BEACON LOST** event to the high layer protocol management entities. The corresponding inaccessibility period is simply given by:

$$T_{ina\leftarrow nosync} = \left(T_{BSD} \cdot \left(2^{BO} + 1\right)\right) \cdot nrLost \tag{8}$$

There are a number of causes for inaccessibility due to loss of node synchronization: a burst of electromagnetic interference in the medium; disturbances in the node receiver circuitry; collisions derived from the hidden terminal problem or node mobility; glitches in the actual PAN coordinator or even its failure. Based on the information it owns, the high layer protocol management entities may take a decision on the appropriate recovery action.

4.4   Orphan Node

If the high layer protocol management entities decide that the node was orphaned, a request is issued to the MAC layer to start an *orphan scan* recovery action, over a specified set of logical channels.

For each logical channel: a MAC orphan notification command is sent; as reply, a MAC realignment command from the coordinator, previously associated, is awaited for during a given period. While the node does not receive the MAC realignment command, the network is inaccessible. Once such MAC command is received the node terminates the scan and acknowledges the frame reception; the network becomes accessible. The worst-case inaccessibility time is given by:

$$\mathcal{T}^{wc}_{ina\leftarrow orphan} = \mathcal{T}_{ina\leftarrow nosync} + \mathcal{T}_{HLP}(Orphan) +$$

$$\sum_{i=1}^{nrchannels} \{\mathcal{T}^{wc}_{MAC}(Orphan) + nrWait \cdot \mathcal{T}_{BSD}\} + \mathcal{T}^{wc}_{ackDelay} + \mathcal{T}_{ack} \tag{9}$$

where, $\mathcal{T}_{HLP}$ is the normalized (symbol) time taken in the high layer protocol management actions. Should the orphan realignment succeed at the first attempt, the inaccessibility period will be simply given by equation 10.

$$\mathcal{T}^{bc}_{ina\leftarrow orphan} = \mathcal{T}_{ina\leftarrow nosync} + \mathcal{T}_{HLP}(Orphan) + \mathcal{T}^{bc}_{MAC}(Orphan) +$$
$$\mathcal{T}_{HLP}(Realign) + \mathcal{T}^{bc}_{MAC\_ack}(Realign) \tag{10}$$

4.5   Coordinator Realignment

At a coordinator the need to assist MAC layer management actions starts when a MAC orphan notification command is received. Upon processing by high layer protocol management entities, the acknowledged transmission of a MAC realignment command is requested. The time taken in these actions is seen as inaccessibility in this coordinator. The best and worst inaccessibility times are given by equations 11 and 12, respectively.

$$\mathcal{T}^{bc}_{ina\leftarrow realign} = \mathcal{T}_{HLP}(Realign) + \mathcal{T}^{bc}_{MAC\_ack}(Realign) \tag{11}$$
$$\mathcal{T}^{wc}_{ina\leftarrow realign} = \mathcal{T}_{HLP}(Realign) + \mathcal{T}^{wc}_{MAC\_ack}(Realign) \tag{12}$$

4.6   PAN Conflict Detection

The creation and management of a PAN can be performed by any node with sufficient memory, battery life, and power processor. These nodes are called Full Function Devices (FFDs). For this reason, there is a possibility of two different PANs in the same POS may render the same PAN identifier. This situation is called a PAN conflict and it can be detected by a PAN coordinator or by its directly associated nodes.

There are two forms to detect a PAN conflict: a beacon frame with the same PAN identifier is received from different PAN coordinators in the same POS; a PAN coordinator receives a PAN ID conflict notification from a node. The former is a local event. The latter involves the transaction of a MAC PAN ID conflict notification command, which may lead to a period of inaccessibility bounded by equations 13 and 14, respectively.

$$\mathcal{T}^{bc}_{ina\leftarrow PAN\_Conflict} = \mathcal{T}^{bc}_{MAC\_ack}(PAN\_Conflict) \tag{13}$$
$$\mathcal{T}^{wc}_{ina\leftarrow PAN\_Conflict} = \mathcal{T}^{wc}_{MAC\_ack}(PAN\_Conflict) \tag{14}$$

4.7 PAN Conflict Resolution

A node is obliged to signal the PAN CONFLICT to the high layer protocol management entities, which in turn will request the MAC layer to perform an active scan. This scan is realized in all currently used logical channels. Scanning each channel involves the transmission of a MAC beacon request command and wait for replies (beacon frames), during a given period.

The PAN identifiers recorded from the received beacons can be sent to the high layer protocol management entities all at once, as specified in equation 15, or each time a beacon frame is received, as drawn in equation 16. During all this process, the network is inaccessible. The best and worst inaccessibility durations are given by equations 15 and 16, respectively.

$$T_{ina \leftarrow PAN\_R}^{bc} = T_{HLP}(PAN\_Conflict)+$$

$$\sum_{i=1}^{nrchannels} \{T_{MAC}^{bc}(Beacon\_R) + T_{BSD}.(2^n + 1)\} + T_{HLP}(Beacon) \tag{15}$$

$$T_{ina \leftarrow PAN\_R}^{wc} = T_{HLP}(PAN\_Conflict)+$$

$$\sum_{i=1}^{nrchannels} \{T_{MAC}^{wc}(Beacon\_R) + T_{BSD}.(2^n + 1)\} + T_{HLP}(Beacon) \tag{16}$$

where, n is a parameter that determines the total duration of the beacon waiting period at each channel.

If, at the end of the search, the PAN coordinator does not found a beacon frame with its own PAN identifier no further action is taken and the network becomes accessible again. Otherwise, a new PAN identifier is selected and, if necessary, a MAC coordinator realignment command is broadcast. However, some nodes may not be synchronized with the "new" superframe structure, which may induce a loss of synchronization, as explained in Section 4.3.

4.8 GTS Request

The allocation of GTS is performed sending a MAC GTS request command to the associated coordinator, which should be acknowledged. While the node does not receive this acknowledgment, the network is seen as inaccessible. The best and worst inaccessibility times are given by equations 17 and 18, respectively.

$$T_{ina \leftarrow GTS}^{bc} = T_{MAC\_ack}^{bc}(GTS) \tag{17}$$
$$T_{ina \leftarrow GTS}^{wc} = T_{MAC\_ack}^{wc}(GTS) \tag{18}$$

This scenario is extremely important because GTS slots can be used for bandwidth reservation. Solutions advanced in the literature try to solve the problem of real-time communications, over IEEE 802.15.4 standard, using GTS allocation mechanisms. The effectiveness of such solutions should be re-analyzed under the scope of a comprehensive network inaccessibility model.

Table 3. The best and worst cases for $868MHz$ frequency band

Scenario	PHY (868-868.6 MHz)					
	Modulation Technique					
	BPSK		*ASK*		*O-QPSK*	
	best case	worst case	bc	wc	bc	wc
	(ms)	(ms)	(ms)	(ms)	(ms)	(ms)
$t_{ina \leftarrow sbfl}$	——	12337	——	19739	——	9870
$t_{ina \leftarrow mbfl}$	12336	49344	19738	78951	9869	39476
$t_{ina \leftarrow nosync}$	49344	49344	78951	78951	39476	39476
$t_{ina \leftarrow orphan}$	49367	50935	78957	81483	39483	40744
$t_{ina \leftarrow realign}$	16	257	5	300	5	162
$t_{ina \leftarrow PAN\_Conflict}$	14	262	4	300	4	163
$t_{ina \leftarrow PAN\_R}$	12340	12389	19742	19814	9872	9909
$t_{ina \leftarrow GTS}$	8	216	4	296	3	154

4.9 Results

The table 3 presents the inaccessibility times for $868MHz$ frequency, considering default values of constants and parameters defined in the 802.15.4 standard. A data transfer, under normal network conditions, with frame size equal to **64 Bytes**, and using the $BPSK$ modulation, has a duration $t_{Data} \cong$ **26 ms**. The occurrence of some inaccessibility scenarios, presented in table 3, increase significantly this time. Furthermore, the beacon loss scenarios ($BPSK$ modulation) have inaccessibility periods up to 50 seconds, which are unacceptable for most embedded real-time applications, demonstrating the importance of our study.

5   Related Work

There are some related works that study the temporal aspects of the IEEE 802.15.4 standard. Ramachandran et. al. [12], Tang et. al [13] and Jung et. al. [14] made an exhaustive study about the CSMA/CA protocol in beacon-enabled PANs. Each study described a Markov model to understand its possible operation states and temporal aspects of this protocol. The three works consider a one-hop star topology where all nodes are in the transmission range of each other.

Ramachandran et. al. [12] focus their analysis in the throughput and energy consumption of the IEEE 802.15.4, considering the superframe only with CAP, no presence of MAC-level acknowledgements, and communications only from nodes to PAN coordinator, to simplify their model. Further, the authors make a modification in CSMA/CA parameters to improve performance and energy consumption of applications that do not need reliable data transfer, i. e., the use of acknowledgement to transmit their data.

The Markov model described for [13] allows analysis of the impact of the CSMA/CA parameters, the number of contending devices, and the data frame size on the network aspects such as throughput and energy efficiency. The authors utilize two two-dimensional Markov chains to make their analyzes and verifying that CSMA/CA parameters have a large impact on the network performance, being necessary to adjust these parameters for the network traffic conditions.

Further, Jung et. al. [14] analyze the performance of CSMA/CA protocol under unsaturated traffic conditions. Although the initial assumptions about the topology and the transmission range of the nodes, the authors consider that there are no transmission errors and no channel sense errors.

Huang et. al. [15], Hameed et. al. [16] and Koubaa et. al. [17] propose a modification on the IEEE 802.15.4 GTS allocation scheme. making optimizations in the default scheme used for bandwidth reservation.

Huang et. al. [15] propose an adaptive GTS allocation scheme that use two phases: a classification phase utilized for assigning priorities to nodes; and a scheduling phase where the GTS resources are allocated considering the priority numbers, the superframe length, and the GTS capacity of superframe. This changes are inserted without any modification of the IEEE 802.15.4 standard.

Hameed et. al. [16] propose a GTS allocation scheme called "Earliest Due Date GTS allocation". This modification considers the deadline of each GTS request, assigning the GTS slots for nodes with smaller normalize deadlines within each superframe. This algorithm assumes that no collisions and no packet lost occurs during transmissions.

Moreover, [17] uses network calculus to model the IEEE 802.15.4 behaviour and propose an implicit GTS allocation called i-GAME. The i-GAME allows the use of one slot by multiple nodes, considering available bandwidth resources, traffic specification and deadline requirements for accept or reject a GTS request.

Cena et. al. [18] propose the combination of wired and wireless worlds to provide real-time communication in industrial environments. This work presents some means to build an hybrid network that incorporates the best of these worlds. Further, this work shows different forms to implement this combination.

Sokullu et. al. [19] show an investigation on possible MAC sublayer attacks on the IEEE 802.15.4. The scenarios presented in [19] describing some temporal problems caused by these attacks in the temporal behaviour of the IEEE 802.15.4 standard.

6 Conclusions

This paper presents the characterization of inaccessibility in wireless networks and does an exhaustive study of inaccessibility in IEEE 802.15.4 standard. This study was based on beacon-enabled personal area network and describes a relevant set of inaccessibility scenarios present on this type of network. Our study shows that the normal operation of MAC sublayer has hidden times that difficult the support of real-time communications. The control of these times, called inaccessibility, and the handling of omission failures can increase the predictability of the network and can be used for supporting real-time communications in lower levels protocols.

Applications timeouts, or other type of solutions used for control the temporal execution of real-time protocols, can use the knowledge of the inaccessibility times to make a fine adjust on its parameters, and provide an enhanced support for execution of real-time applications.

Future work directions will focus on providing means to reduce the periods of inaccessibility; extending the study to other inaccessibility scenarios including scenarios derived of MAC sublayer attacks; to provide support to signal the periods of inaccessibility to high-layers. Additionally, the results of these future works can be used to improve the support of real-time communications, providing the means of analyzing network delays and message schedulability under a performability perspective.

References

1. Veríssimo, P., Rodrigues, L., Baptista, M.: AMp: A Highly Parallel Atomic Multicast Protocol. SIGCOMM Comput. Commun. Rev. 19(4), 83–93 (1989)
2. Veríssimo, P., Marques, J.A.: Reliable broadcast for fault-tolerance on local computer networks. In: Proceedings of the Ninth Symposium on Reliable Distributed Systems, Alabama, USA, pp. 24–90. IEEE, Los Alamitos (1990)
3. Rufino, J., Verissimo, P., Arroz, G., Almeida, C.: Control of Inaccessibility in CANELy. In: 2006 IEEE International Workshop on Factory Communication Systems, Torino, Italy, June 2006, pp. 34–43 (2006)
4. Verissimo, P., Rufino, J., Ming, L.: How hard is hard real-time communication on field-buses? In: Twenty-Seventh Annual International Symposium on Fault-Tolerant Computing, 1997. FTCS-27. Digest of Papers, June 1997, pp. 112–121 (1997)
5. Rufino, J., Verissimo, P.: A study on the Inaccessibility Characteristics of ISO 8802/4 Token-Bus LANs. In: 11th Annual Joint Conference of the IEEE Computer and Communication Societies, INFOCOM 1992, Florence, Italy, May 1992, vol. 2, pp. 958–967 (1992)
6. Rufino, J., Craveiro, J., Schoofs, T., Tatibana, C., Windsor, J.: AIR Technology: A Step Towards ARINC 653 in Space. In: Eurospace DASIA 2009, Istanbul, Turkey (May 2009)
7. Veríssimo, P., Rufino, J., Rodrigues, L.: Enforcing Real-Time Behaviour on LAN-Based Protocols. In: 10th IFAC Workshop on Distributed Computer Control Systems (September 1991)
8. Karl, H., Willig, A.: Protocols and Architectures for Wireless Sensor Networks. John Wiley and Sons. Ltd., Chichester (2005)
9. IEEE 802.15.4 Standard: Part 15.4: Wireless Medium Access Control (MAC) and Physical Layer (PHY) Specifications for Low-Rate Wireless Personal Area Networks (WPANs). IEEE Standard 802.15.4 Working Group Std., Revision of IEEE Std. 802.15.4-2003 (2006)
10. Gutierrez, J., Naeve, M., Callaway, E., Bourgeois, M., Mitter, V., Heile, B.: IEEE 802.15.4: A Developing Standard for Low-Power Low-Cost Wireless Personal Area Networks. IEEE Network 15(5), 12–19 (2001)
11. Souza, J.L.R., Rufino, J.: Characterization of inaccessibility in ieee 802.15.4: A complete study. Technical report, AIR-II Technical Report RT-09-01 (2009)

12. Ramachandran, I., Das, A.K., Roy, S.: Analysis of the contention access period of IEEE 802.15.4 MAC. ACM Transactions on Sensor Networks (TOSN) 3(1), 4 (2007)
13. He, J., Tang, Z., Chen, H.H., Zhang, Q.: An accurate and scalable analytical model for IEEE 802.15.4 slotted CSMA/CA networks. IEEE Transactions on Wireless Communications 8(1), 440–448 (2009)
14. Jung, C., Hwang, H., Sung, D., Hwang, G.: Enhanced Markov Chain Model and Throughput Analysis of the Slotted CSMA/CA for IEEE 802.15.4 Under Unsaturated Traffic Conditions. IEEE Transactions on Vehicular Technology 58(1), 473–478 (2009)
15. Huang, Y.K., Pang, A.C., Hung, H.N.: An Adaptive GTS Allocation Scheme for IEEE 802.15.4. IEEE Transactions on Parallel and Distributed Systems 19(5), 641–651 (2008)
16. Hameed, M., Trsek, H., Graeser, O., Jasperneite, J.: Performance investigation and optimization of IEEE 802.15.4 for industrial wireless sensor networks. In: IEEE International Conference on Emerging Technologies and Factory Automation, 2008. ETFA 2008, September 2008, pp. 1016–1022 (2008)
17. Koubâa, A., Cunha, A., Alves, M., Tovar, E.: i-GAME: An Implicit GTS Allocation Mechanism in IEEE 802.15.4, theory and practice. Springer Real-Time Systems Journal 39(1-3), 169–204 (2008)
18. Cena, G., Valenzano, A., Vitturi, S.: Hybrid Wired/Wireless Networks for Real-Time Communications. IEEE Industrial Electronics Magazine 2(1), 8–20 (2008)
19. Sokullu, R., Korkmaz, I., Dagdeviren, O., Mitseva, A., Prasad, N.R.: An Investigation on IEEE 802.15.4 MAC Layer Attacks. In: The 10th International Symposium on Wireless Personal Multimedia Communications, Jaipur, India (December 2007)

FemtoNode: Reconfigurable and Customizable Architecture for Wireless Sensor Networks*

Rodrigo Schmidt Allgayer, Marcelo Götz, and Carlos Eduardo Pereira

Departamento de Engenharia Elétrica
Universidade Federal do Rio Grande do Sul - UFRGS
Av. Osvaldo Aranha, 103 - Porto Alegre, Brazil - CEP90035-190
{allgayer,mgoetz,cpereira}@ece.ufrgs.br

Abstract. With the growth and the development of new applications for Wireless Sensor Networks (WSN), sensor nodes are able to handle more complex events that require higher processing performance and hardware flexibility. These new features intend to meet the requirements of various applications, as well as to provide customized platforms that have only the needed resources. WSNs often need a flexible architecture able to adapt to design and environment changes. The use of reconfigurable architectures is an alternative to bring more flexibility and more processing capability for the sensor node. This paper proposes a reconfigurable and customizable sensor node called FemtoNode which has a reconfigurable platform and a wireless module to support applications for WSNs, using an object-oriented language Java as specification language of its architecture. The proposed concepts were validated with a case study of an heterogeneous wireless sensor network composed of sensors nodes based on different platforms, whose results are described in this work.

Keywords: Wireless Sensor Networks, Reconfigurable Architecture, Embedded Systems, Object-oriented Programming.

1 Introduction

Wireless Sensor Networks (WSN) have been developed along MEMS (Micro-Electro-Mechanical Systems) technological evolution. Applications for WSN are emerging in various areas such as military, medical, industrial, agriculture and domestic, as well as for human hostile and danger environments [2]. These networks evolved from ad-hoc wireless communication networks, or Manet (Mobile Ad-Hoc Networks), which don't need an infrastructure to provide a communication among nodes due to its self-organization characteristics. However, WSNs have some special requirements in order to couple with a (usual) large number of nodes, high failures rate and limited power. These aspects require a different architecture, in despite of that, used in conventional networks [1].

---

* This work has been partly funded by the Brazilian research agencie CNPq.

A. Rettberg et al. (Eds.): IESS 2009, IFIP AICT 310, pp. 302–309, 2009.

Usually, a WSN is designed to support a specific application. In such case, sensor nodes have only minimal and necessary resources allowing the WSN to meet the requirements of this particular application. However, this approach lacks in flexibility, since it cannot be optimally designed for a dynamic application, whose requirements may change over the time (e.g.: a WSN inserted in a changing environment).

Thus, a sensor node used in such a WSN needs a flexible architecture able to adapt to design and environment changes. The use of reconfigurable architectures is an alternative to bring more flexibility and more processing capability for the sensor-node [7]. Compared with ASICs (Application Specific Integrated Circuit) based architectures, which have a high cost in production setup, reconfigurable architectures enable a reduction in these costs because its architecture can be adapted to the target application. Additionally, reconfigurability allows reduction in time development, and it enables the development of generic platforms to deal with a greater number of applications.

In order to allow the designer and the application to profit from those reconfigurable computing benefits, this paper proposes a flexible platform for a sensor node, called FemtoNode. This proposal comprises a methodology (based on object-oriented Java language) to assist designer in specification and synthesis of a sensor node on a reconfigurable platform.

The text of the paper is presented as follows: Section 2 presents a brief state-of-the-art analysis of some nodes based on reconfigurable architectures. The FemtoNode customizable hardware architecture is described in Section 3. Then, Section 4 presents an API (Application Programming Interface) developed for FemtoNode. In the following, a case study is presented in Section 5 and, finally, Section 6 draws some concluding remarks and directions of the future work.

2   Related Work

Some studies that use reconfigurable architectures in wireless sensor network are discussed below. In [10,4] a sensor node called RANS-300 (Reconfigurable Architecture for Sensor Network - 300kgates) was developed incorporating reconfigurable hardware resources to improve and to expand the set of features and monitor executed by conventional sensor nodes. These features allow the processing of complex events that requires high computational efficiency and accuracy. The sensor node has the ability to disable these features when not needed, thus minimizing energy consumption. Another feature is the reconfiguration of the hardware's architecture, which enables adaptation and tolerance to permanent failures.

The characteristic of reconfigurability is also present in [16], where it is proposed a framework, called REWISE (Reconfigurable Wireless Intelligent Sensor Network), for WSNs. This framework proposes that sensor nodes can be reconfigured at runtime through the network infrastructure. The dynamic reconfiguration of the sensor node is performed based on situations such as: changes in the objectives of the network mission, needs to update the nodes, repair errors, and adapt to changes at the environment.

Furthermore, the reconfigurable architectures can be used not only to accelerate data processing, but also to provide a hardware architecture to implement a bigger number of wireless communication modules. The sensor node proposed in [11] contains 4 wireless communication modules that increase the data transfer rate and decrease communication latency, even by sending and receiving data simultaneously. This node can play the role of a gateway in order to interconnect different WSN.

However, we found that the use of reconfigurable architectures in WSN increase flexibility in the sensor node to deal with new application's requirements. These feature allows a WSN node to meet dynamic reconfiguration during runtime as well as reconfiguration on design-time. An increase in the processing of collected information may be used with help of processors or co-processors synthesized, for example, in programmable logic devices.

Among the studies reviewed, is was not found a research about the use and optimization of architectures dedicated for application requirements. The actual microcontrollers have several resources that often are not used, which lead to additional energy consumption of the sensor node. So, the use of a tool to carry out the synthesis of a dedicated microcontroller is important for applications in WSNs.

Other features that were not presented are the use of an object-oriented programming language to assist the reuse of code, and by the portability of the developed applications. The synthesis of a microcontroller, which implement a virtual machine that complies with the Java specification, introduce code reuse and application portability for the sensor node.

Seeking to fill gaps presented in this analysis, it was proposed the creation of a reconfigurable and customizable sensor node based on Java, called FemtoNode.

3   FemtoNode Architecture

The architecture of a sensor node aims to efficiently support specific application needs. It requires a dedicated processing module, including a wireless communication interface, which meets both energy and performance requirements, as well as footprint constrains. The fact that application requirements or operation/environmental conditions may change during system operation imposes a major challenge: how a generic sensor node architecture can be designed and tailored to the current application requirements?

FemtoNode is an alternative addressed to contribute with this challenge. It is a customizable sensor node, based on reconfigurable hardware, a customizable ASIP (Application-Specific Instruction-set Processor), and on a wireless communication interface. The FemtoNode is configured according to application requirements. Currently, FemtoNode does not support dynamic reconfiguration, which is planned as future work.

FemtoNode uses the RT-FemtoJava processor [9], a stack-based microcontroller that natively executes Java byte-codes. It implements an execution engine for Java in hardware, through a stack machine that is compatible with the specification of Java Virtual Machine. The customized code application is generated by the Sashimi [9,14] design environment.

Sashimi tool allows the use of a high-level object-oriented language not only for programming the application, but also for the complete specification of the system containing the microcontroller. Sashimi makes the automatic extraction of the subset of Java instructions needed to implement the application. For each system a specific microcontroller (with an adapted set of instructions) can be generated, and self-adapt its software. The code includes a VHDL description of the processor core and ROM (programs) and RAM (variables) memories. Therefore, the result is an optimized use of the hardware resources and software for each application. Furthermore, Sashimi environment had been extended to incorporate an API that supports concurrent tasks, implementing the RTSJ (Real-Time Specification for Java) [15] standard, allowing FemtoNode to support real-time constraints.

As RT-FemtoJava is customizable, its code can be optimized according to the application requirements, reducing the occupied hardware area, and also the power consumption and dissipation requirements. The customizable hardware architecture of FemtoNode allows the use of sensor node as either a low- or high-end node. If the application requires higher performance resources to handle more complex data, such as image processing, additional available resources in the FemtoNode architecture, these features can be included. However, if the application is aimed to process simple data, such as those from presence sensors, a reduced set of resources in the architecture is used. This feature benefits the sensor node, because energy consumption is a great concern in wireless sensor networks, due to the limited energy resource. Besides, reducing the unused resources during the sensor node architecture synthesis allows the implementation

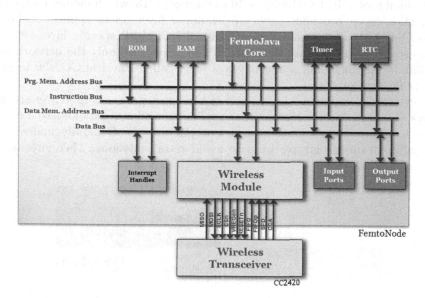

Fig. 1. Hardware Architecture of FemtoNode

in reconfigurable architectures with fewer available logical units, which provides great application portability between these architectures.

In the current implementation, FemtoNode includes a wireless transceiver CC2420 [8], from Texas Instruments, which utilizes IEEE 802.15.4 standard communication protocol specified for wireless sensor network applications.

A module adapter described in VHDL performs the interface with the wireless transceiver. This module uses data and address buses to communicate with the processor, performing data exchange and allowing the transceiver parameters configuration. An interruption system informs the processor when a reception was made. Figure 1 shows such FemtoNode's architecture.

To easiest the use of the wireless communication module by the application developers, a communication API (called API-Wireless) was developed and incorporated into FemtoJava framework. This API-Wireless abstracts details of communication means between sensor nodes, offering a simplified form for configuration of data transfer module.

4   API-Wireless

Aiming to offer an easier way to use FemtoNode resources for application's developers, an API was developed, called API-Wireless. APIs can be defined as a set of public classes with functions and procedures that enable and facilitate application development. Thus, API-Wireless makes communication hardware transparent, offering a simple way to access the wireless communication module by methods.

API-Wireless was developed based on API-COM [5,6] which was developed for Sashimi tool. API-COM follows ISO-OSI model [13] which defines each communication layer, providing service from upper layer up to application layer. API-COM split the communication protocol into three specific layers: transport, network and datalink. However, API-Wireless uses only the network and datalink layers, including a new physical layer called Physical_CC2420 to perform radio configuration.

Unlike traditional networks, the use of transport protocols in WSNs are not always necessary. Most sensor network applications admits data loss, so a mechanism to ensure data transmission is not justified [1]. Generally nodes send data information in multiple ways to avoid retransmissions. Therefore, many

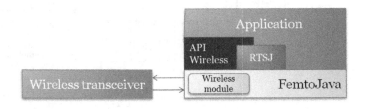

Fig. 2. FemtoNode Architecture with API-Wireless

applications use only physical, datalink and network layers to develop protocols for WSNs.

FemtoNode architecture, including the API-Wireless, is shown in Figure 2. API-Wireless is located between application and wireless module. The application can use API to access resources from wireless communication or to use directly the resources of RT-FemtoJava microcontroller.

5 Case Study

Distributed networks of wireless sensors in industrial environments benefit the application by introducing flexibility and adaptability into the processes, improving their quality and reliability. These applications have several benefits on installation and maintenance of devices, support for remote monitoring, reduction of costs and problems related to data communication cables and their repair [3,17]. Another advantage is the possibility of placing sensors and actuators in places of difficult access, where sensors with data cables wouldn't be possible to be installed.

Based on benefits of using WSNs in industrial applications, a case study was proposed using an industrial control process application. This case study is used to validate the architecture created in this paper using the implementation of a network of heterogeneous sensors and actuators. This network consists of sensor nodes and actuator nodes with platforms that have different characteristics, both hardware and software, with support for Java applications. This sophisticated application demonstrates the need for an approach to deal with distributed objects.

The proposed network for validation consists of two types of sensor-nodes: FemtoNode and Sunspot [12]. Tests were performed using a distributed control in an industrial plant measuring the temperature distribution. This process consists of three components: sensor, controller and actuator. The sensor is responsible for measuring the temperature, it can be composed of a network of wireless sensors, where each sensor measures the temperature of a certain point of the process and sends it to the controller. The controller receives data from the sensors and, through a control algorithm, sends the data to the actuator. The actuator is responsible for performing the action in the system through a heat source, in this case, a thermal resistance.

SunSPOTs (incluir referencia para SunSPOTs aqui) are responsible for temperature sensing and system actuating, in the other hand FemtoNode performs the control algorithm based on sensor information and sends the results to the actuator.

In this application the FemtoNode with the controller code was implemented in a FPGA Virtex-II [18] from Xilinx.

Application code was generated using compilers for different devices. Sashimi tool was used to compile the code for ROM and RAM memory of FemtoJava for further synthesis on a reconfigurable architecture in the FemtoNode. Sunspot's application was generated with a cross-compiler for ARM7 microcontroller which is inside of SunSpot.

6   Conclusions and Future Work

The architecture presented in this paper, called FemtoNode, introduce flexibility with the use of a reconfigurable architecture, and a softcore microcontroller in its architecture, which can be adapted to application needs. Moreover, only required hardware is synthesized into the FPGA, reducing the amount of logic required and energy consumption.

The use of Java language allows an easy application specification and code reuse for other applications, by exploring object-oriented concepts. Heterogeneous sensor networks, which have different kinds of hardware platforms in the same network, can use the portability of this language to solve the resources incompatibility.

Wireless communication is important in sensor network because it enable information exchange between nodes in an efficient way. However, this type of communication consumes a large amount of energy and a choice of a correct protocol communication is needed for the network's performance. Thus, the choice of IEEE802.15.4 protocol for the FemtoNode was appropriate because it presents a low power consumption and a reduced data transfer rate addressed to WSN applications that do not have a large amount of transmitted data.

Abstraction of communication mechanisms for application developer is useful and it was included in this work with the development of an API-Wireless, which presents resources to send and receive data as well as the configuration of the wireless communication module.

As future work, dynamic reconfiguration feature is going to be incorporated into FemtoNode. This feature will enable FemtoNode to be dynamically customized in the case of, for instance, changing communication requirements. By this means, FemtoNode will support a broad spectrum of application types.

References

1. Akyildiz, I.F., Su, W., Sankarasubramaniam, Y., Cayirci, E.: A survey on sensor networks. IEEE Communications Magazine 40(8), 102–114 (2002)
2. Arampatzis, T., Lygeros, J., Manesis, S.: A survey of applications of wireless sensors and wireless sensor networks. In: Proceedings of International Symposium on Control and Automation Intelligent Control, Limassol, Cyprus, June 2005, pp. 719–724. IEEE, New York (2005)
3. Bonivento, A., Carloni, L.P., Sangiovanni-Vincentelli, A.: Platform-based design of wireless sensor networks for industrial applications. In: Proceedings of Conference on Design, automation and test in Europe - DATE 2006, Munich, Germany, pp. 1103–1107. European Design and Automation Association, Leuven (2006)
4. Caldas, R.B., Correa Jr., F.L., Nacif, J.A., Roque, T.R., Ruiz, L.B., Fernandas, A.O., da Mata, J.M., Coelho Jr., C.: Low power/high performance self-adapting sensor node architecture. In: Proceedings of 10th IEEE Conference on Emerging Technologies and Factory Automation - ETFA 2005, Catania, Italy, September 2005, vol. 2, p. 976. IEEE, New York (2005)
5. da Silva Jr., E.T.: Adaptativo para Sistemas Embarcados e de Tempo-Real. PhD thesis, Instituto de Informática, Universidade Federal do Rio Grande do Sul, Porto Alegre (2008)

6. da Silva Jr., E.T., Freitas, E.P., Wagner, F.R., Carvalho, F.C., Pereira, C.E.: Java framework for distributed real-time embedded systems. In: Proceedings of IEEE International Symposium on Object-Oriented Real-Time Distributed Computing - ISORC 2006, Gyeongju, Korea, April 2006, pp. 85–92. IEEE Computer Society, Los Alamitos (2006)
7. Hinkelmann, H., Zipf, P., Glesner, M.: A domain-specific dynamically reconfigurable hardware platform for wireless sensor networks. In: Proceedings of International Conference on Field-Programmable Technology, December 2007, pp. 313–316 (2007)
8. Texas Instruments. 2.4GHz IEEE802.15.4 / ZigBee-ready RF Transceiver. Texas Instruments (2007), http://focus.ti.com/lit/ds/symlink/cc2420.pdf/
9. Ito, S.A., Carro, L., Jacobi, R.P.: Making java work for microcontroller applications. IEEE Design and Test of Computers 18(5), 100–110 (2001)
10. Corrêa Jr., F.L.: Nó sensor com arquitetura reconfigurável para redes de sensores sem fio. Master's thesis, Instituto de Ciências Exatas, Universidade Federal de Minas Gerais, Belo Horizonte, Brasil (2004)
11. Kohvakka, M., Arpinen, T., Hannikainen, M., Hamalainen, T.D.: High-performance multi-radio wsn platform. In: Proceedings of the 2nd international workshop on Multi-hop ad hoc networks: from theory to reality, pp. 95–97. ACM, New York (2006)
12. Sun Microsystems. Sunspot (2009), http://www.sunspotworld.com/
13. Tanenbaum, A.S.: Computer Networks, 4th edn. Prentice Hall, New Jersey (2003)
14. Universidade Federal do Rio Grande do Sul - UFRGS, Porto Alegre, Brasil. SASHIMI: manual do usuário (2006)
15. Wehrmeister, M.A., Pereira, C.E., Becker, L.B.: Optimizing the generation of object-oriented real-time embedded applications based on the real-time specification for java. In: Proceedings of the Conference on Design, automation and test in Europe - DATE 2006, Munich, Germany, pp. 806–811. European Design and Automation Association, Leuven (2006)
16. Wilder, J.L., Uzelac, V., Milenkovic, A., Jovanov, E.: Runtime hardware reconfiguration in wireless sensor networks. In: Proceedings of the 40th Southeastern Symposium on System Theory, March 2008, pp. 154–158 (2008)
17. Willig, A.: Recent and emerging topics in wireless industrial communications: a selection. IEEE Transactions on Industrial Informatics 4(2), 102–124 (2008)
18. Xilinx. Xilinx University Program Virtex-II Pro Development System. Xilinx (April 2008)

Efficient Modeling of Embedded Systems Using Computer-Aided Recoding

Rainer Dömer

Center for Embedded Computer Systems
University of California, Irvine
doemer@uci.edu

Abstract. The design of embedded computing systems faces a serious productivity gap due to the increasing complexity of their hardware and software components. One solution to address this problem is the modeling at higher levels of abstraction. However, writing proper executable system models is challenging, error-prone, and very time-consuming.

This tutorial outlines a novel modeling technique called *computer-aided recoding* which automates the process of specifying and modeling embedded systems by use of advanced computer-aided design (CAD) techniques. Using a designer-controlled approach with automated source code transformations, computer-aided recoding can derive an executable parallel system model directly from available sequential reference code. As a result, system modeling is streamlined, enabling a shorter design time and higher productivity.

Keywords: Embedded System Design, Specification and Modeling, Computer-Aided Recoding.

1 Introduction

Embedded computing systems, such as video-enabled mobile phones and reliable medical devices, are omnipresent and pervasive in our everyday life. The design of these systems, however, is very challenging due to hard design constraints, including strict timing, multi-core functionality, low power, low price, and short time-to-market. Moreover, we face a growing design productivity gap due to the increasing complexity of the embedded hardware and software components.

The International Technology Roadmap for Semiconductors (ITRS) lists modeling at higher levels of abstraction as key to overcome the productivity gap [1]. Much like the quality of an architectural blue-print determines the quality of the resulting building, the model of an embedded system is the key to its successful implementation. However, writing proper executable system models is challenging, error-prone, and very time-consuming. For a simple MP3 decoder application, our experiments have shown that more than 90% of the overall design time was spent in creating and editing the system model [2]. Other studies also confirm that the model specification phase is a serious bottleneck in embedded system design.

A. Rettberg et al. (Eds.): IESS 2009, IFIP AICT 310, pp. 310–311, 2009.

2 Computer-Aided Recoding

In this tutorial, we present *computer-aided recoding,* a new specification and modeling technique that automates various steps in the process of writing embedded system models. Computer-aided recoding is a designer-controlled approach that relies on automated source code transformations available to the system designer in form of a "smart" integrated development environment [2]. In this approach, the designer makes the decisions, whereas the tool automatically transforms the source code.

Specifically, we discuss several types of source code transformations, including code and data partitioning to create parallel and flexible system models [3], pointer recoding to eliminate unwanted pointers in given C reference code [4], creation of structural hierarchy to properly organize the initially unstructured "flat" application code [5], and exposing potential parallelism and creating explicit communication and synchronization in the system model [6]. Using our prototype implementation of an interactive source recoder [2], we provide experimental results that demonstrate the effectiveness of the approach and show significant gains in design productivity.

3 Conclusion

Computer-aided recoding can derive an executable parallel system model directly from available sequential reference code. Automatic source code transformations relieve the system designer from complex code analysis and tedious coding tasks, allowing uninterrupted focus on system modeling and design space exploration. As a result, modeling writing is streamlined, enabling a shorter design time and higher productivity, as well as quality improvements in the end design.

References

1. International Semiconductor Industry Association: International Technology Roadmap for Semiconductors (ITRS) (2007), http://www.itrs.net
2. Chandraiah, P., Dömer, R.: An Interactive Model Re-Coder for Efficient SoC Specification. In: Rettberg, A., Zanella, M., Dömer, R., Gerstlauer, A., Rammig, F. (eds.) Proceedings of the International Embedded Systems Symposium, Embedded System Design: Topics, Techniques and Trends. Springer, Irvine (2007)
3. Chandraiah, P., Dömer, R.: Designer-Controlled Generation of Parallel and Flexible Heterogeneous MPSoC Specification. In: Proceedings of the Design Automation Conference 2007, San Diego, California (June 2007)
4. Chandraiah, P., Dömer, R.: Pointer Re-coding for Creating Definitive MPSoC Models. In: Proceedings of the International Conference on Hardware/Software Codesign and System Synthesis, Salzburg, Austria (September 2007)
5. Chandraiah, P., Dömer, R.: Automatic Re-coding of Reference Code into Structured and Analyzable SoC Models. In: Proceedings of the Asia and South Pacific Design Automation Conference 2008, Seoul, Korea (January 2008)
6. Chandraiah, P., Dömer, R.: Code and Data Structure Partitioning for Parallel and Flexible MPSoC Specification Using Designer-Controlled Re-Coding. IEEE Transactions on Computer-Aided Design of Integrated Circuits and Systems 27(6), 1078–1090 (2008)

New Challenges for Designers of Fault Tolerant Embedded Systems Based on Future Technologies

Luigi Carro and Carlos Arthur Lang Lisboa

Instituto de Informática, Programa de Pós-Graduação em Computação, UFRGS
Av. Bento Gonçalves, 9500 – Bloco IV – Prédio 67 – 91501-970 – Porto Alegre – RS - Brazil
{carro,calisboa}@inf.ufrgs.br

Abstract. The major challenges that will be faced by designers of embedded systems based on future technologies are discussed. While providing many benefits, those technologies bring along several problems, such as higher defect rates, higher sensitivity to radiation induced transient faults, and the possibility of occurrence of multiple simultaneous faults and long duration transients. The main characteristics of future technologies are presented and the new challenges imposed to designers highlighted. Classic and recently proposed mitigation techniques are reviewed and the weaknesses that will impair their application to those technologies discussed. Recent research works aiming to cope with this new scenario are presented, analyzed and discussed, taking into account their impact on area, performance and power consumption. Strategies to cope with those challenges at different design levels are discussed and research paths that may lead to the solution of the problems are proposed.

Keywords: Transient faults, future technologies, mitigation techniques, embedded systems.

1 Introduction

As the technology evolves, faster and smaller devices become available for manufacturing circuits that while more efficient, are more sensitive to the effects of radiation. The high transistor density, reducing the distance between neighbor devices, makes possible the occurrence of multiple upsets caused by a single particle hit. The achievable high speed, reducing the clock cycles of circuits, leads to transient pulses lasting longer than one cycle. All those facts preclude the use of several existing soft error mitigation techniques based on temporal redundancy, and require the development of innovative fault tolerant techniques to cope with this challenging new scenario.

In this tutorial the works that point to this new scenario are briefly presented, and existing mitigation techniques are analyzed, showing their weaknesses to cope with multiple simultaneous faults and long duration transients (LDTs). The need for innovative solutions to face these challenges is highlighted and recently proposed candidate techniques to deal with faults at different abstraction levels are presented and discussed.

A. Rettberg et al. (Eds.): IESS 2009, IFIP AICT 310, pp. 312–313, 2009.
© IFIP International Federation for Information Processing 2009

2 Summary

The collision of an energetic particle with the silicon substrate of CMOS circuits causes the deposition of a charge that may affect the state of the hit device. If the collected charge is larger than the critical charge of the device, it may change the transistor's state, thereby inducing what is called a transient fault. After a given time, this charge dissipates and the device resumes its previous state. The time lapse since the charge is collected until it is dissipated is called the transient width. If the transient width is long enough, the wrong state may be latched by a storage element in the circuit, causing what is called a soft error, since the circuit is still able to store new correct values in the future.

When the predicted transient widths are contrasted with the evolution of typical circuit propagation delays across technologies, one can see that they don't scale at the same pace. For small energy particles, there is almost no variation in the transient widths, while for higher energy ones the variation is still far below that of the propagation delays. In parallel, the decreasing dimensions of devices make the occurrence of multiple simultaneous faults a growing concern for designers, since most of current mitigation techniques rely on the single fault model and cannot cope with simultaneous faults.

These facts lead to the prediction of a new scenario, in which many currently used soft errors mitigation techniques will no longer succeed.

Techniques based on temporal redundancy, which sample the outputs of a circuit twice, and then compare the obtained values in order to detect transient errors, use a fixed time interval between the two samplings. This interval must be larger than the maximum expected transient width, otherwise two equally erroneous output values might be considered correct. In order to cope with long duration transients, the time between samplings should be larger, but since the duration of the transients may become equal to or larger than the cycle time of the circuits, this alternative is precluded by the unbearable performance penalty it imposes.

In turn, classic techniques based on space redundancy, such as duplication with comparison (DWC) and triple modular redundancy (TMR), despite being able to cope with LDTs, still impose very high area and power consumption overheads, which are very scarce resources in the embedded systems arena. Other techniques, working at component or circuit level, will also become .

Given this scenario, the development of innovative mitigation techniques to deal with LDTs and multiple simultaneous faults becomes mandatory.

In this tutorial, recently proposed techniques are analyzed in order to determine their adequacy to cope with those problems. Furthermore, it is shown that the mitigation of faults at the lower abstraction levels of digital systems usually implies higher overheads than those imposed by higher level mitigation techniques.

The use of algorithm or system level mitigation techniques is then evaluated as a possible path to the hardening of complete systems against radiation induced faults, and some proposed works that adopted this strategy are presented and discussed.

Finally, it is shown that a combination of different techniques, working at distinct abstraction levels, maybe the best approach to be adopted, since errors at the lower levels of a system may even impair the ability of the system to deal with faults at the higher levels.

Author Index